INJUSTICE

GODS AMONG US: YEAR FOUR

VOLUME 2

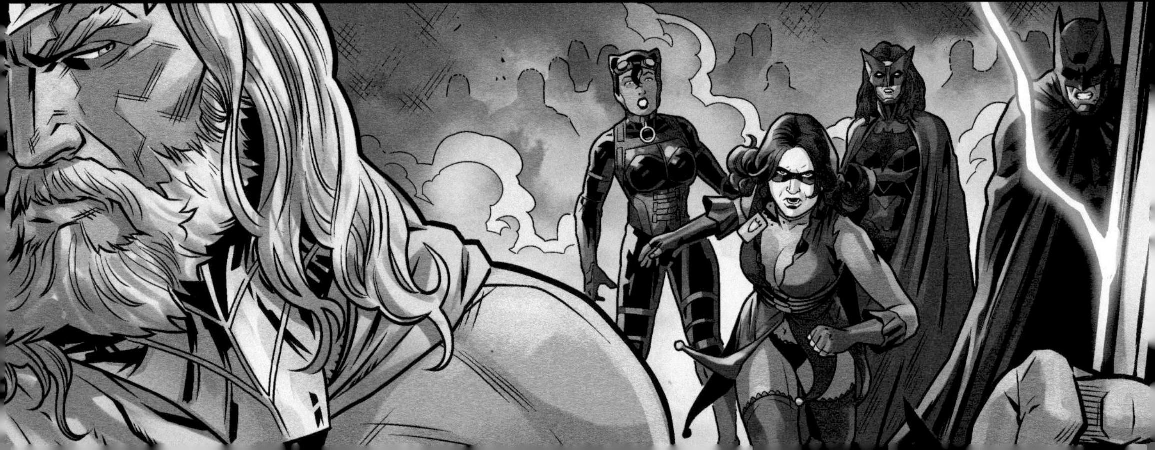

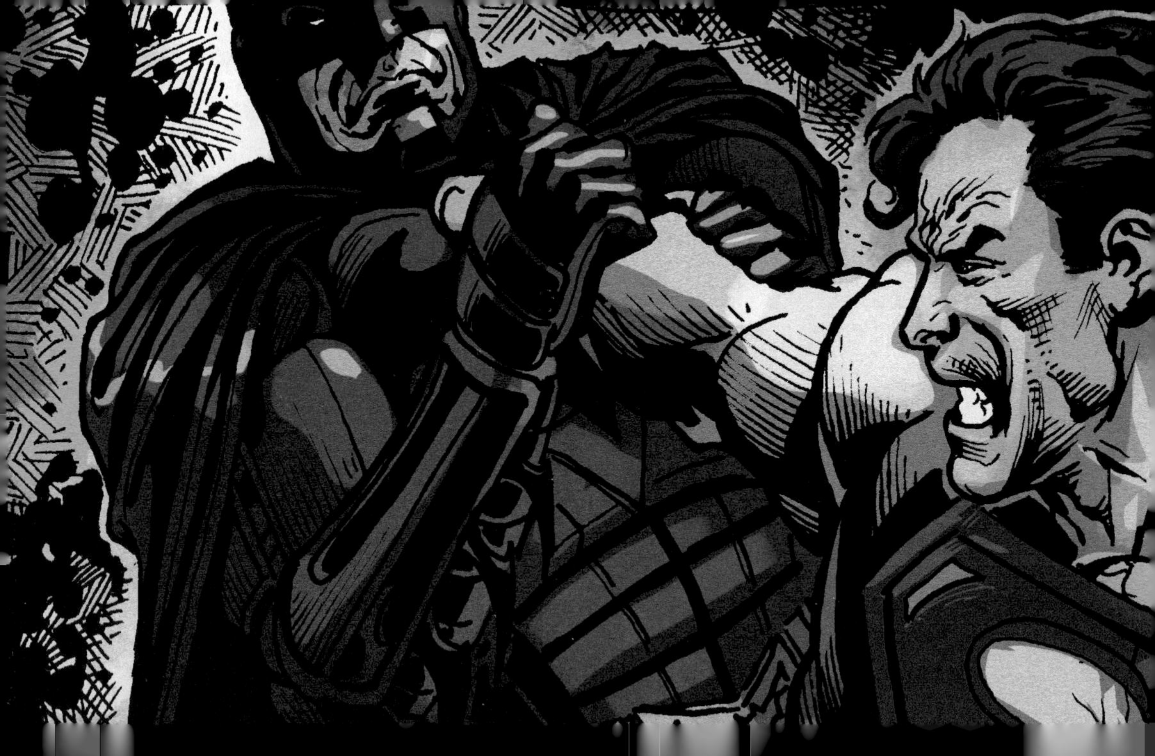

STICE

U S: YEAR FOUR
VOLUME 2

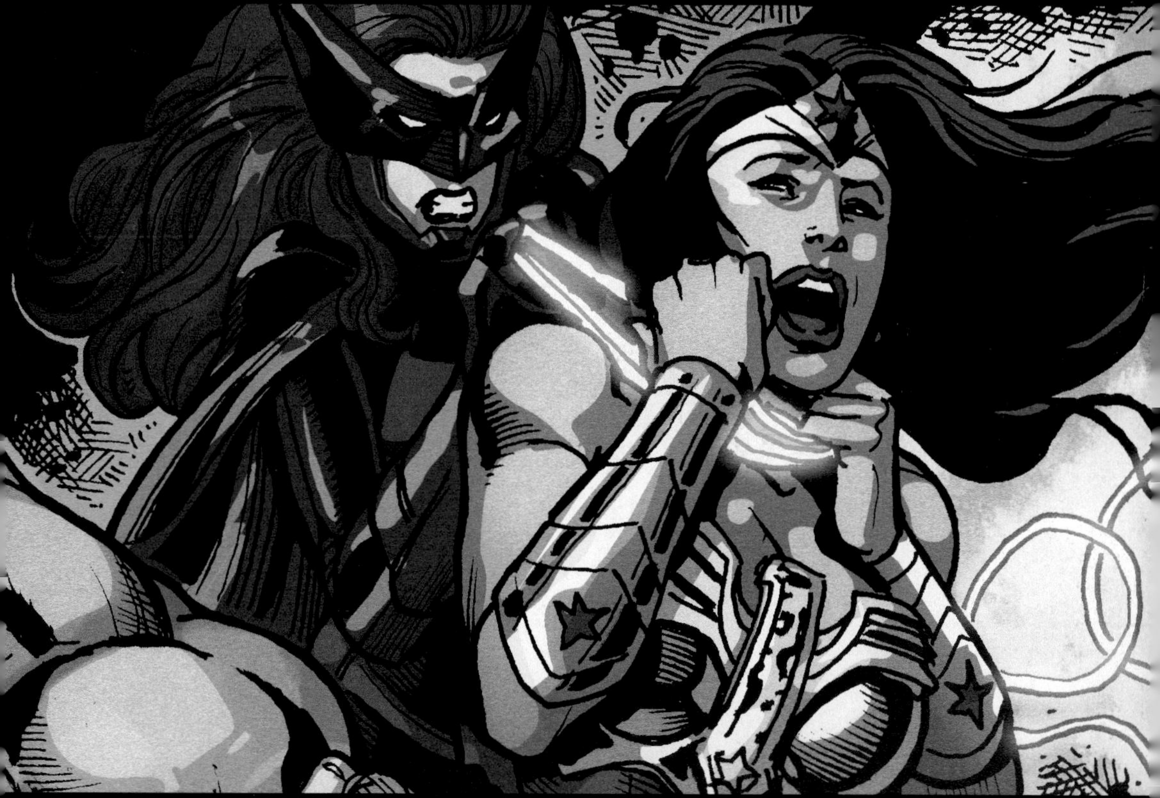

SUPERMAN Created by JERRY SIEGEL and JOE SHUSTER.
By Special Arrangement with the Jerry Siegel Family.

BASED ON THE VIDEO GAME *INJUSTICE: GODS AMONG US*

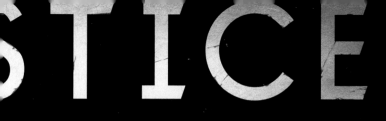

Jim Chadwick Editor – Original Series
David Piña Assistant Editor – Original Series
Jeb Woodard Group Editor – Collected Editions
Paul Santos Editor – Collected Edition
Steve Cook Design Director – Books
Louis Prandi Publication Design

Bob Harras Senior VP – Editor-in-Chief, DC Comics

Diane Nelson President
Dan DiDio and Jim Lee Co-Publishers
Geoff Johns Chief Creative Officer
Amit Desai Senior VP – Marketing & Global Franchise Management
Nairi Gardiner Senior VP – Finance
Sam Ades VP – Digital Marketing
Bobbie Chase VP – Talent Development
Mark Chiarello Senior VP – Art, Design & Collected Editions
John Cunningham VP – Content Strategy
Anne DePies VP – Strategy Planning & Reporting
Don Falletti VP – Manufacturing Operations
Lawrence Ganem VP – Editorial Administration & Talent Relations
Alison Gill Senior VP – Manufacturing & Operations
Hank Kanalz Senior VP – Editorial Strategy & Administration
Jay Kogan VP – Legal Affairs
Derek Maddalena Senior VP – Sales & Business Development
Jack Mahan VP – Business Affairs
Dan Miron VP – Sales Planning & Trade Development
Nick Napolitano VP – Manufacturing Administration
Carol Roeder VP – Marketing
Eddie Scannell VP – Mass Account & Digital Sales
Courtney Simmons Senior VP – Publicity & Communications
Jim (Ski) Sokolowski VP – Comic Book Specialty & Newsstand Sales
Sandy Yi Senior VP – Global Franchise Management

INJUSTICE: GODS AMONG US: YEAR FOUR VOLUME 2

Published by DC Comics. Compilation and all new material Copyright © 2016 DC Comics. All Rights Reserved. Originally published in single magazine form in INJUSTICE: GODS AMONG US: YEAR FOUR 8-12, INJUSTICE: GODS AMONG US: YEAR FOUR ANNUAL 1. Copyright © 2015, 2016 DC Comics. All Rights Reserved. All characters, their distinctive likenesses and related elements featured in this publication are trademarks of DC Comics. The stories, characters and incidents featured in this publication are entirely fictional. DC Comics does not read or accept unsolicited submissions of ideas, stories or artwork.

DC Comics, 2900 West Alameda Ave., Burbank, CA 91505
Printed by RR Donnelley, Salem, VA, USA. 7/15/16. First Printing.
ISBN: 978-1-4012-6268-6

Library of Congress Cataloging-in-Publication Data is available.

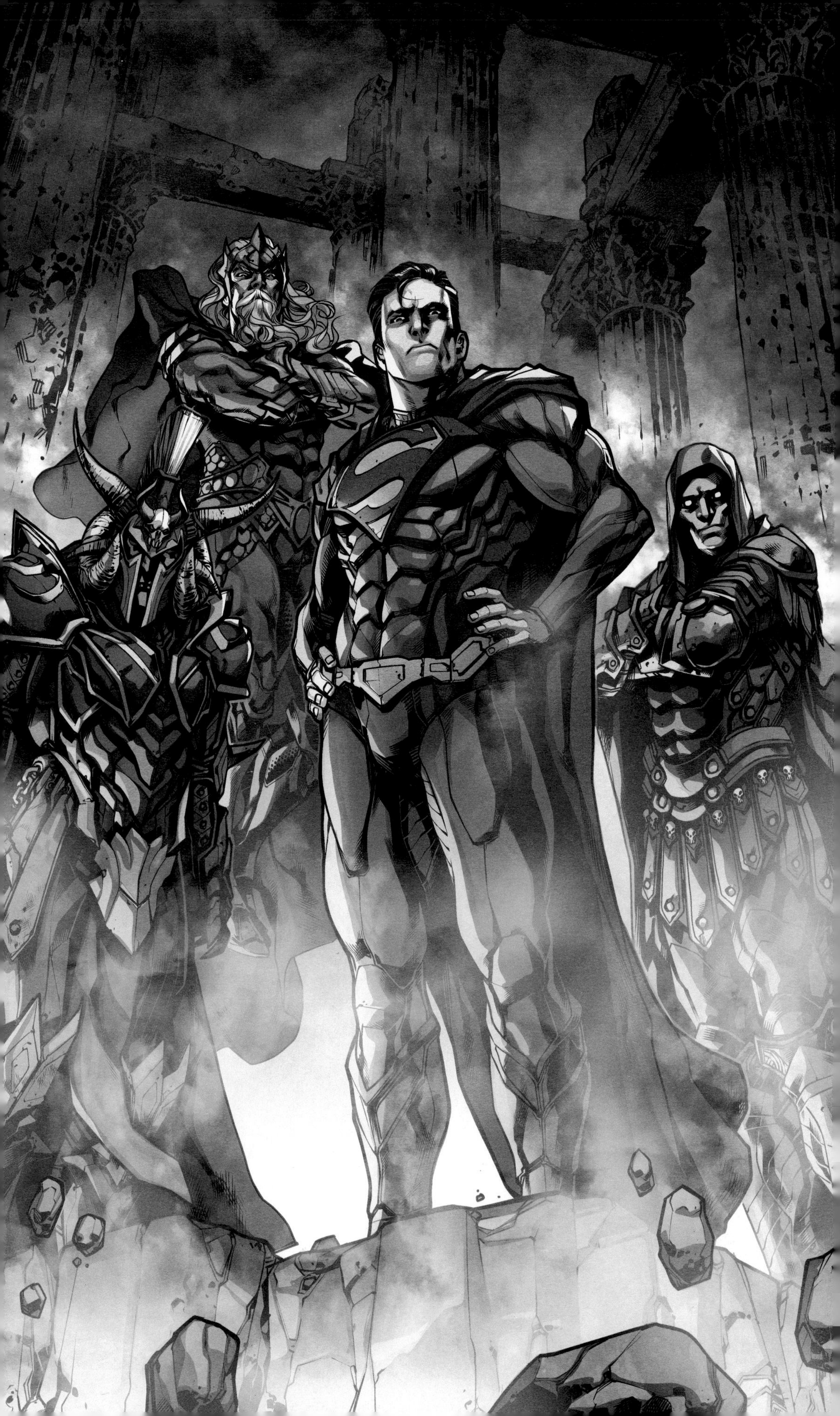

"Exile" **Brian Buccellato** Writer **Bruno Redondo** **Tom Derenick** **Juan Albarran** Artists
J. Nanjan **Rex Lokus** Colorists Cover Art by **Neil Googe & Rex Lokus**

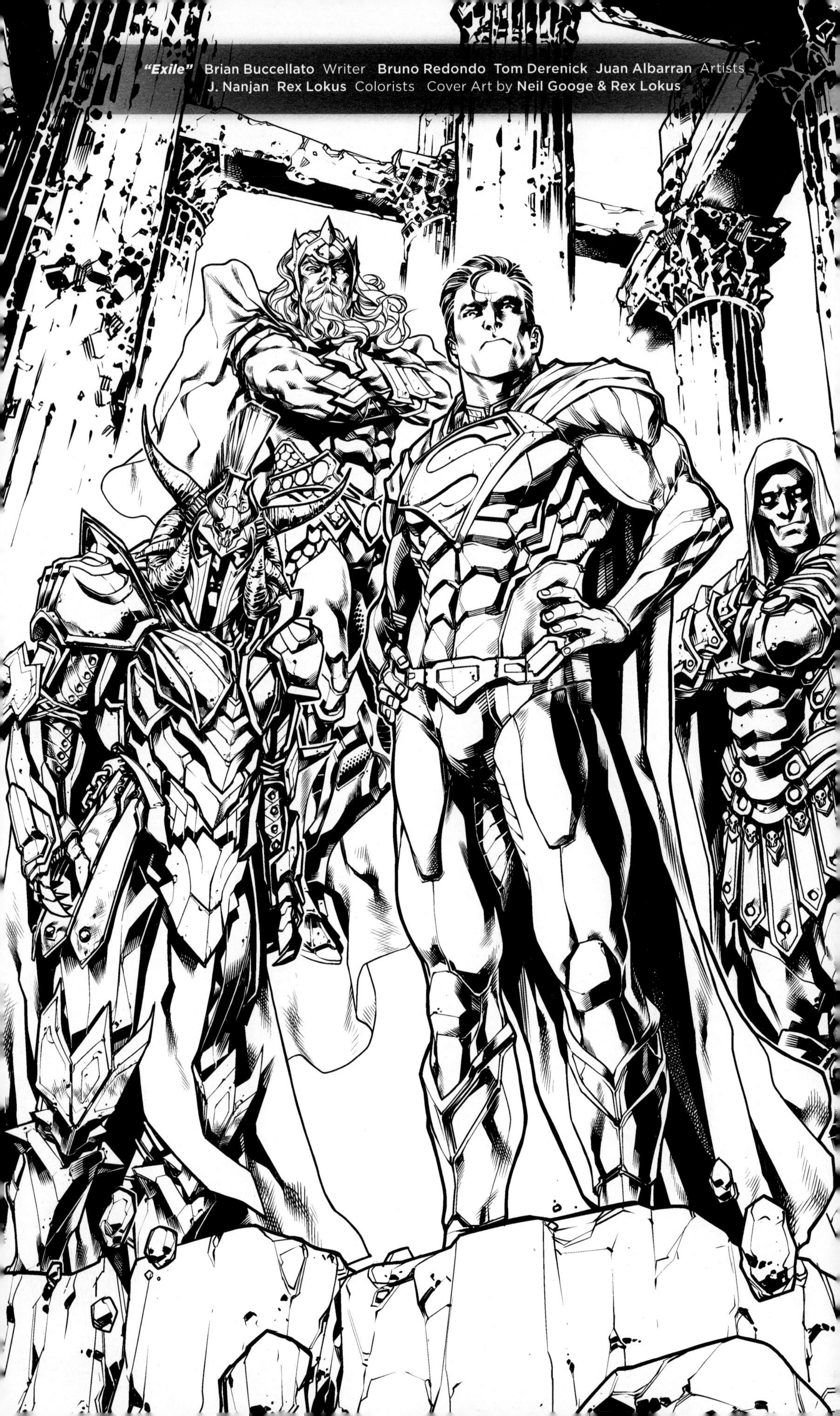

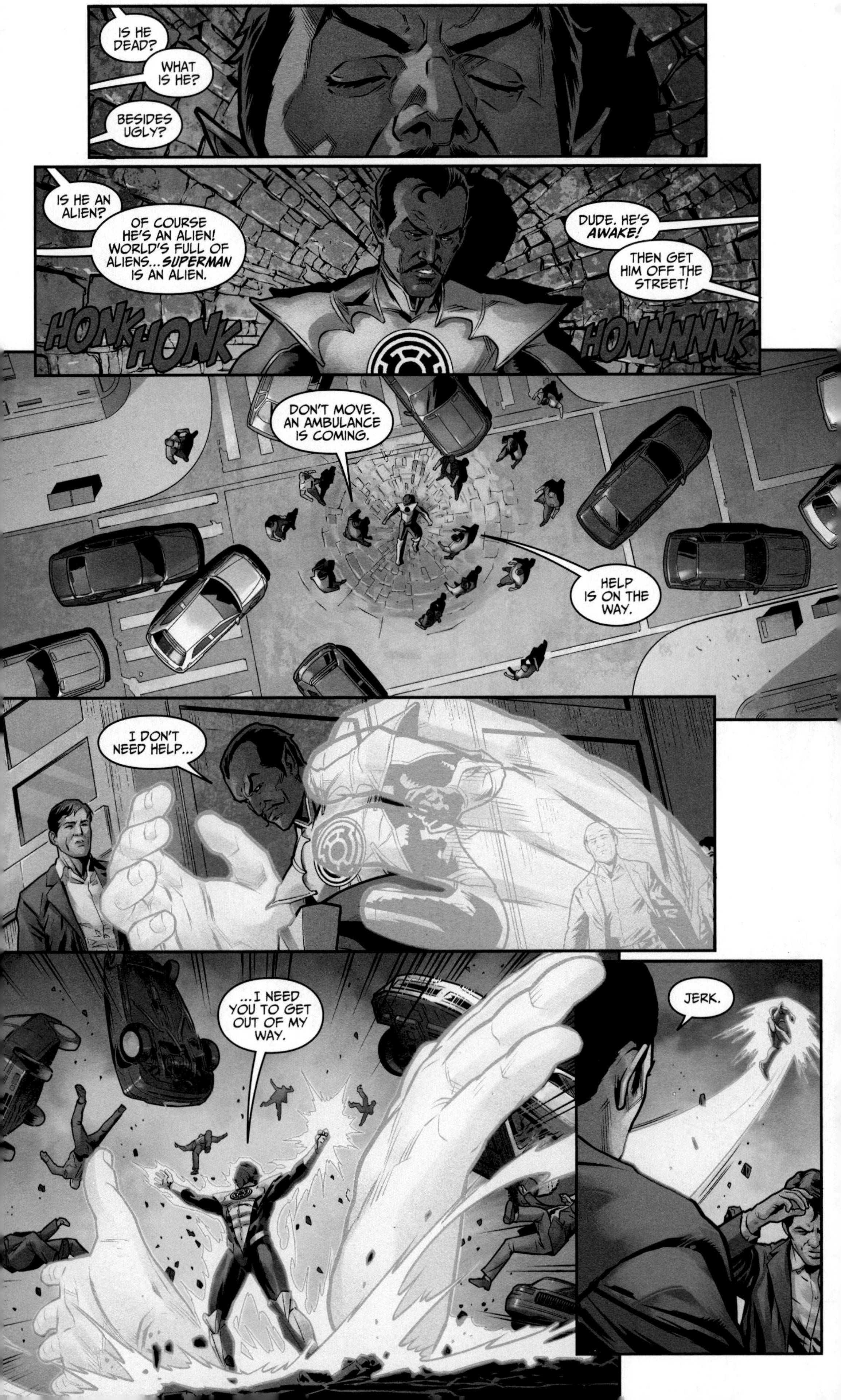
IS HE DEAD?
WHAT IS HE?
BESIDES UGLY?
IS HE AN ALIEN?
OF COURSE HE'S AN ALIEN! WORLD'S FULL OF ALIENS...SUPERMAN IS AN ALIEN.
DUDE. HE'S AWAKE!
THEN GET HIM OFF THE STREET!
HONK HONK
HONNNNNK
DON'T MOVE. AN AMBULANCE IS COMING.
HELP IS ON THE WAY.
I DON'T NEED HELP...
...I NEED YOU TO GET OUT OF MY WAY.
JERK.

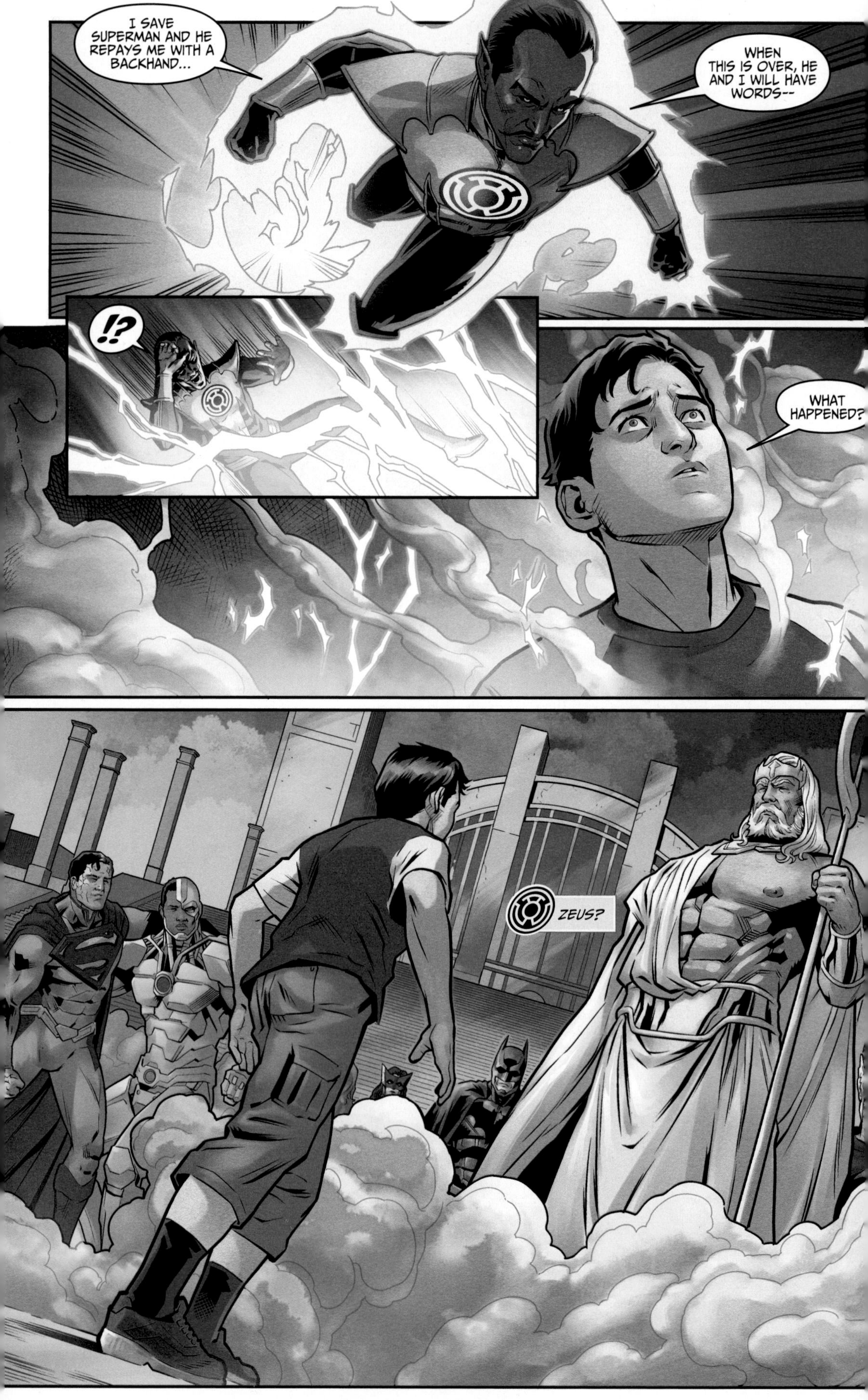
I SAVE SUPERMAN AND HE REPAYS ME WITH A BACKHAND...
WHEN THIS IS OVER, HE AND I WILL HAVE WORDS--
!?
WHAT HAPPENED?
ZEUS?

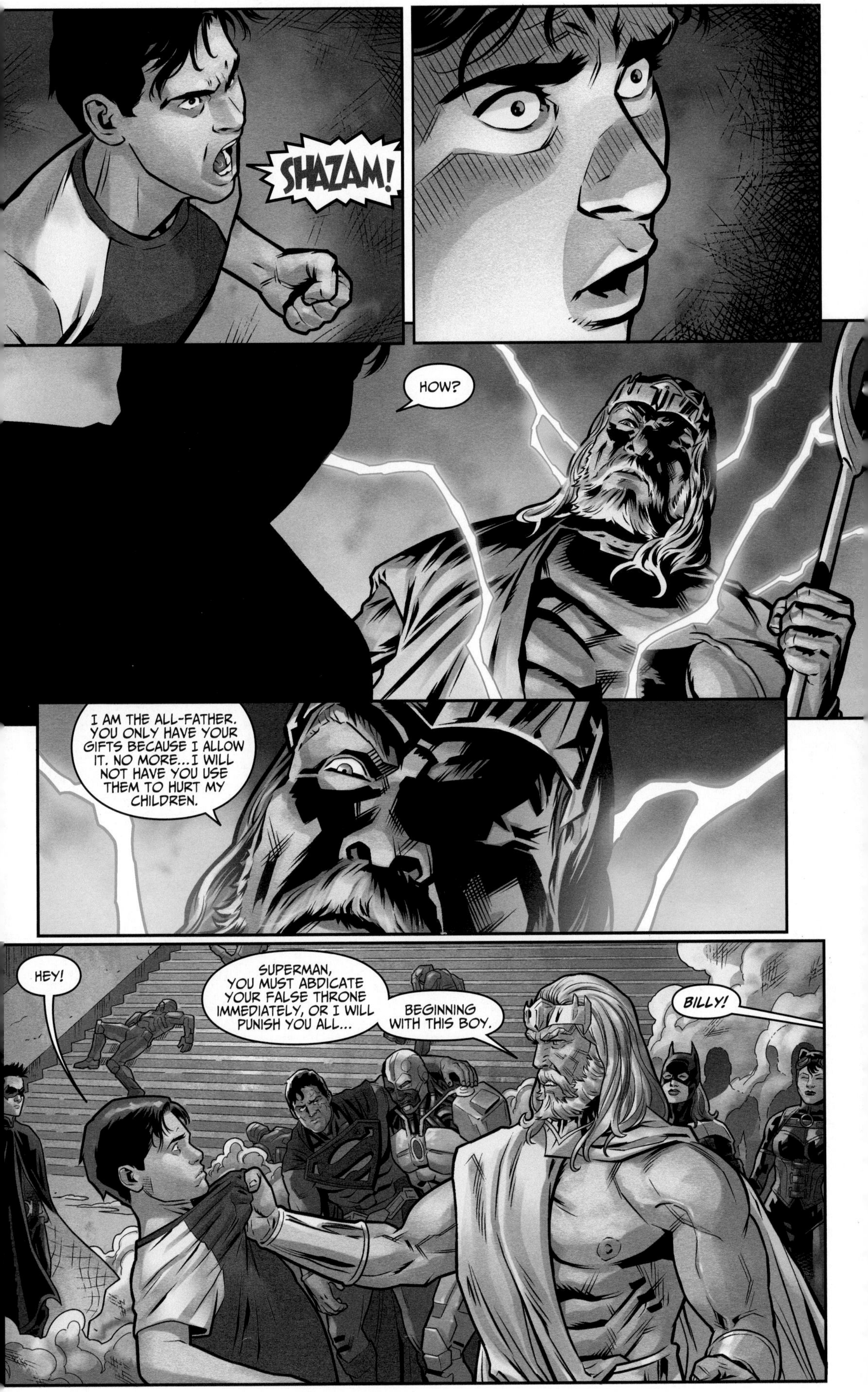
SHAZAM!
HOW?
I AM THE ALL-FATHER. YOU ONLY HAVE YOUR GIFTS BECAUSE I ALLOW IT. NO MORE...I WILL NOT HAVE YOU USE THEM TO HURT MY CHILDREN.
HEY!
SUPERMAN, YOU MUST ABDICATE YOUR FALSE THRONE IMMEDIATELY, OR I WILL PUNISH YOU ALL...
BEGINNING WITH THIS BOY.
BILLY!

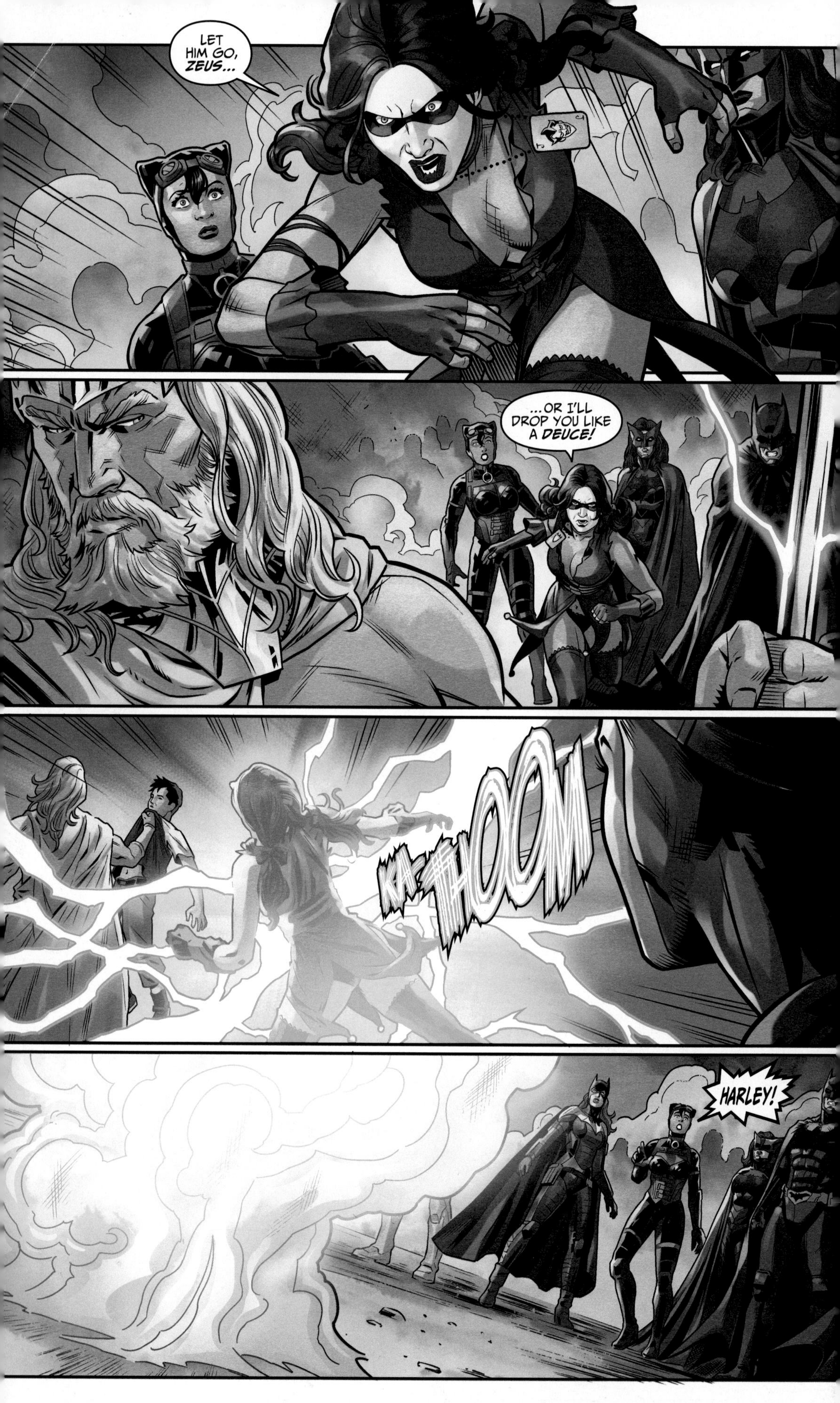
LET HIM GO, ZEUS...
...OR I'LL DROP YOU LIKE A DEUCE!
KA-THOOM
HARLEY!

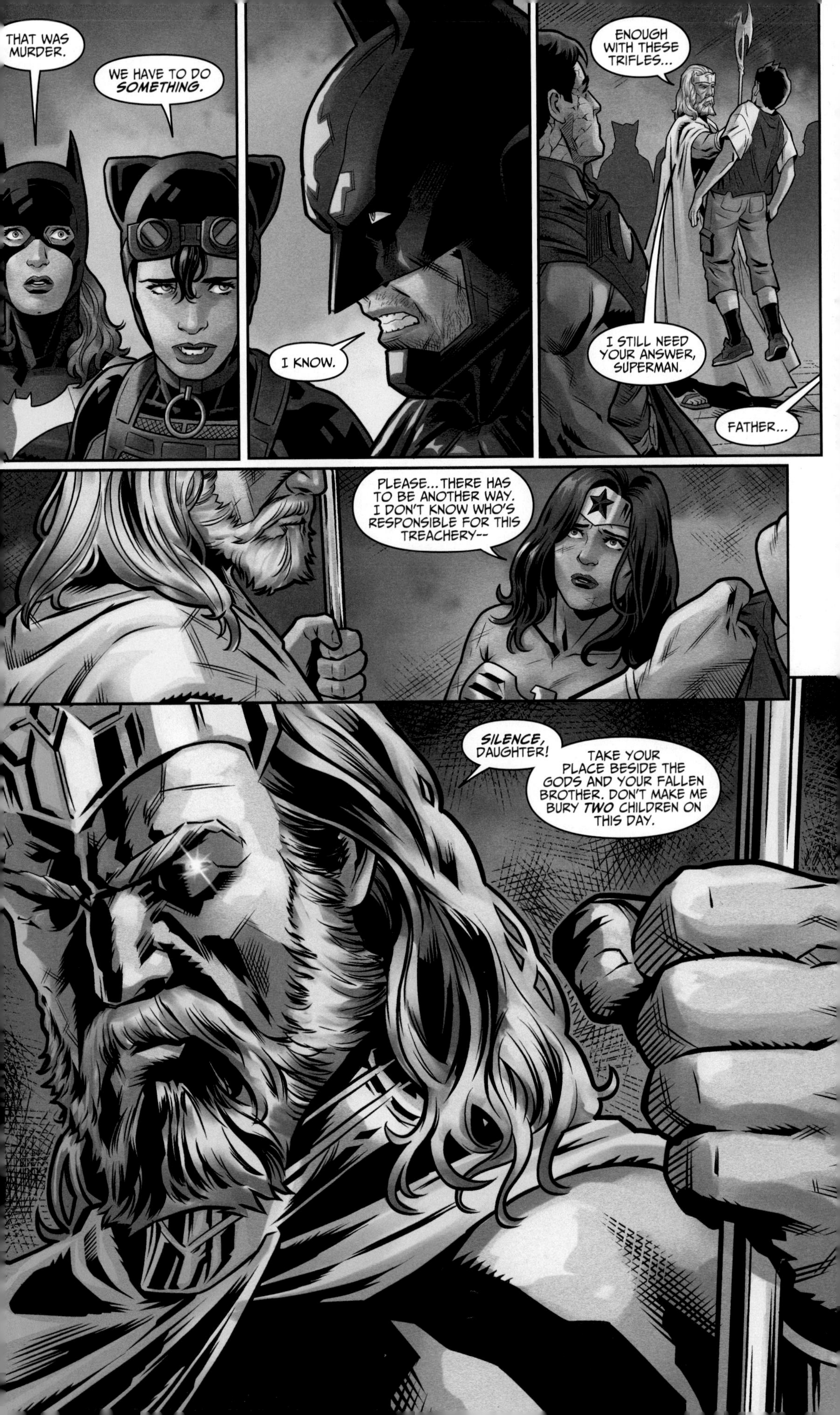
THAT WAS MURDER.
WE HAVE TO DO *SOMETHING.*
I KNOW.
ENOUGH WITH THESE TRIFLES...
I STILL NEED YOUR ANSWER, SUPERMAN.
FATHER...
PLEASE...THERE HAS TO BE ANOTHER WAY. I DON'T KNOW WHO'S RESPONSIBLE FOR THIS TREACHERY--
SILENCE, DAUGHTER!
TAKE YOUR PLACE BESIDE THE GODS AND YOUR FALLEN BROTHER. DON'T MAKE ME BURY *TWO* CHILDREN ON THIS DAY.

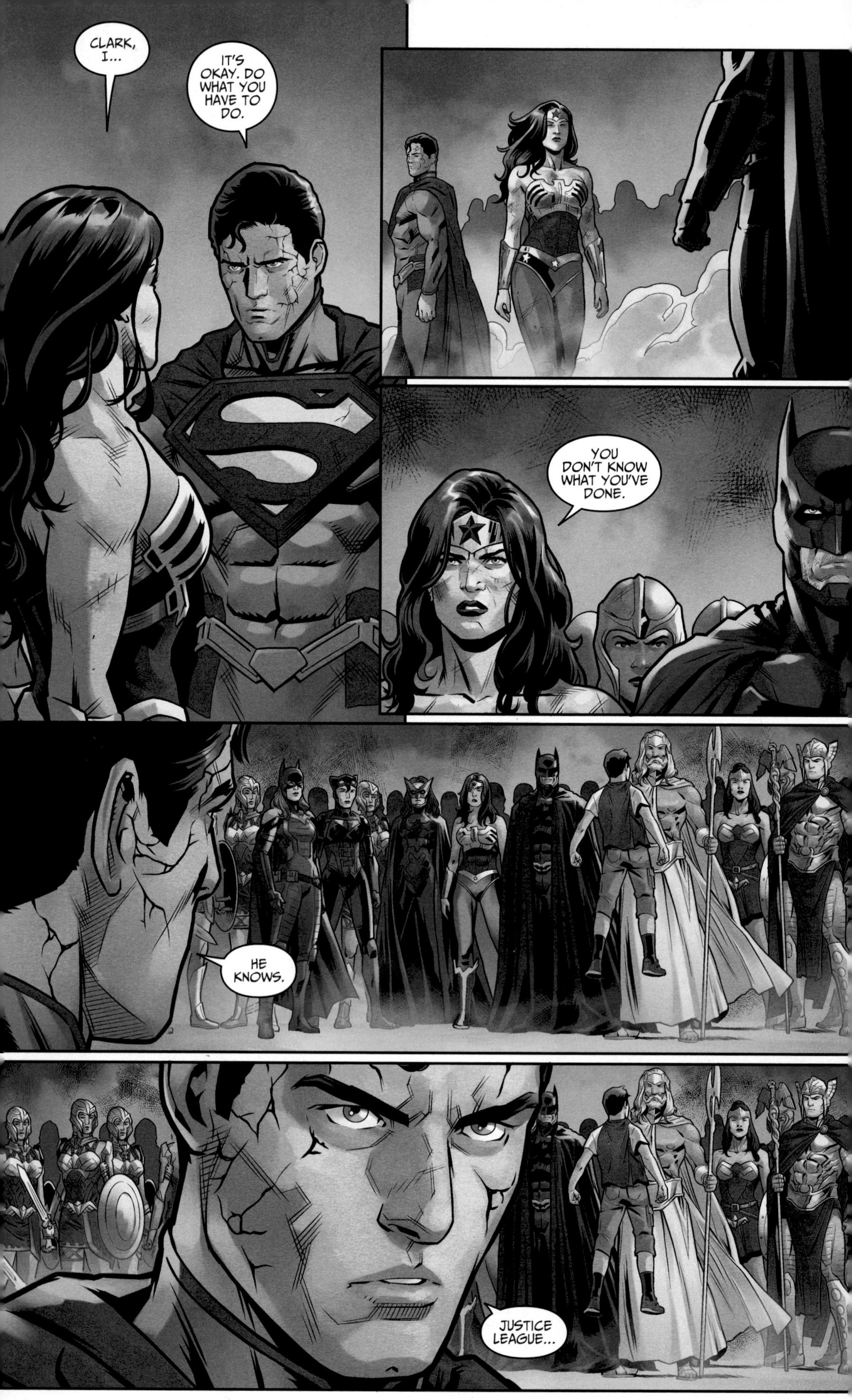
CLARK, I...
IT'S OKAY. DO WHAT YOU HAVE TO DO.
YOU DON'T KNOW WHAT YOU'VE DONE.
HE KNOWS.
JUSTICE LEAGUE...

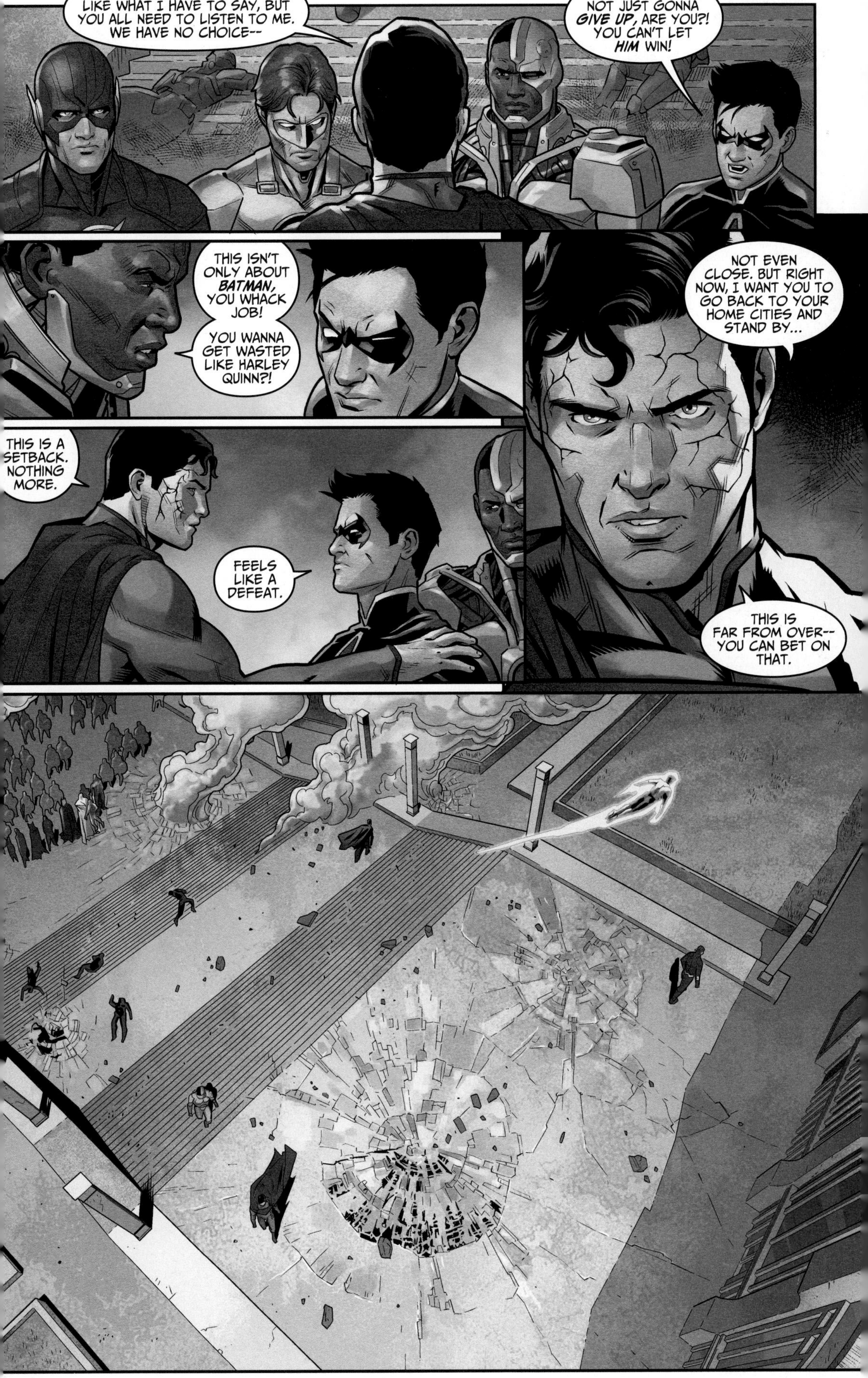
YOU'RE NOT GOING TO LIKE WHAT I HAVE TO SAY, BUT YOU ALL NEED TO LISTEN TO ME. WE HAVE NO CHOICE--
YOU'RE NOT JUST GONNA GIVE UP, ARE YOU?! YOU CAN'T LET HIM WIN!
THIS ISN'T ONLY ABOUT BATMAN, YOU WHACK JOB!
YOU WANNA GET WASTED LIKE HARLEY QUINN?!
THIS IS A SETBACK. NOTHING MORE.
FEELS LIKE A DEFEAT.
NOT EVEN CLOSE. BUT RIGHT NOW, I WANT YOU TO GO BACK TO YOUR HOME CITIES AND STAND BY...
THIS IS FAR FROM OVER-- YOU CAN BET ON THAT.

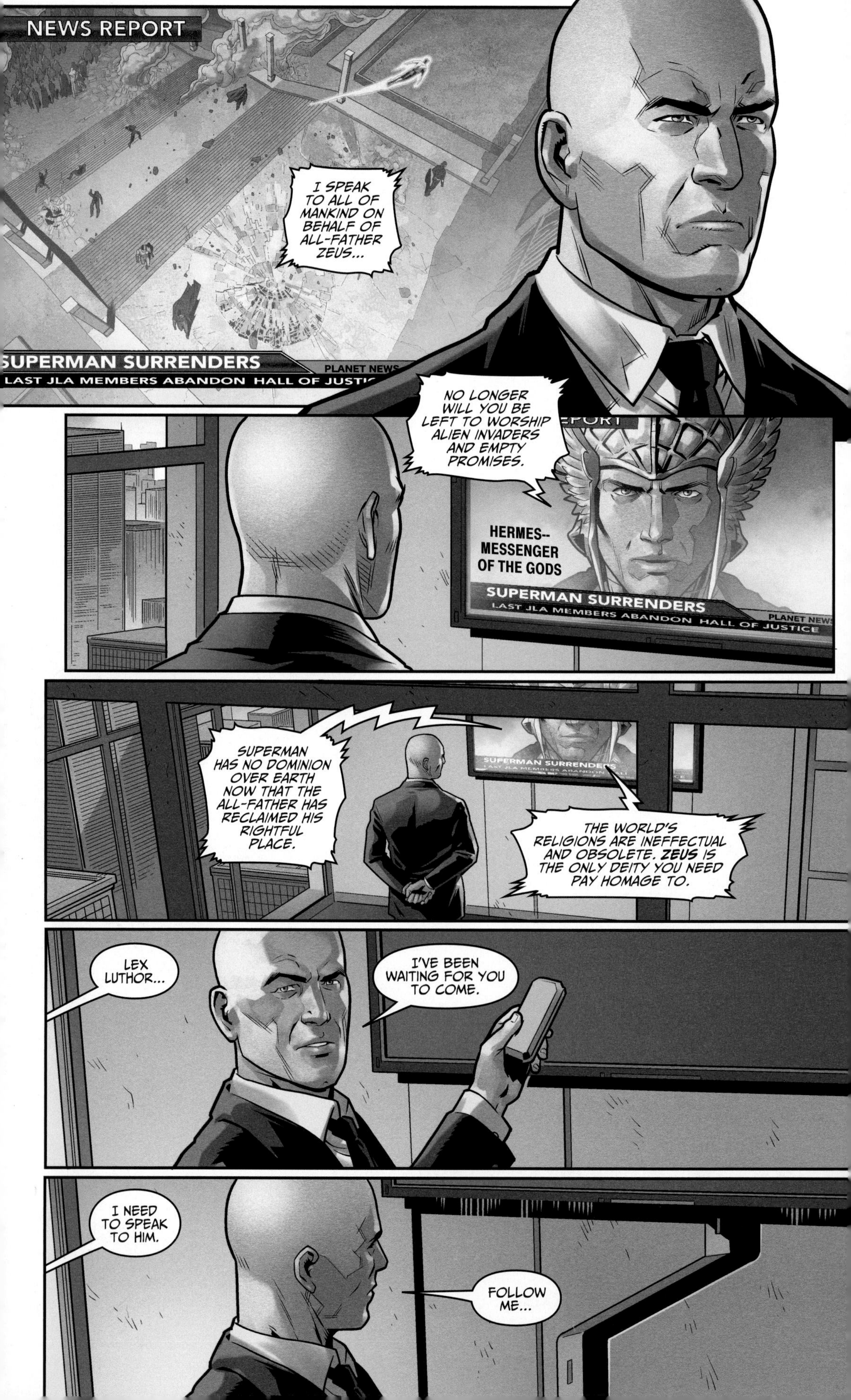
NEWS REPORT
I SPEAK TO ALL OF MANKIND ON BEHALF OF ALL-FATHER ZEUS...
SUPERMAN SURRENDERS
PLANET NEWS
LAST JLA MEMBERS ABANDON HALL OF JUSTICE
NO LONGER WILL YOU BE LEFT TO WORSHIP ALIEN INVADERS AND EMPTY PROMISES.
HERMES--MESSENGER OF THE GODS
SUPERMAN SURRENDERS
LAST JLA MEMBERS ABANDON HALL OF JUSTICE
PLANET NEWS
SUPERMAN HAS NO DOMINION OVER EARTH NOW THAT THE ALL-FATHER HAS RECLAIMED HIS RIGHTFUL PLACE.
THE WORLD'S RELIGIONS ARE INEFFECTUAL AND OBSOLETE. **ZEUS** IS THE ONLY DEITY YOU NEED PAY HOMAGE TO.
LEX LUTHOR...
I'VE BEEN WAITING FOR YOU TO COME.
I NEED TO SPEAK TO HIM.
FOLLOW ME...

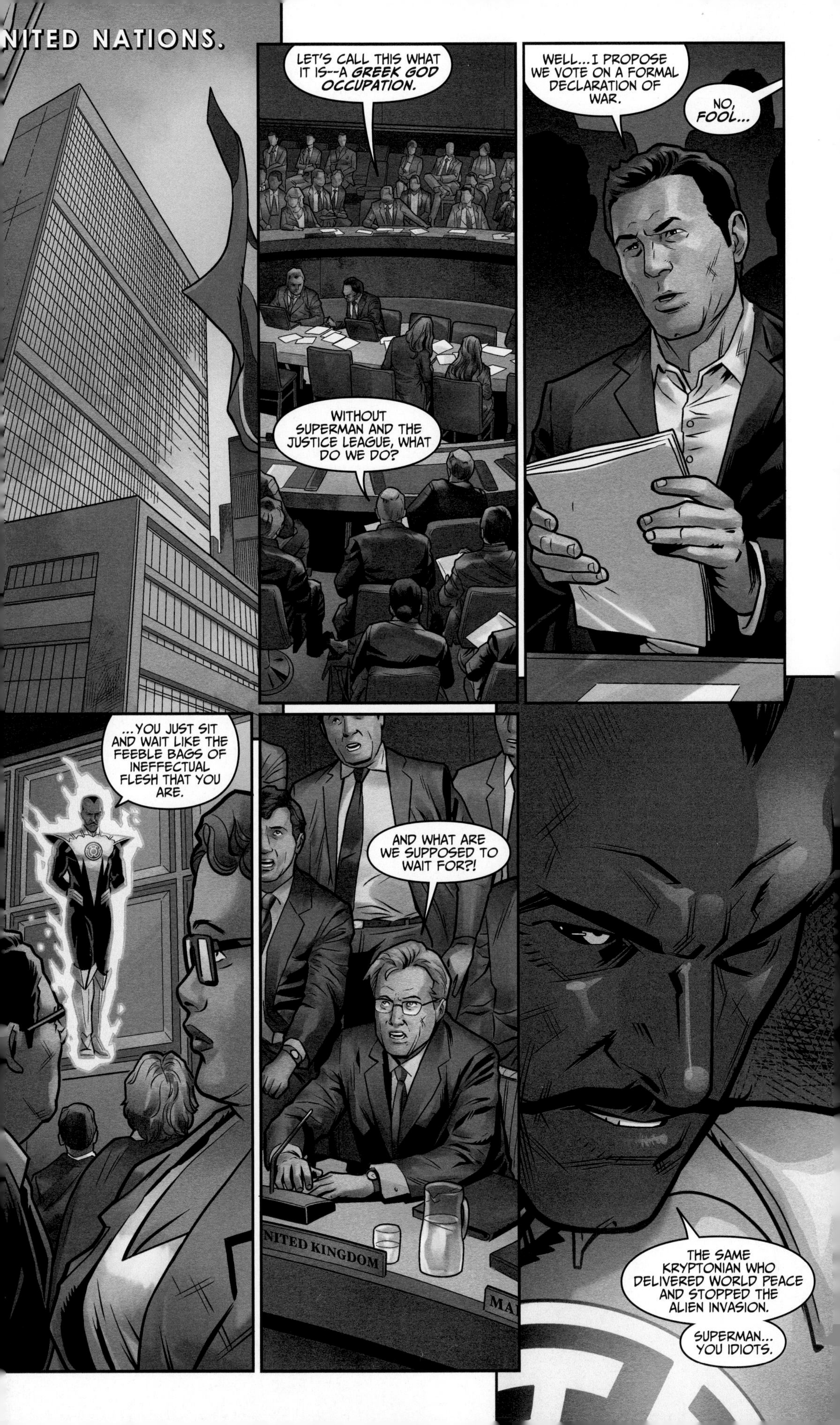
NITED NATIONS.
LET'S CALL THIS WHAT IT IS--A GREEK GOD OCCUPATION.
WITHOUT SUPERMAN AND THE JUSTICE LEAGUE, WHAT DO WE DO?
WELL...I PROPOSE WE VOTE ON A FORMAL DECLARATION OF WAR.
NO, FOOL...
...YOU JUST SIT AND WAIT LIKE THE FEEBLE BAGS OF INEFFECTUAL FLESH THAT YOU ARE.
AND WHAT ARE WE SUPPOSED TO WAIT FOR?!
NITED KINGDOM
THE SAME KRYPTONIAN WHO DELIVERED WORLD PEACE AND STOPPED THE ALIEN INVASION.
SUPERMAN... YOU IDIOTS.

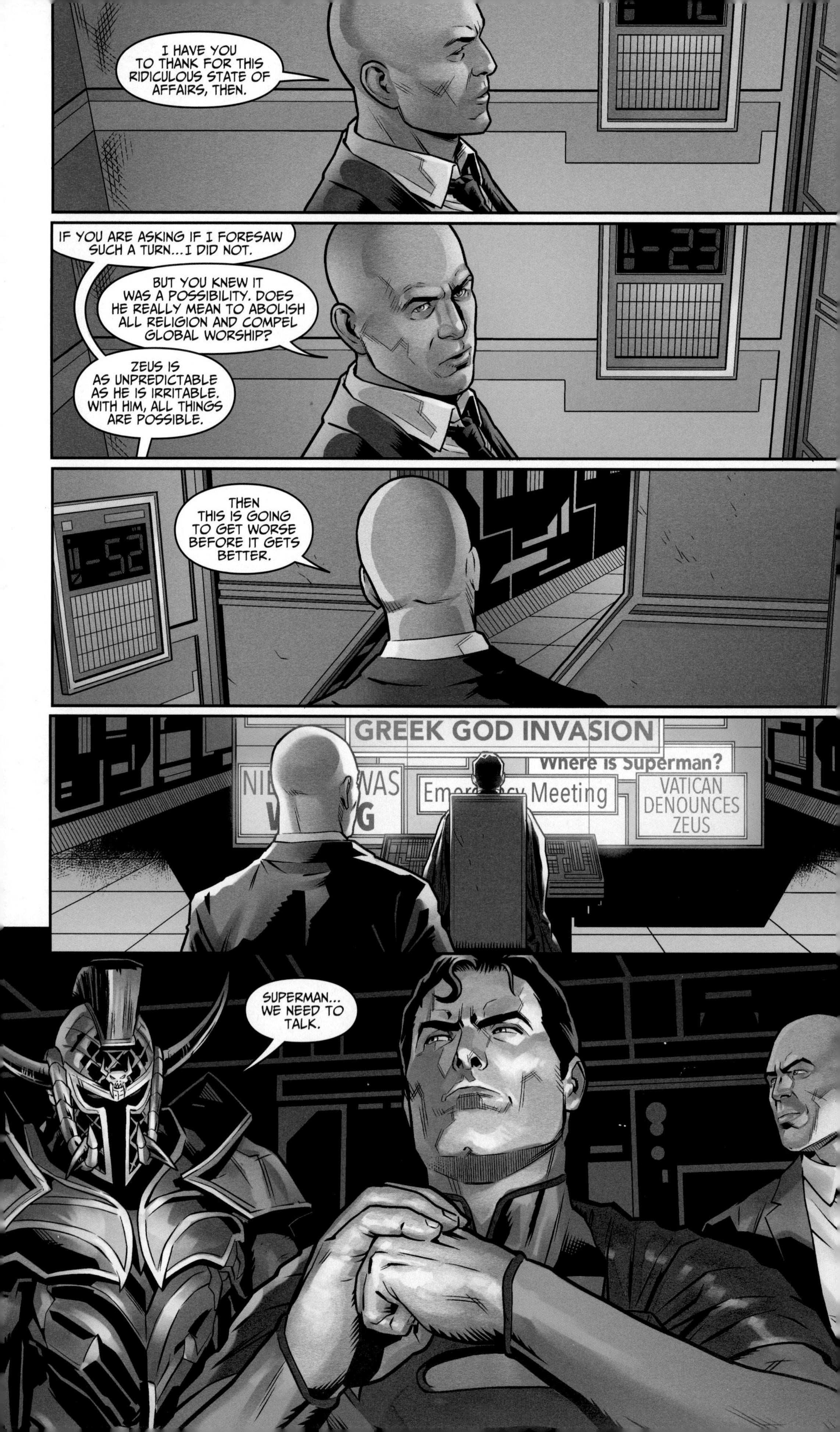

I HAVE YOU TO THANK FOR THIS RIDICULOUS STATE OF AFFAIRS, THEN.
IF YOU ARE ASKING IF I FORESAW SUCH A TURN...I DID NOT.
BUT YOU KNEW IT WAS A POSSIBILITY. DOES HE REALLY MEAN TO ABOLISH ALL RELIGION AND COMPEL GLOBAL WORSHIP?
ZEUS IS AS UNPREDICTABLE AS HE IS IRRITABLE. WITH HIM, ALL THINGS ARE POSSIBLE.
THEN THIS IS GOING TO GET WORSE BEFORE IT GETS BETTER.
GREEK GOD INVASION
Where is Superman?
VATICAN DENOUNCES ZEUS
SUPERMAN... WE NEED TO TALK.

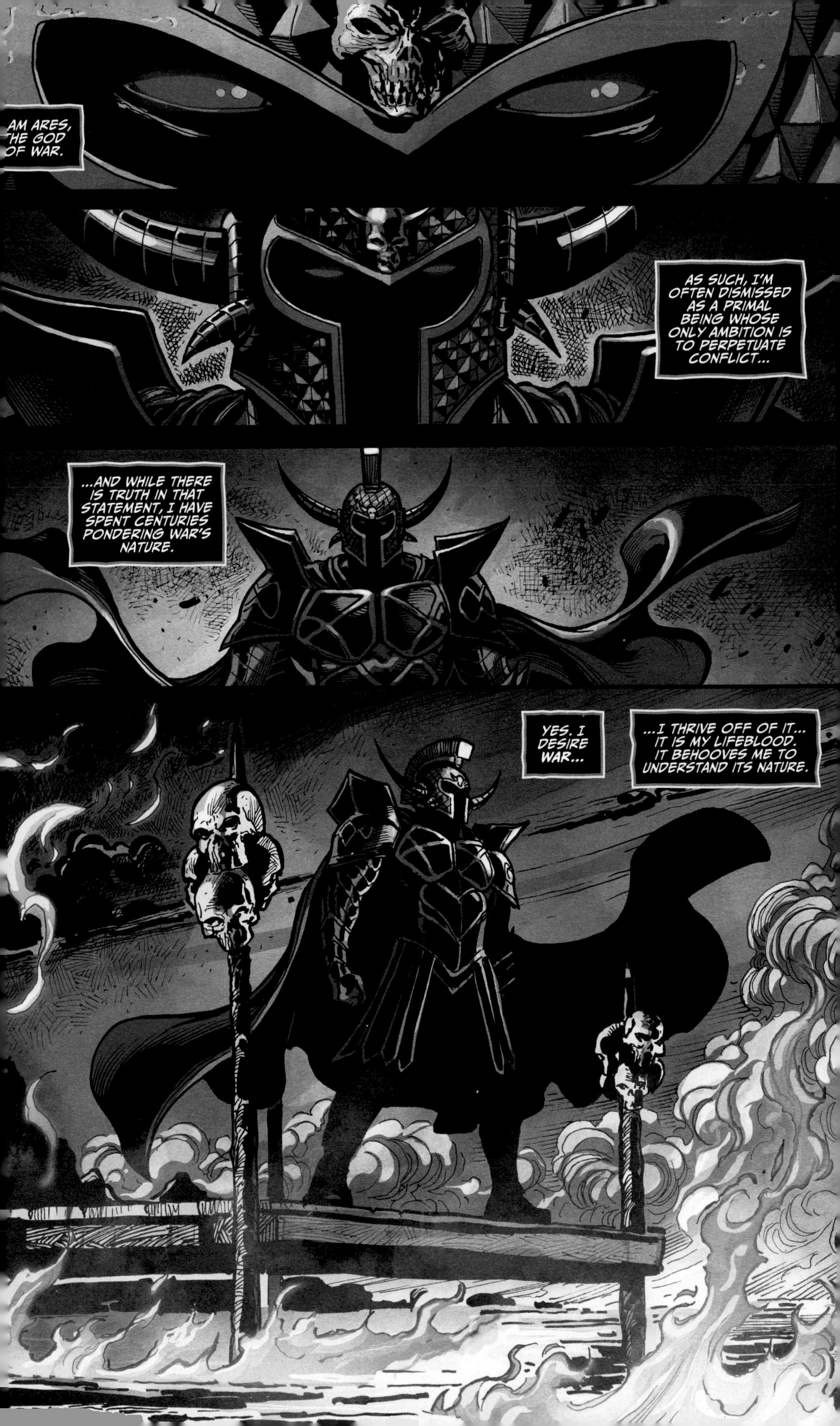
AM ARES, THE GOD OF WAR.
AS SUCH, I'M OFTEN DISMISSED AS A PRIMAL BEING WHOSE ONLY AMBITION IS TO PERPETUATE CONFLICT...
...AND WHILE THERE IS TRUTH IN THAT STATEMENT, I HAVE SPENT CENTURIES PONDERING WAR'S NATURE.
YES. I DESIRE WAR...
...I THRIVE OFF OF IT... IT IS MY LIFEBLOOD. IT BEHOOVES ME TO UNDERSTAND ITS NATURE.

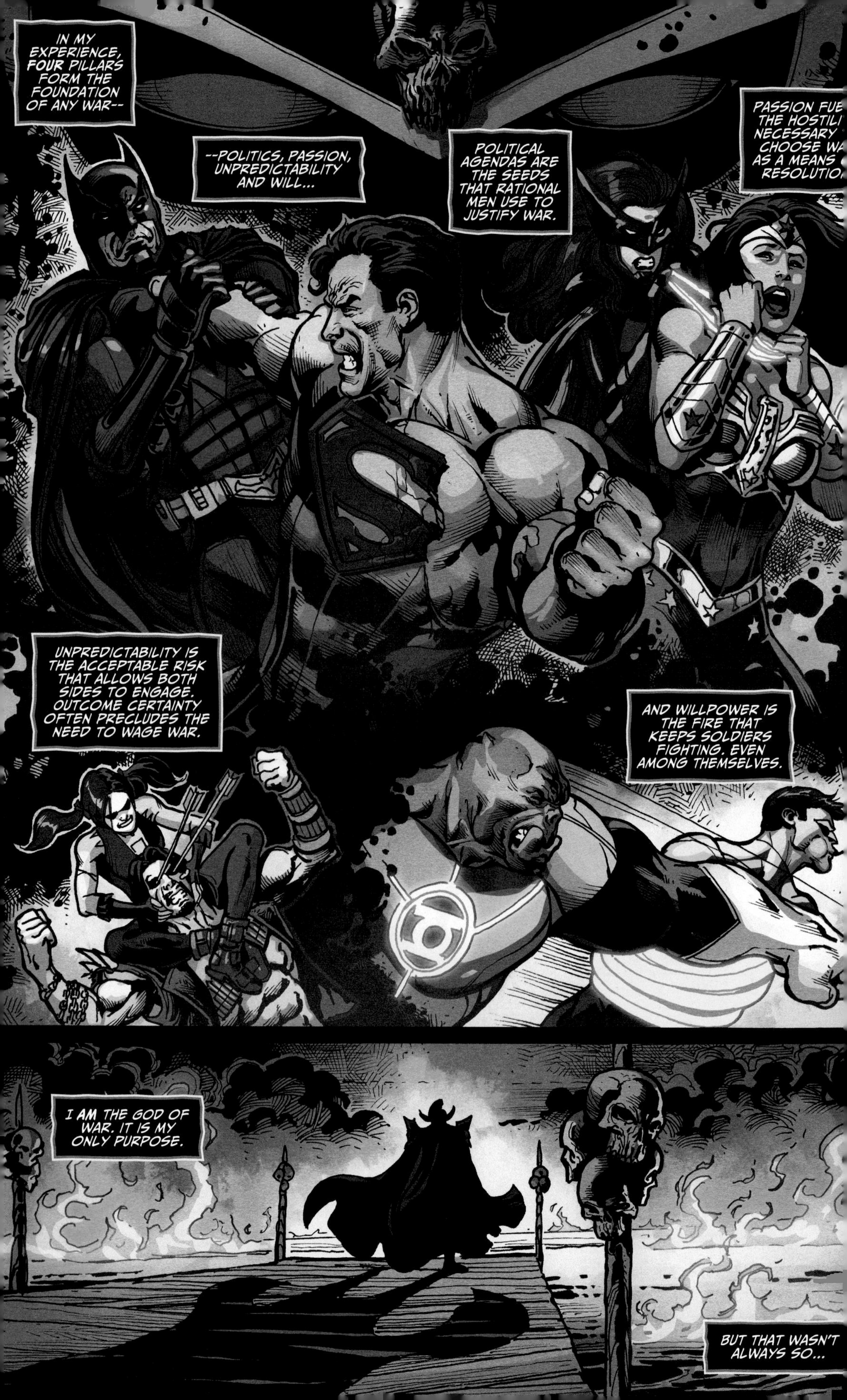

IN MY EXPERIENCE, FOUR PILLARS FORM THE FOUNDATION OF ANY WAR--
--POLITICS, PASSION, UNPREDICTABILITY AND WILL...
POLITICAL AGENDAS ARE THE SEEDS THAT RATIONAL MEN USE TO JUSTIFY WAR.
PASSION FUE THE HOSTILI NECESSARY CHOOSE WA AS A MEANS RESOLUTIO
UNPREDICTABILITY IS THE ACCEPTABLE RISK THAT ALLOWS BOTH SIDES TO ENGAGE. OUTCOME CERTAINTY OFTEN PRECLUDES THE NEED TO WAGE WAR.
AND WILLPOWER IS THE FIRE THAT KEEPS SOLDIERS FIGHTING. EVEN AMONG THEMSELVES.
I AM THE GOD OF WAR. IT IS MY ONLY PURPOSE.
BUT THAT WASN'T ALWAYS SO...

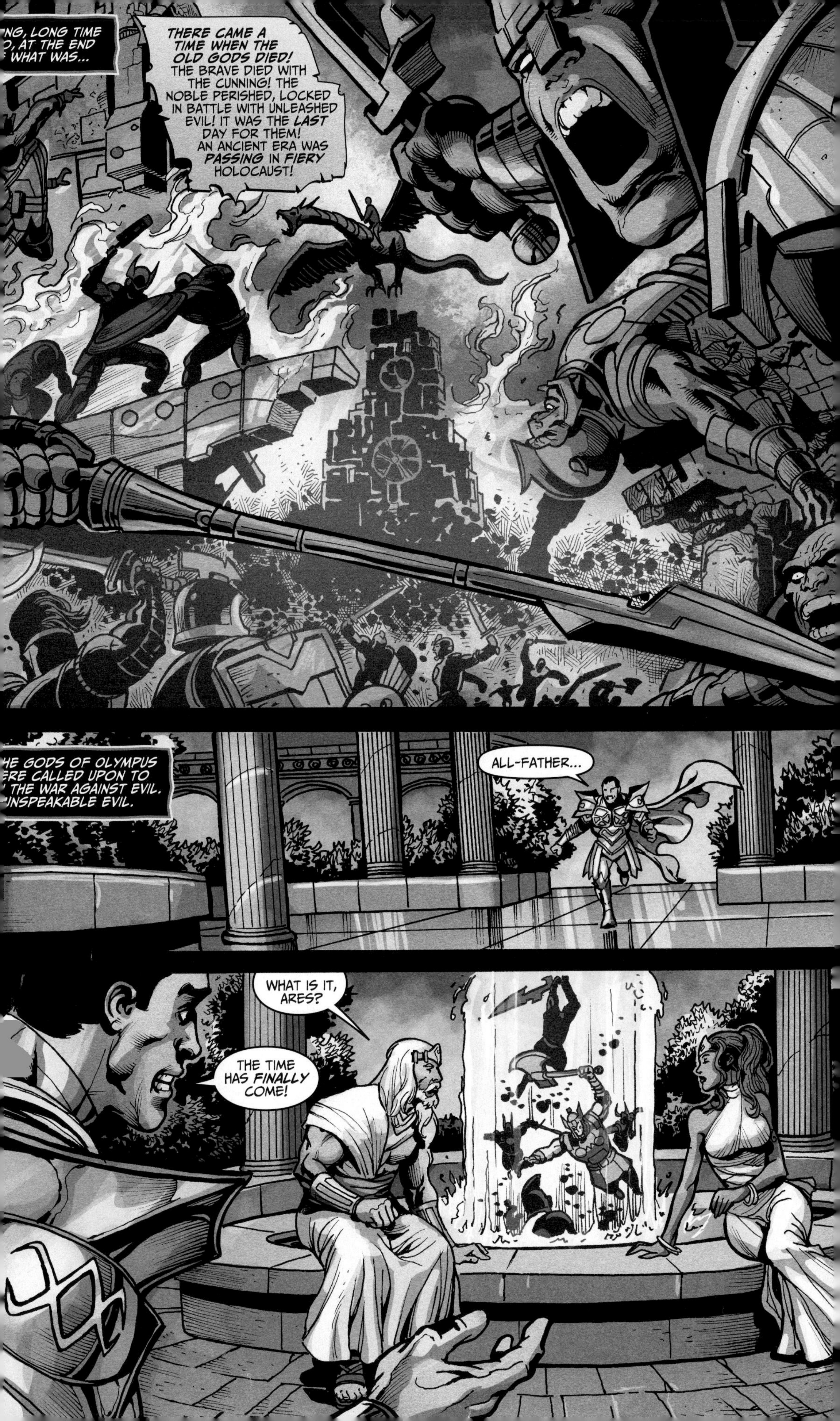

NG, LONG TIME
O, AT THE END
WHAT WAS...
THERE CAME A TIME WHEN THE OLD GODS DIED! THE BRAVE DIED WITH THE CUNNING! THE NOBLE PERISHED, LOCKED IN BATTLE WITH UNLEASHED EVIL! IT WAS THE LAST DAY FOR THEM! AN ANCIENT ERA WAS PASSING IN FIERY HOLOCAUST!
HE GODS OF OLYMPUS
ERE CALLED UPON TO
THE WAR AGAINST EVIL.
UNSPEAKABLE EVIL.
ALL-FATHER...
WHAT IS IT, ARES?
THE TIME HAS FINALLY COME!

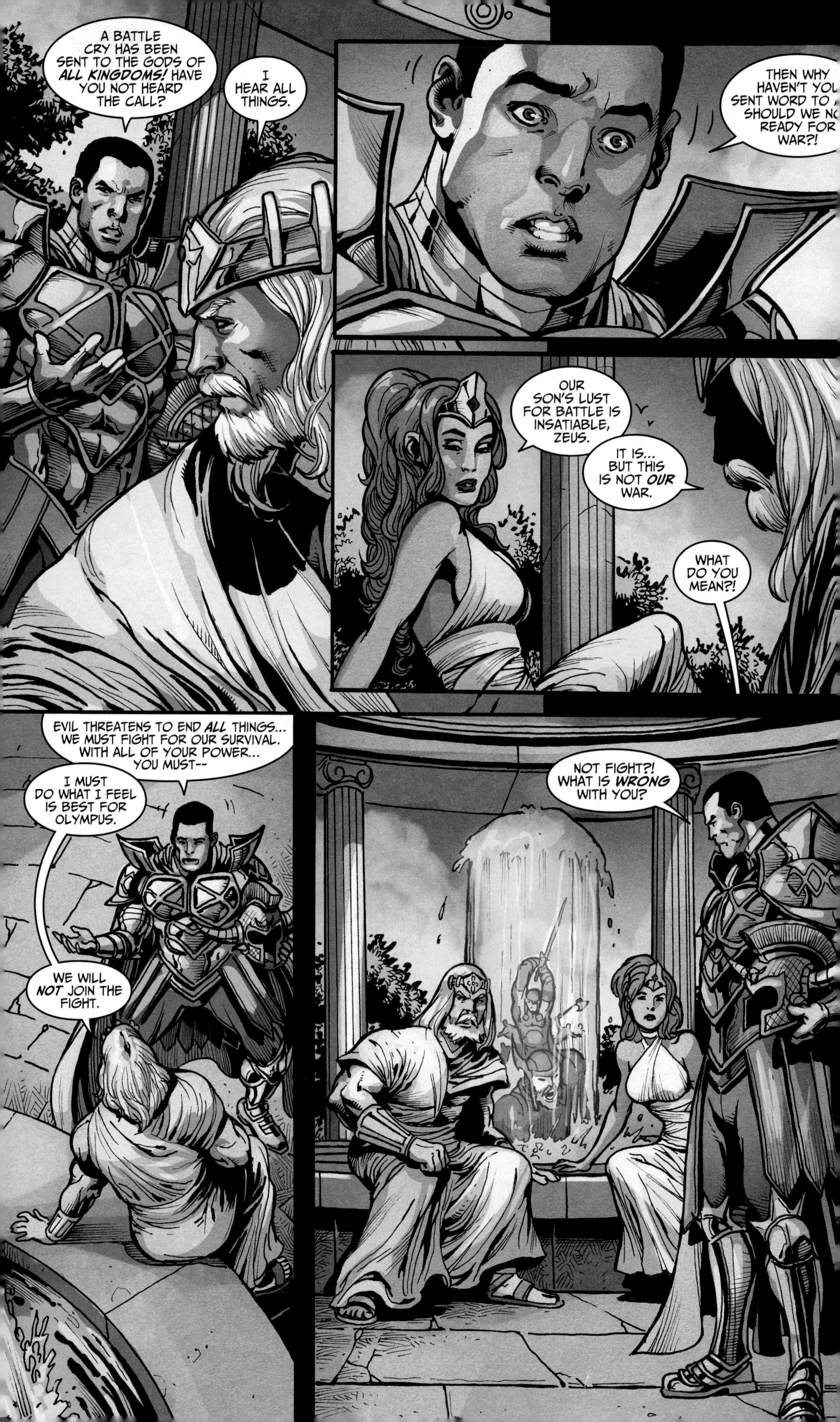
A BATTLE CRY HAS BEEN SENT TO THE GODS OF ALL KINGDOMS! HAVE YOU NOT HEARD THE CALL?
I HEAR ALL THINGS.
THEN WHY HAVEN'T YOU SENT WORD TO ... SHOULD WE N... READY FOR WAR?!
OUR SON'S LUST FOR BATTLE IS INSATIABLE, ZEUS.
IT IS... BUT THIS IS NOT OUR WAR.
WHAT DO YOU MEAN?!
EVIL THREATENS TO END ALL THINGS... WE MUST FIGHT FOR OUR SURVIVAL. WITH ALL OF YOUR POWER... YOU MUST--
I MUST DO WHAT I FEEL IS BEST FOR OLYMPUS.
WE WILL NOT JOIN THE FIGHT.
NOT FIGHT?! WHAT IS WRONG WITH YOU?

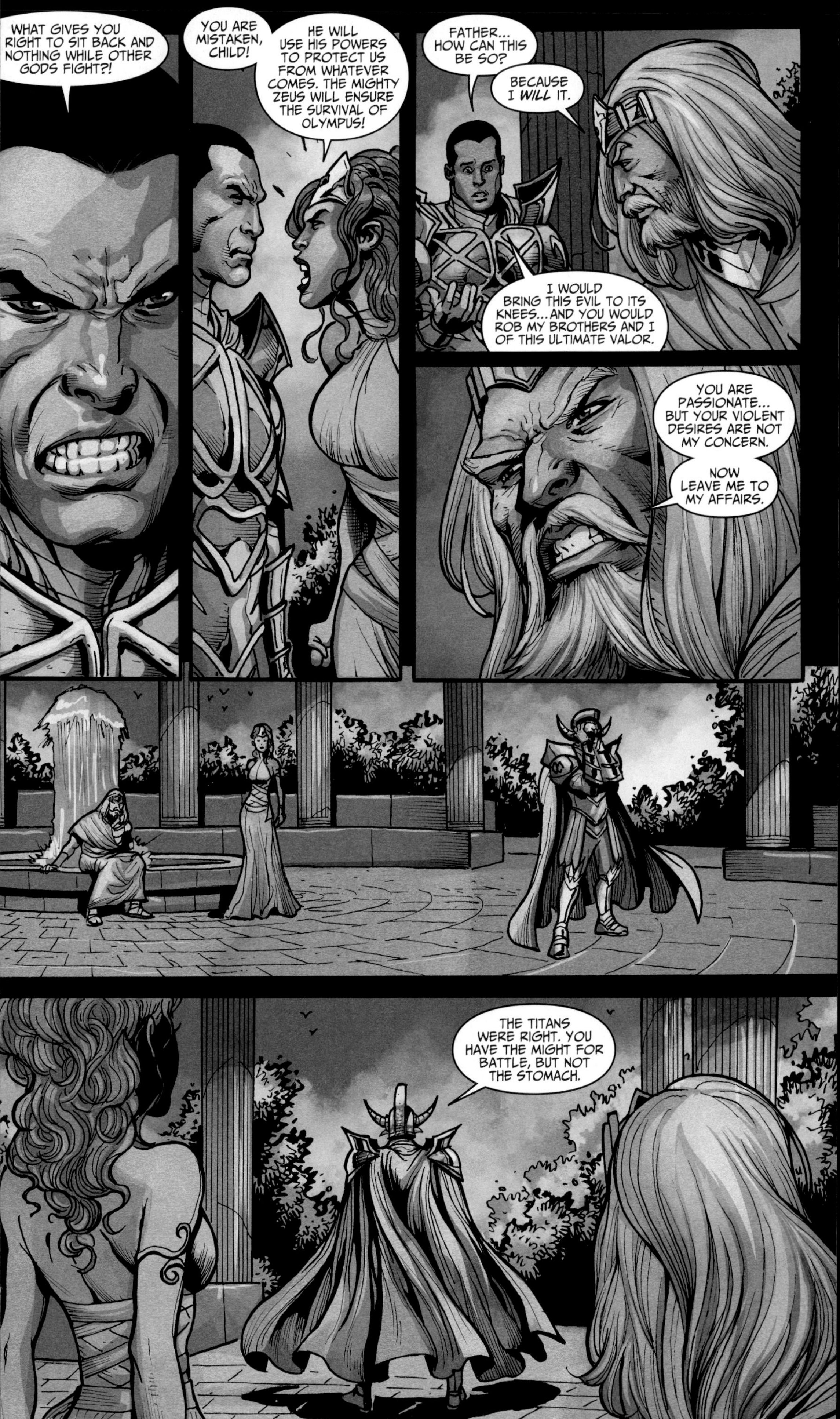
WHAT GIVES YOU RIGHT TO SIT BACK AND NOTHING WHILE OTHER GODS FIGHT?!
YOU ARE MISTAKEN, CHILD!
HE WILL USE HIS POWERS TO PROTECT US FROM WHATEVER COMES. THE MIGHTY ZEUS WILL ENSURE THE SURVIVAL OF OLYMPUS!
FATHER... HOW CAN THIS BE SO?
BECAUSE I **WILL** IT.
I WOULD BRING THIS EVIL TO ITS KNEES... AND YOU WOULD ROB MY BROTHERS AND I OF THIS ULTIMATE VALOR.
YOU ARE PASSIONATE... BUT YOUR VIOLENT DESIRES ARE NOT MY CONCERN.
NOW LEAVE ME TO MY AFFAIRS.
THE TITANS WERE RIGHT. YOU HAVE THE MIGHT FOR BATTLE, BUT NOT THE STOMACH.

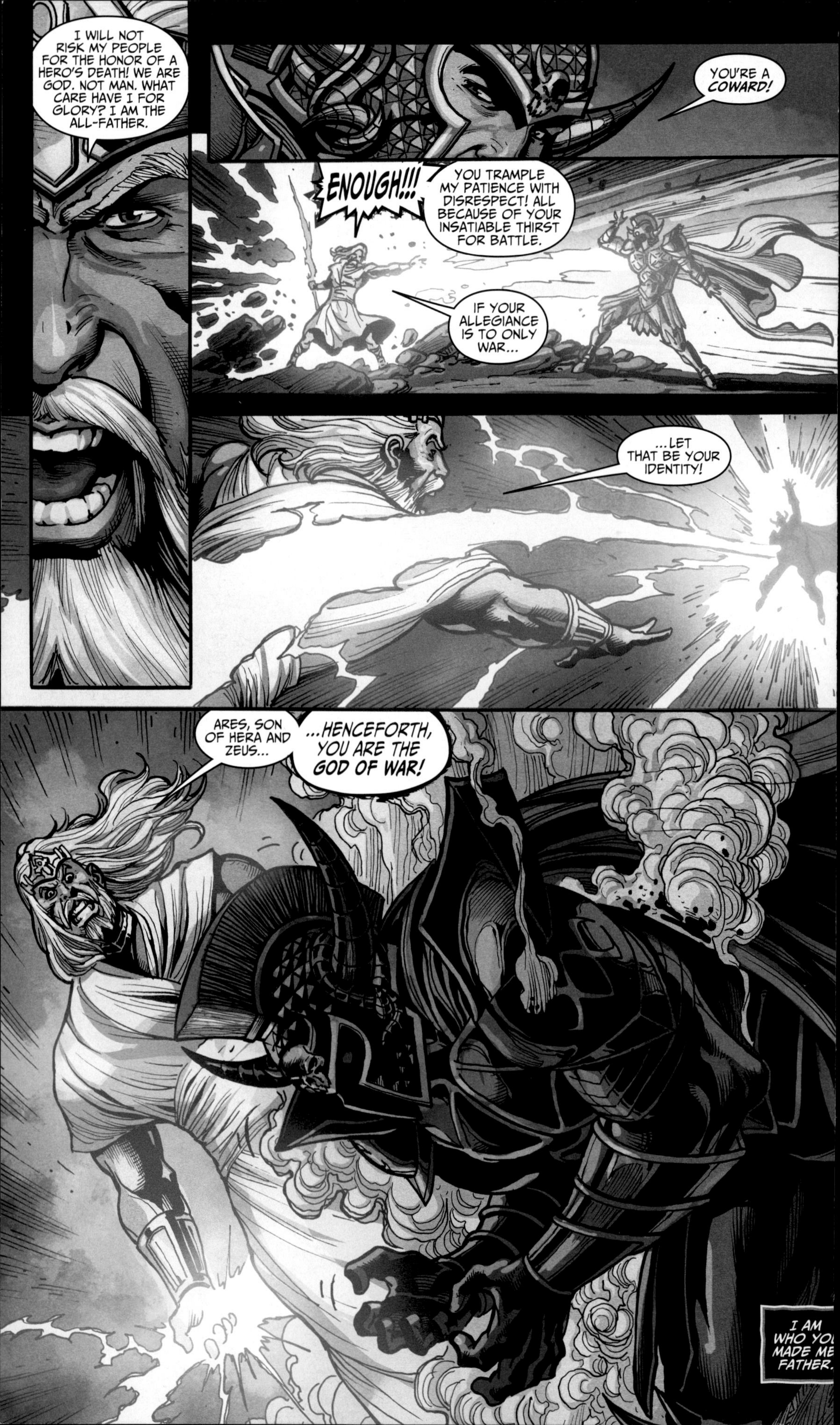
I WILL NOT RISK MY PEOPLE FOR THE HONOR OF A HERO'S DEATH! WE ARE GOD. NOT MAN. WHAT CARE HAVE I FOR GLORY? I AM THE ALL-FATHER.
YOU'RE A *COWARD!*
ENOUGH!!!
YOU TRAMPLE MY PATIENCE WITH DISRESPECT! ALL BECAUSE OF YOUR INSATIABLE THIRST FOR BATTLE.
IF YOUR ALLEGIANCE IS TO ONLY WAR...
...LET THAT BE YOUR IDENTITY!
ARES, SON OF HERA AND ZEUS...
...HENCEFORTH, YOU ARE THE GOD OF WAR!
I AM WHO YO MADE ME FATHER.

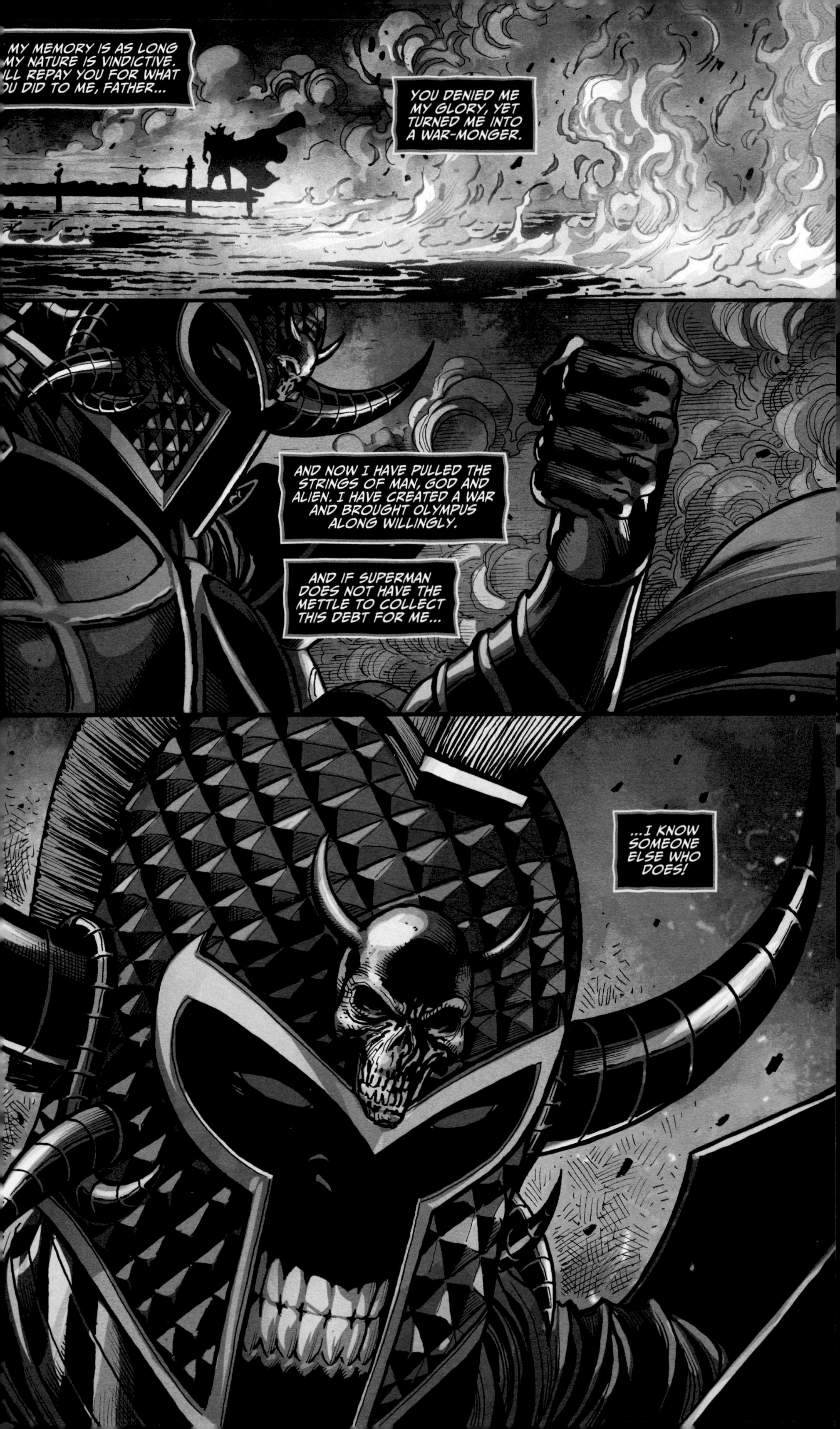
MY MEMORY IS AS LONG
MY NATURE IS VINDICTIVE.
ILL REPAY YOU FOR WHAT
OU DID TO ME, FATHER...
YOU DENIED ME MY GLORY, YET TURNED ME INTO A WAR-MONGER.
AND NOW I HAVE PULLED THE STRINGS OF MAN, GOD AND ALIEN. I HAVE CREATED A WAR AND BROUGHT OLYMPUS ALONG WILLINGLY.
AND IF SUPERMAN DOES NOT HAVE THE METTLE TO COLLECT THIS DEBT FOR ME...
...I KNOW SOMEONE ELSE WHO DOES!

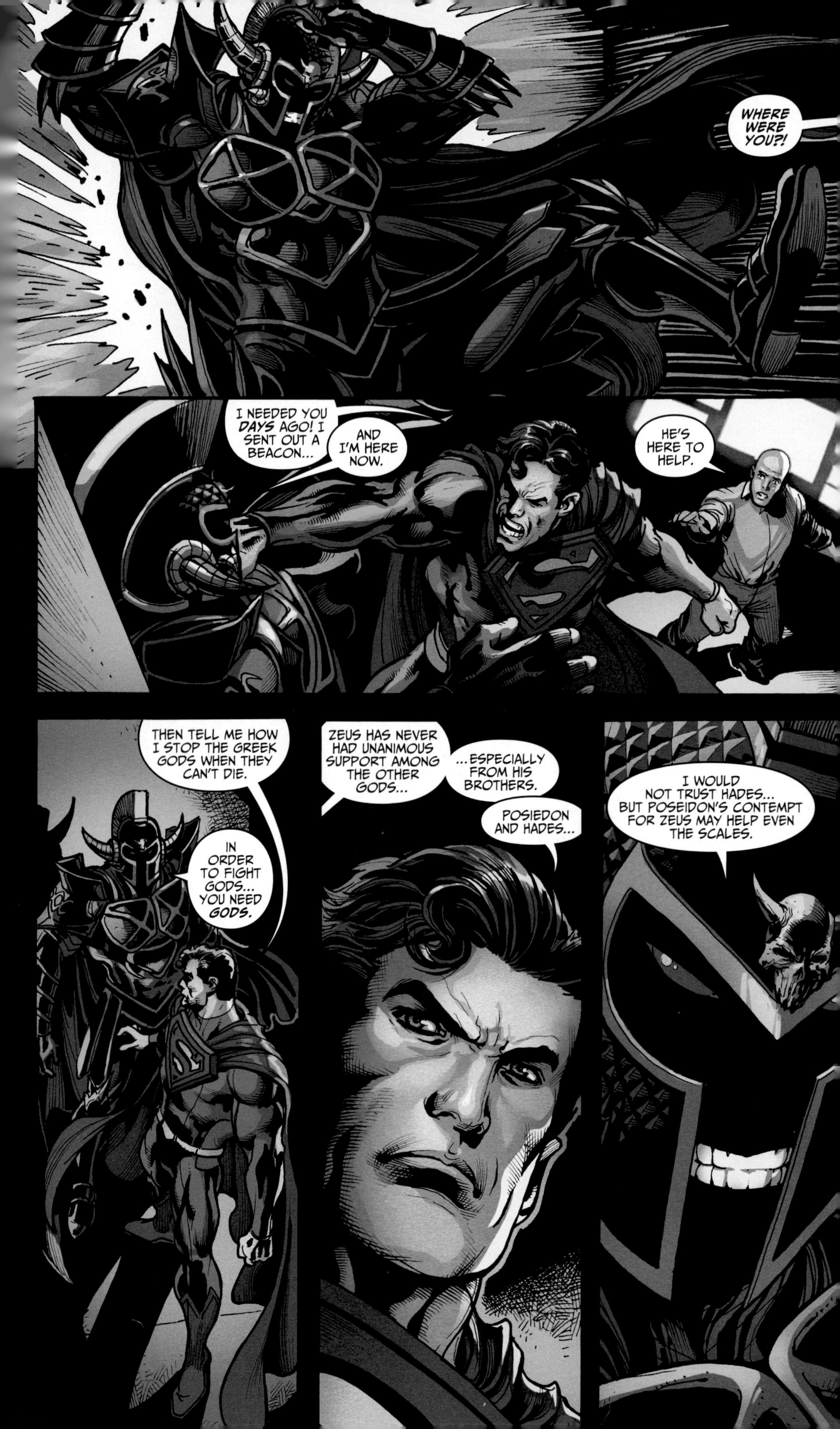
WHERE WERE YOU?!
I NEEDED YOU *DAYS* AGO! I SENT OUT A BEACON...
AND I'M HERE NOW.
HE'S HERE TO HELP.
THEN TELL ME HOW I STOP THE GREEK GODS WHEN THEY CAN'T DIE.
IN ORDER TO FIGHT GODS... YOU NEED *GODS.*
ZEUS HAS NEVER HAD UNANIMOUS SUPPORT AMONG THE OTHER GODS...
...ESPECIALLY FROM HIS BROTHERS.
POSIEDON AND HADES...
I WOULD NOT TRUST HADES... BUT POSEIDON'S CONTEMPT FOR ZEUS MAY HELP EVEN THE SCALES.

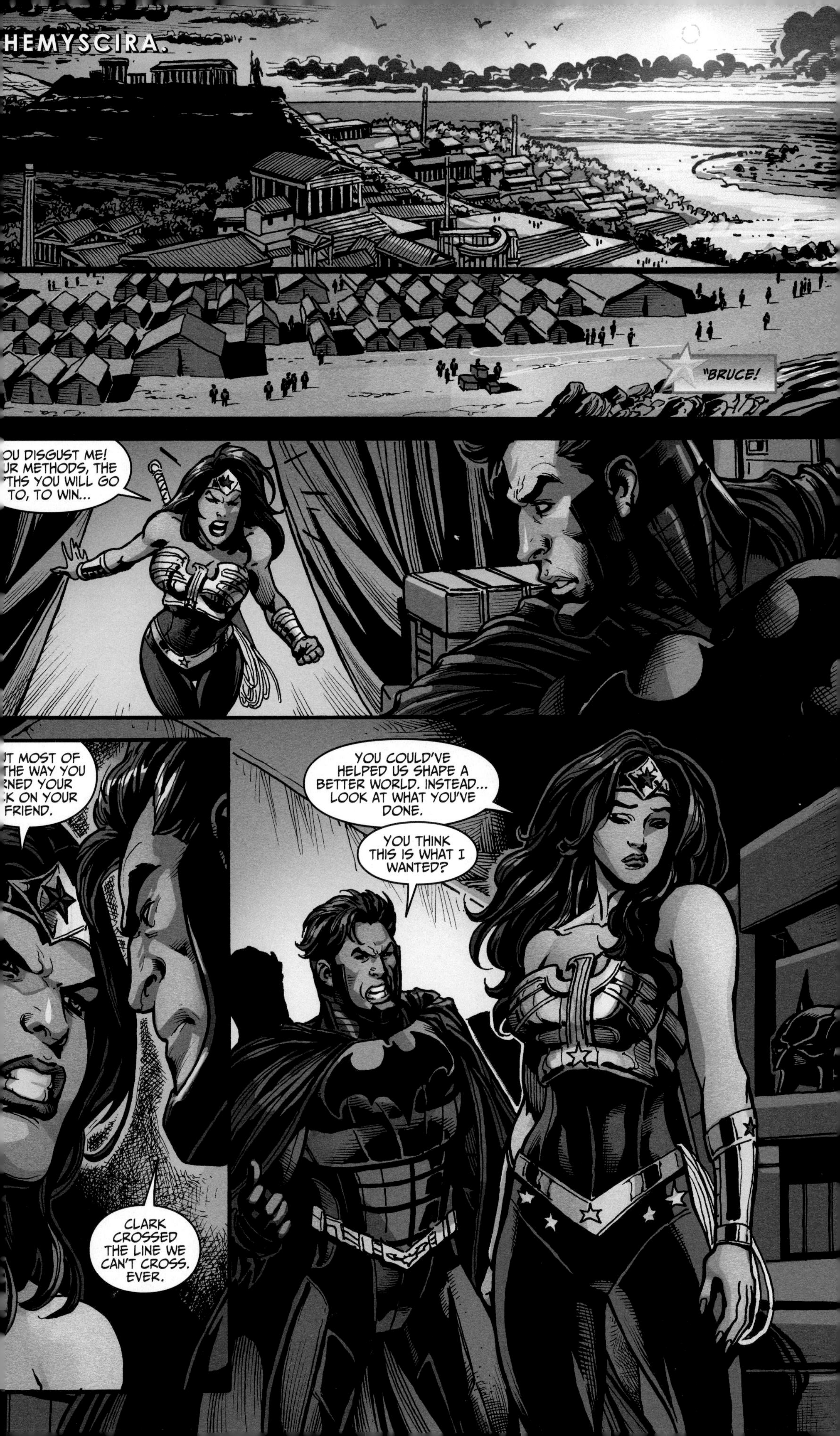
HEMYSCIRA.
"BRUCE!
OU DISGUST ME! UR METHODS, THE THS YOU WILL GO TO, TO WIN...
T MOST OF THE WAY YOU RNED YOUR K ON YOUR FRIEND.
CLARK CROSSED THE LINE WE CAN'T CROSS. EVER.
YOU COULD'VE HELPED US SHAPE A BETTER WORLD. INSTEAD... LOOK AT WHAT YOU'VE DONE.
YOU THINK THIS IS WHAT I WANTED?

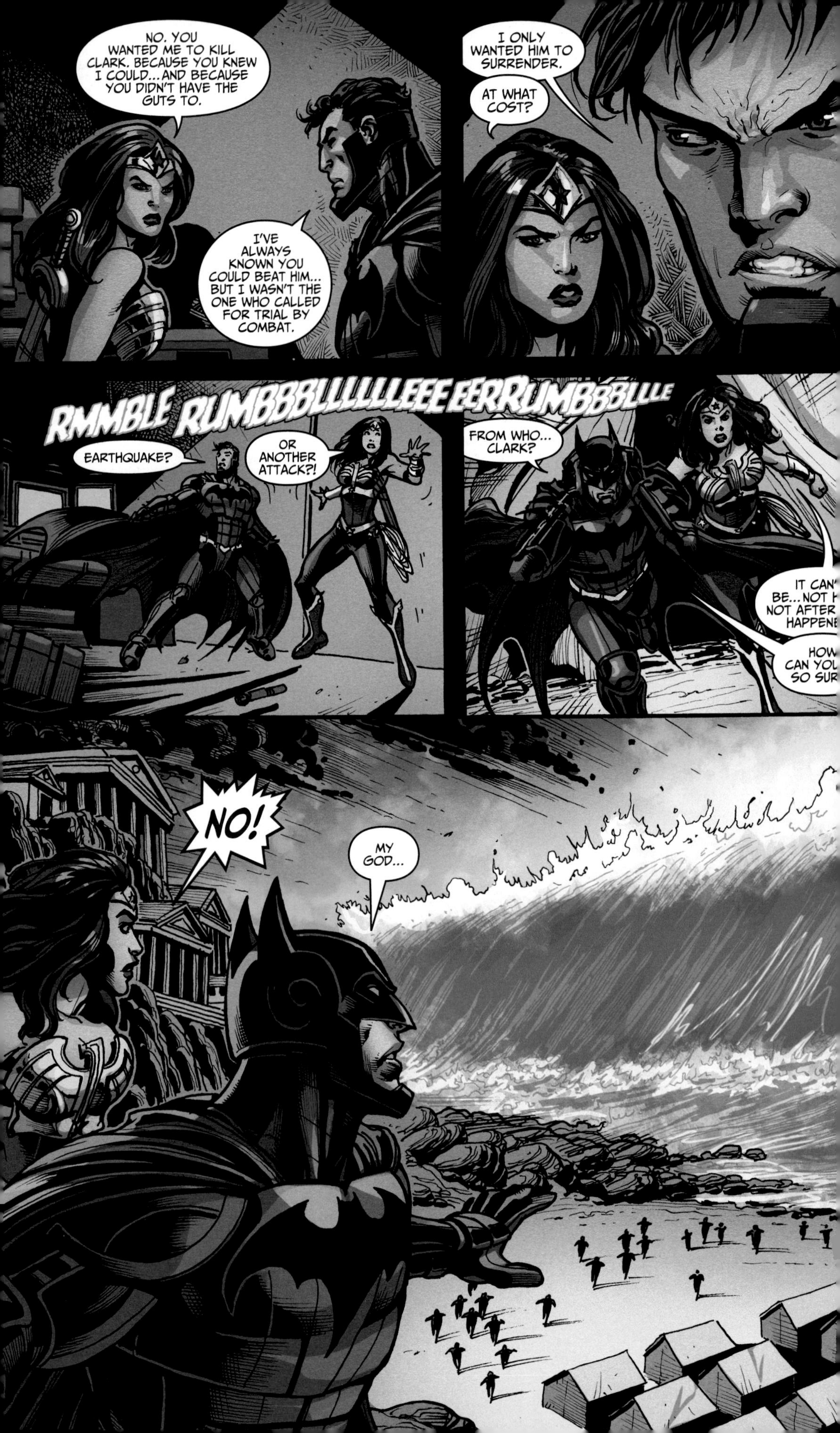
NO. YOU WANTED ME TO KILL CLARK. BECAUSE YOU KNEW I COULD...AND BECAUSE YOU DIDN'T HAVE THE GUTS TO.
I'VE ALWAYS KNOWN YOU COULD BEAT HIM... BUT I WASN'T THE ONE WHO CALLED FOR TRIAL BY COMBAT.
I ONLY WANTED HIM TO SURRENDER.
AT WHAT COST?
RMMBLE RUMBBBLLLLLLLEEEEERRUMBBBLLLE
EARTHQUAKE?
OR ANOTHER ATTACK?!
FROM WHO... CLARK?
NO!
MY GOD...

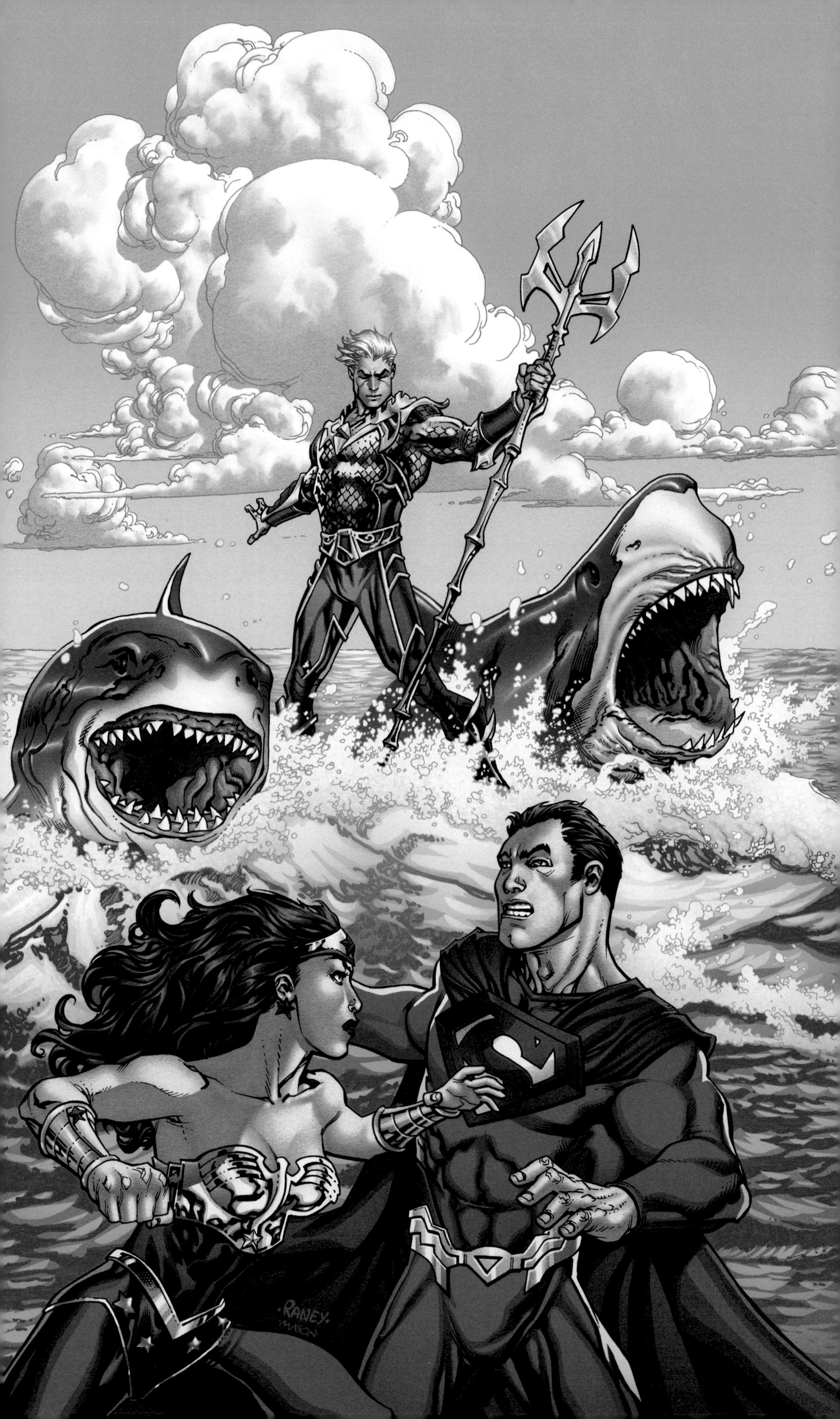
RANEY
MASON

"Making Waves" **Brian Buccellato** Writer **Xermanico** **Mike S. Miller** Artists **J. Nanjan** **Rex Lokus** Colorists
Cover Art by **Tom Raney & Thomas Mason**

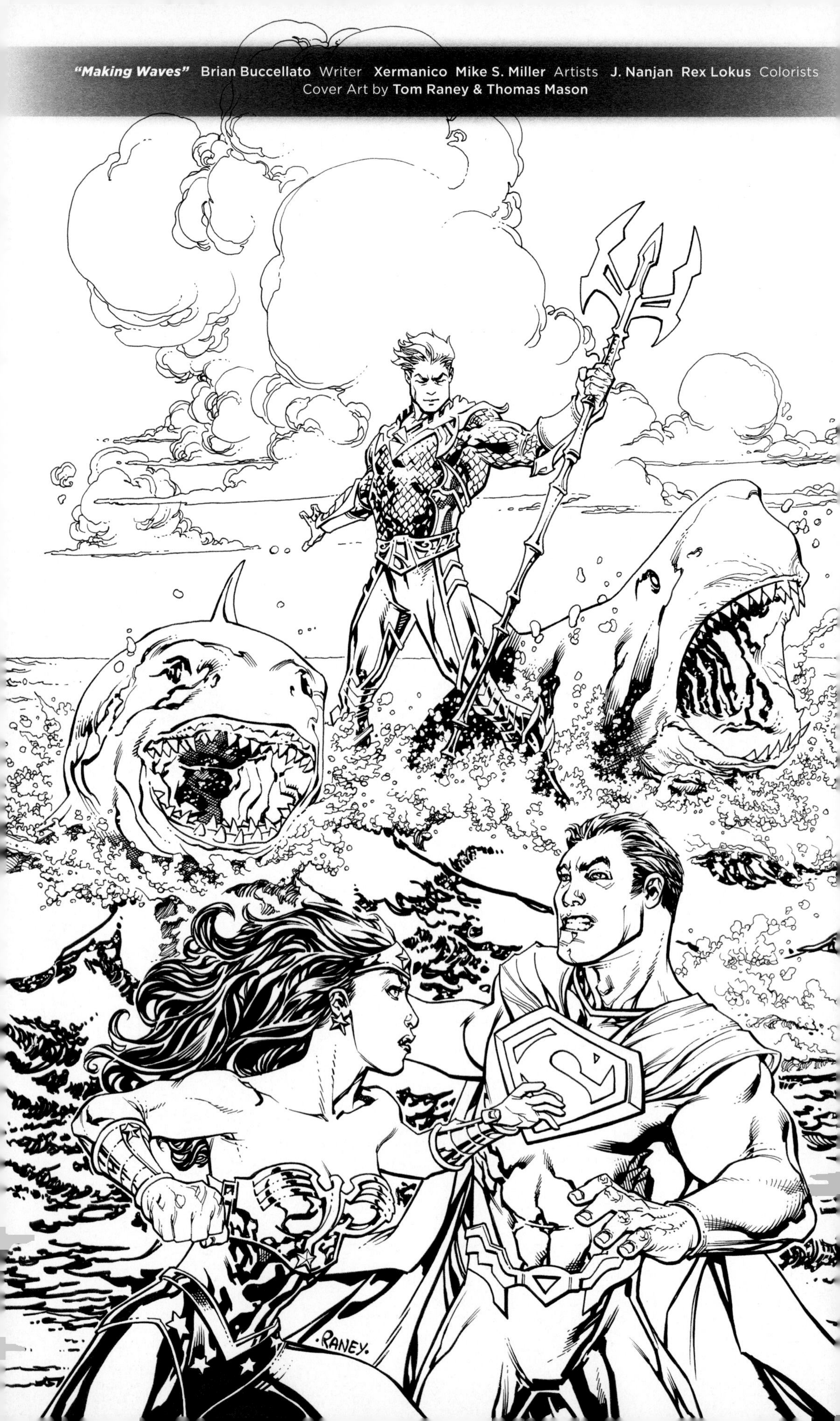

RANEY

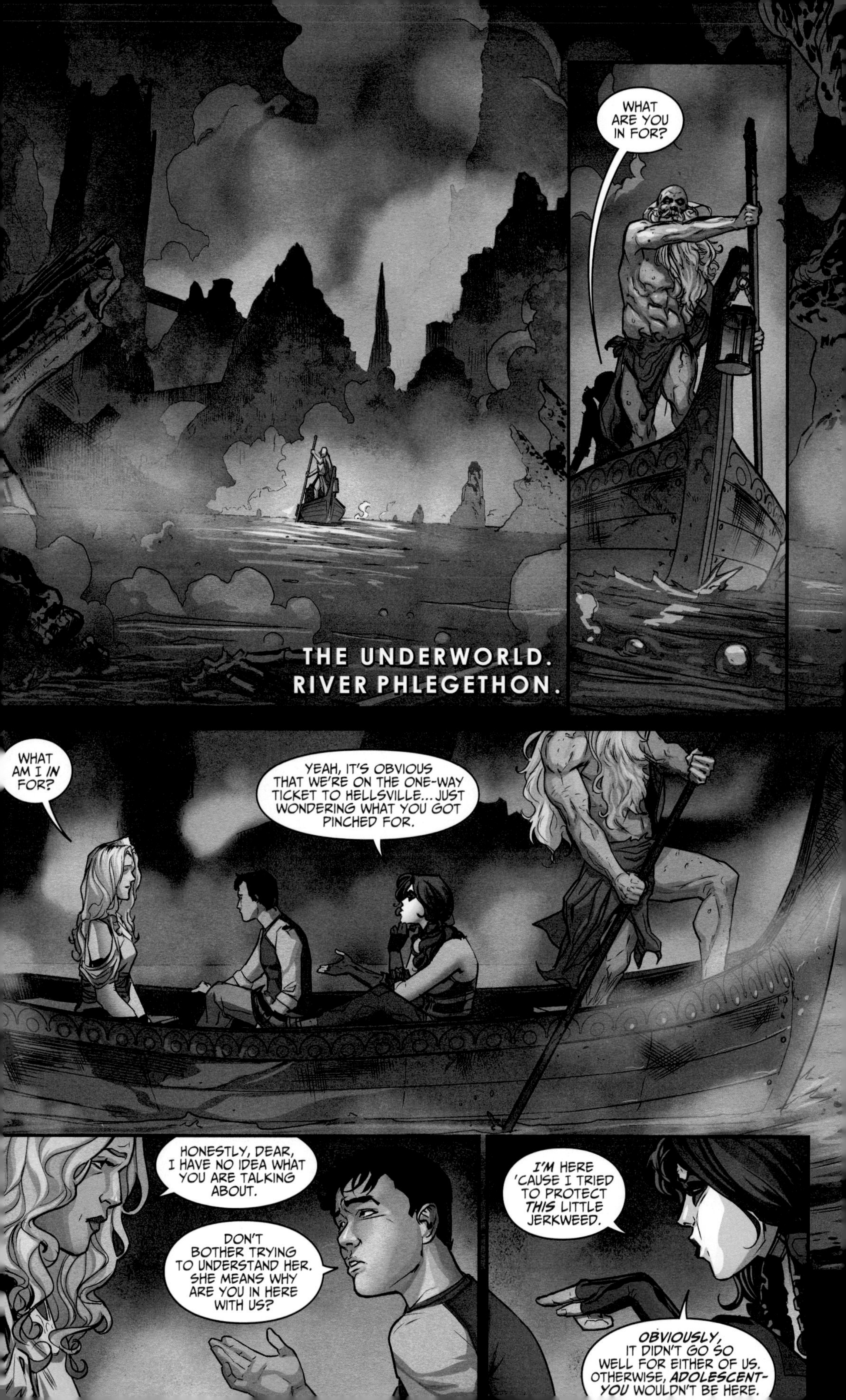

THE UNDERWORLD. RIVER PHLEGETHON.
WHAT ARE YOU IN FOR?
WHAT AM I *IN* FOR?
YEAH, IT'S OBVIOUS THAT WE'RE ON THE ONE-WAY TICKET TO HELLSVILLE... JUST WONDERING WHAT YOU GOT PINCHED FOR.
HONESTLY, DEAR, I HAVE NO IDEA WHAT YOU ARE TALKING ABOUT.
DON'T BOTHER TRYING TO UNDERSTAND HER. SHE MEANS WHY ARE YOU IN HERE WITH US?
I'M HERE 'CAUSE I TRIED TO PROTECT *THIS* LITTLE JERKWEED.
OBVIOUSLY, IT DIDN'T GO SO WELL FOR EITHER OF US. OTHERWISE, ***ADOLESCENT-YOU*** WOULDN'T BE HERE.

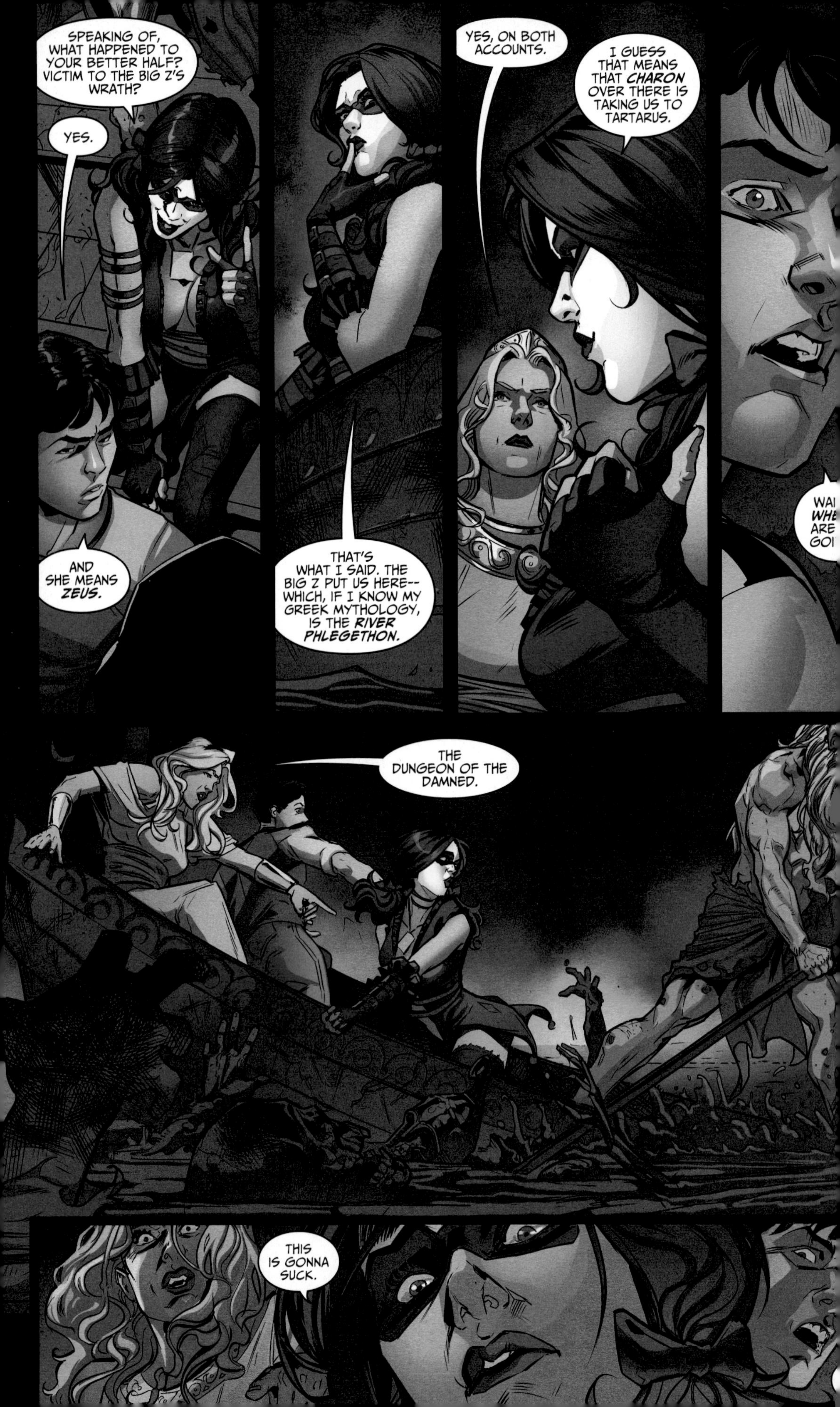
SPEAKING OF, WHAT HAPPENED TO YOUR BETTER HALF? VICTIM TO THE BIG Z'S WRATH?
YES.
AND SHE MEANS *ZEUS.*
THAT'S WHAT I SAID. THE BIG Z PUT US HERE-- WHICH, IF I KNOW MY GREEK MYTHOLOGY, IS THE *RIVER PHLEGETHON.*
YES, ON BOTH ACCOUNTS.
I GUESS THAT MEANS THAT *CHARON* OVER THERE IS TAKING US TO TARTARUS.
THE DUNGEON OF THE DAMNED.
THIS IS GONNA SUCK.

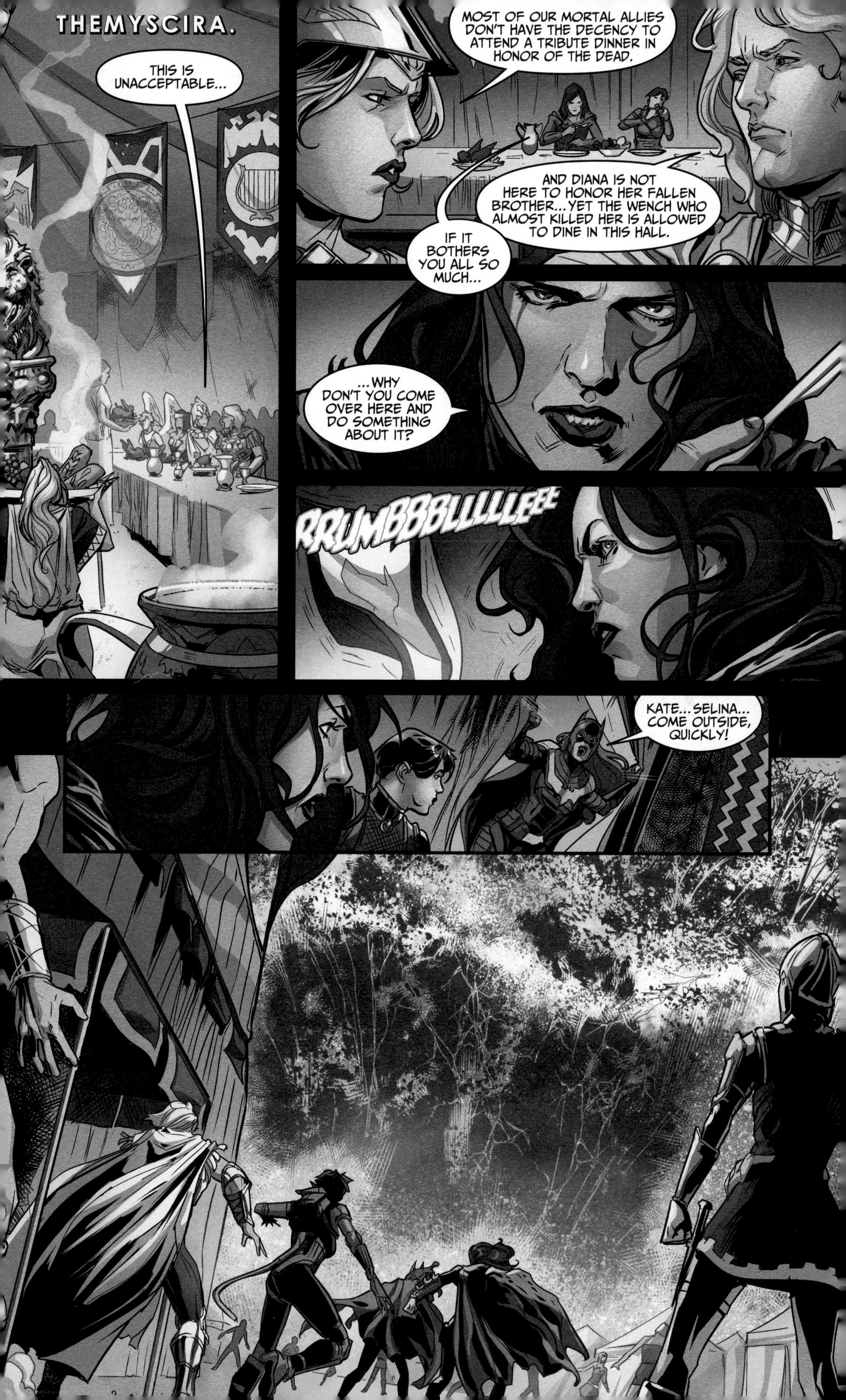
THEMYSCIRA.
THIS IS UNACCEPTABLE...
MOST OF OUR MORTAL ALLIES DON'T HAVE THE DECENCY TO ATTEND A TRIBUTE DINNER IN HONOR OF THE DEAD.
AND DIANA IS NOT HERE TO HONOR HER FALLEN BROTHER...YET THE WENCH WHO ALMOST KILLED HER IS ALLOWED TO DINE IN THIS HALL.
IF IT BOTHERS YOU ALL SO MUCH...
...WHY DON'T YOU COME OVER HERE AND DO SOMETHING ABOUT IT?
RRUMBBBLLLLLEEE
KATE...SELINA... COME OUTSIDE, QUICKLY!

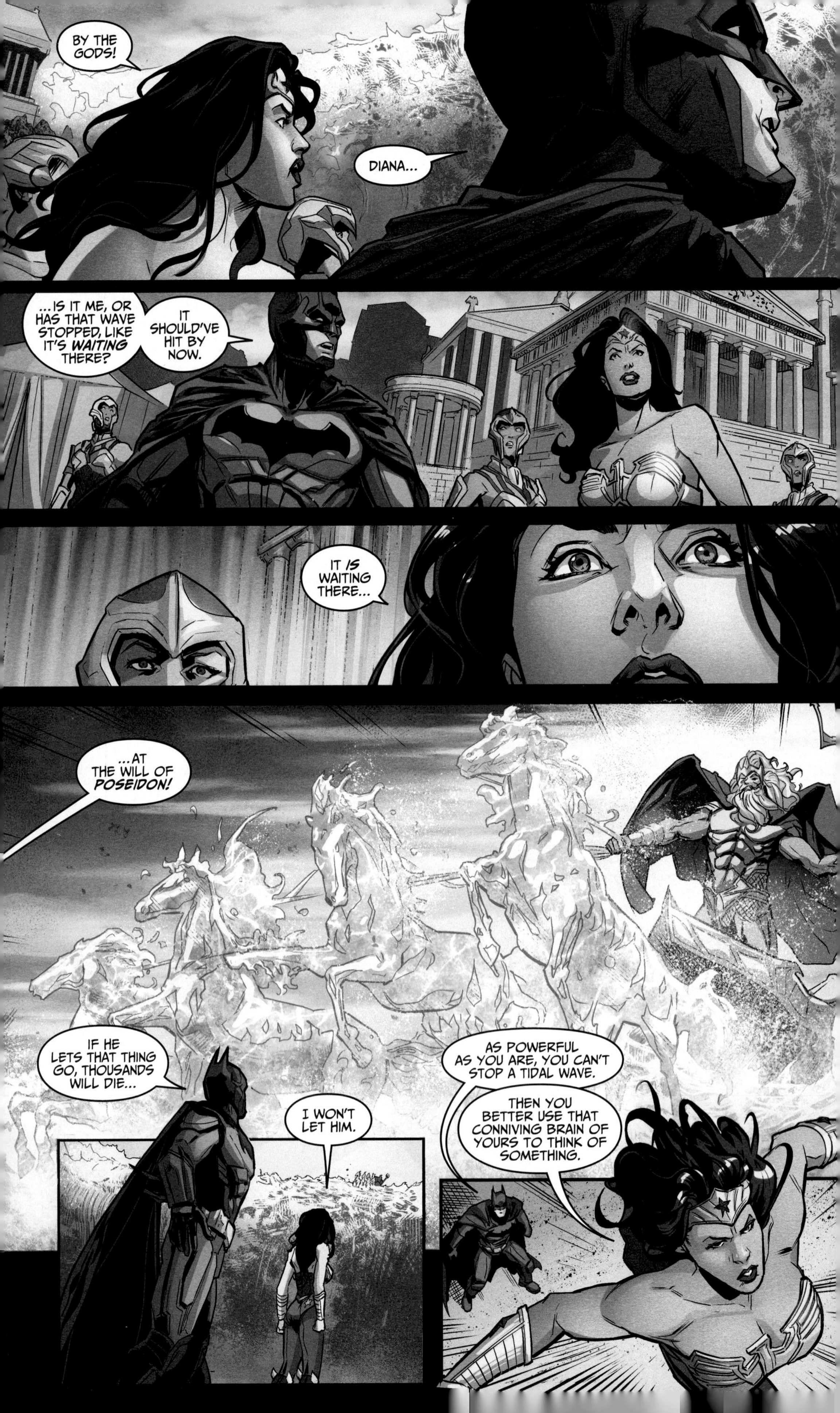
BY THE GODS!
DIANA...
...IS IT ME, OR HAS THAT WAVE STOPPED, LIKE IT'S *WAITING* THERE?
IT SHOULD'VE HIT BY NOW.
IT *IS* WAITING THERE...
...AT THE WILL OF *POSEIDON!*
IF HE LETS THAT THING GO, THOUSANDS WILL DIE...
I WON'T LET HIM.
AS POWERFUL AS YOU ARE, YOU CAN'T STOP A TIDAL WAVE.
THEN YOU BETTER USE THAT CONNIVING BRAIN OF YOURS TO THINK OF SOMETHING.

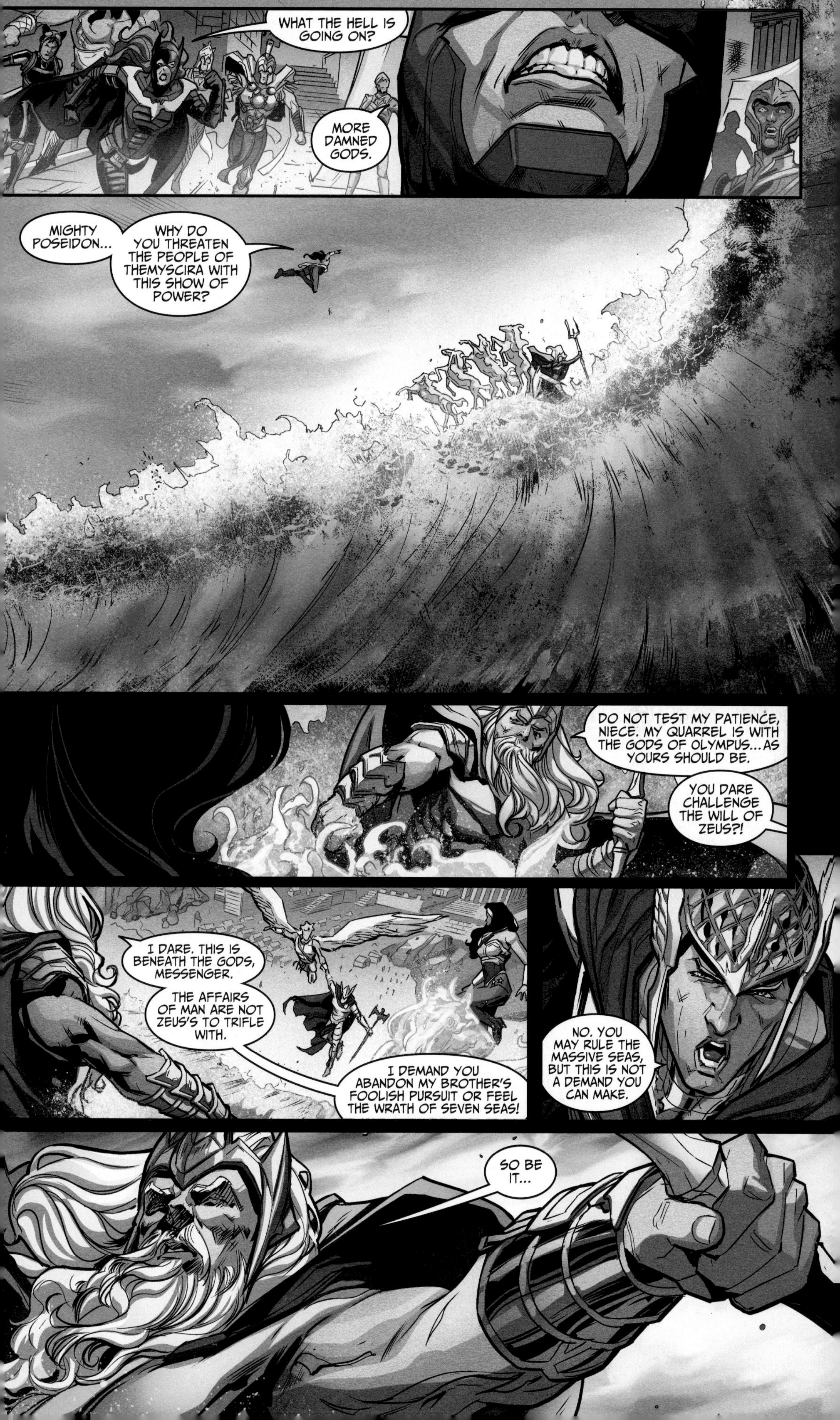
WHAT THE HELL IS GOING ON?
MORE DAMNED GODS.
MIGHTY POSEIDON...
WHY DO YOU THREATEN THE PEOPLE OF THEMYSCIRA WITH THIS SHOW OF POWER?
DO NOT TEST MY PATIENCE, NIECE. MY QUARREL IS WITH THE GODS OF OLYMPUS... AS YOURS SHOULD BE.
YOU DARE CHALLENGE THE WILL OF ZEUS?!
I DARE. THIS IS BENEATH THE GODS, MESSENGER.
THE AFFAIRS OF MAN ARE NOT ZEUS'S TO TRIFLE WITH.
I DEMAND YOU ABANDON MY BROTHER'S FOOLISH PURSUIT OR FEEL THE WRATH OF SEVEN SEAS!
NO. YOU MAY RULE THE MASSIVE SEAS, BUT THIS IS NOT A DEMAND YOU CAN MAKE.
SO BE IT...

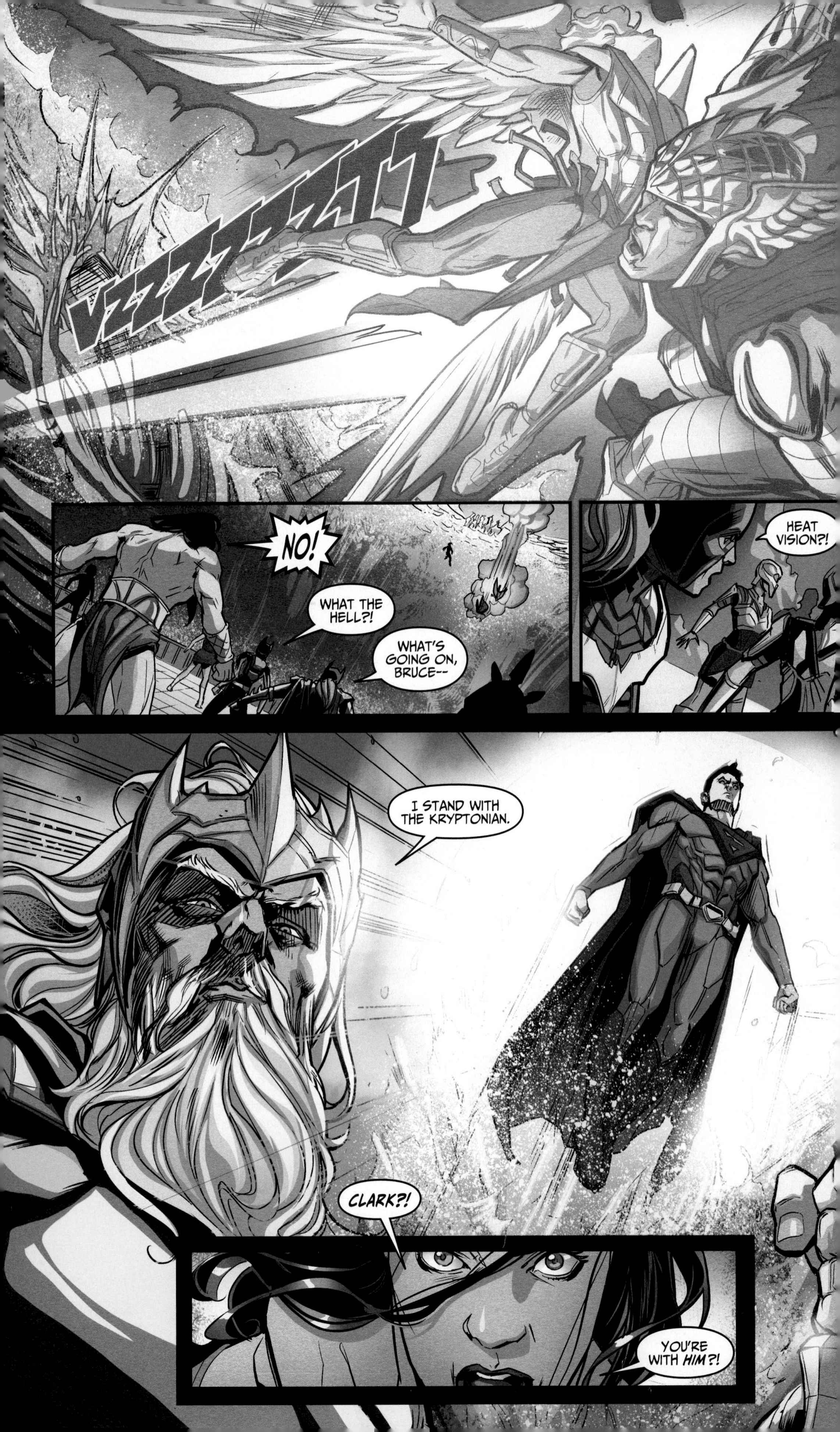

VZZZZZZZAAT
NO!
WHAT THE HELL?!
WHAT'S GOING ON, BRUCE--
HEAT VISION?!
I STAND WITH THE KRYPTONIAN.
CLARK?!
YOU'RE WITH HIM?!

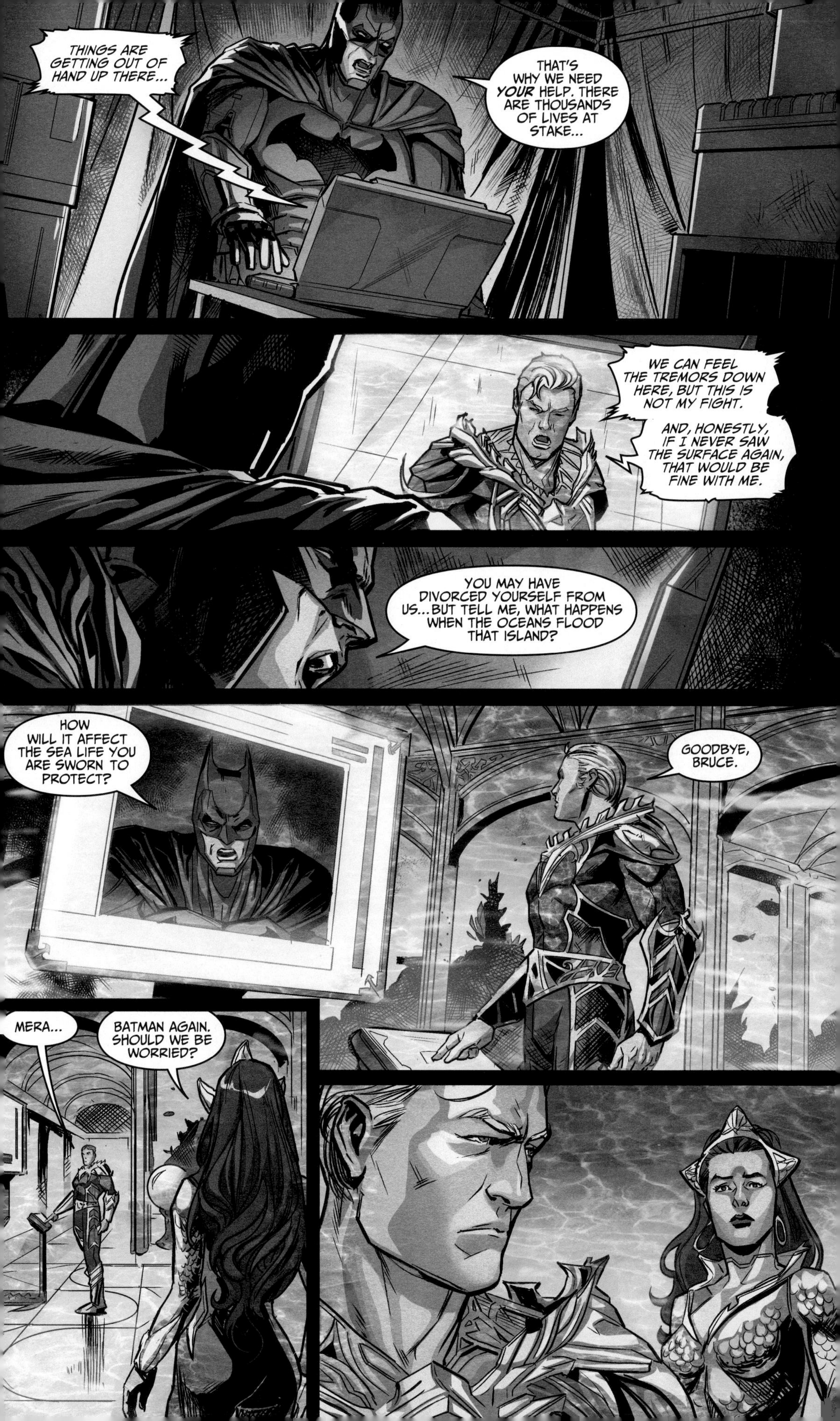
THINGS ARE GETTING OUT OF HAND UP THERE...
THAT'S WHY WE NEED YOUR HELP. THERE ARE THOUSANDS OF LIVES AT STAKE...
WE CAN FEEL THE TREMORS DOWN HERE, BUT THIS IS NOT MY FIGHT.
AND, HONESTLY, IF I NEVER SAW THE SURFACE AGAIN, THAT WOULD BE FINE WITH ME.
YOU MAY HAVE DIVORCED YOURSELF FROM US...BUT TELL ME, WHAT HAPPENS WHEN THE OCEANS FLOOD THAT ISLAND?
HOW WILL IT AFFECT THE SEA LIFE YOU ARE SWORN TO PROTECT?
GOODBYE, BRUCE.
MERA...
BATMAN AGAIN. SHOULD WE BE WORRIED?

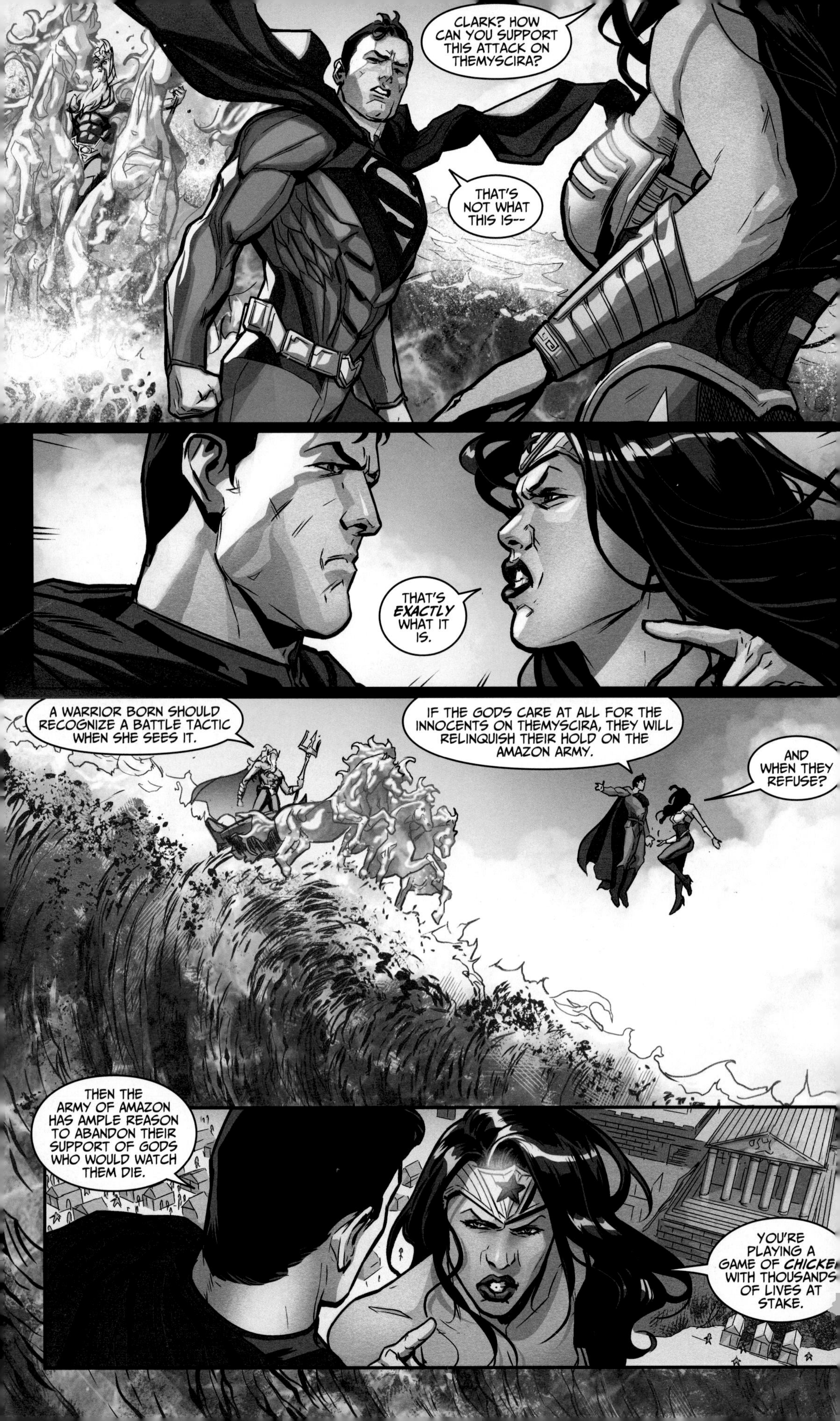
CLARK? HOW CAN YOU SUPPORT THIS ATTACK ON THEMYSCIRA?
THAT'S NOT WHAT THIS IS--
THAT'S EXACTLY WHAT IT IS.
A WARRIOR BORN SHOULD RECOGNIZE A BATTLE TACTIC WHEN SHE SEES IT.
IF THE GODS CARE AT ALL FOR THE INNOCENTS ON THEMYSCIRA, THEY WILL RELINQUISH THEIR HOLD ON THE AMAZON ARMY.
AND WHEN THEY REFUSE?
THEN THE ARMY OF AMAZON HAS AMPLE REASON TO ABANDON THEIR SUPPORT OF GODS WHO WOULD WATCH THEM DIE.
YOU'RE PLAYING A GAME OF CHICKE WITH THOUSANDS OF LIVES AT STAKE.

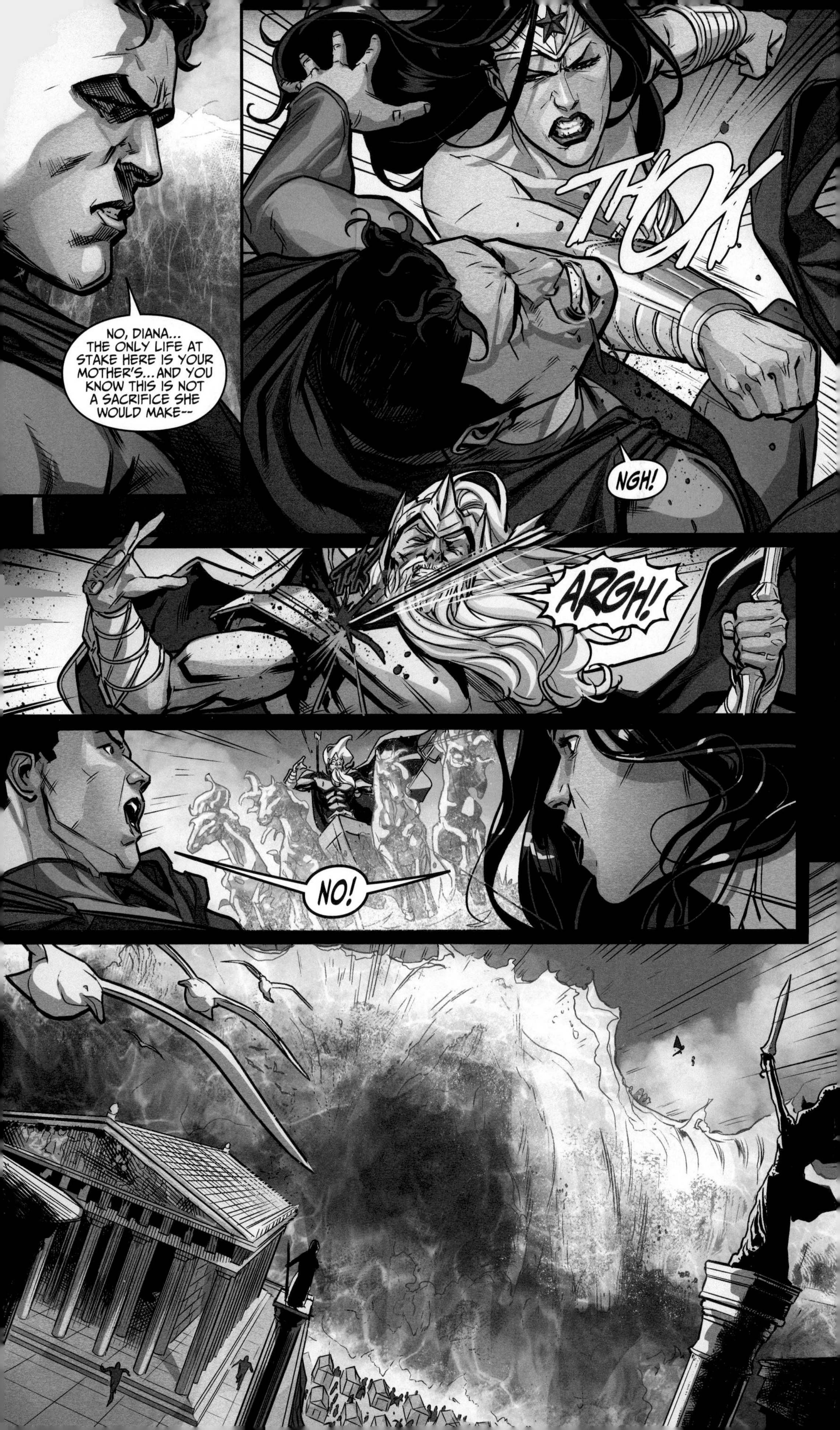
NO, DIANA... THE ONLY LIFE AT STAKE HERE IS YOUR MOTHER'S...AND YOU KNOW THIS IS NOT A SACRIFICE SHE WOULD MAKE--
THOK
NGH!
ARGH!
NO!

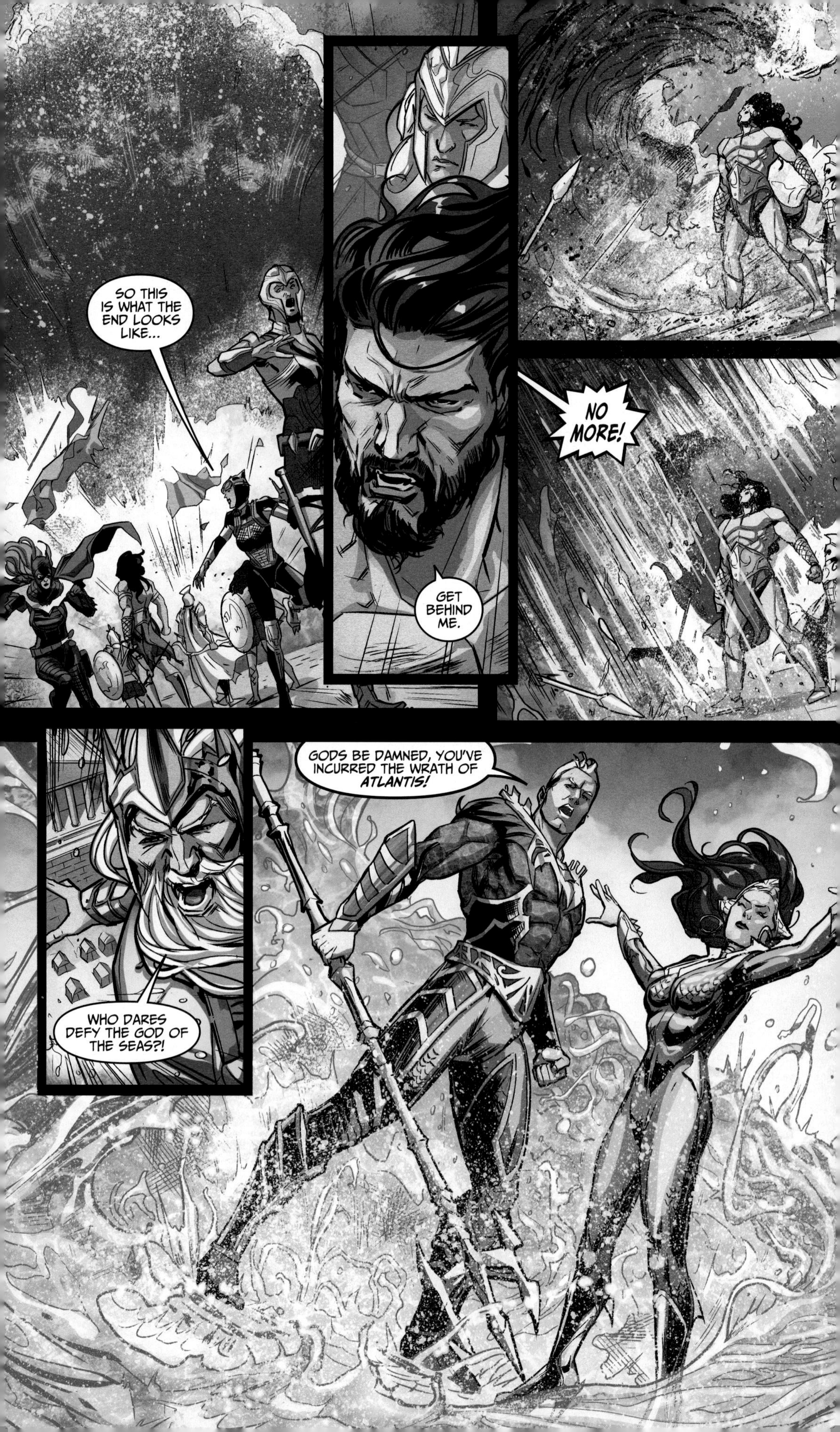
SO THIS IS WHAT THE END LOOKS LIKE...
GET BEHIND ME.
NO MORE!
WHO DARES DEFY THE GOD OF THE SEAS?!
GODS BE DAMNED, YOU'VE INCURRED THE WRATH OF *ATLANTIS!*

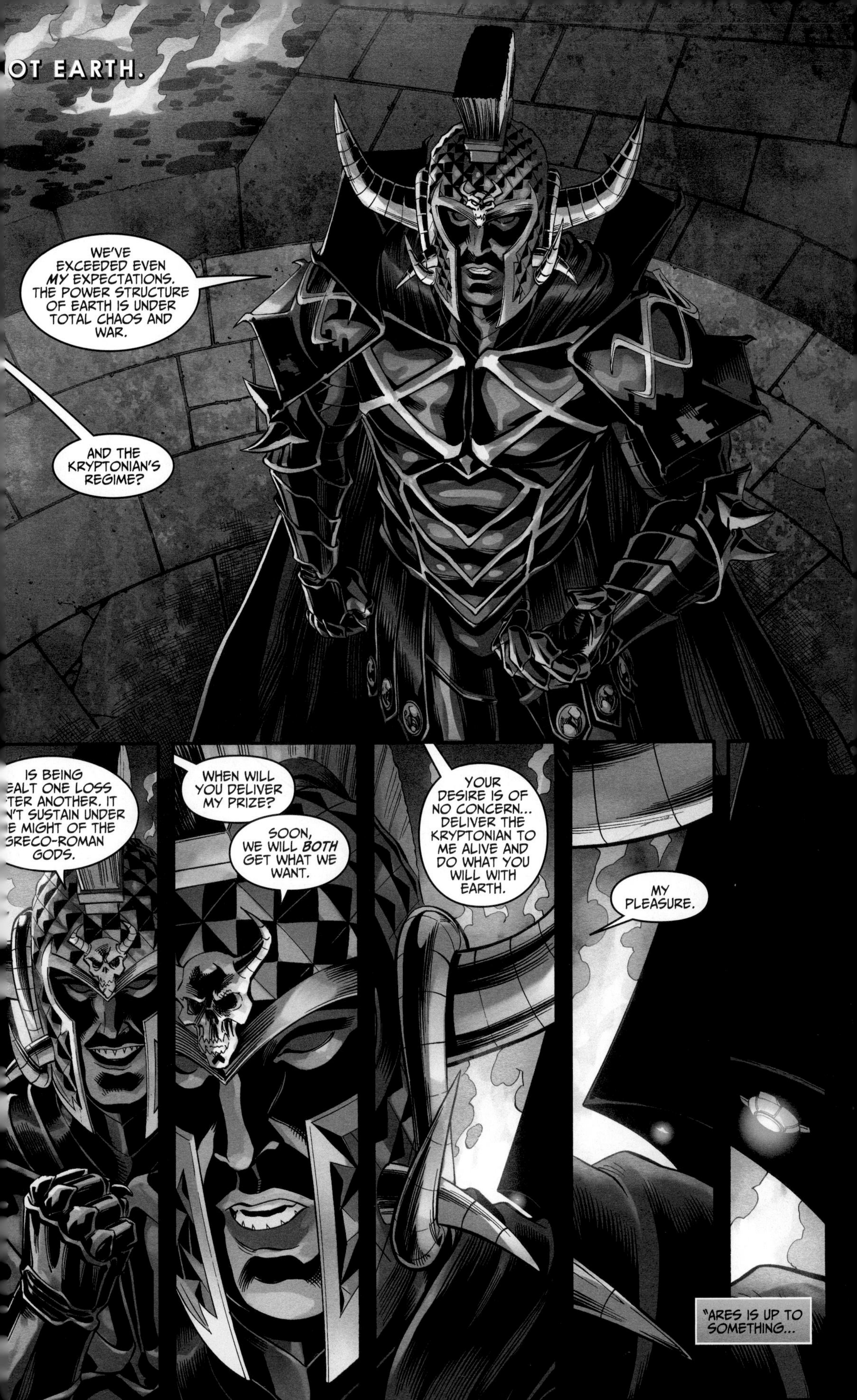
OT EARTH.
WE'VE EXCEEDED EVEN *MY* EXPECTATIONS. THE POWER STRUCTURE OF EARTH IS UNDER TOTAL CHAOS AND WAR.
AND THE KRYPTONIAN'S REGIME?
IS BEING
EALT ONE LOSS
TER ANOTHER. IT
N'T SUSTAIN UNDER
E MIGHT OF THE
GRECO-ROMAN
GODS.
WHEN WILL YOU DELIVER MY PRIZE?
SOON, WE WILL *BOTH* GET WHAT WE WANT.
YOUR DESIRE IS OF NO CONCERN... DELIVER THE KRYPTONIAN TO ME ALIVE AND DO WHAT YOU WILL WITH EARTH.
MY PLEASURE.
"ARES IS UP TO SOMETHING...

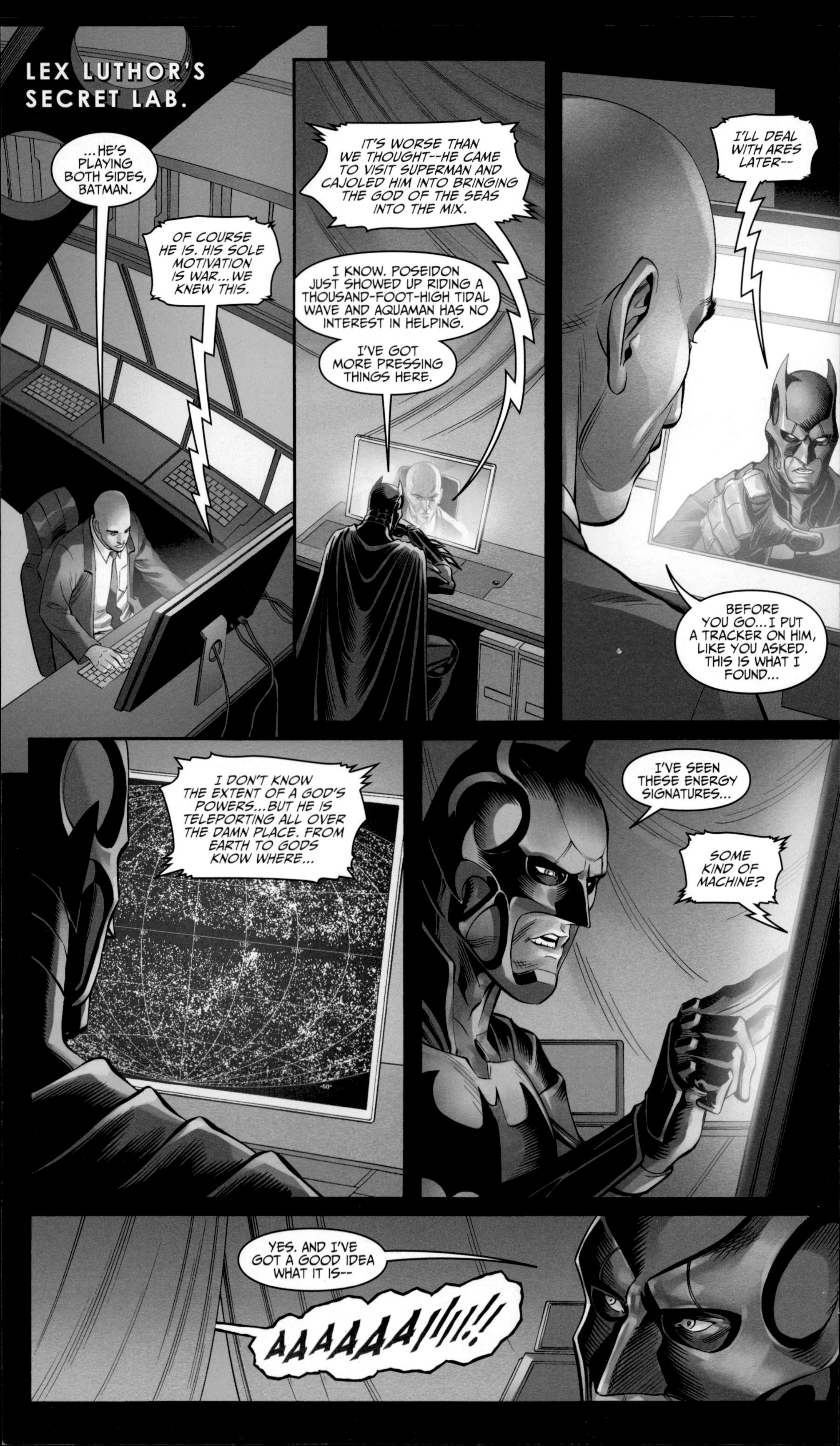

LEX LUTHOR'S SECRET LAB.
...HE'S PLAYING BOTH SIDES, BATMAN.
OF COURSE HE IS. HIS SOLE MOTIVATION IS WAR...WE KNEW THIS.
IT'S WORSE THAN WE THOUGHT--HE CAME TO VISIT SUPERMAN AND CAJOLED HIM INTO BRINGING THE GOD OF THE SEAS INTO THE MIX.
I KNOW. POSEIDON JUST SHOWED UP RIDING A THOUSAND-FOOT-HIGH TIDAL WAVE AND AQUAMAN HAS NO INTEREST IN HELPING.
I'VE GOT MORE PRESSING THINGS HERE.
I'LL DEAL WITH ARES LATER--
BEFORE YOU GO...I PUT A TRACKER ON HIM, LIKE YOU ASKED. THIS IS WHAT I FOUND...
I DON'T KNOW THE EXTENT OF A GOD'S POWERS...BUT HE IS TELEPORTING ALL OVER THE DAMN PLACE. FROM EARTH TO GODS KNOW WHERE...
I'VE SEEN THESE ENERGY SIGNATURES...
SOME KIND OF MACHINE?
YES. AND I'VE GOT A GOOD IDEA WHAT IT IS--
AAAAAA!!!!!!

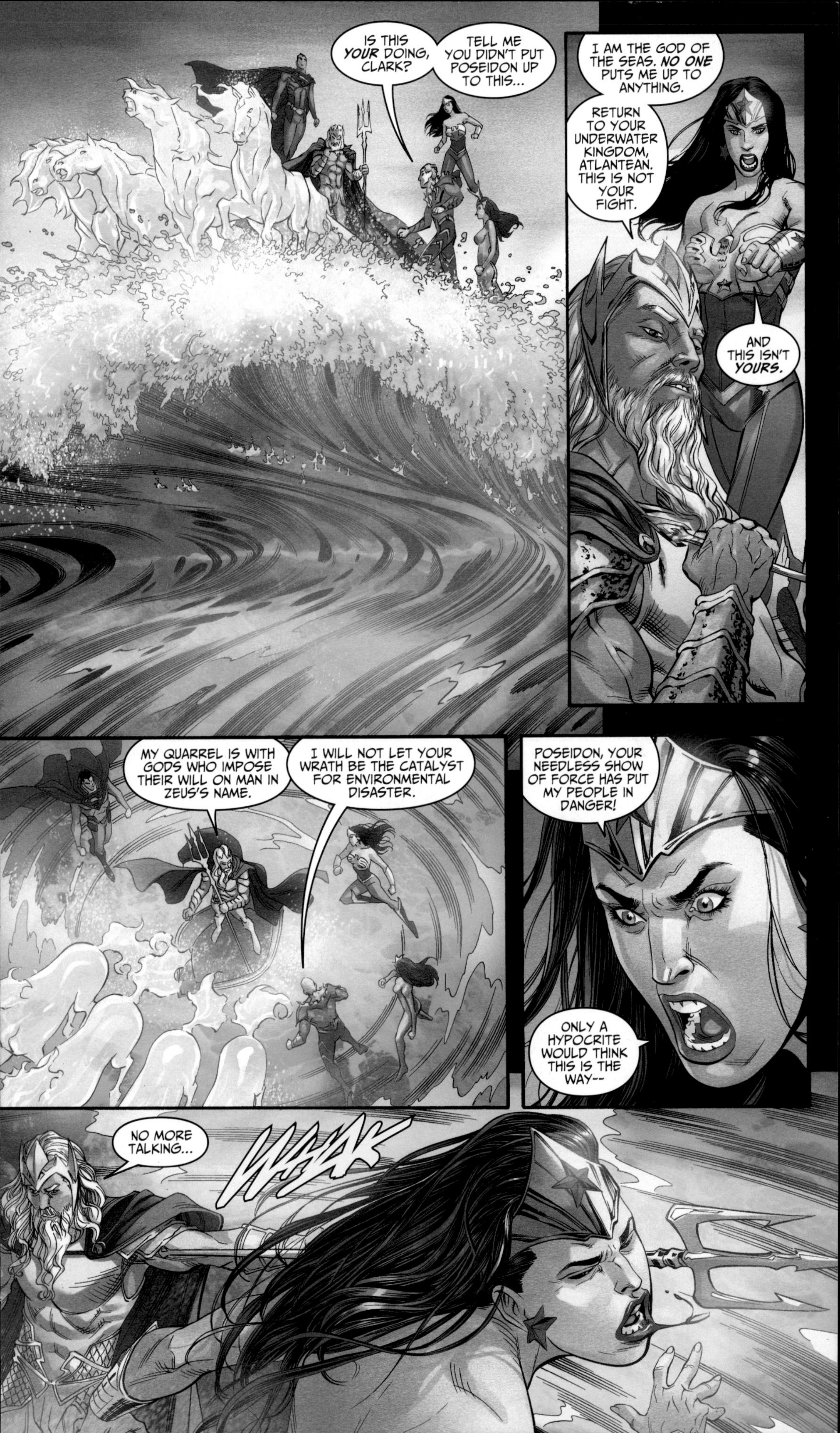
IS THIS YOUR DOING, CLARK?
TELL ME YOU DIDN'T PUT POSEIDON UP TO THIS...
I AM THE GOD OF THE SEAS. NO ONE PUTS ME UP TO ANYTHING.
RETURN TO YOUR UNDERWATER KINGDOM, ATLANTEAN. THIS IS NOT YOUR FIGHT.
AND THIS ISN'T YOURS.
MY QUARREL IS WITH GODS WHO IMPOSE THEIR WILL ON MAN IN ZEUS'S NAME.
I WILL NOT LET YOUR WRATH BE THE CATALYST FOR ENVIRONMENTAL DISASTER.
POSEIDON, YOUR NEEDLESS SHOW OF FORCE HAS PUT MY PEOPLE IN DANGER!
ONLY A HYPOCRITE WOULD THINK THIS IS THE WAY--
NO MORE TALKING...
WHAK

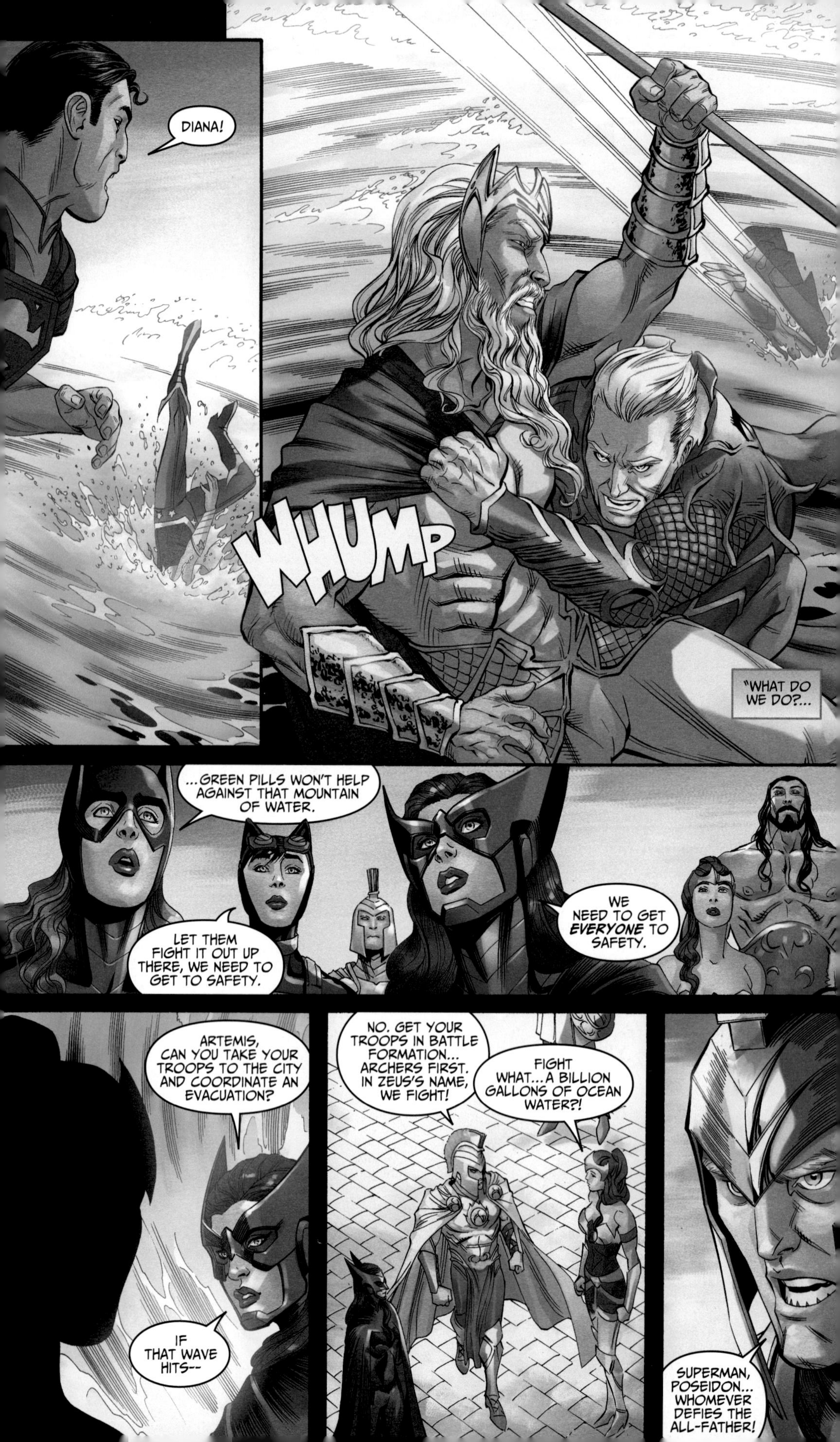
DIANA!
WHUMP
"WHAT DO WE DO?...
...GREEN PILLS WON'T HELP AGAINST THAT MOUNTAIN OF WATER.
LET THEM FIGHT IT OUT UP THERE, WE NEED TO GET TO SAFETY.
WE NEED TO GET EVERYONE TO SAFETY.
ARTEMIS, CAN YOU TAKE YOUR TROOPS TO THE CITY AND COORDINATE AN EVACUATION?
IF THAT WAVE HITS--
NO. GET YOUR TROOPS IN BATTLE FORMATION... ARCHERS FIRST. IN ZEUS'S NAME, WE FIGHT!
FIGHT WHAT...A BILLION GALLONS OF OCEAN WATER?!
SUPERMAN, POSEIDON... WHOMEVER DEFIES THE ALL-FATHER!

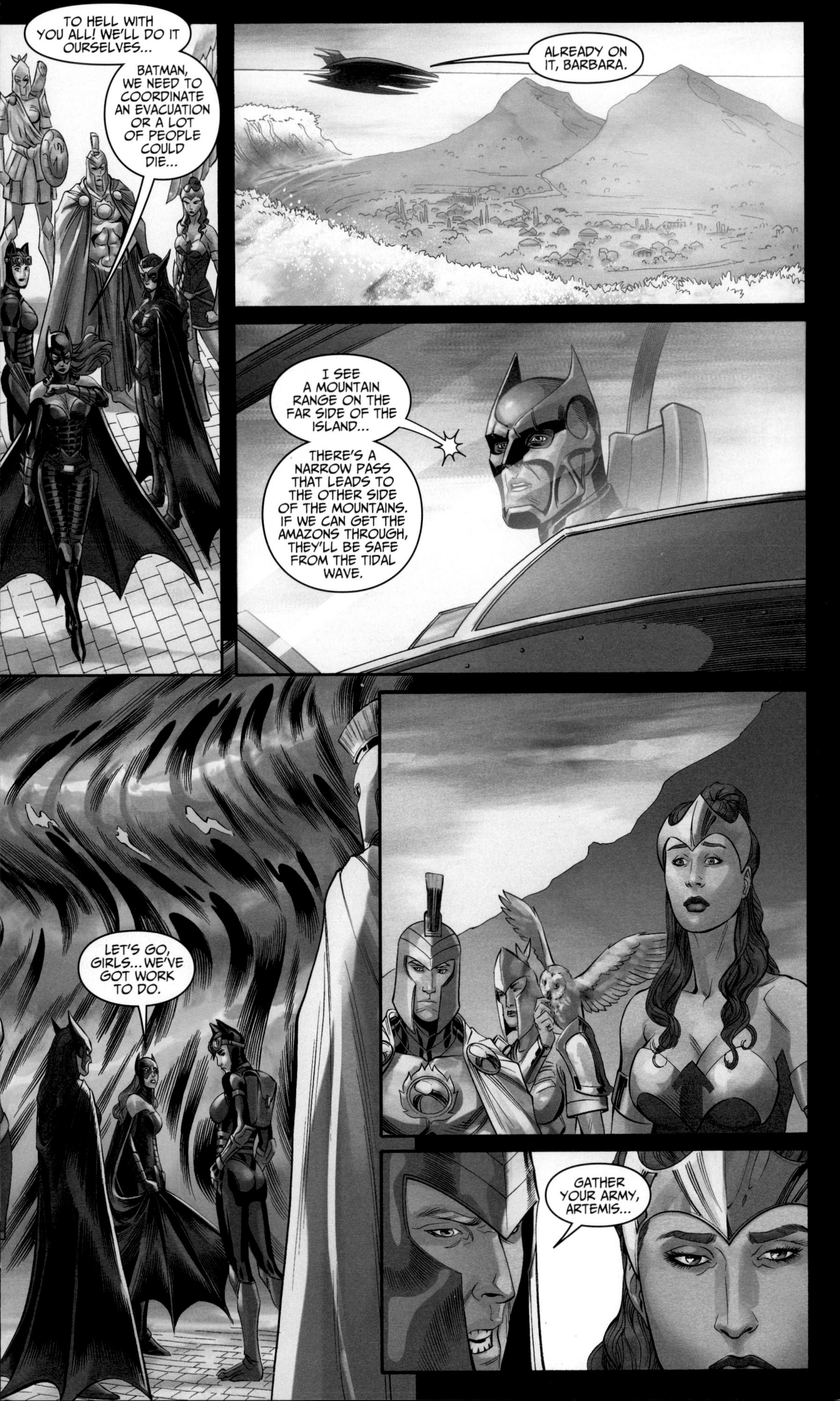
TO HELL WITH YOU ALL! WE'LL DO IT OURSELVES...
BATMAN, WE NEED TO COORDINATE AN EVACUATION OR A LOT OF PEOPLE COULD DIE...
ALREADY ON IT, BARBARA.
I SEE A MOUNTAIN RANGE ON THE FAR SIDE OF THE ISLAND...
THERE'S A NARROW PASS THAT LEADS TO THE OTHER SIDE OF THE MOUNTAINS. IF WE CAN GET THE AMAZONS THROUGH, THEY'LL BE SAFE FROM THE TIDAL WAVE.
LET'S GO, GIRLS...WE'VE GOT WORK TO DO.
GATHER YOUR ARMY, ARTEMIS...

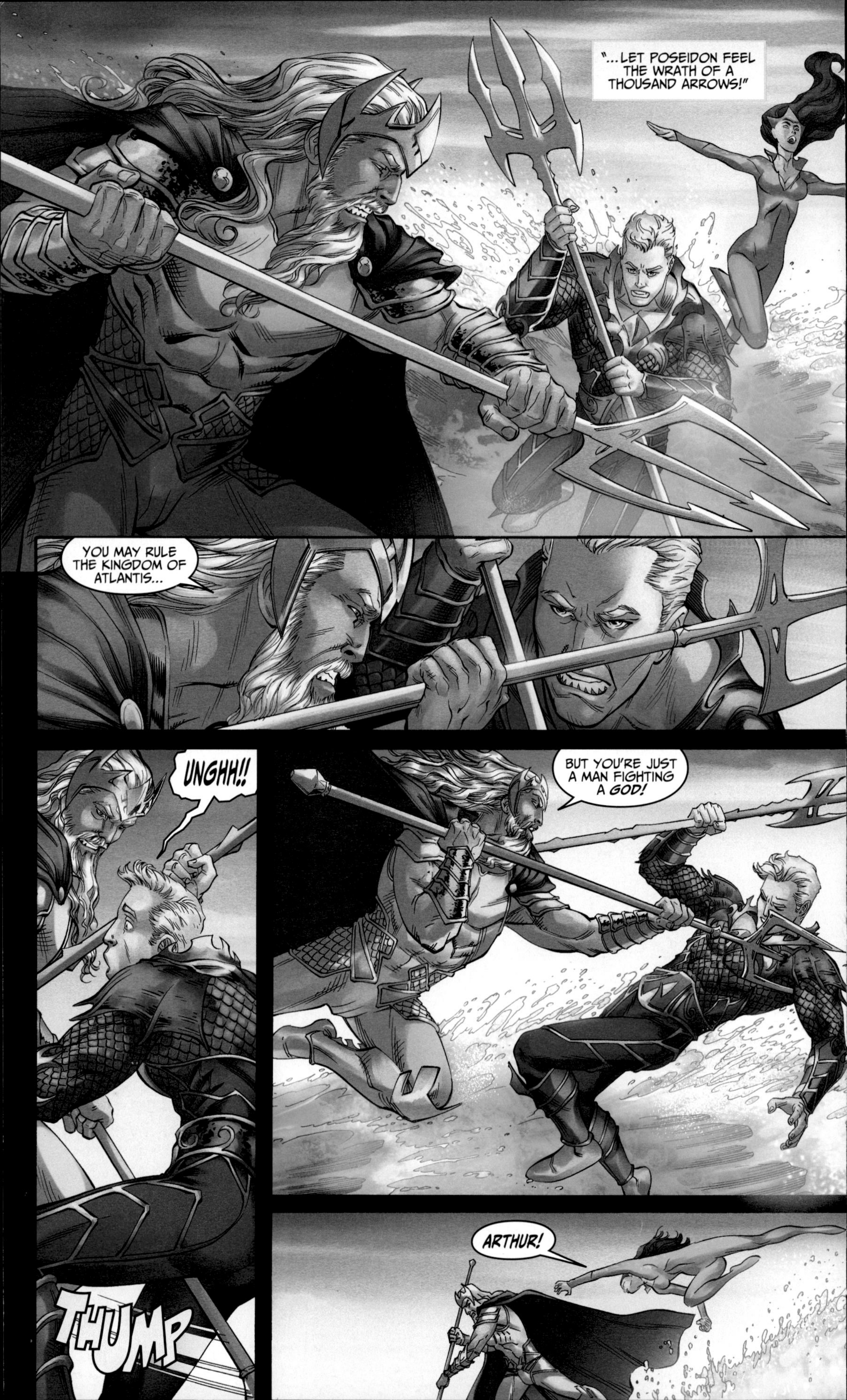
"...LET POSEIDON FEEL THE WRATH OF A THOUSAND ARROWS!"
YOU MAY RULE THE KINGDOM OF ATLANTIS...
UNGHH!!
BUT YOU'RE JUST A MAN FIGHTING A *GOD*!
THUMP
ARTHUR!

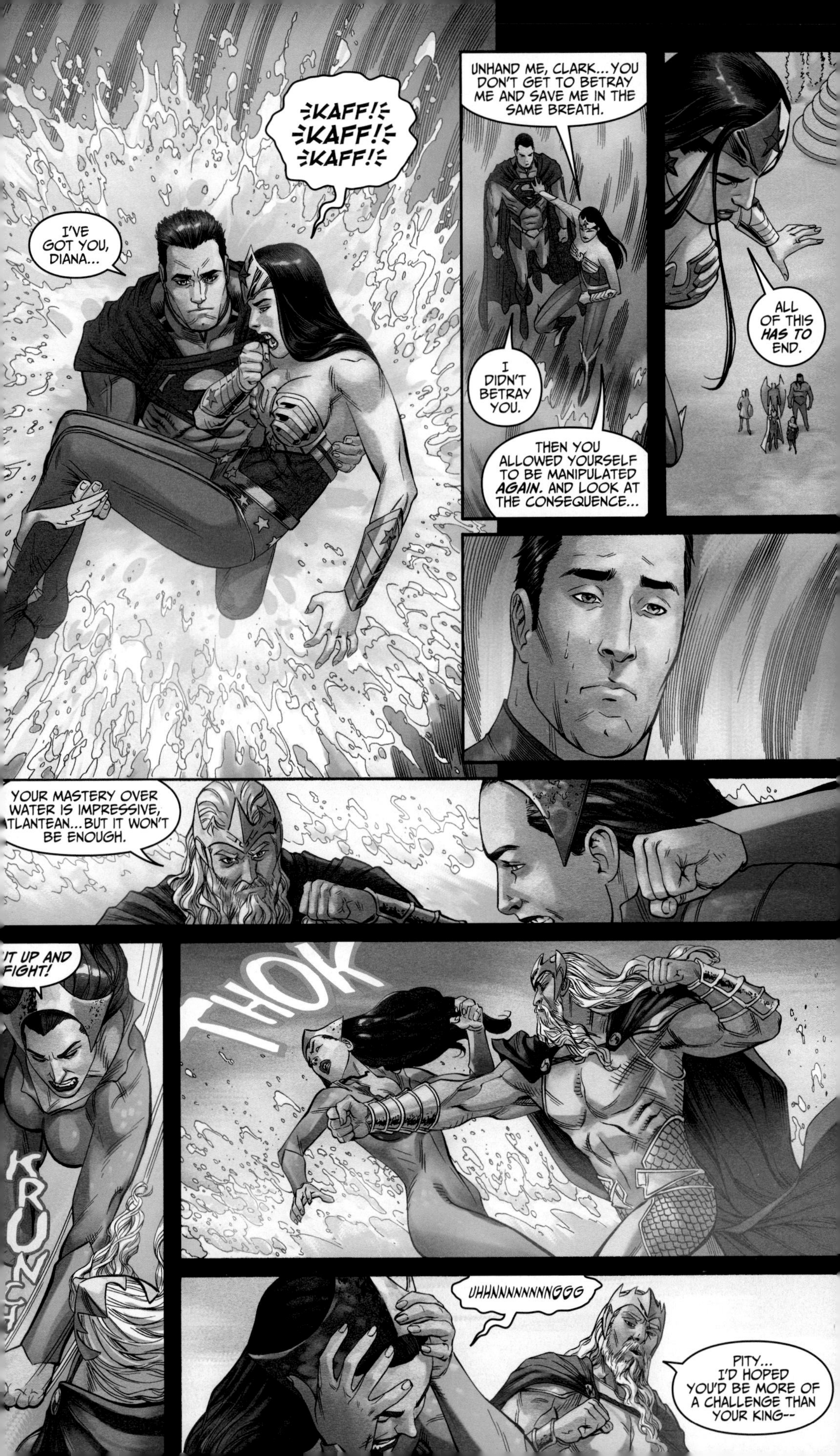

KAFF! KAFF! KAFF!
I'VE GOT YOU, DIANA...
UNHAND ME, CLARK...YOU DON'T GET TO BETRAY ME AND SAVE ME IN THE SAME BREATH.
I DIDN'T BETRAY YOU.
THEN YOU ALLOWED YOURSELF TO BE MANIPULATED AGAIN. AND LOOK AT THE CONSEQUENCE...
ALL OF THIS HAS TO END.
YOUR MASTERY OVER WATER IS IMPRESSIVE, TLANTEAN...BUT IT WON'T BE ENOUGH.
IT UP AND FIGHT!
KRUNCH
THOK
UHHNNNNNNNNGGG
PITY... I'D HOPED YOU'D BE MORE OF A CHALLENGE THAN YOUR KING--

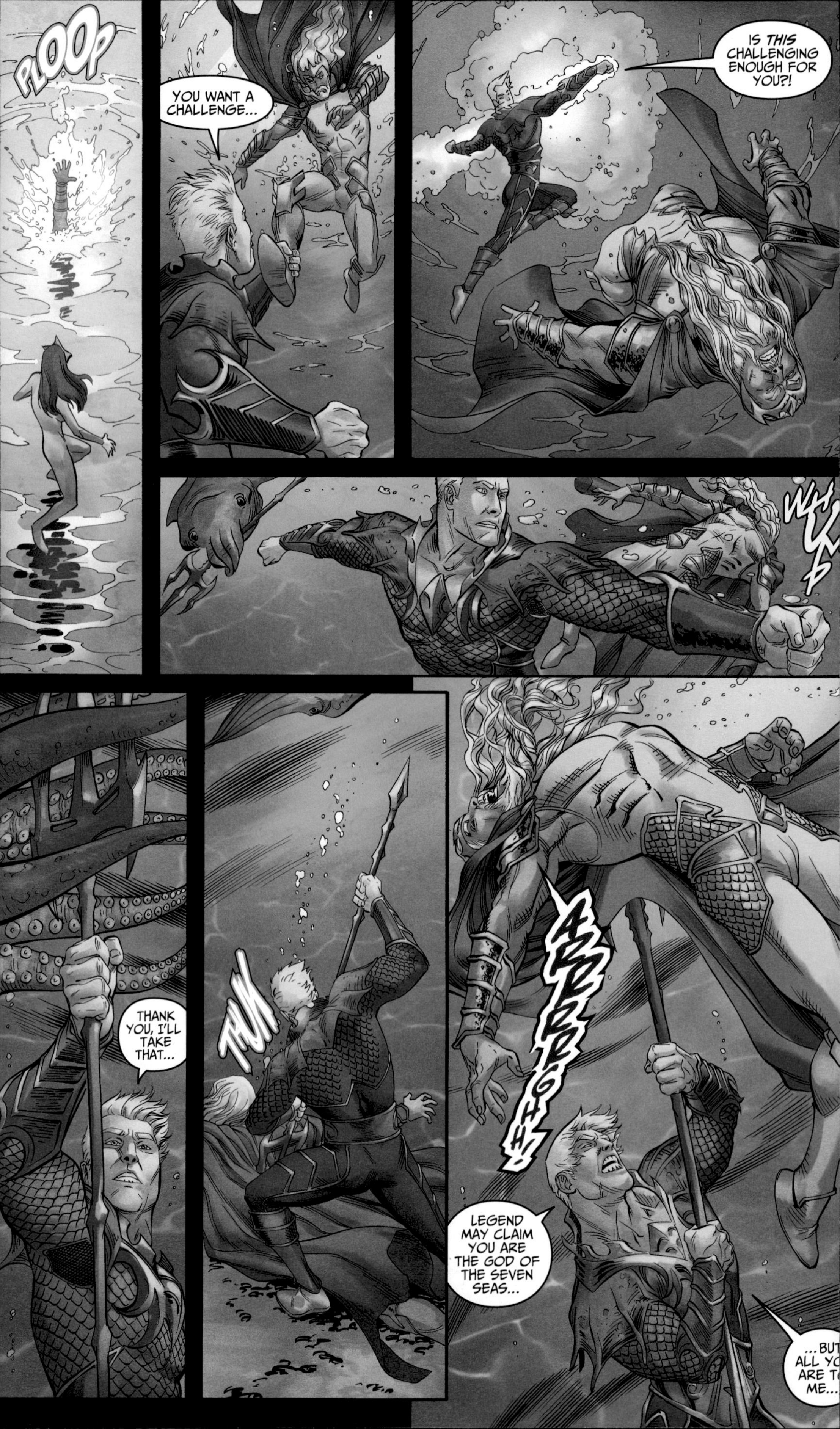
PLOOP
YOU WANT A CHALLENGE...
IS *THIS* CHALLENGING ENOUGH FOR YOU?!
WHUD
THANK YOU, I'LL TAKE THAT...
THUK
AARRRGHHH!
LEGEND MAY CLAIM YOU ARE THE GOD OF THE SEVEN SEAS...
...BUT ALL YO ARE T ME...

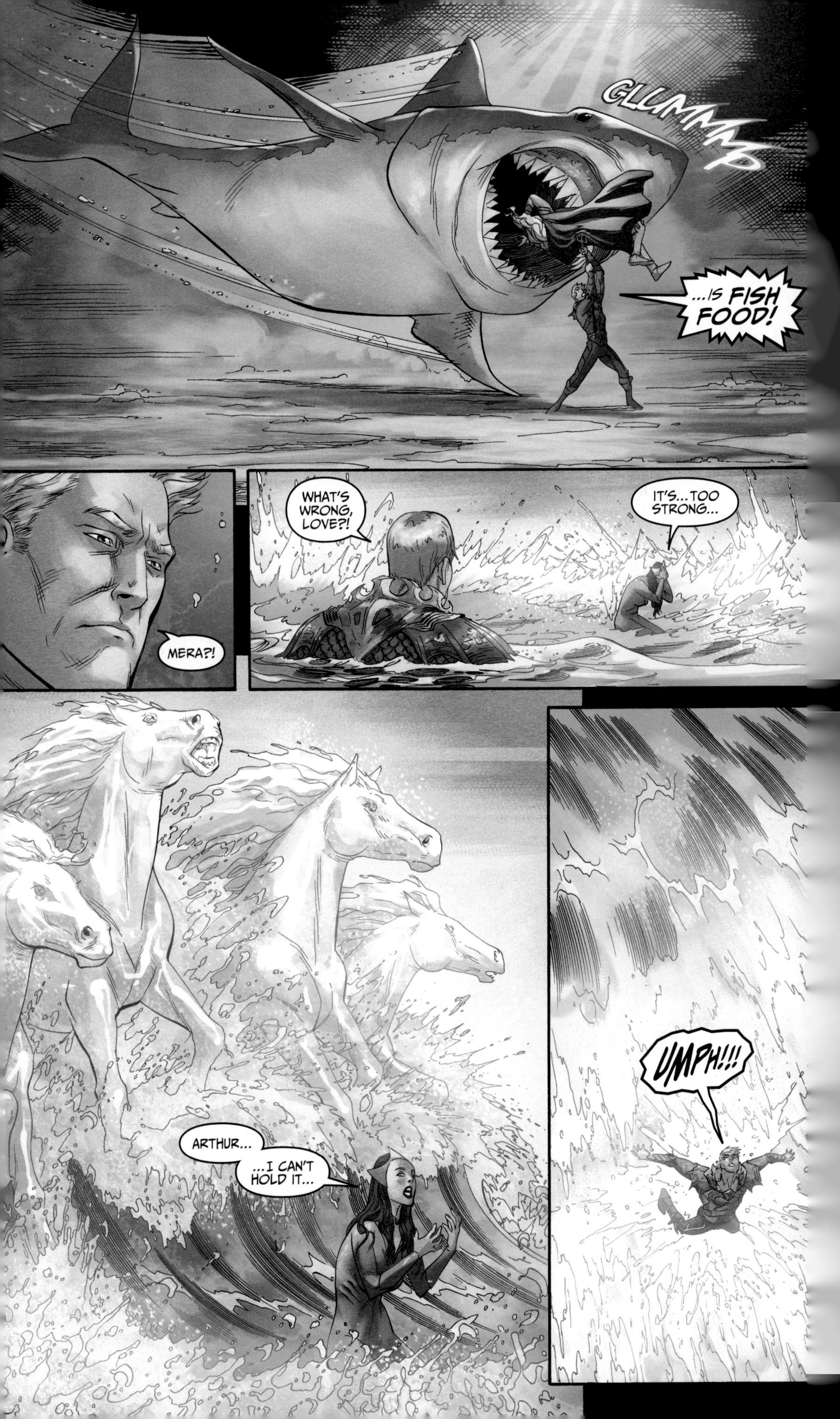
GLLLMMMP
...IS FISH FOOD!
MERA?!
WHAT'S WRONG, LOVE?!
IT'S...TOO STRONG...
ARTHUR...
...I CAN'T HOLD IT...
UMPH!!!

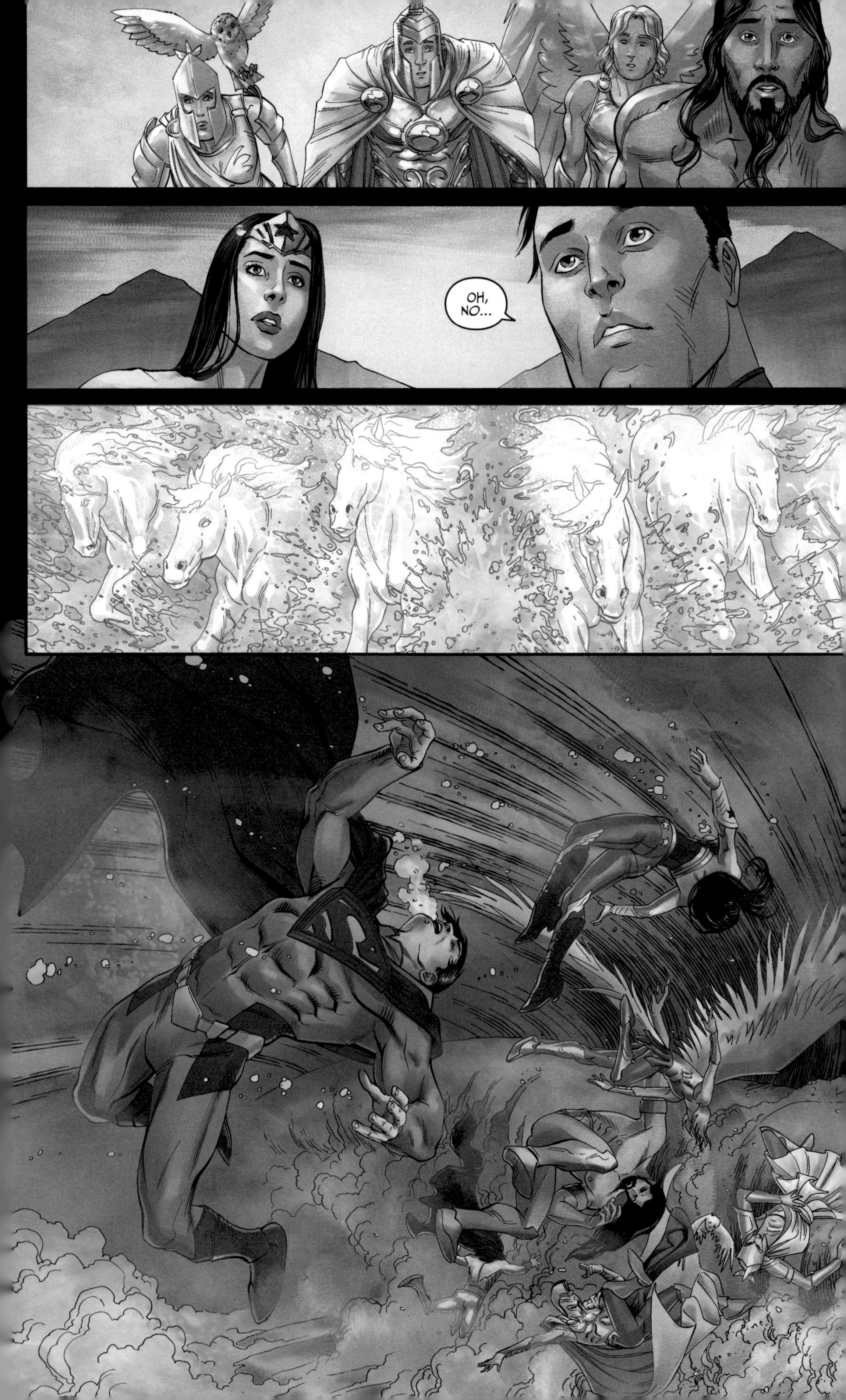
OH, NO...

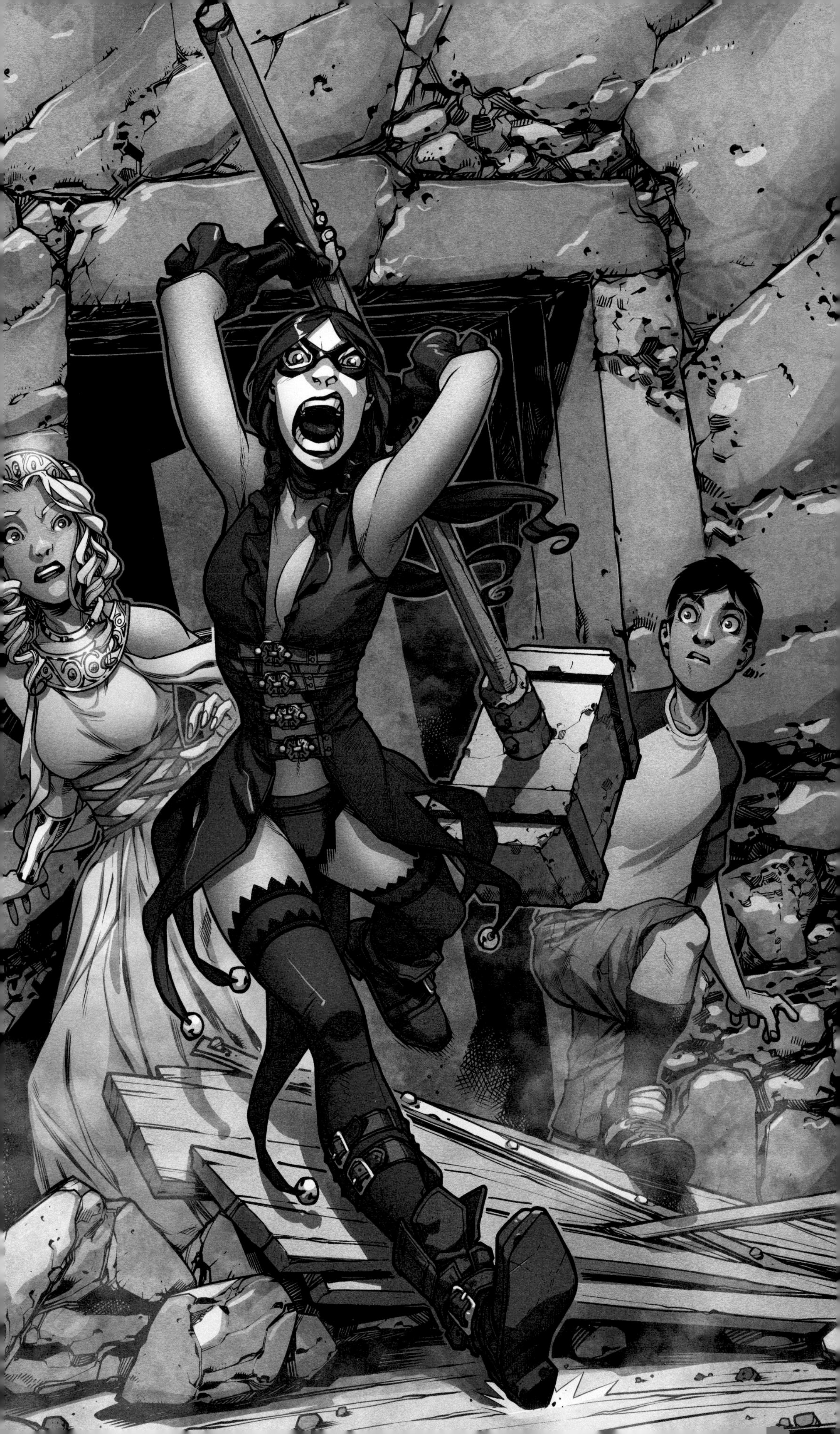

"Stupid Tartarus" **Brian Buccellato** Writer **Xermanico Bruno Redondo Juan Albarran** Artists
Rex Lokus Colorist Cover Art by **Neil Googe & Rex Lokus**

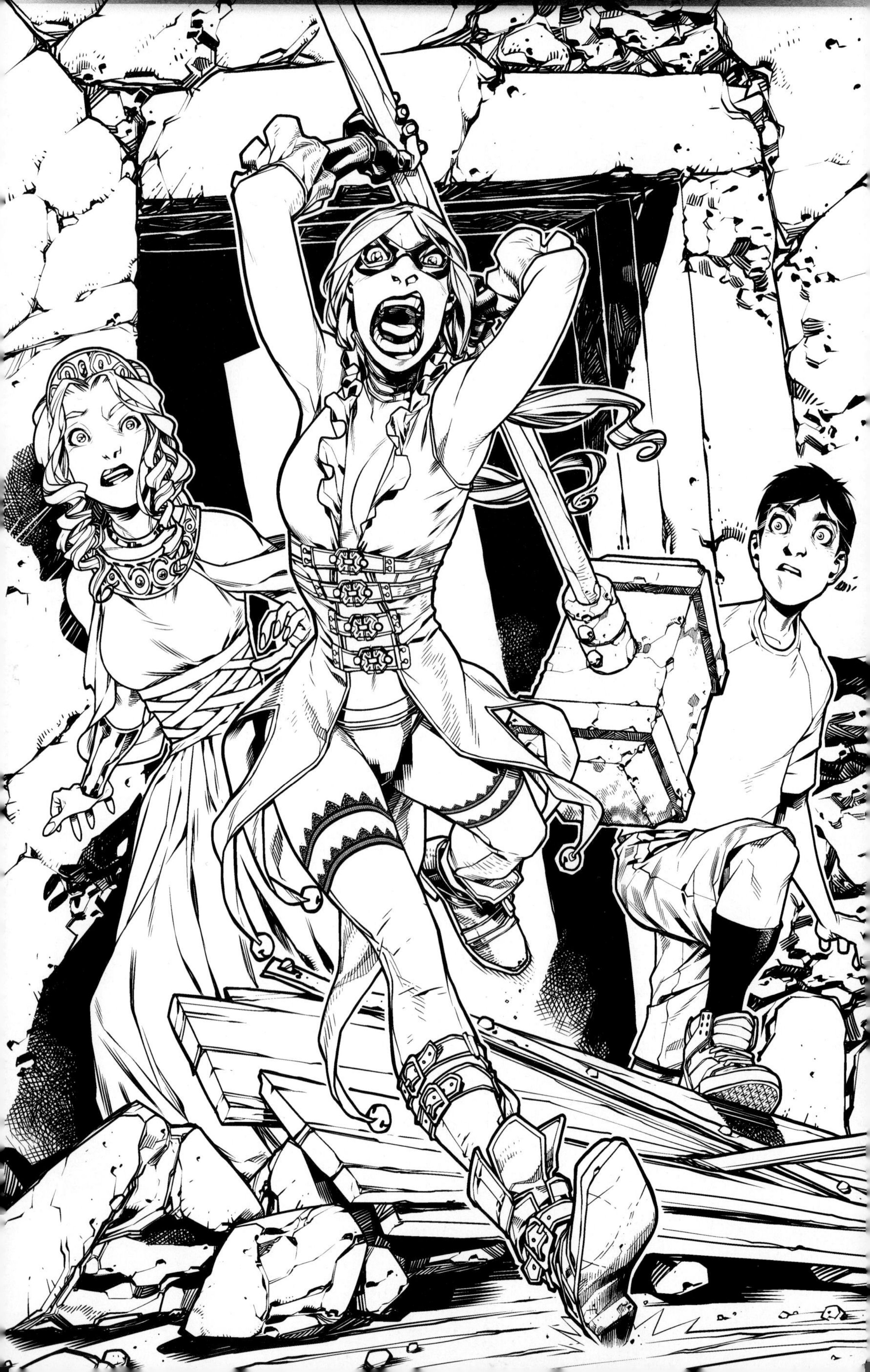

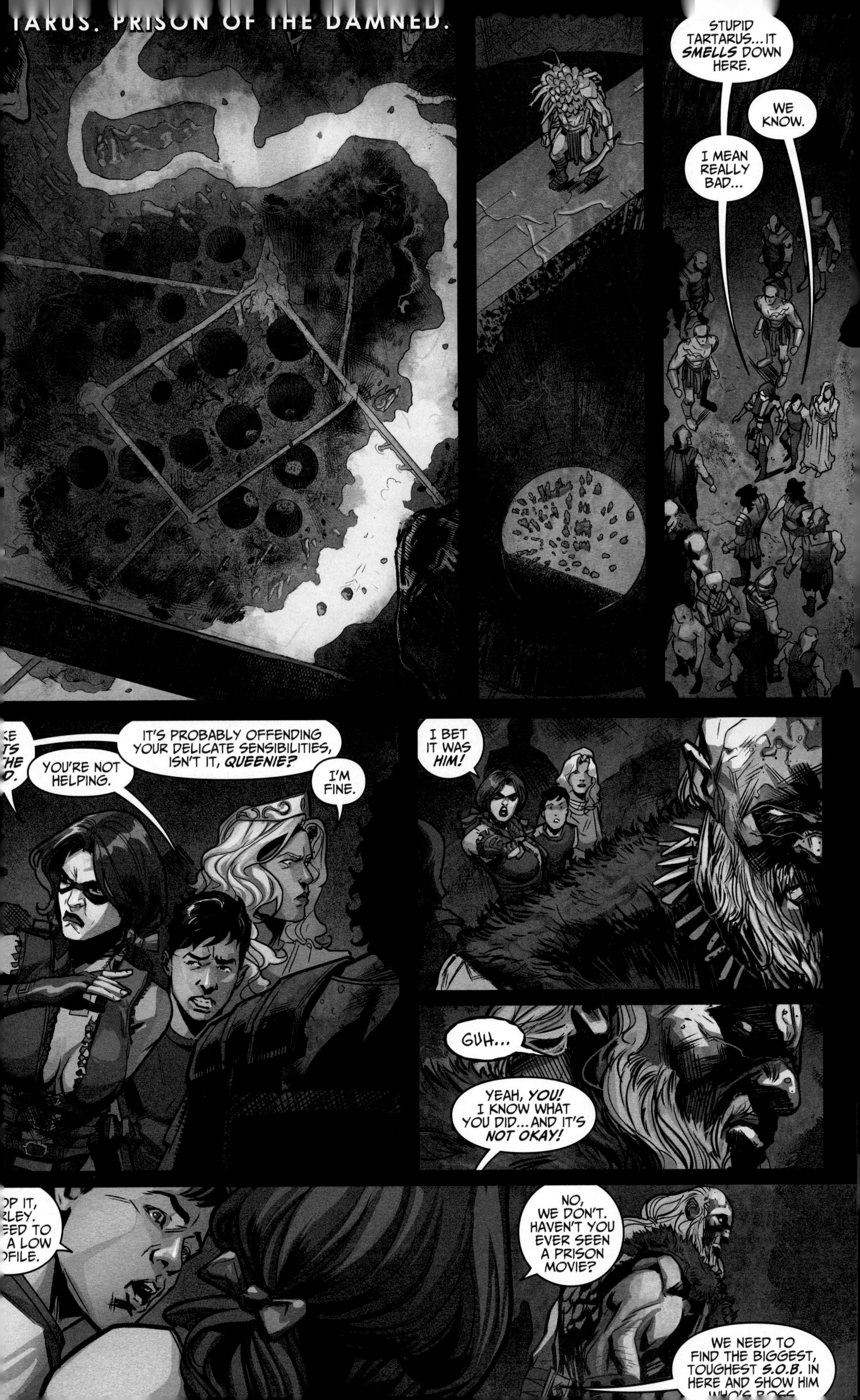
TARUS. PRISON OF THE DAMNED.
STUPID TARTARUS... IT SMELLS DOWN HERE.
WE KNOW.
I MEAN REALLY BAD...
IT'S PROBABLY OFFENDING YOUR DELICATE SENSIBILITIES, ISN'T IT, QUEENIE?
YOU'RE NOT HELPING.
I'M FINE.
I BET IT WAS HIM!
GUH...
YEAH, YOU! I KNOW WHAT YOU DID... AND IT'S NOT OKAY!
NO, WE DON'T. HAVEN'T YOU EVER SEEN A PRISON MOVIE?
WE NEED TO FIND THE BIGGEST, TOUGHEST S.O.B. IN HERE AND SHOW HIM

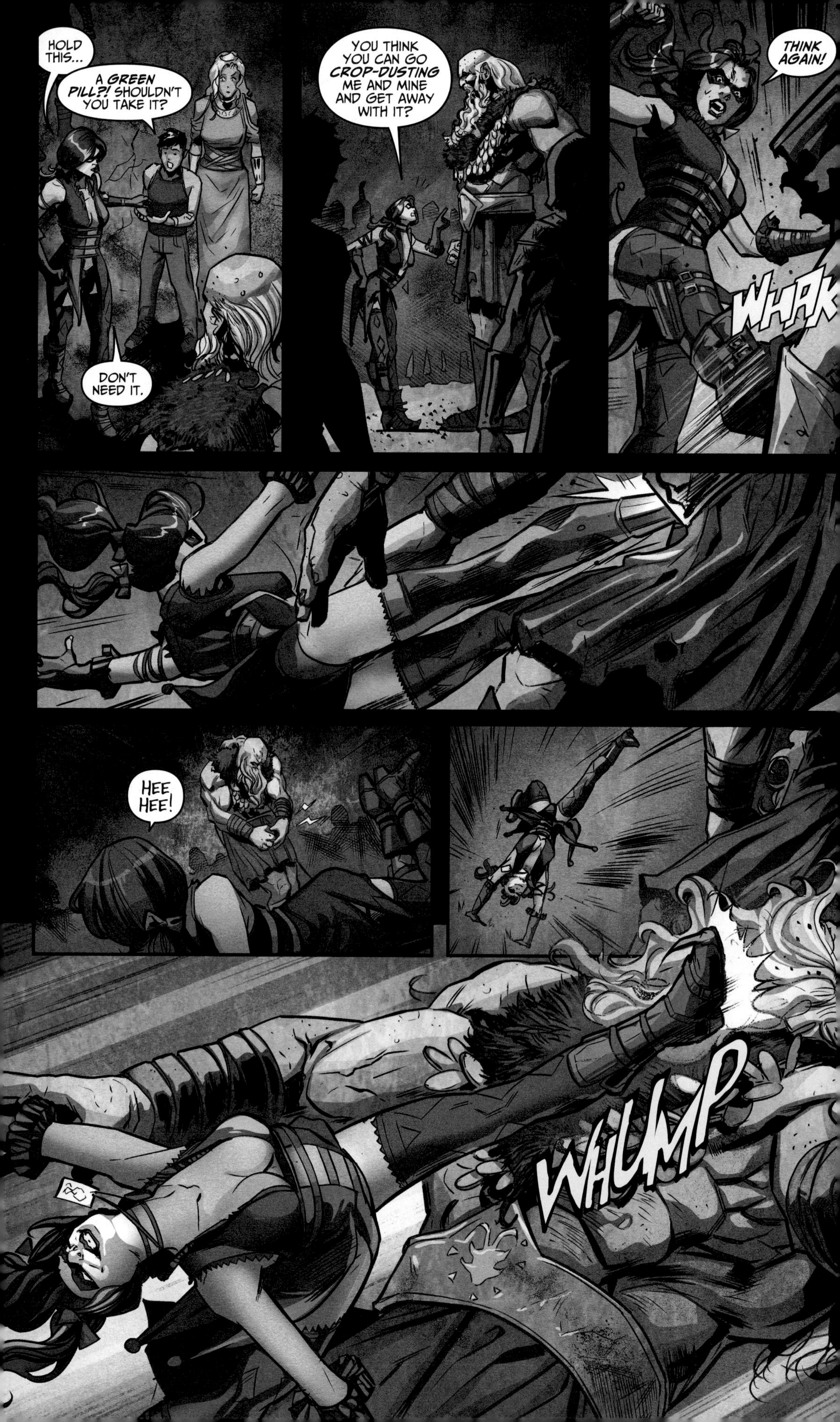

HOLD THIS...
A GREEN PILL?! SHOULDN'T YOU TAKE IT?
DON'T NEED IT.
YOU THINK YOU CAN GO CROP-DUSTING ME AND MINE AND GET AWAY WITH IT?
THINK AGAIN!
WHAK
HEE HEE!
WHUMP

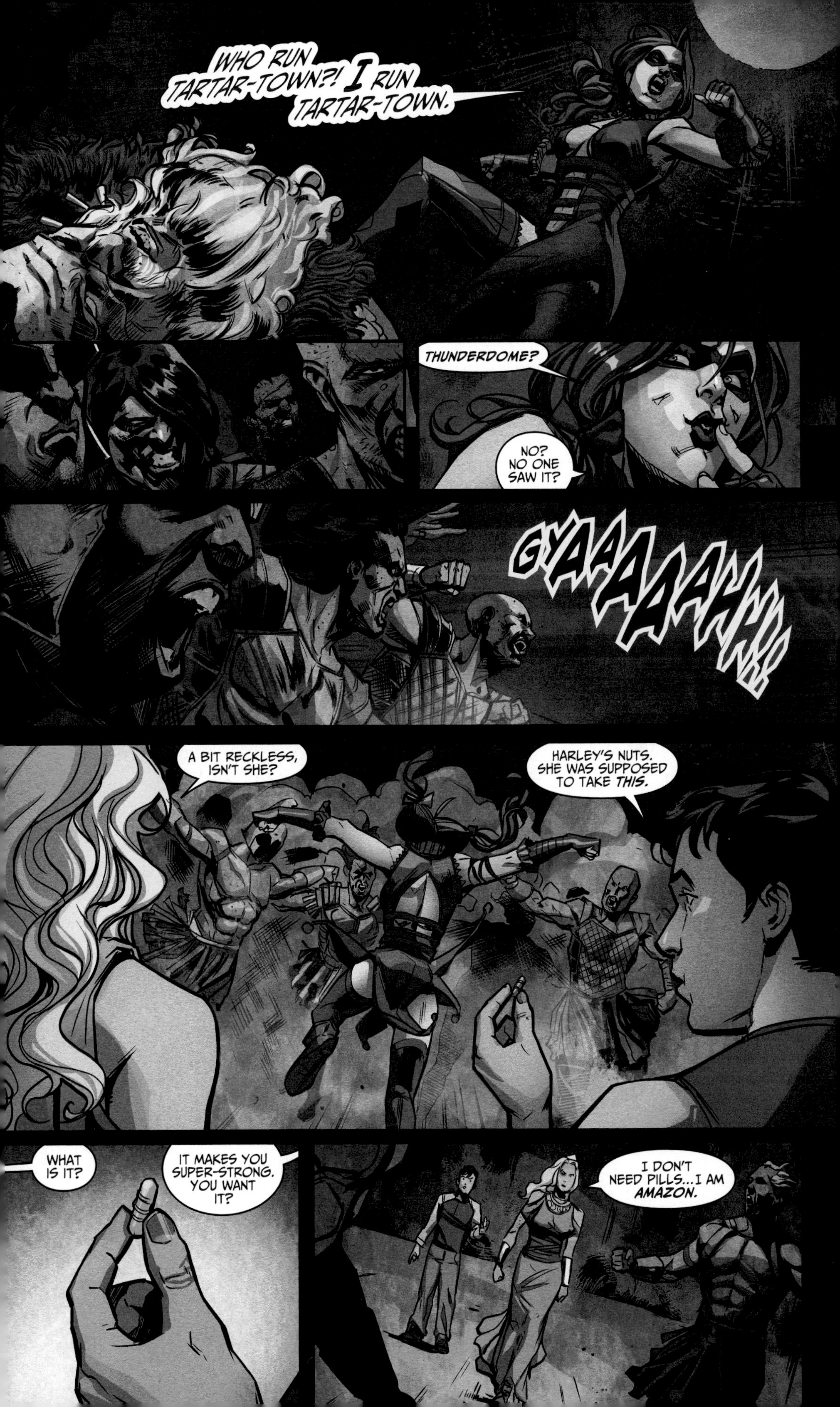
WHO RUN TARTAR-TOWN?! I RUN TARTAR-TOWN.
THUNDERDOME?
NO? NO ONE SAW IT?
GYAAAAAAH!!
A BIT RECKLESS, ISN'T SHE?
HARLEY'S NUTS. SHE WAS SUPPOSED TO TAKE THIS.
WHAT IS IT?
IT MAKES YOU SUPER-STRONG. YOU WANT IT?
I DON'T NEED PILLS...I AM AMAZON.

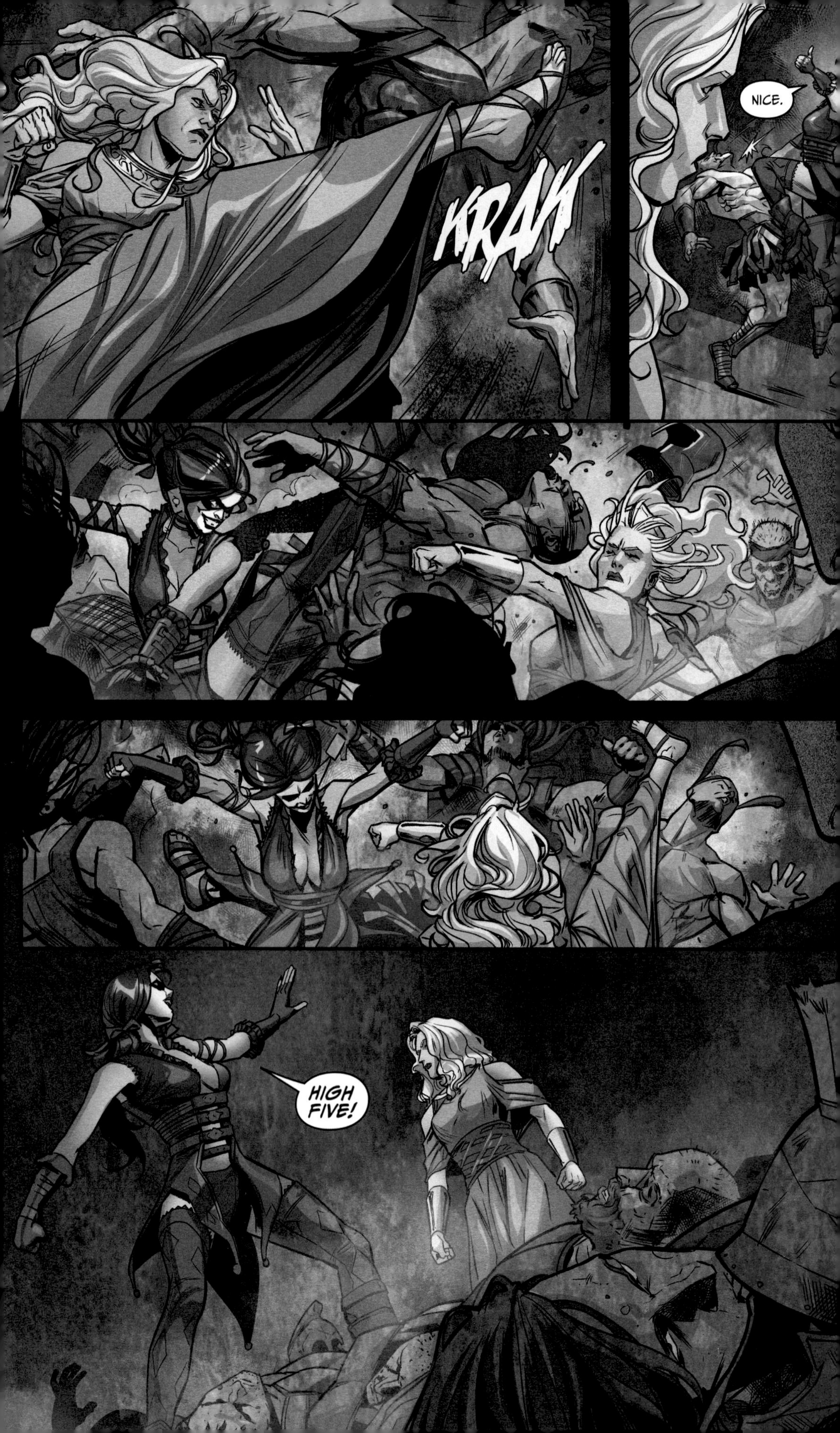
KRAK
NICE.
HIGH FIVE!

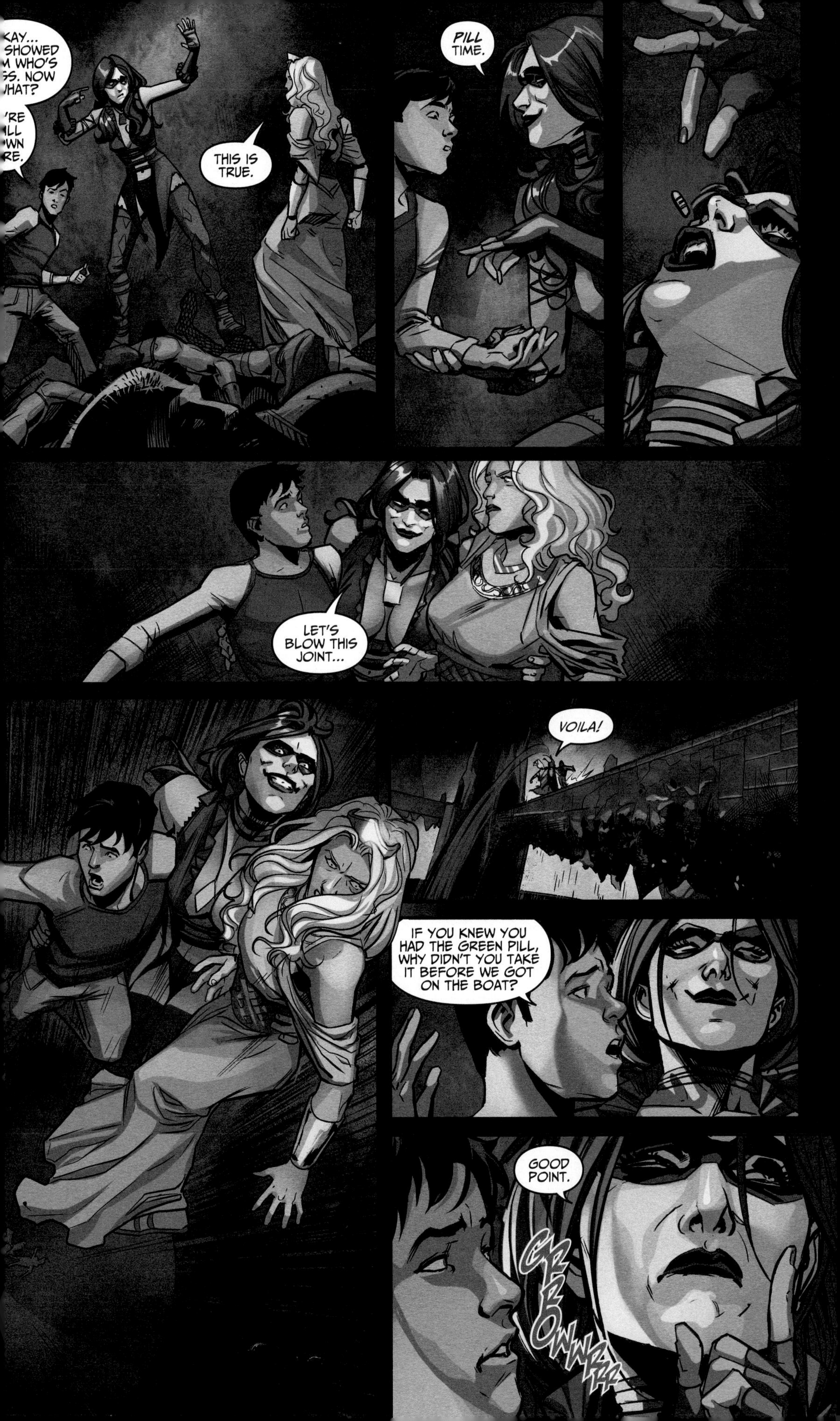
KAY... SHOWED M WHO'S SS. NOW WHAT?
'RE ILL OWN RE.
THIS IS TRUE.
PILL TIME.
LET'S BLOW THIS JOINT...
VOILA!
IF YOU KNEW YOU HAD THE GREEN PILL, WHY DIDN'T YOU TAKE IT BEFORE WE GOT ON THE BOAT?
GOOD POINT.

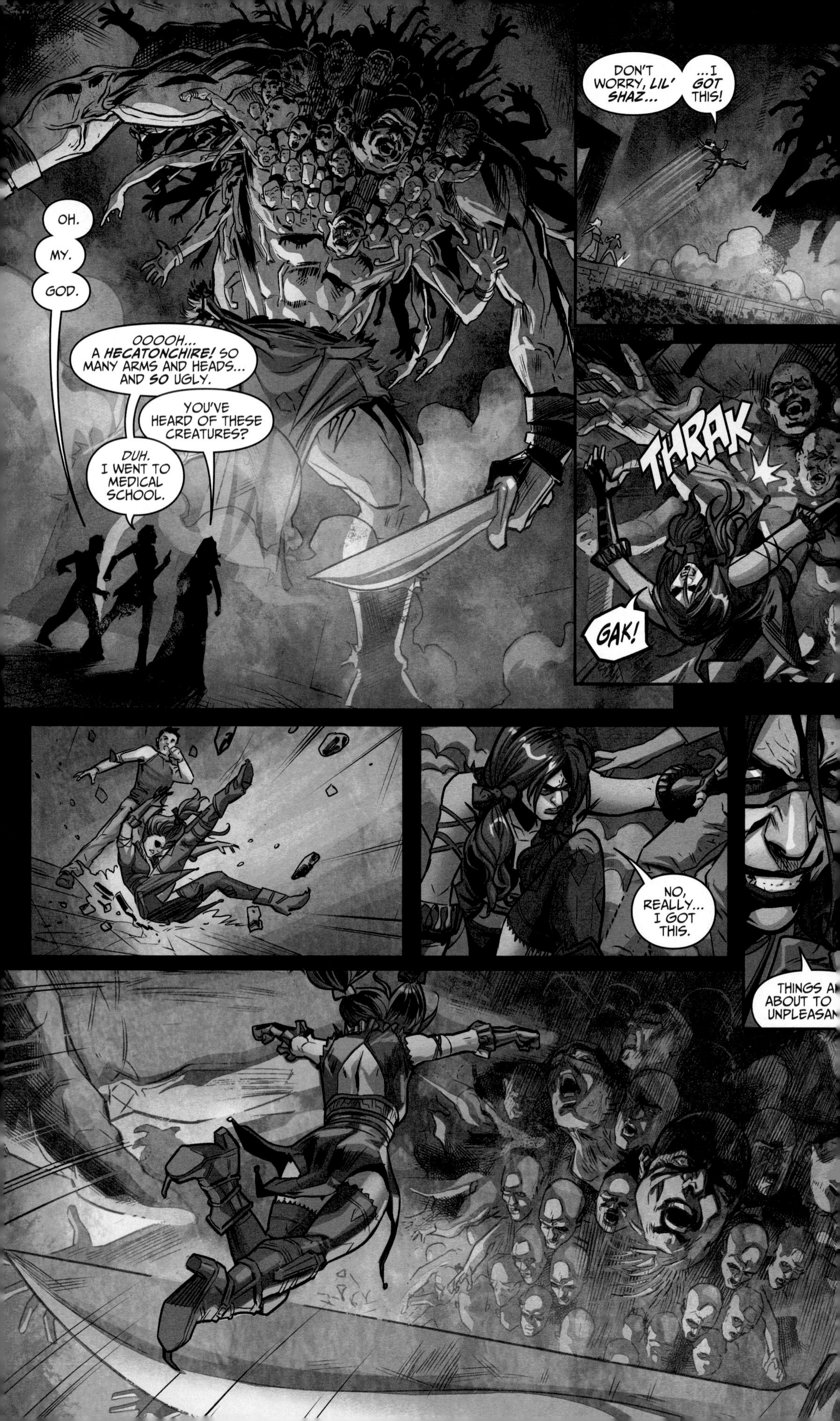
OH.
MY.
GOD.
OOOOH... A HECATONCHIRE! SO MANY ARMS AND HEADS... AND SO UGLY.
YOU'VE HEARD OF THESE CREATURES?
DUH. I WENT TO MEDICAL SCHOOL.
DON'T WORRY, LIL' SHAZ...
...I GOT THIS!
THRAK
GAK!
NO, REALLY... I GOT THIS.

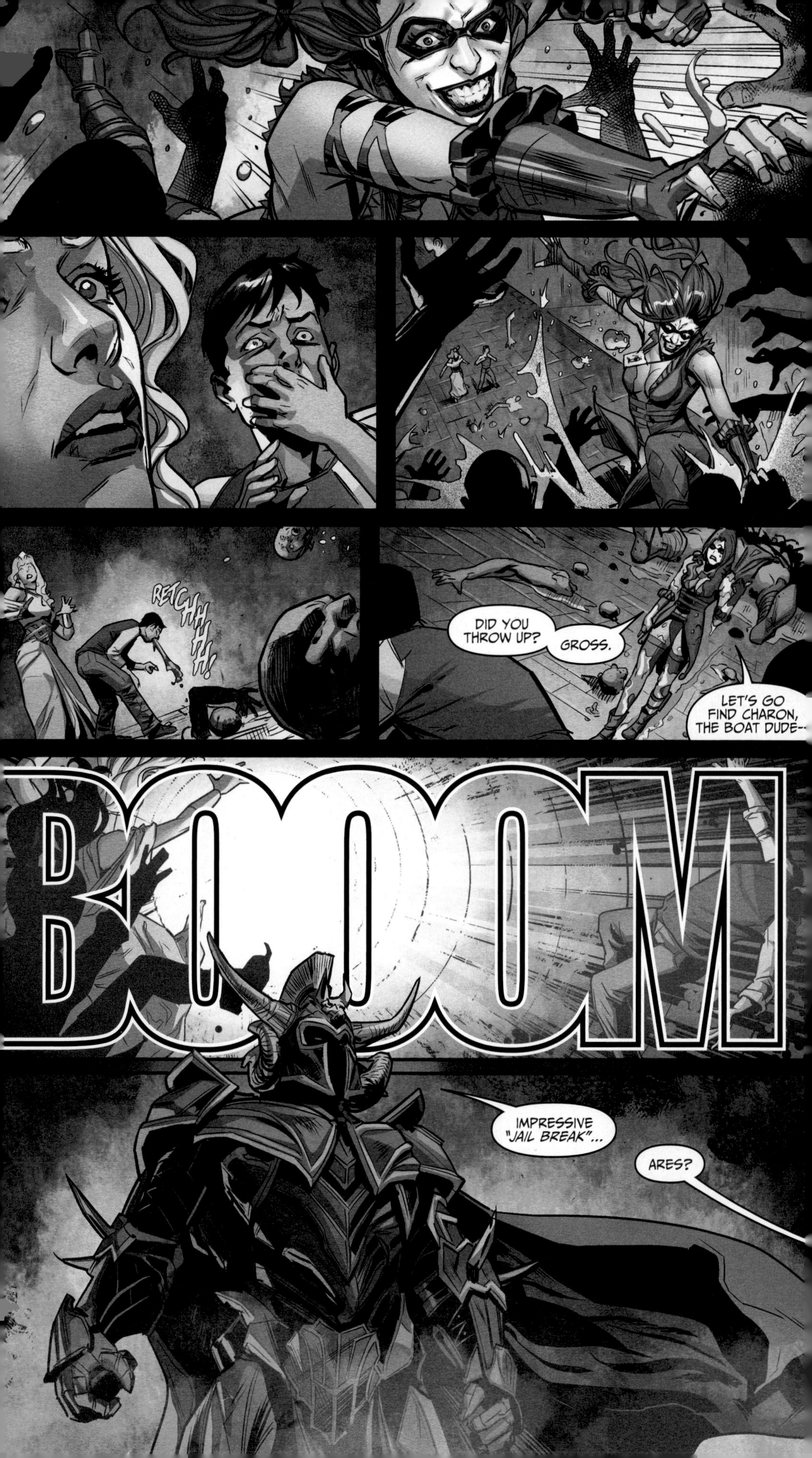
RETCHHHHH!
DID YOU THROW UP?
GROSS.
LET'S GO FIND CHARON, THE BOAT DUDE--
BOOOOM
IMPRESSIVE "JAIL BREAK"...
ARES?

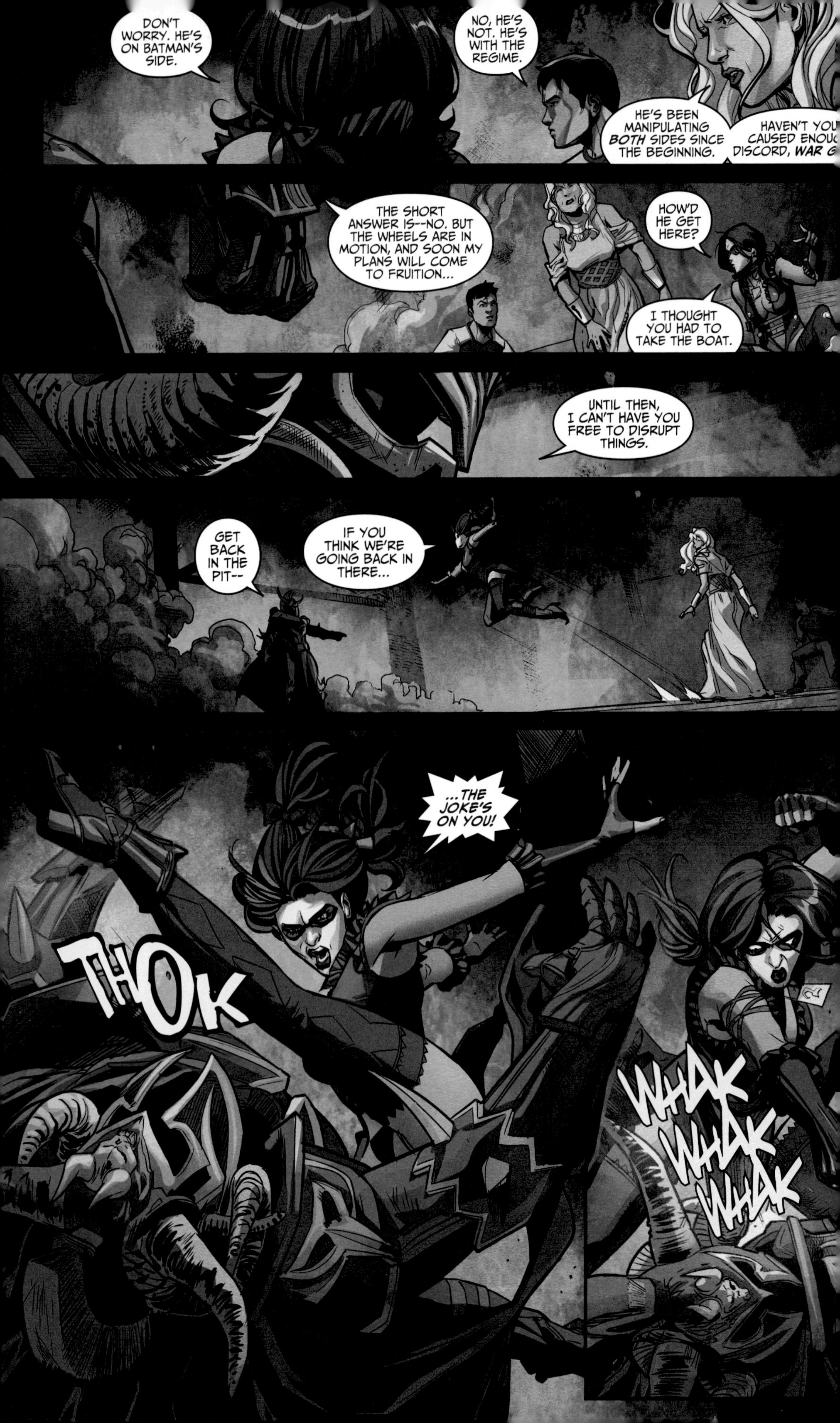
DON'T WORRY. HE'S ON BATMAN'S SIDE.
NO, HE'S NOT. HE'S WITH THE REGIME.
HE'S BEEN MANIPULATING BOTH SIDES SINCE THE BEGINNING.
HAVEN'T YOU CAUSED ENOUG DISCORD, WAR G
THE SHORT ANSWER IS--NO. BUT THE WHEELS ARE IN MOTION, AND SOON MY PLANS WILL COME TO FRUITION...
HOW'D HE GET HERE?
I THOUGHT YOU HAD TO TAKE THE BOAT.
UNTIL THEN, I CAN'T HAVE YOU FREE TO DISRUPT THINGS.
GET BACK IN THE PIT--
IF YOU THINK WE'RE GOING BACK IN THERE...
...THE JOKE'S ON YOU!
THOK
WHAK WHAK WHAK

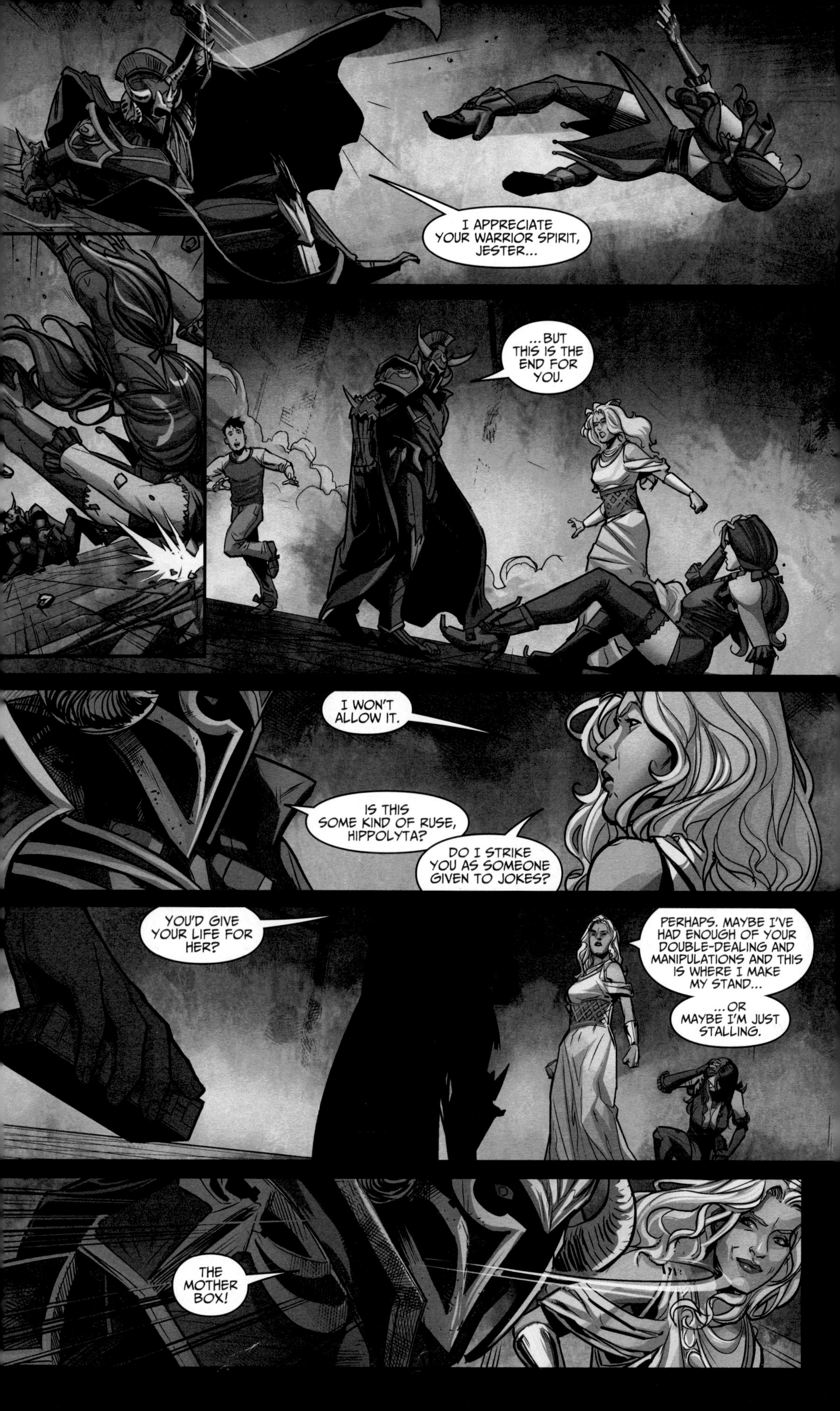
I APPRECIATE YOUR WARRIOR SPIRIT, JESTER...
...BUT THIS IS THE END FOR YOU.
I WON'T ALLOW IT.
IS THIS SOME KIND OF RUSE, HIPPOLYTA?
DO I STRIKE YOU AS SOMEONE GIVEN TO JOKES?
YOU'D GIVE YOUR LIFE FOR HER?
PERHAPS. MAYBE I'VE HAD ENOUGH OF YOUR DOUBLE-DEALING AND MANIPULATIONS AND THIS IS WHERE I MAKE MY STAND...
...OR MAYBE I'M JUST STALLING.
THE MOTHER BOX!

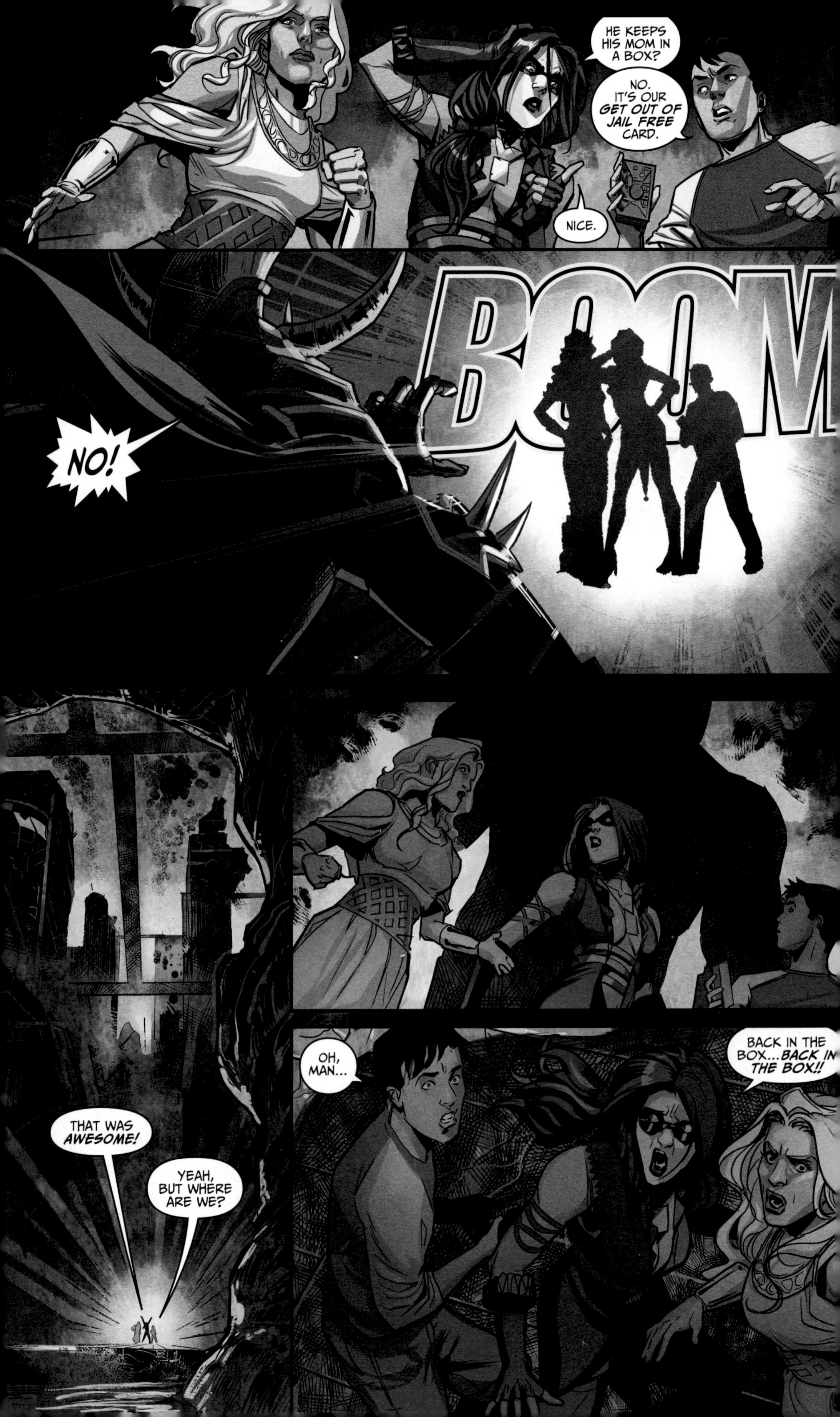
HE KEEPS HIS MOM IN A BOX?
NO. IT'S OUR ***GET OUT OF JAIL FREE*** CARD.
NICE.
BOOM
NO!
THAT WAS ***AWESOME!***
YEAH, BUT WHERE ARE WE?
OH, MAN...
BACK IN THE BOX...***BACK IN THE BOX!!***

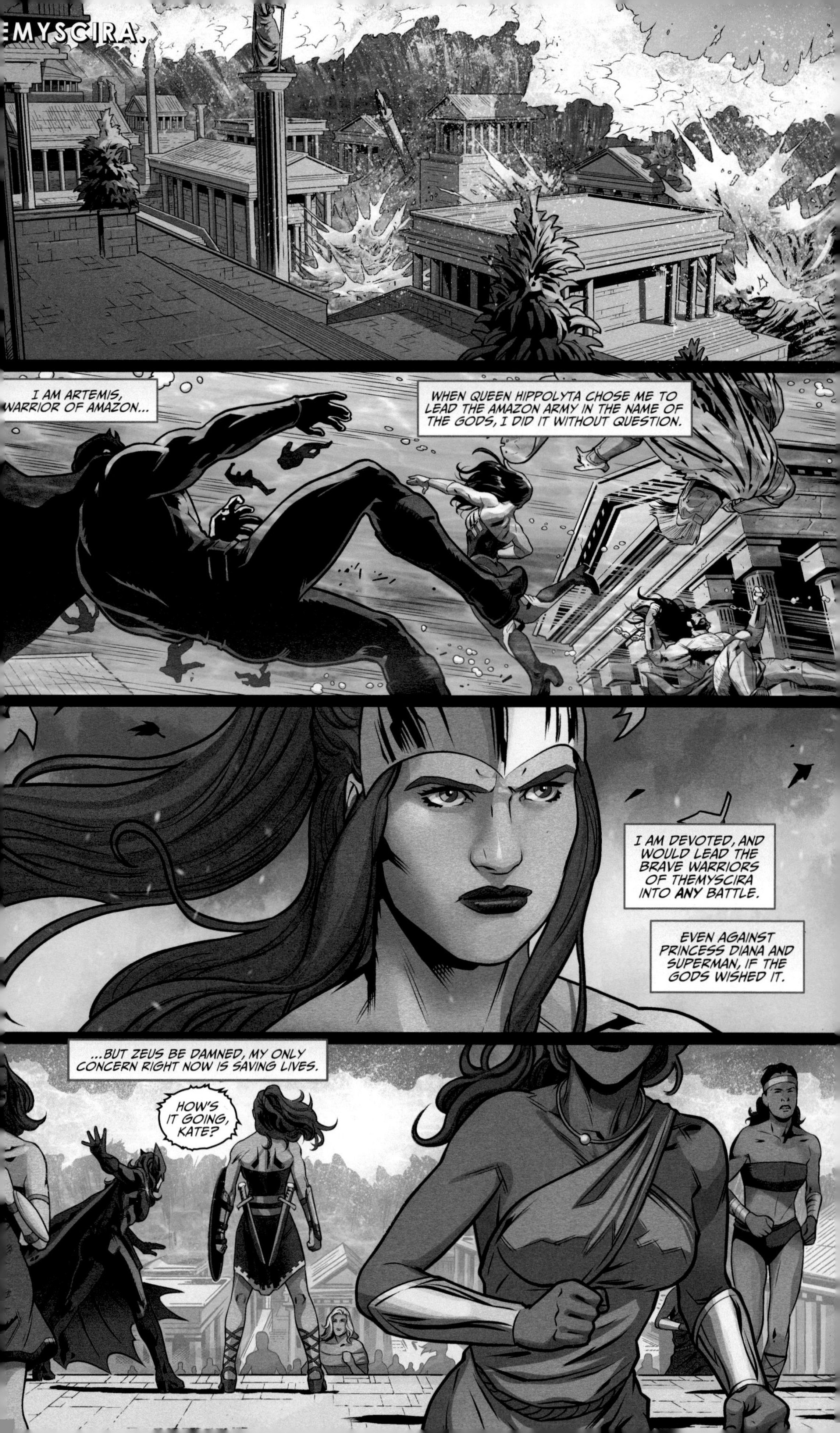

EMYSCIRA.
I AM ARTEMIS, WARRIOR OF AMAZON...
WHEN QUEEN HIPPOLYTA CHOSE ME TO LEAD THE AMAZON ARMY IN THE NAME OF THE GODS, I DID IT WITHOUT QUESTION.
I AM DEVOTED, AND WOULD LEAD THE BRAVE WARRIORS OF THEMYSCIRA INTO ANY BATTLE.
EVEN AGAINST PRINCESS DIANA AND SUPERMAN, IF THE GODS WISHED IT.
...BUT ZEUS BE DAMNED, MY ONLY CONCERN RIGHT NOW IS SAVING LIVES.
HOW'S IT GOING, KATE?

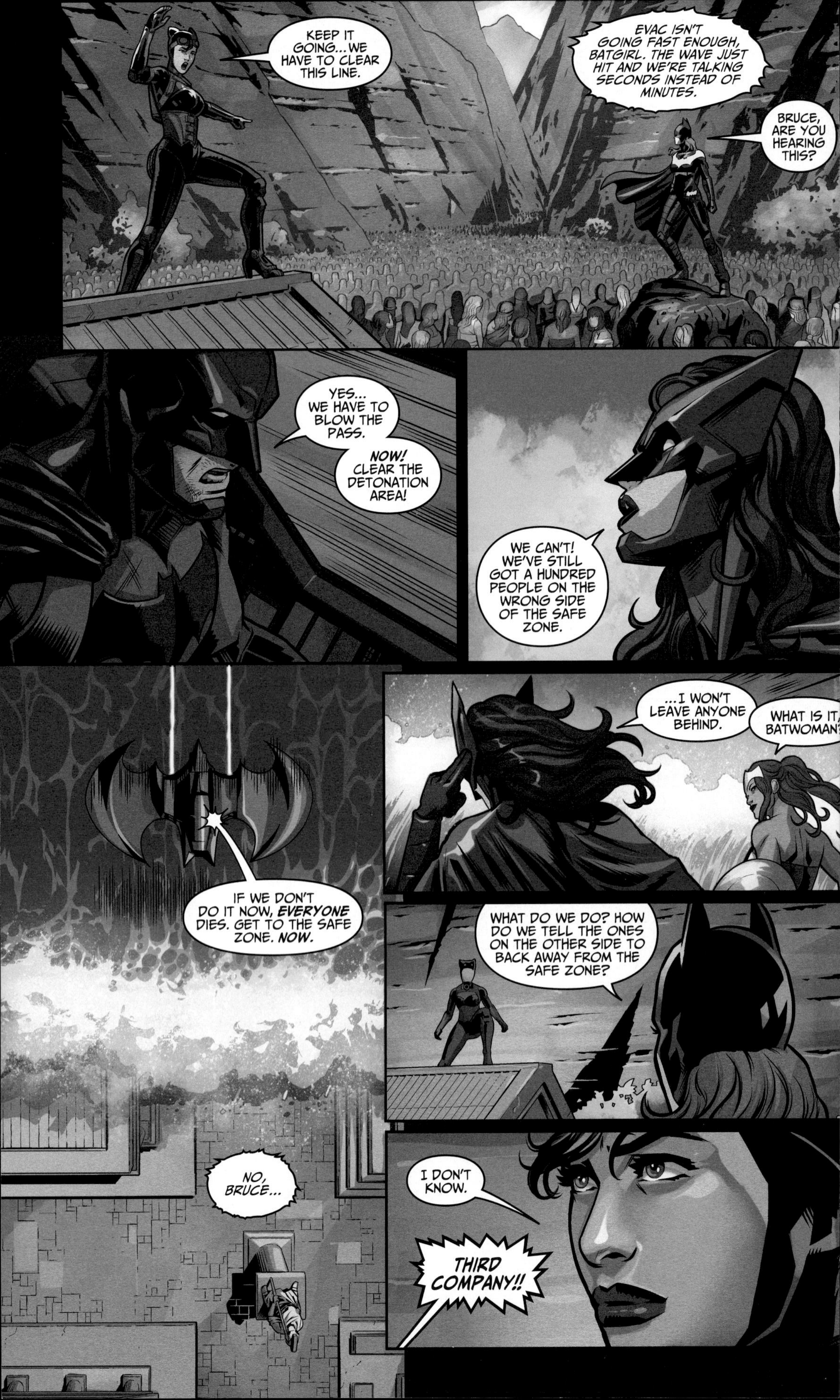

KEEP IT GOING...WE HAVE TO CLEAR THIS LINE.
EVAC ISN'T GOING FAST ENOUGH, BATGIRL. THE WAVE JUST HIT AND WE'RE TALKING SECONDS INSTEAD OF MINUTES.
BRUCE, ARE YOU HEARING THIS?
YES... WE HAVE TO BLOW THE PASS.
NOW! CLEAR THE DETONATION AREA!
WE CAN'T! WE'VE STILL GOT A HUNDRED PEOPLE ON THE WRONG SIDE OF THE SAFE ZONE.
IF WE DON'T DO IT NOW, EVERYONE DIES. GET TO THE SAFE ZONE. NOW.
NO, BRUCE...
...I WON'T LEAVE ANYONE BEHIND.
WHAT IS IT, BATWOMAN?
WHAT DO WE DO? HOW DO WE TELL THE ONES ON THE OTHER SIDE TO BACK AWAY FROM THE SAFE ZONE?
I DON'T KNOW.
THIRD COMPANY!!

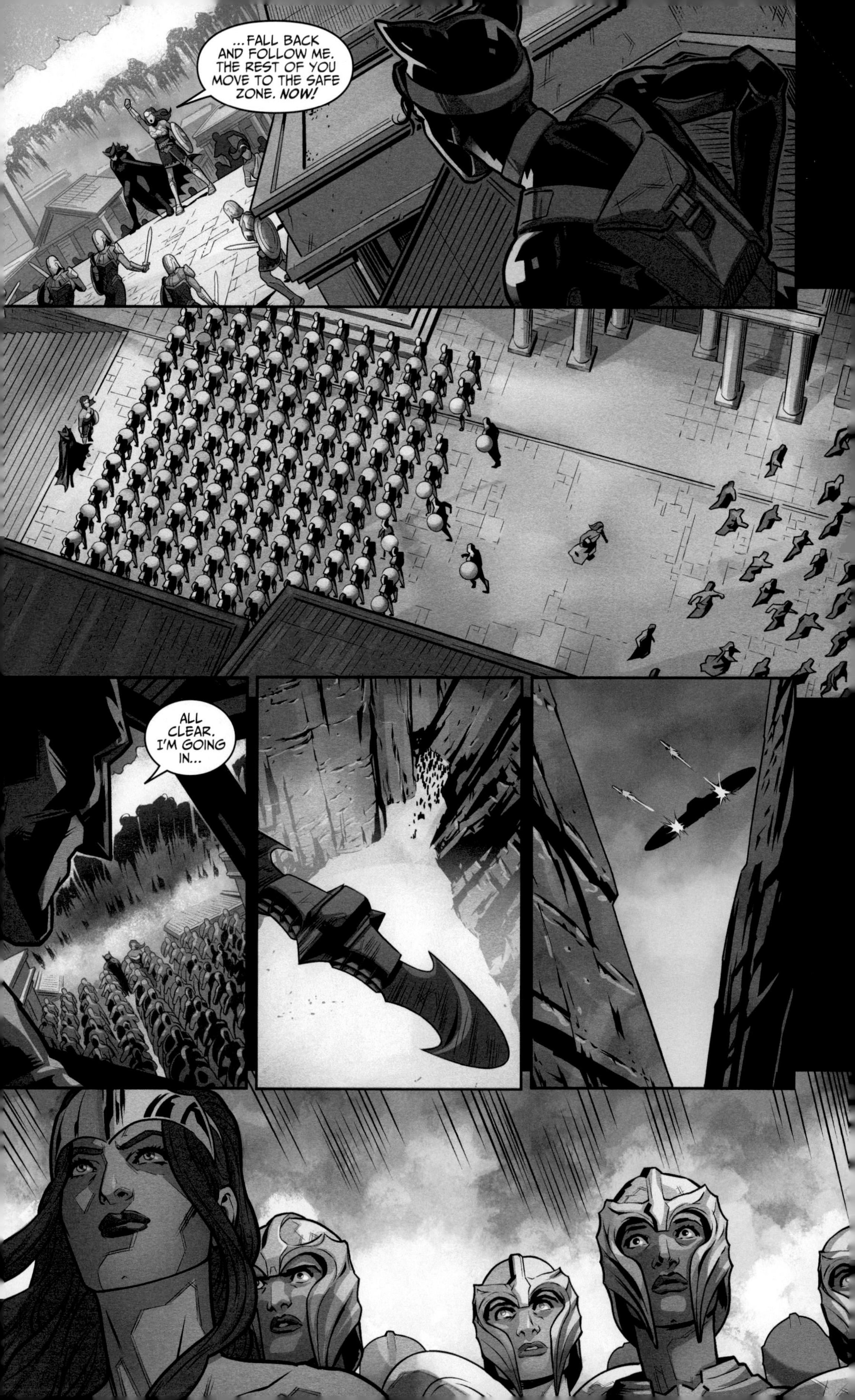
...FALL BACK AND FOLLOW ME. THE REST OF YOU MOVE TO THE SAFE ZONE. NOW!
ALL CLEAR. I'M GOING IN...

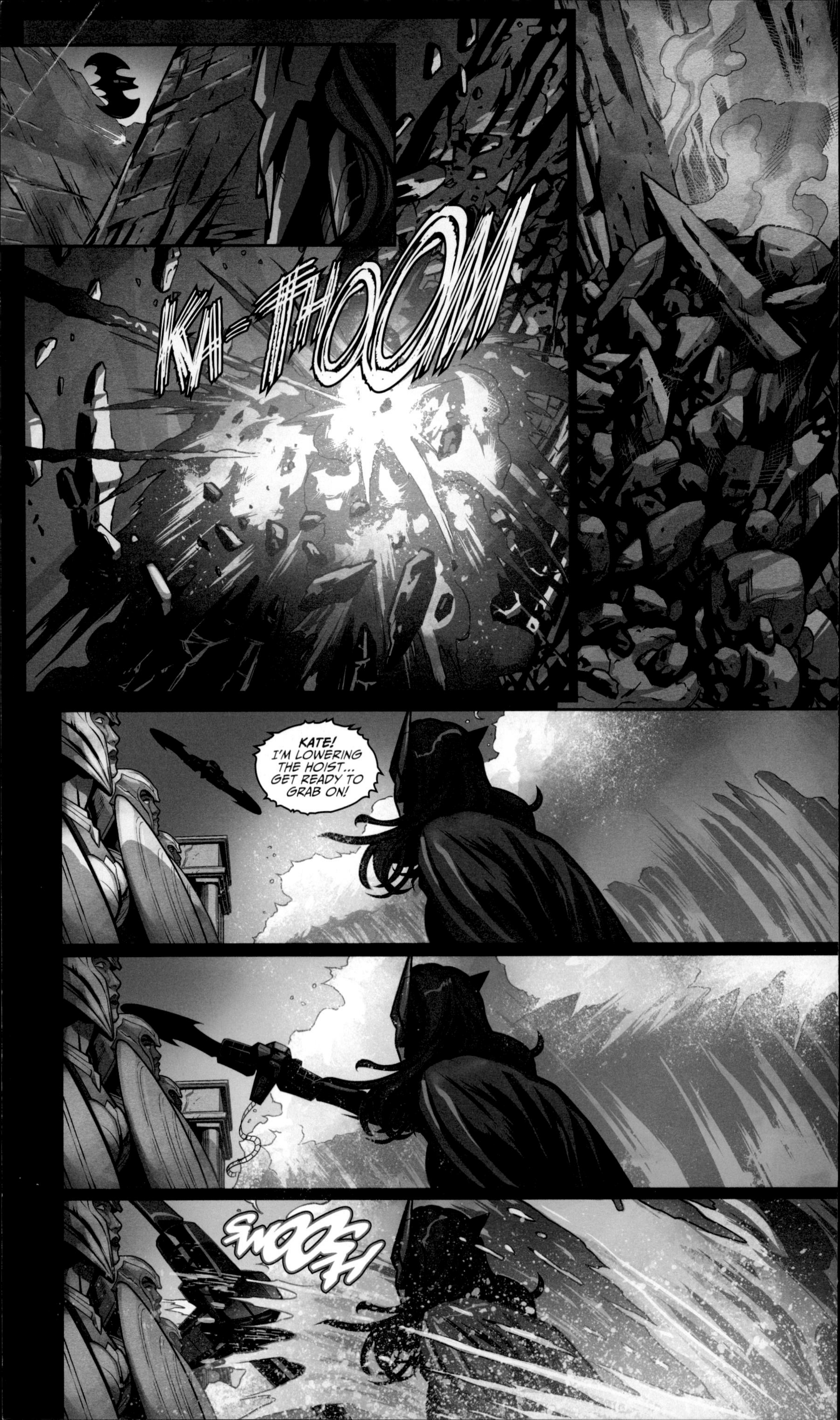
KA-THOOM
KATE! I'M LOWERING THE HOIST... GET READY TO GRAB ON!
SWOOSH

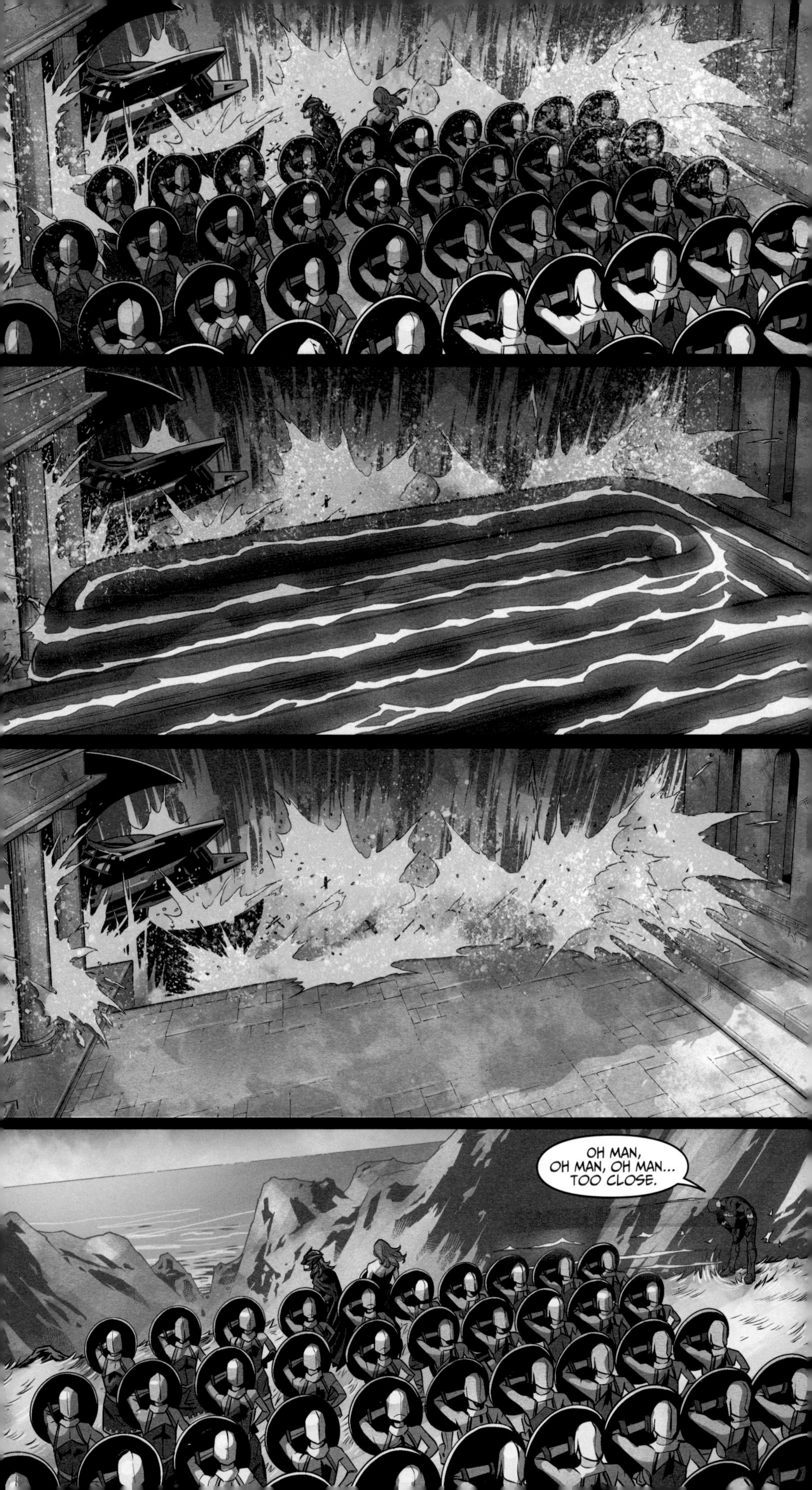
OH MAN, OH MAN, OH MAN... TOO CLOSE.

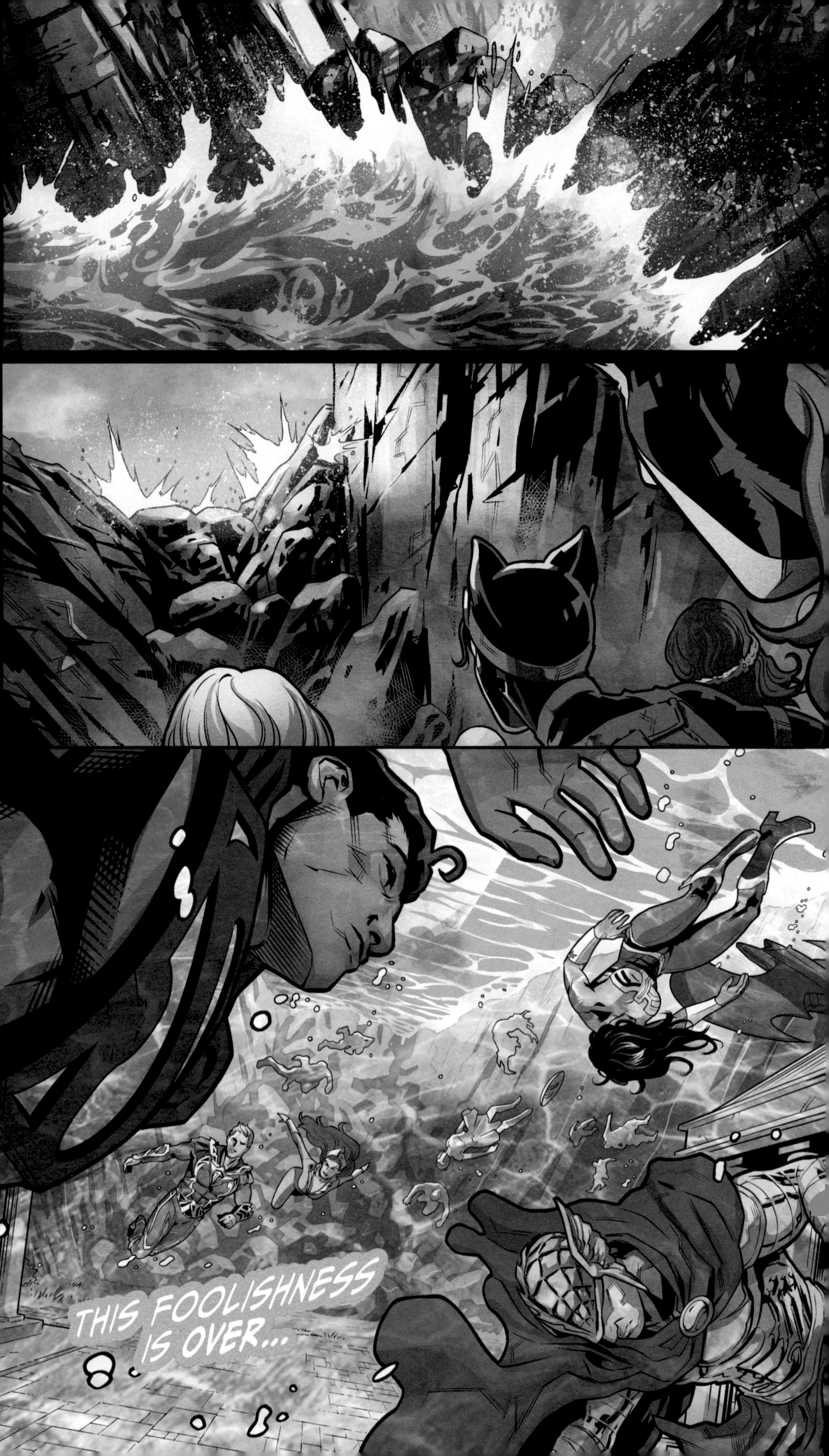
THIS FOOLISHNESS IS OVER...

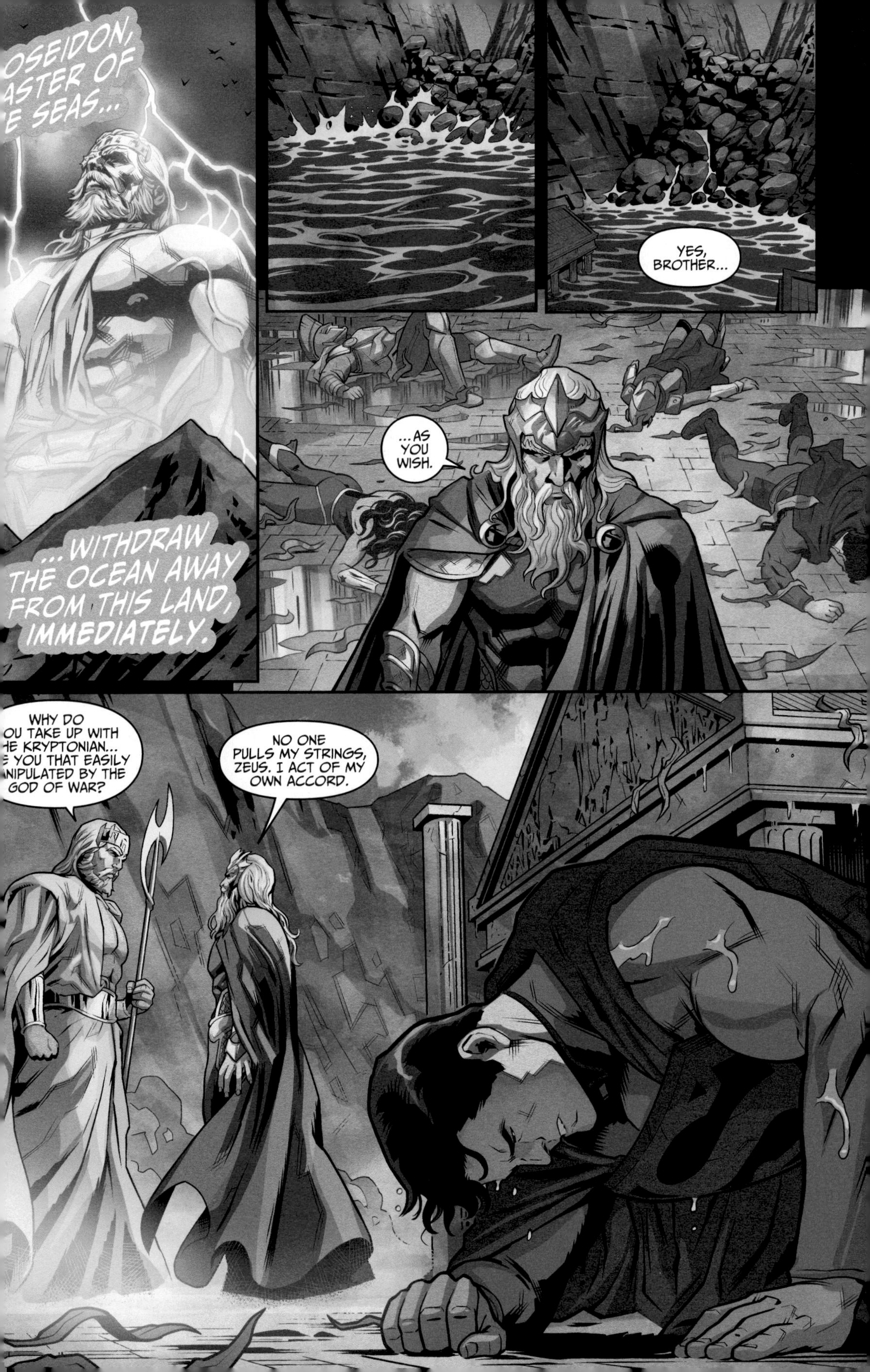
OSEIDON,
ASTER OF
E SEAS...
...WITHDRAW THE OCEAN AWAY FROM THIS LAND, IMMEDIATELY.
YES, BROTHER...
...AS YOU WISH.
WHY DO
OU TAKE UP WITH
HE KRYPTONIAN...
E YOU THAT EASILY
ANIPULATED BY THE
GOD OF WAR?
NO ONE PULLS MY STRINGS, ZEUS. I ACT OF MY OWN ACCORD.

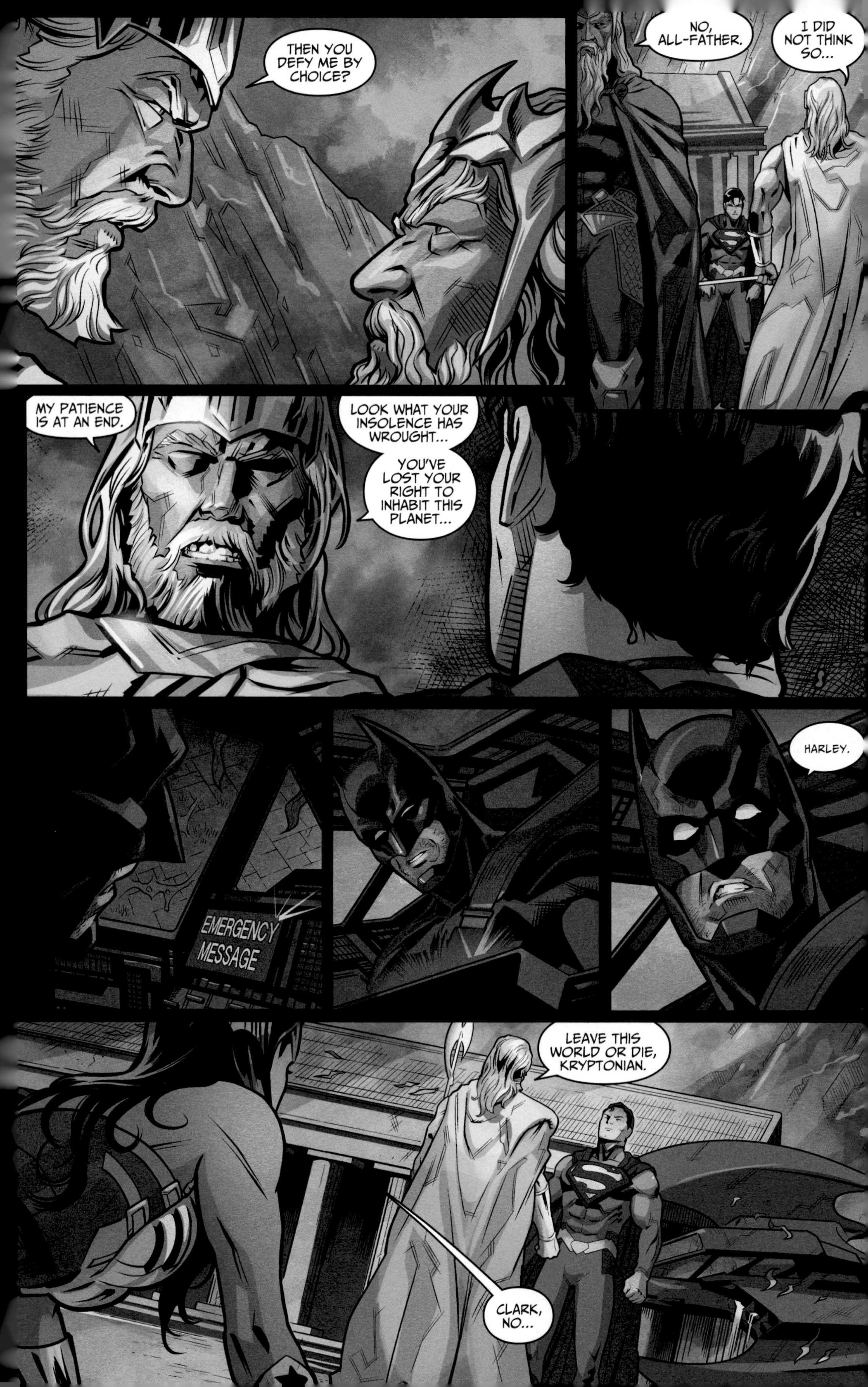
THEN YOU DEFY ME BY CHOICE?
NO, ALL-FATHER.
I DID NOT THINK SO...
MY PATIENCE IS AT AN END.
LOOK WHAT YOUR INSOLENCE HAS WROUGHT...
YOU'VE LOST YOUR RIGHT TO INHABIT THIS PLANET...
EMERGENCY MESSAGE
HARLEY.
LEAVE THIS WORLD OR DIE, KRYPTONIAN.
CLARK, NO...

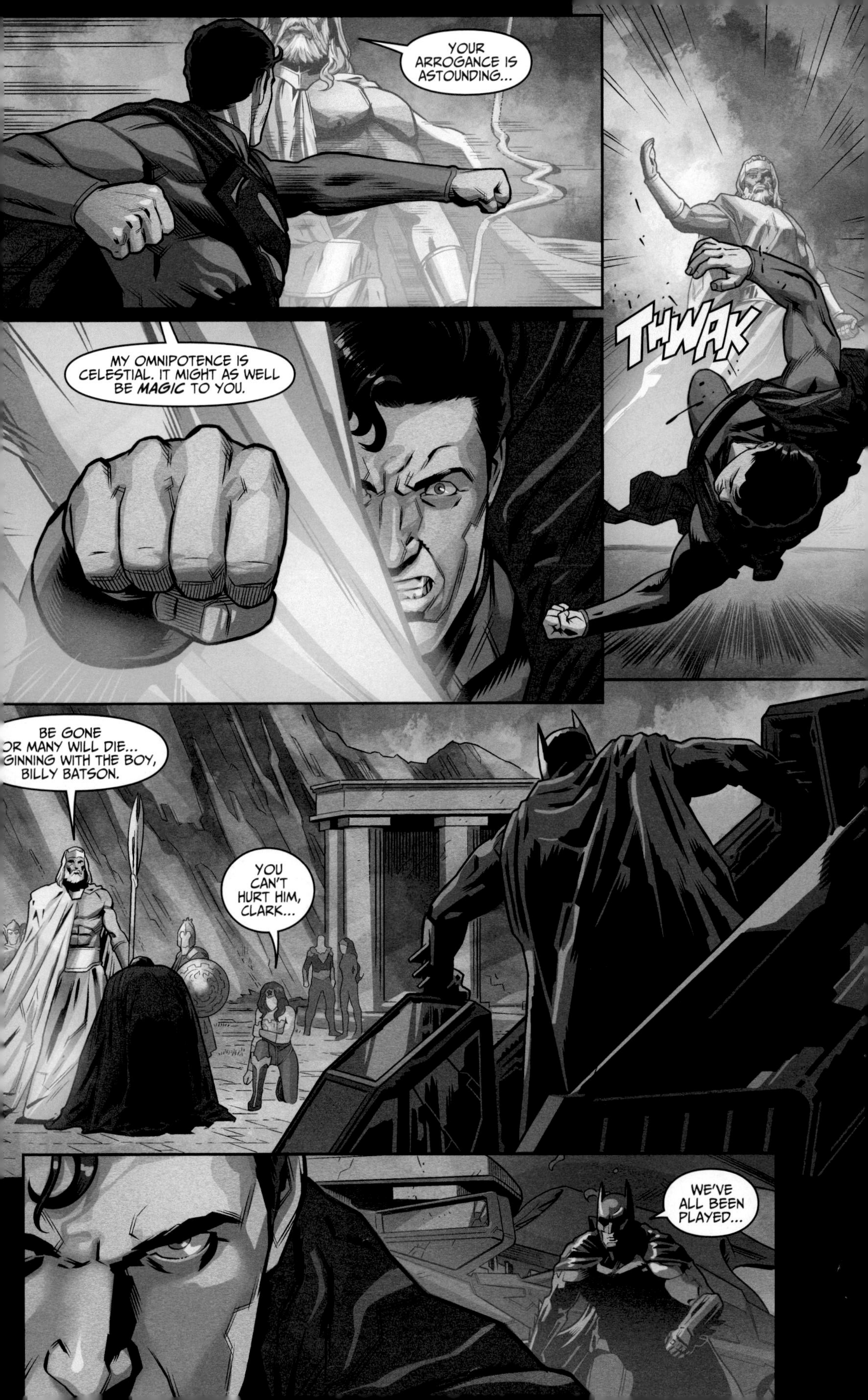
YOUR ARROGANCE IS ASTOUNDING...
THWAK
MY OMNIPOTENCE IS CELESTIAL. IT MIGHT AS WELL BE *MAGIC* TO YOU.
BE GONE OR MANY WILL DIE... GINNING WITH THE BOY, BILLY BATSON.
YOU CAN'T HURT HIM, CLARK...
WE'VE ALL BEEN PLAYED...

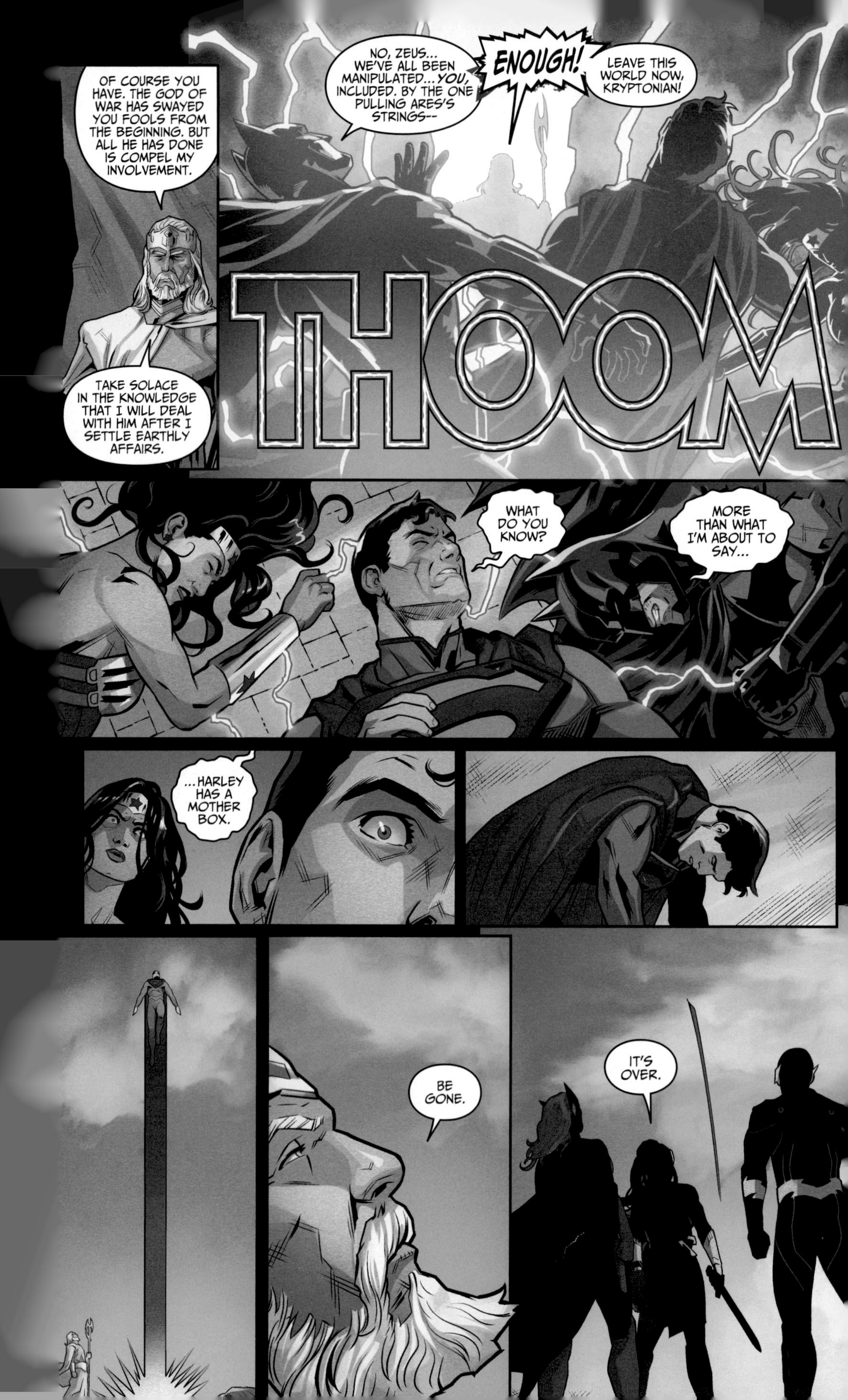
OF COURSE YOU HAVE. THE GOD OF WAR HAS SWAYED YOU FOOLS FROM THE BEGINNING. BUT ALL HE HAS DONE IS COMPEL MY INVOLVEMENT.
TAKE SOLACE IN THE KNOWLEDGE THAT I WILL DEAL WITH HIM AFTER I SETTLE EARTHLY AFFAIRS.
NO, ZEUS... WE'VE ALL BEEN MANIPULATED... *YOU*, INCLUDED. BY THE ONE PULLING ARES'S STRINGS--
ENOUGH!
LEAVE THIS WORLD NOW, KRYPTONIAN!
THOOM
WHAT DO YOU KNOW?
MORE THAN WHAT I'M ABOUT TO SAY...
...HARLEY HAS A MOTHER BOX.
BE GONE.
IT'S OVER.

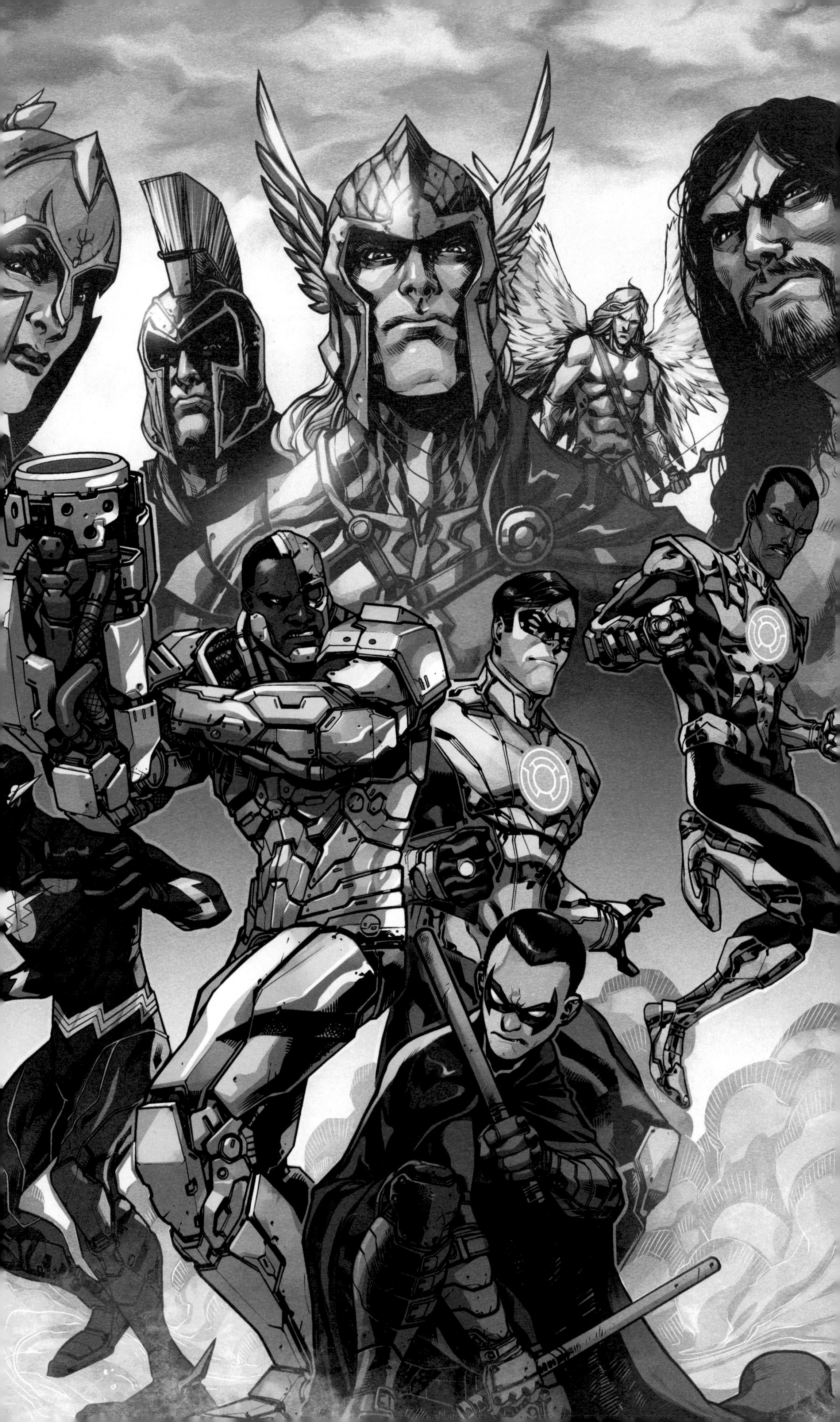

"The Dark Side" **Brian Buccellato** Writer **Tom Derenick Xermanico** Artists
J. Nanjan Rex Lokus Colorists Cover Art by **Neil Googe & Rex Lokus**

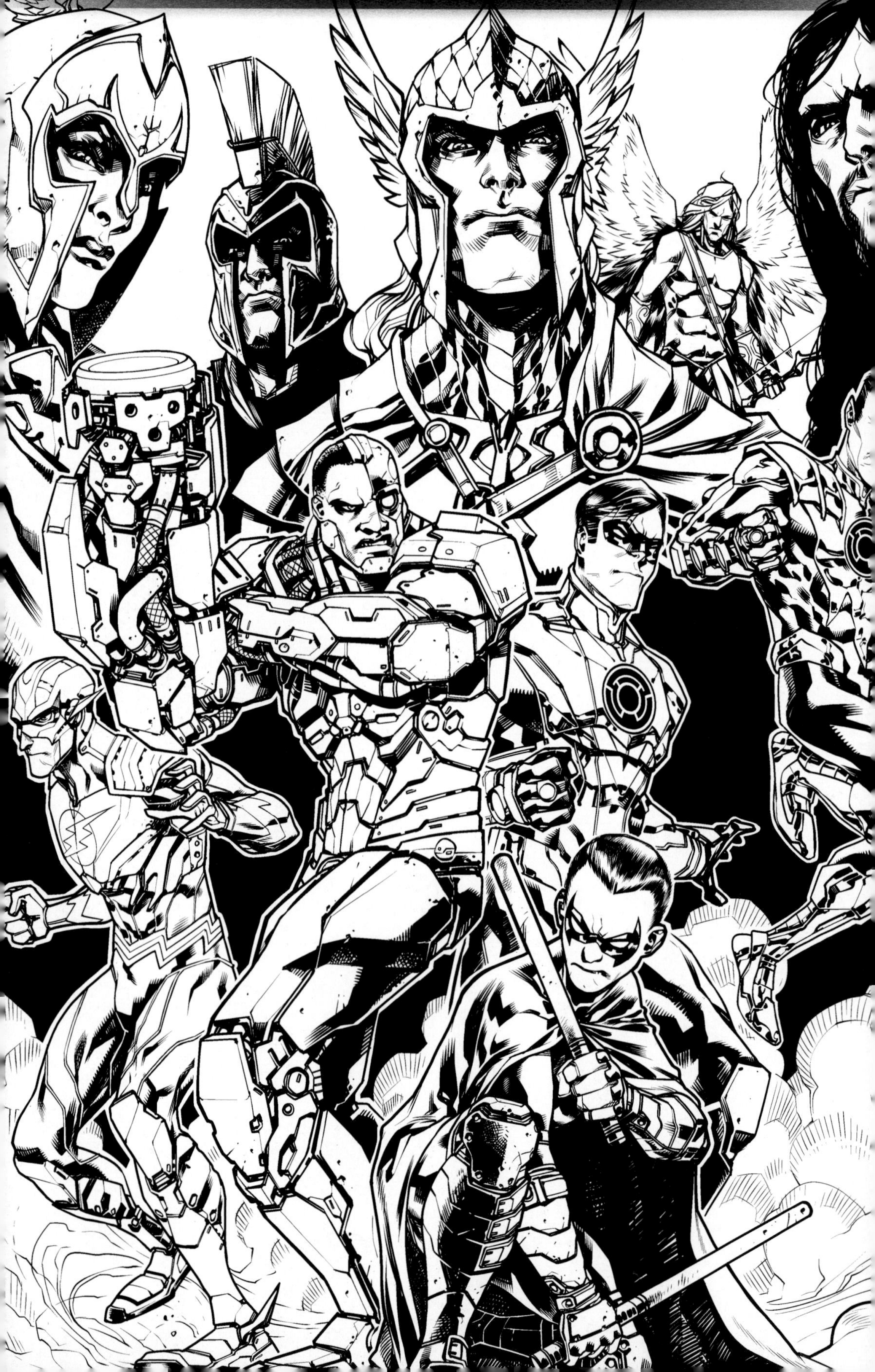

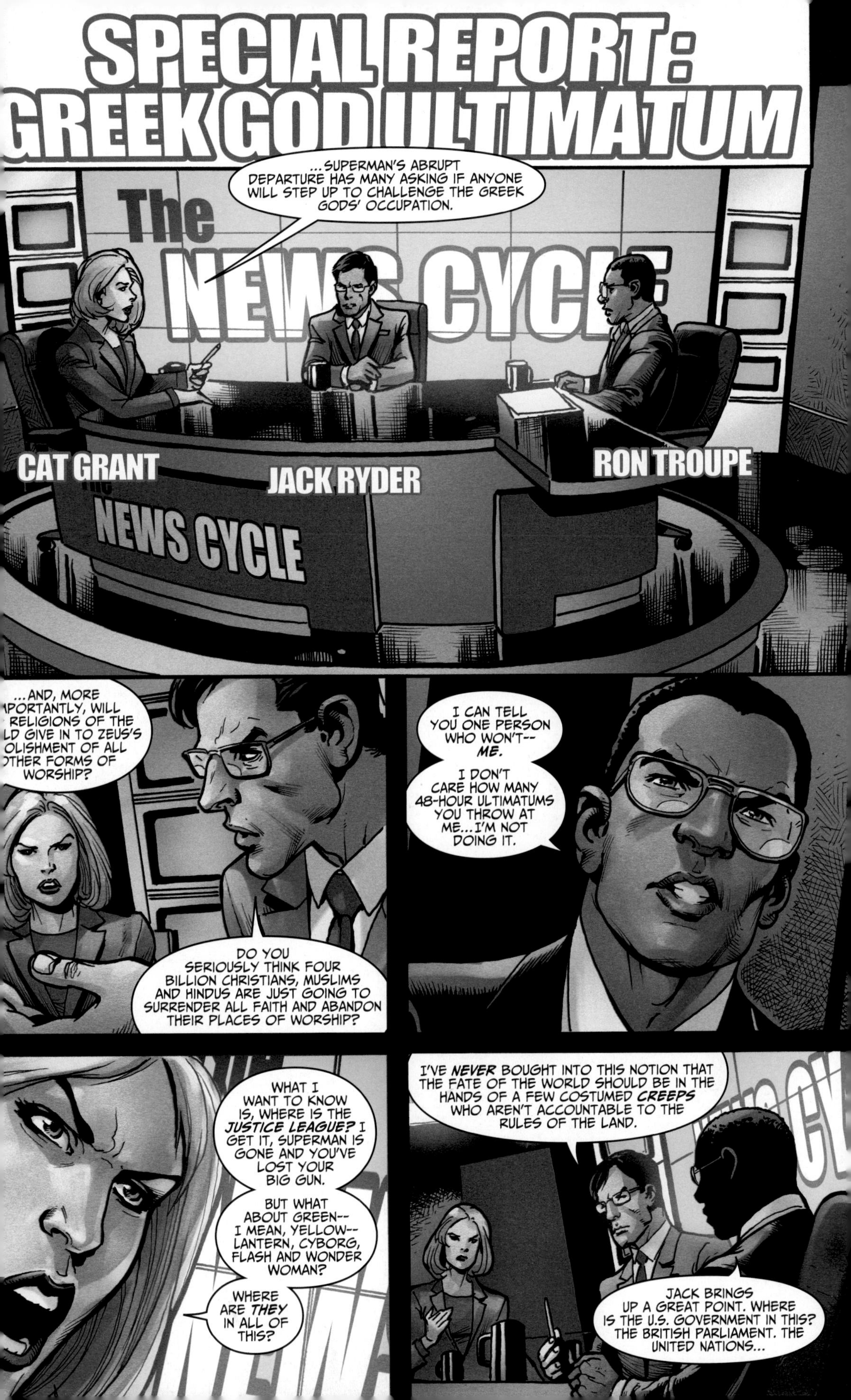
SPECIAL REPORT: GREEK GOD ULTIMATUM
...SUPERMAN'S ABRUPT DEPARTURE HAS MANY ASKING IF ANYONE WILL STEP UP TO CHALLENGE THE GREEK GODS' OCCUPATION.
The NEWS CYCLE
CAT GRANT
JACK RYDER
RON TROUPE
NEWS CYCLE
...AND, MORE PORTANTLY, WILL RELIGIONS OF THE LD GIVE IN TO ZEUS'S OLISHMENT OF ALL OTHER FORMS OF WORSHIP?
DO YOU SERIOUSLY THINK FOUR BILLION CHRISTIANS, MUSLIMS AND HINDUS ARE JUST GOING TO SURRENDER ALL FAITH AND ABANDON THEIR PLACES OF WORSHIP?
I CAN TELL YOU ONE PERSON WHO WON'T-- ME.
I DON'T CARE HOW MANY 48-HOUR ULTIMATUMS YOU THROW AT ME...I'M NOT DOING IT.
WHAT I WANT TO KNOW IS, WHERE IS THE JUSTICE LEAGUE? I GET IT, SUPERMAN IS GONE AND YOU'VE LOST YOUR BIG GUN.
BUT WHAT ABOUT GREEN-- I MEAN, YELLOW-- LANTERN, CYBORG, FLASH AND WONDER WOMAN?
WHERE ARE THEY IN ALL OF THIS?
I'VE NEVER BOUGHT INTO THIS NOTION THAT THE FATE OF THE WORLD SHOULD BE IN THE HANDS OF A FEW COSTUMED CREEPS WHO AREN'T ACCOUNTABLE TO THE RULES OF THE LAND.
JACK BRINGS UP A GREAT POINT. WHERE IS THE U.S. GOVERNMENT IN THIS? THE BRITISH PARLIAMENT. THE UNITED NATIONS...

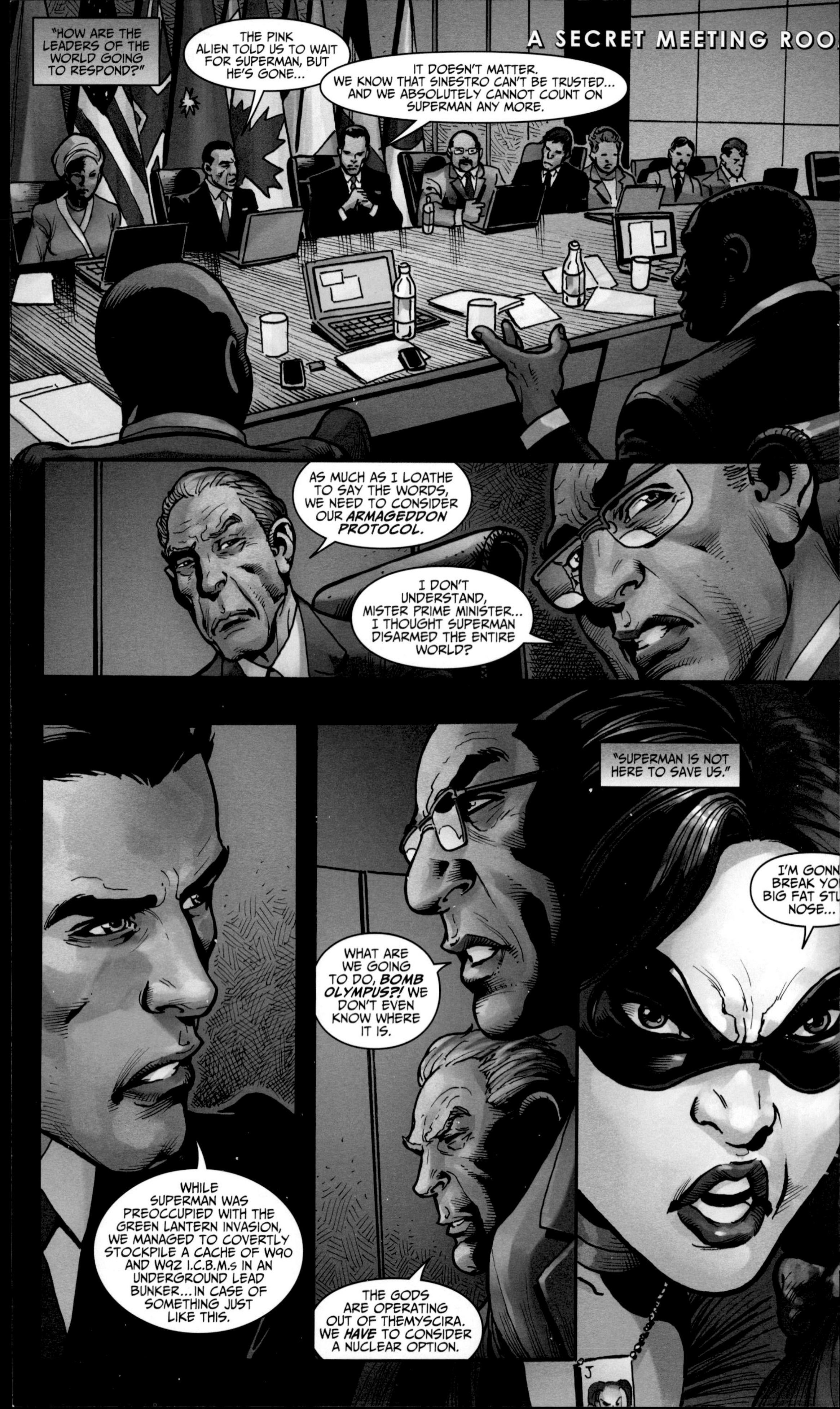
A SECRET MEETING ROO
"HOW ARE THE LEADERS OF THE WORLD GOING TO RESPOND?"
THE PINK ALIEN TOLD US TO WAIT FOR SUPERMAN, BUT HE'S GONE...
IT DOESN'T MATTER. WE KNOW THAT SINESTRO CAN'T BE TRUSTED... AND WE ABSOLUTELY CANNOT COUNT ON SUPERMAN ANY MORE.
AS MUCH AS I LOATHE TO SAY THE WORDS, WE NEED TO CONSIDER OUR ARMAGEDDON PROTOCOL.
I DON'T UNDERSTAND, MISTER PRIME MINISTER... I THOUGHT SUPERMAN DISARMED THE ENTIRE WORLD?
WHILE SUPERMAN WAS PREOCCUPIED WITH THE GREEN LANTERN INVASION, WE MANAGED TO COVERTLY STOCKPILE A CACHE OF W90 AND W92 I.C.B.M.s IN AN UNDERGROUND LEAD BUNKER...IN CASE OF SOMETHING JUST LIKE THIS.
WHAT ARE WE GOING TO DO, BOMB OLYMPUS?! WE DON'T EVEN KNOW WHERE IT IS.
THE GODS ARE OPERATING OUT OF THEMYSCIRA. WE HAVE TO CONSIDER A NUCLEAR OPTION.
"SUPERMAN IS NOT HERE TO SAVE US."
I'M GONN BREAK YO BIG FAT STU NOSE...

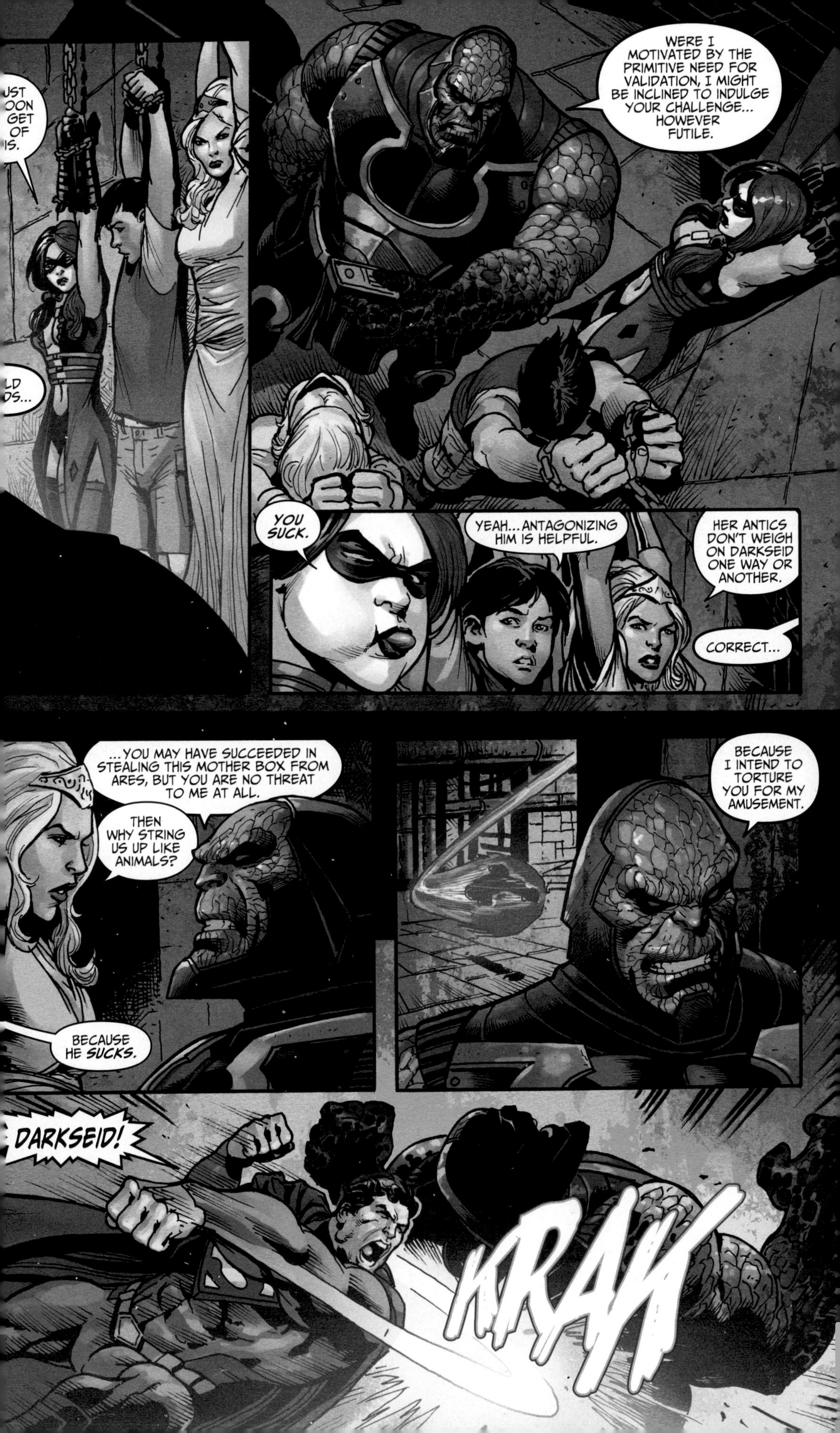
WERE I MOTIVATED BY THE PRIMITIVE NEED FOR VALIDATION, I MIGHT BE INCLINED TO INDULGE YOUR CHALLENGE... HOWEVER FUTILE.
YOU SUCK.
YEAH...ANTAGONIZING HIM IS HELPFUL.
HER ANTICS DON'T WEIGH ON DARKSEID ONE WAY OR ANOTHER.
CORRECT...
...YOU MAY HAVE SUCCEEDED IN STEALING THIS MOTHER BOX FROM ARES, BUT YOU ARE NO THREAT TO ME AT ALL.
THEN WHY STRING US UP LIKE ANIMALS?
BECAUSE HE SUCKS.
BECAUSE I INTEND TO TORTURE YOU FOR MY AMUSEMENT.
DARKSEID!
KRAK

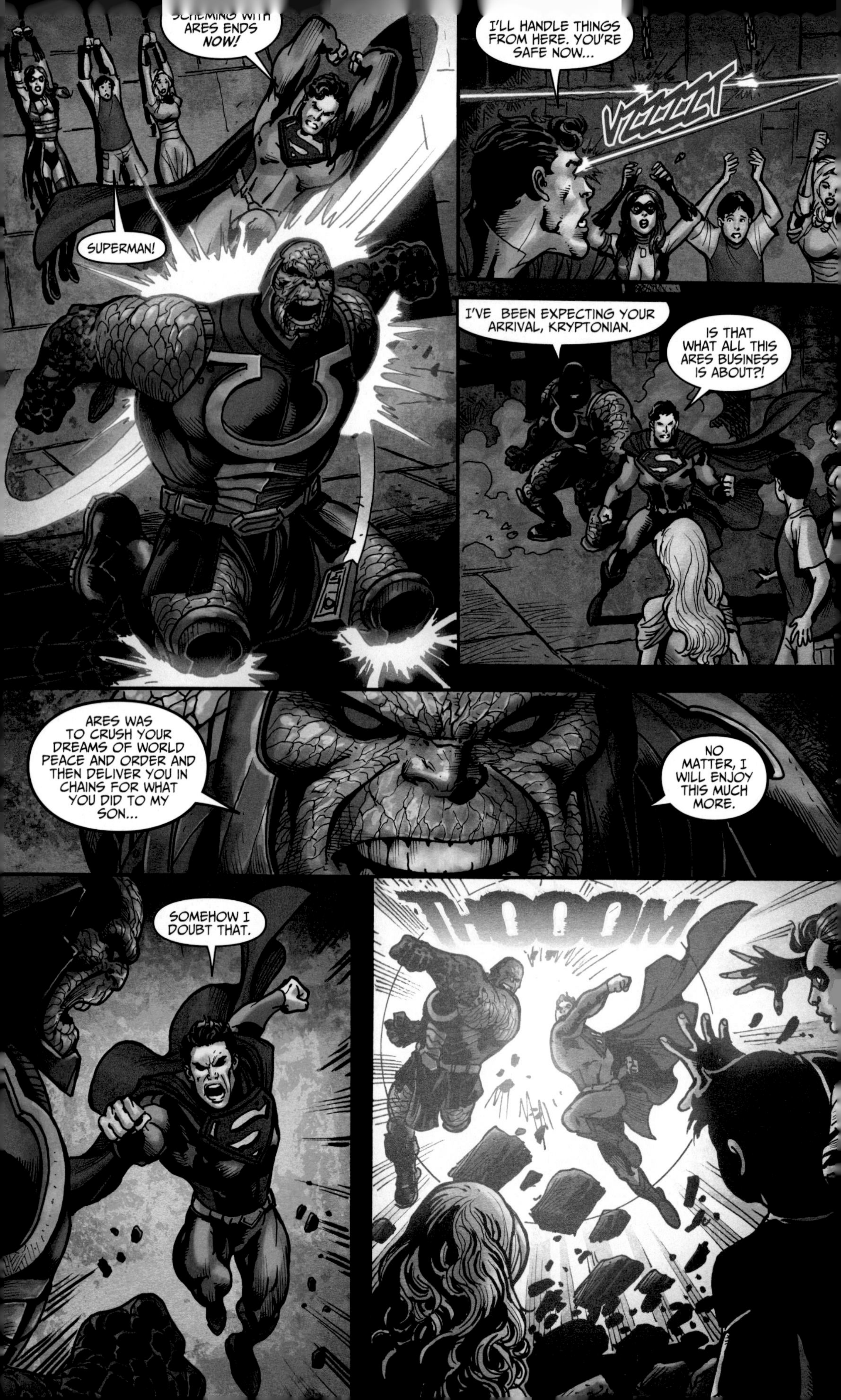
SCHEMING WITH ARES ENDS NOW!
SUPERMAN!
I'LL HANDLE THINGS FROM HERE. YOU'RE SAFE NOW...
I'VE BEEN EXPECTING YOUR ARRIVAL, KRYPTONIAN.
IS THAT WHAT ALL THIS ARES BUSINESS IS ABOUT?!
ARES WAS TO CRUSH YOUR DREAMS OF WORLD PEACE AND ORDER AND THEN DELIVER YOU IN CHAINS FOR WHAT YOU DID TO MY SON...
NO MATTER, I WILL ENJOY THIS MUCH MORE.
SOMEHOW I DOUBT THAT.
THOOOM

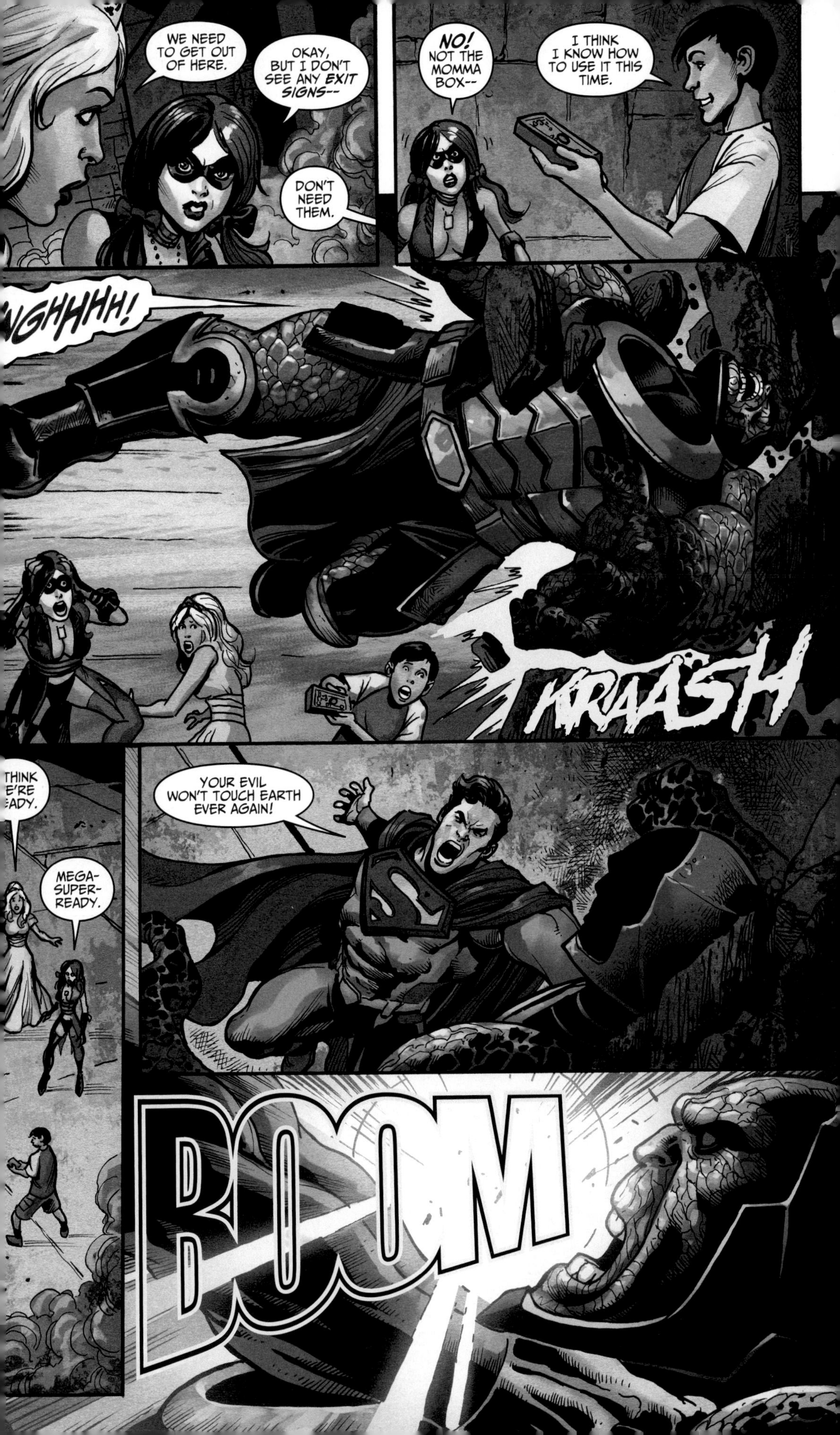
WE NEED TO GET OUT OF HERE.
OKAY, BUT I DON'T SEE ANY EXIT SIGNS--
DON'T NEED THEM.
NO! NOT THE MOMMA BOX--
I THINK I KNOW HOW TO USE IT THIS TIME.
NGHHHH!
KRAASH
THINK E'RE EADY.
MEGA-SUPER-READY.
YOUR EVIL WON'T TOUCH EARTH EVER AGAIN!
BOOM

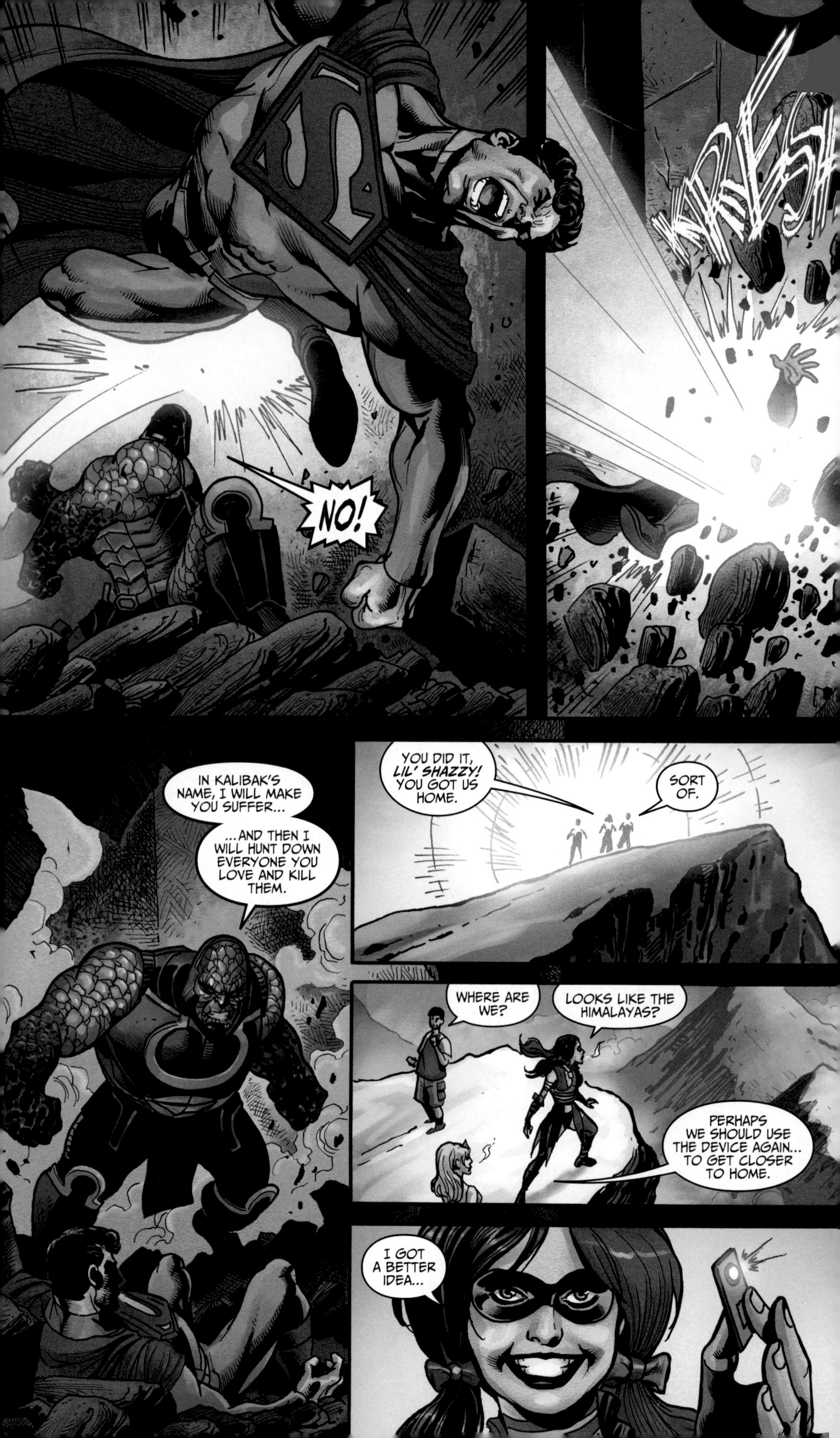
NO!
KRESH
IN KALIBAK'S NAME, I WILL MAKE YOU SUFFER...
...AND THEN I WILL HUNT DOWN EVERYONE YOU LOVE AND KILL THEM.
YOU DID IT, LIL' SHAZZY! YOU GOT US HOME.
SORT OF.
WHERE ARE WE?
LOOKS LIKE THE HIMALAYAS?
PERHAPS WE SHOULD USE THE DEVICE AGAIN... TO GET CLOSER TO HOME.
I GOT A BETTER IDEA...

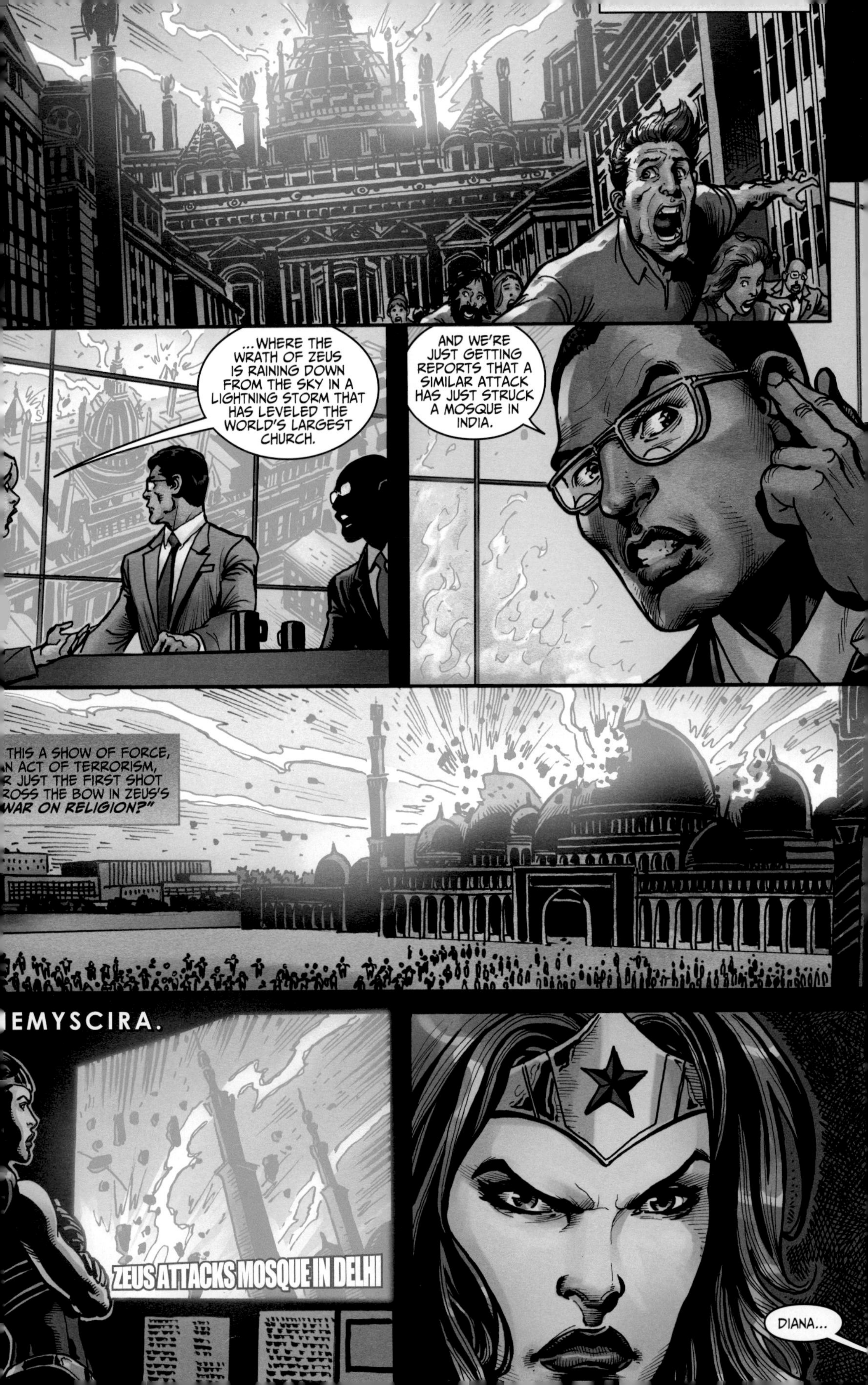
...WHERE THE WRATH OF ZEUS IS RAINING DOWN FROM THE SKY IN A LIGHTNING STORM THAT HAS LEVELED THE WORLD'S LARGEST CHURCH.
AND WE'RE JUST GETTING REPORTS THAT A SIMILAR ATTACK HAS JUST STRUCK A MOSQUE IN INDIA.
THIS A SHOW OF FORCE, N ACT OF TERRORISM, R JUST THE FIRST SHOT ROSS THE BOW IN ZEUS'S WAR ON RELIGION?"
EMYSCIRA.
ZEUS ATTACKS MOSQUE IN DELHI
DIANA...

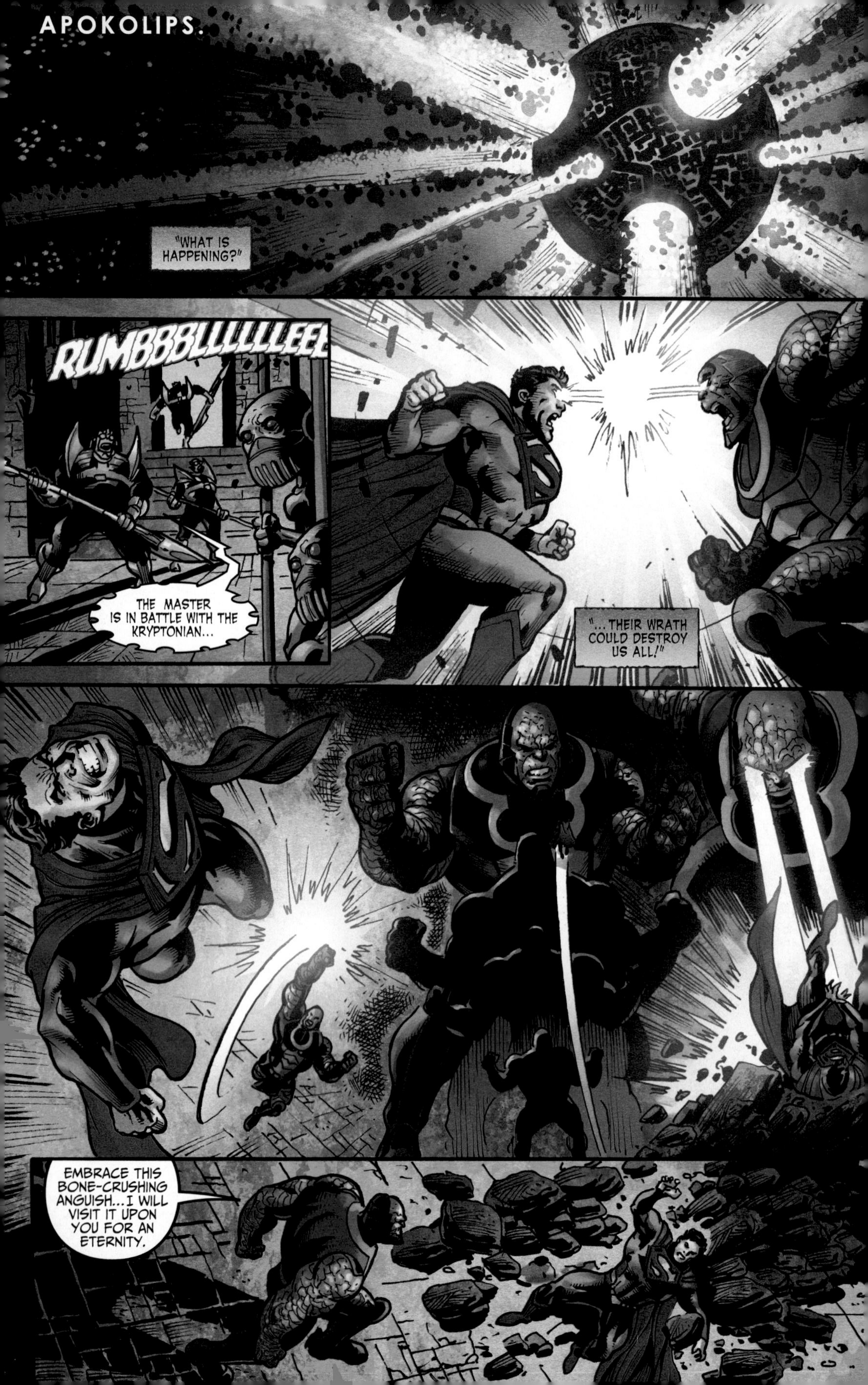
APOKOLIPS.
"WHAT IS HAPPENING?"
RUMBBBLLLLLLLEEE
THE MASTER IS IN BATTLE WITH THE KRYPTONIAN...
"...THEIR WRATH COULD DESTROY US ALL!"
EMBRACE THIS BONE-CRUSHING ANGUISH...I WILL VISIT IT UPON YOU FOR AN ETERNITY.

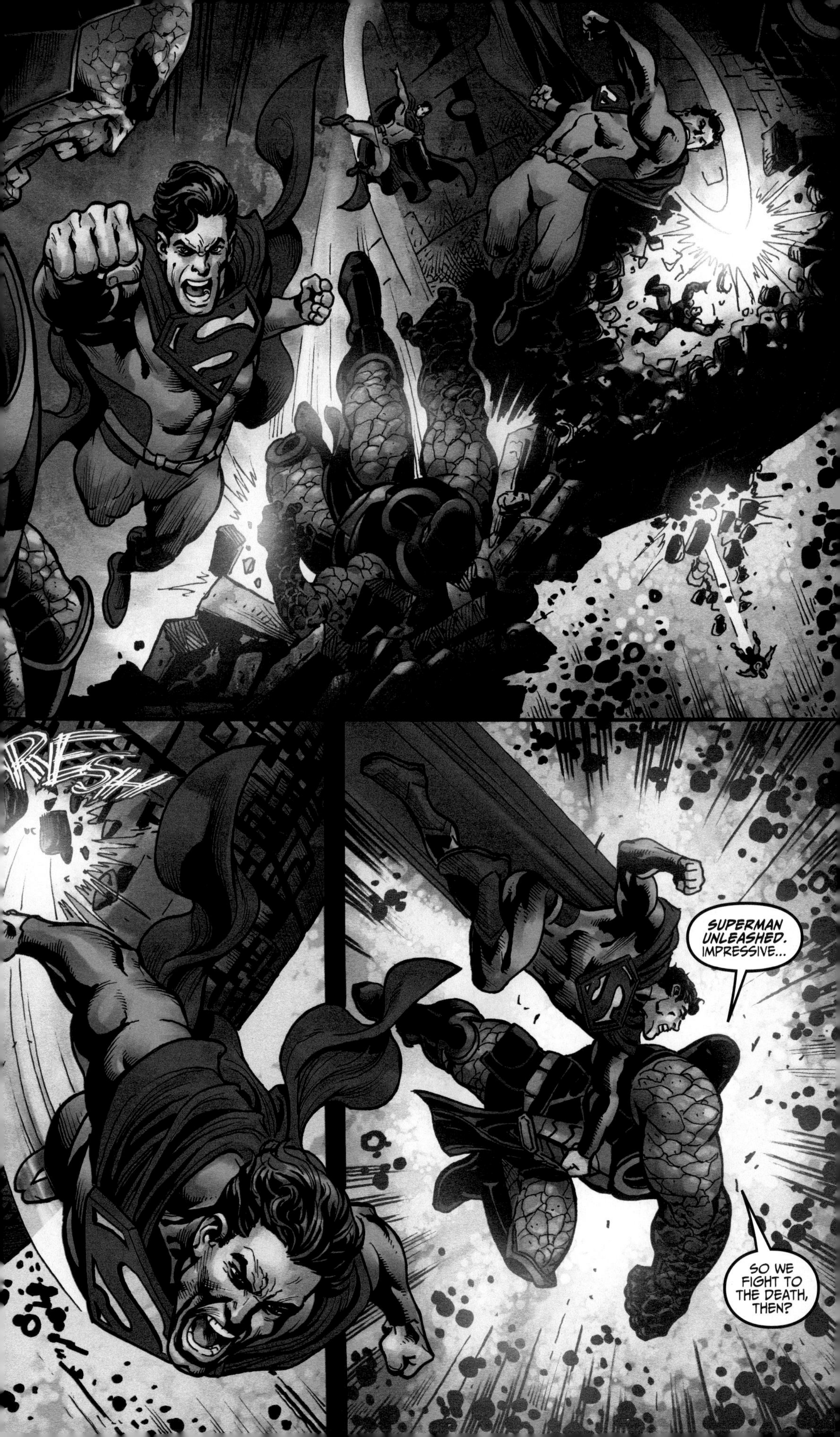
RESH
SUPERMAN UNLEASHED. IMPRESSIVE...
SO WE FIGHT TO THE DEATH, THEN?

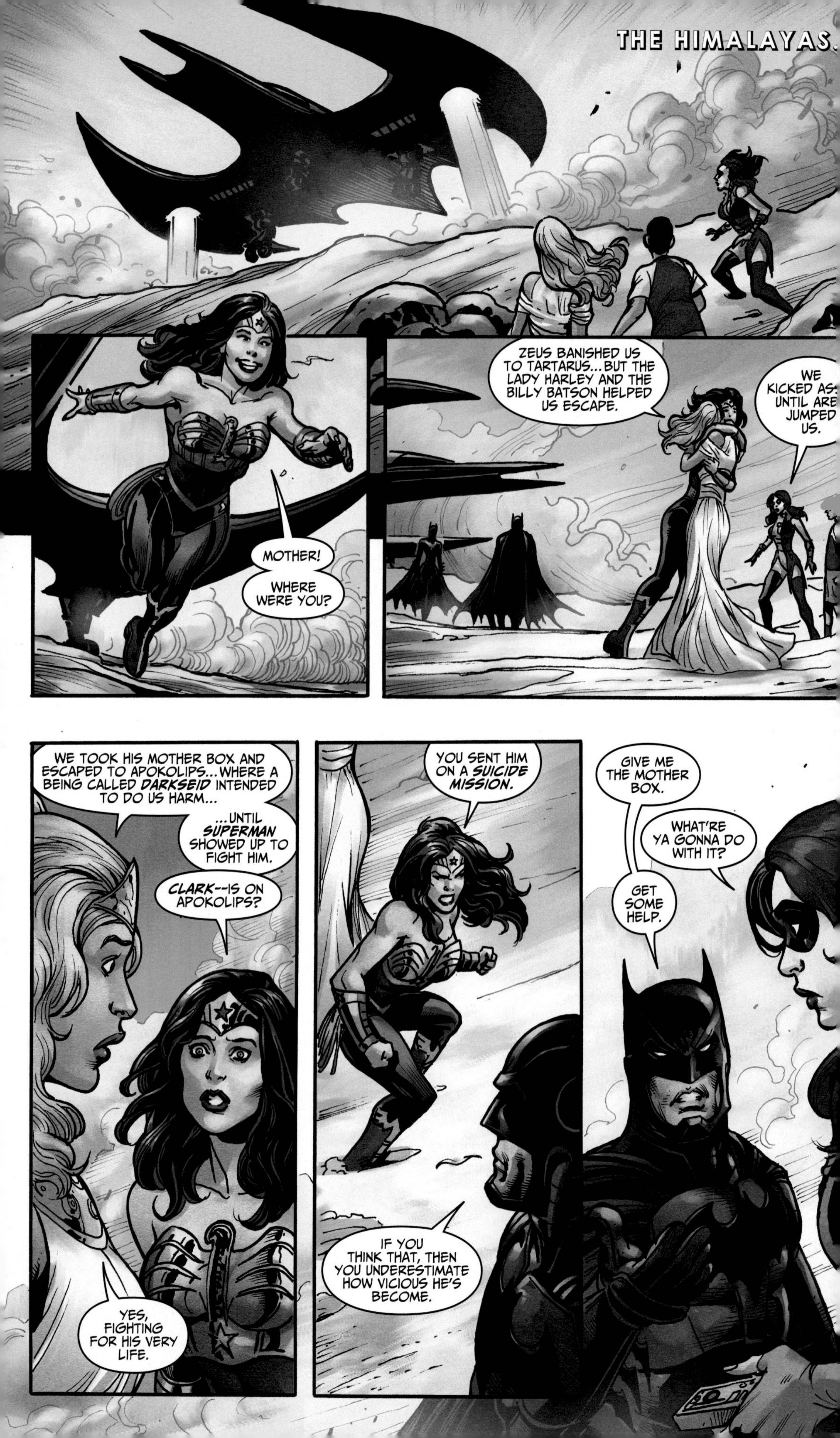
THE HIMALAYAS.
MOTHER!
WHERE WERE YOU?
ZEUS BANISHED US TO TARTARUS...BUT THE LADY HARLEY AND THE BILLY BATSON HELPED US ESCAPE.
WE KICKED AS UNTIL ARE JUMPED US.
WE TOOK HIS MOTHER BOX AND ESCAPED TO APOKOLIPS...WHERE A BEING CALLED DARKSEID INTENDED TO DO US HARM...
...UNTIL SUPERMAN SHOWED UP TO FIGHT HIM.
CLARK--IS ON APOKOLIPS?
YES, FIGHTING FOR HIS VERY LIFE.
YOU SENT HIM ON A SUICIDE MISSION.
IF YOU THINK THAT, THEN YOU UNDERESTIMATE HOW VICIOUS HE'S BECOME.
GIVE ME THE MOTHER BOX.
WHAT'RE YA GONNA DO WITH IT?
GET SOME HELP.

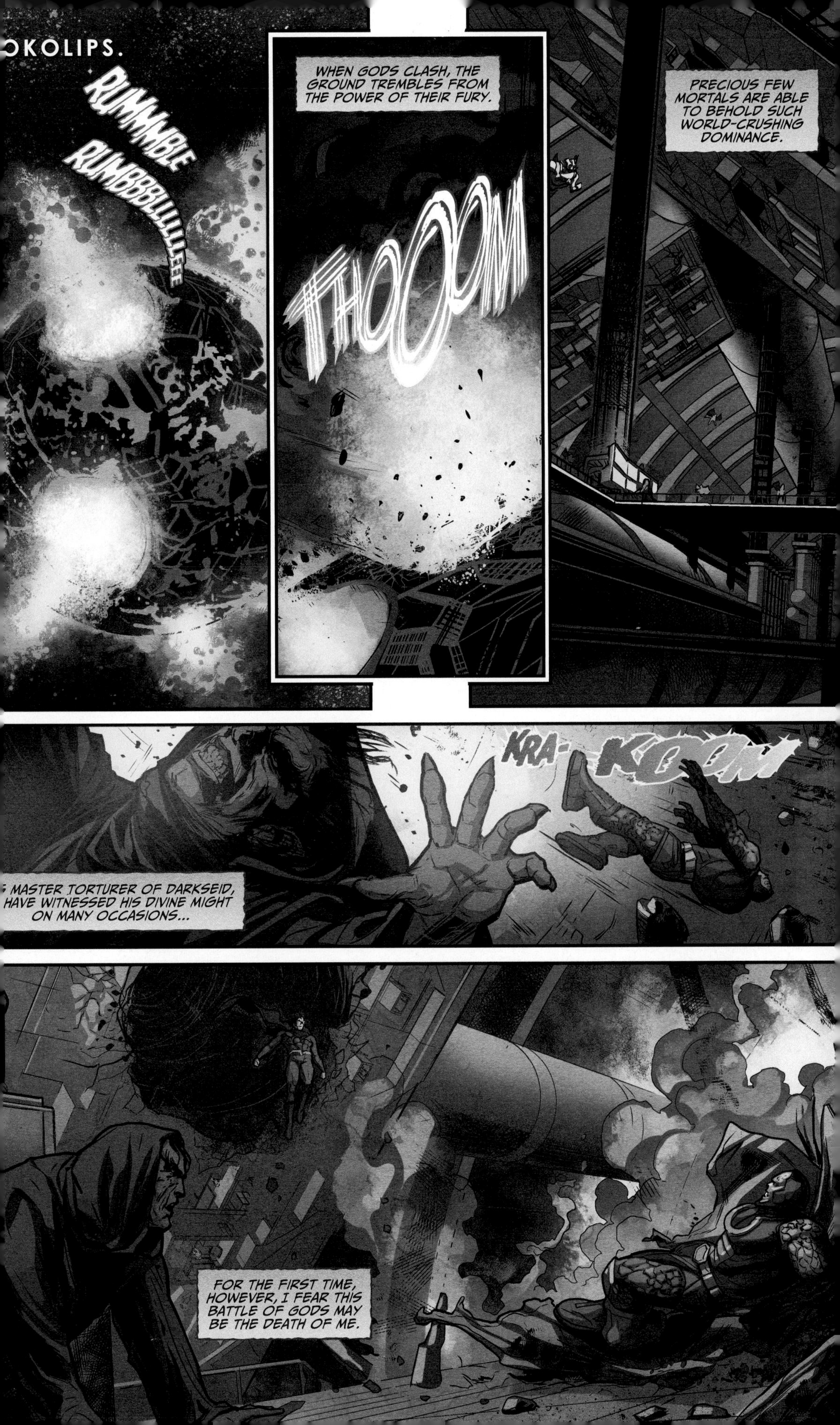
OKOLIPS.
RUMMMBLE
RUMBBBLLLLLLLEEE
WHEN GODS CLASH, THE GROUND TREMBLES FROM THE POWER OF THEIR FURY.
THOOOOM
PRECIOUS FEW MORTALS ARE ABLE TO BEHOLD SUCH WORLD-CRUSHING DOMINANCE.
KRA-KOOM
MASTER TORTURER OF DARKSEID, HAVE WITNESSED HIS DIVINE MIGHT ON MANY OCCASIONS...
FOR THE FIRST TIME, HOWEVER, I FEAR THIS BATTLE OF GODS MAY BE THE DEATH OF ME.

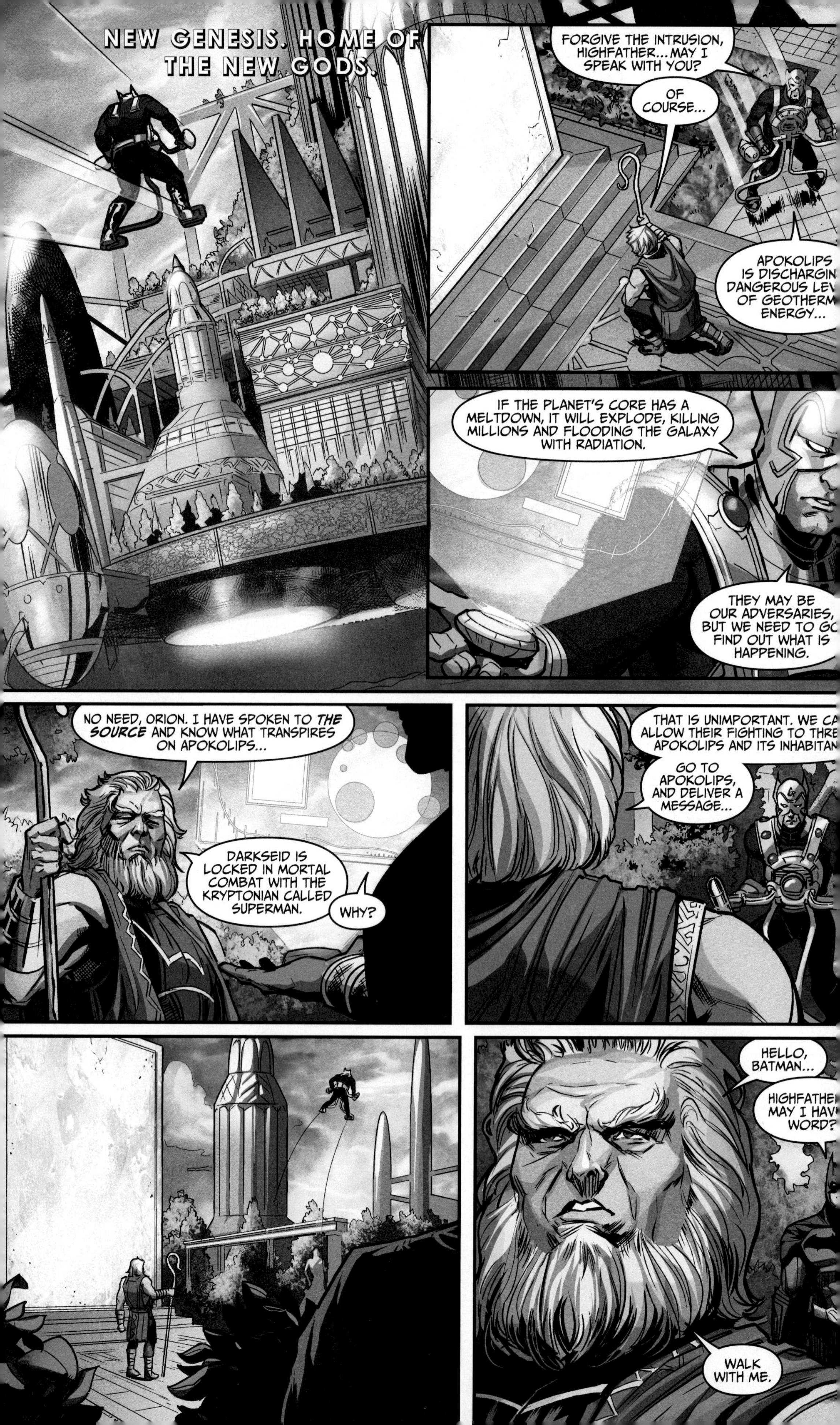
NEW GENESIS. HOME OF THE NEW GODS.
FORGIVE THE INTRUSION, HIGHFATHER... MAY I SPEAK WITH YOU?
OF COURSE...
APOKOLIPS IS DISCHARGIN DANGEROUS LEV OF GEOTHERM ENERGY...
IF THE PLANET'S CORE HAS A MELTDOWN, IT WILL EXPLODE, KILLING MILLIONS AND FLOODING THE GALAXY WITH RADIATION.
THEY MAY BE OUR ADVERSARIES, BUT WE NEED TO GO FIND OUT WHAT IS HAPPENING.
NO NEED, ORION. I HAVE SPOKEN TO THE SOURCE AND KNOW WHAT TRANSPIRES ON APOKOLIPS...
DARKSEID IS LOCKED IN MORTAL COMBAT WITH THE KRYPTONIAN CALLED SUPERMAN.
WHY?
THAT IS UNIMPORTANT. WE CA ALLOW THEIR FIGHTING TO THRE APOKOLIPS AND ITS INHABITAN
GO TO APOKOLIPS, AND DELIVER A MESSAGE...
HELLO, BATMAN...
HIGHFATHE MAY I HAV WORD?
WALK WITH ME.

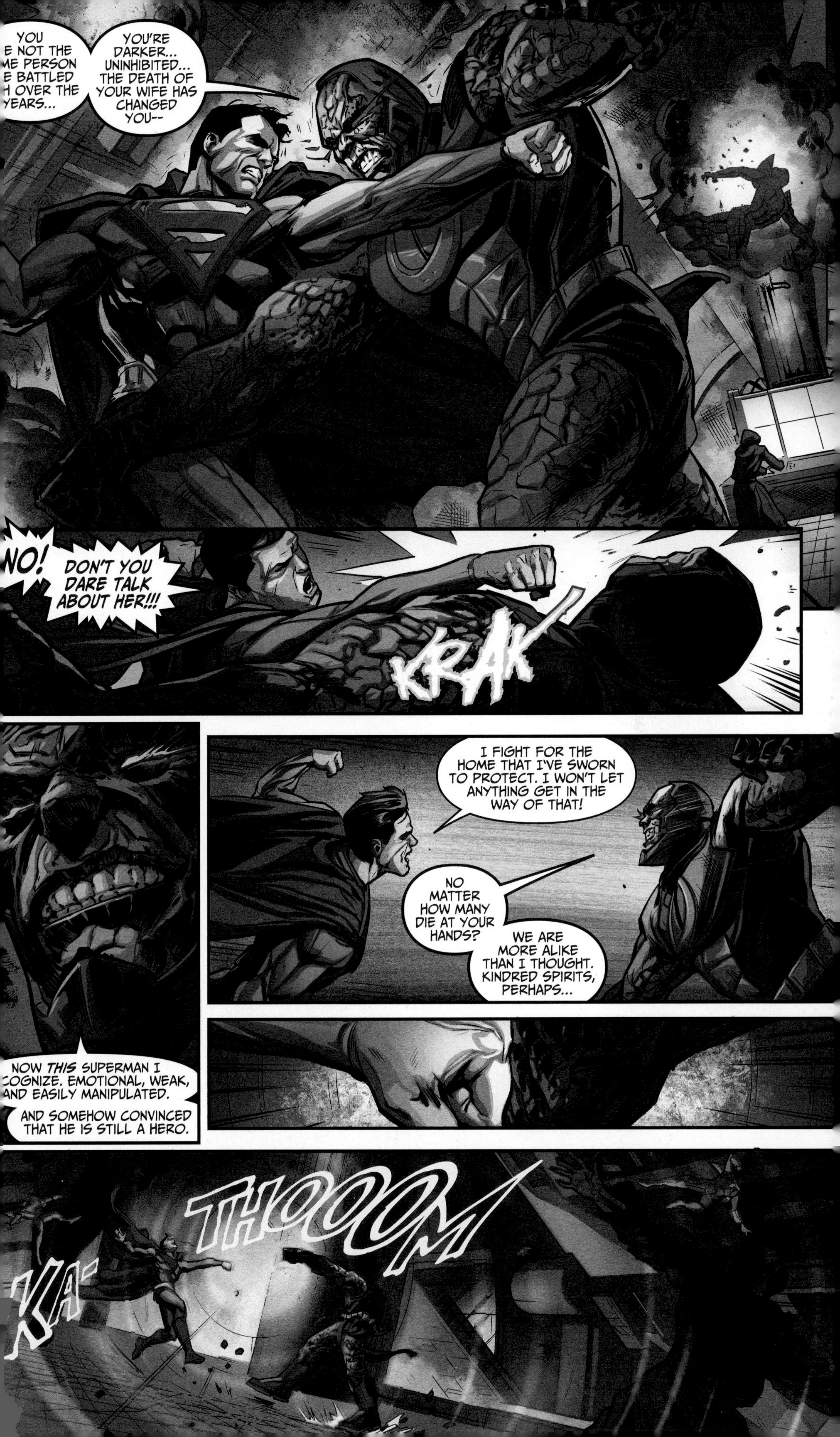
YOU
E NOT THE
ME PERSON
E BATTLED
H OVER THE
YEARS...
YOU'RE DARKER... UNINHIBITED... THE DEATH OF YOUR WIFE HAS CHANGED YOU--
NO!
DON'T YOU DARE TALK ABOUT HER!!!
KRAK
I FIGHT FOR THE HOME THAT I'VE SWORN TO PROTECT. I WON'T LET ANYTHING GET IN THE WAY OF THAT!
NO MATTER HOW MANY DIE AT YOUR HANDS?
WE ARE MORE ALIKE THAN I THOUGHT. KINDRED SPIRITS, PERHAPS...
NOW THIS SUPERMAN I
COGNIZE. EMOTIONAL, WEAK,
AND EASILY MANIPULATED.
AND SOMEHOW CONVINCED THAT HE IS STILL A HERO.
KA-THOOOM

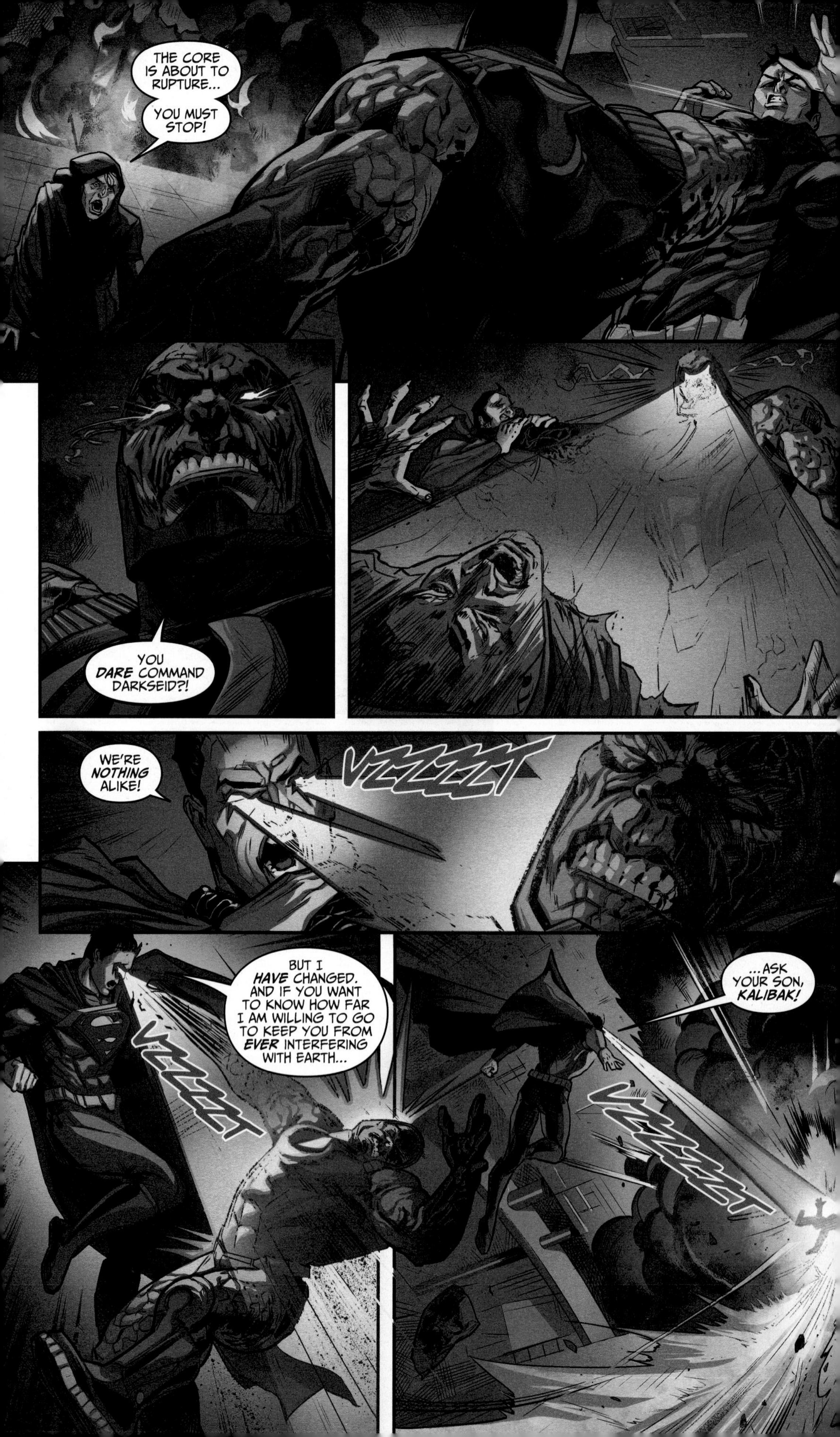
THE CORE IS ABOUT TO RUPTURE...
YOU MUST STOP!
YOU DARE COMMAND DARKSEID?!
WE'RE NOTHING ALIKE!
VZZZZT
BUT I HAVE CHANGED. AND IF YOU WANT TO KNOW HOW FAR I AM WILLING TO GO TO KEEP YOU FROM EVER INTERFERING WITH EARTH...
VZZZT
...ASK YOUR SON, KALIBAK!
VZZZZT

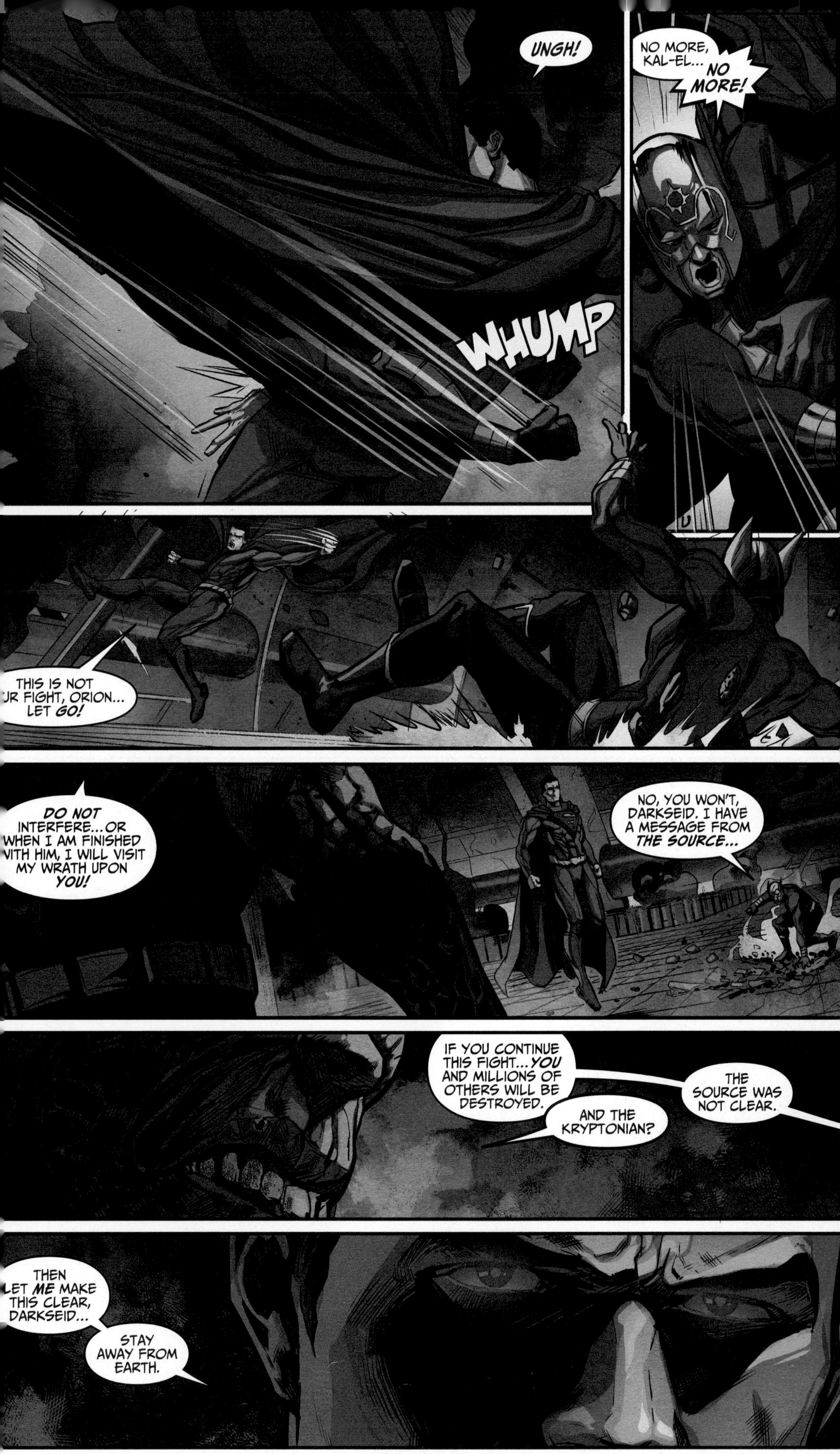

UNGH!
NO MORE, KAL-EL... NO MORE!
WHUMP
THIS IS NOT ...R FIGHT, ORION... LET GO!
DO NOT INTERFERE...OR WHEN I AM FINISHED ...VITH HIM, I WILL VISIT MY WRATH UPON YOU!
NO, YOU WON'T, DARKSEID. I HAVE A MESSAGE FROM THE SOURCE...
IF YOU CONTINUE THIS FIGHT...YOU AND MILLIONS OF OTHERS WILL BE DESTROYED.
AND THE KRYPTONIAN?
THE SOURCE WAS NOT CLEAR.
THEN ...ET ME MAKE THIS CLEAR, DARKSEID...
STAY AWAY FROM EARTH.

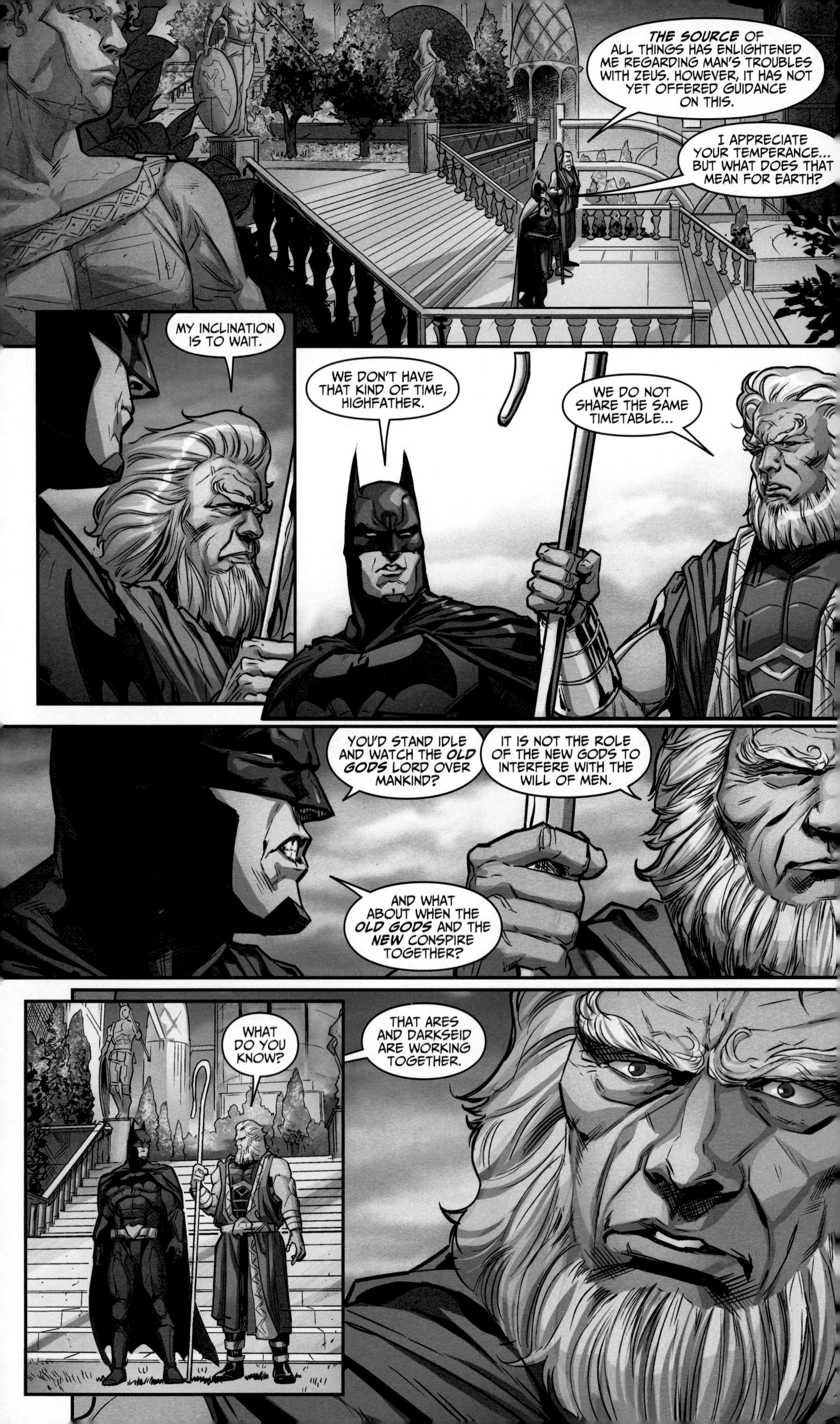
THE SOURCE OF ALL THINGS HAS ENLIGHTENED ME REGARDING MAN'S TROUBLES WITH ZEUS. HOWEVER, IT HAS NOT YET OFFERED GUIDANCE ON THIS.
I APPRECIATE YOUR TEMPERANCE... BUT WHAT DOES THAT MEAN FOR EARTH?
MY INCLINATION IS TO WAIT.
WE DON'T HAVE THAT KIND OF TIME, HIGHFATHER.
WE DO NOT SHARE THE SAME TIMETABLE...
YOU'D STAND IDLE AND WATCH THE *OLD GODS* LORD OVER MANKIND?
IT IS NOT THE ROLE OF THE NEW GODS TO INTERFERE WITH THE WILL OF MEN.
AND WHAT ABOUT WHEN THE *OLD GODS* AND THE *NEW* CONSPIRE TOGETHER?
WHAT DO YOU KNOW?
THAT ARES AND DARKSEID ARE WORKING TOGETHER.

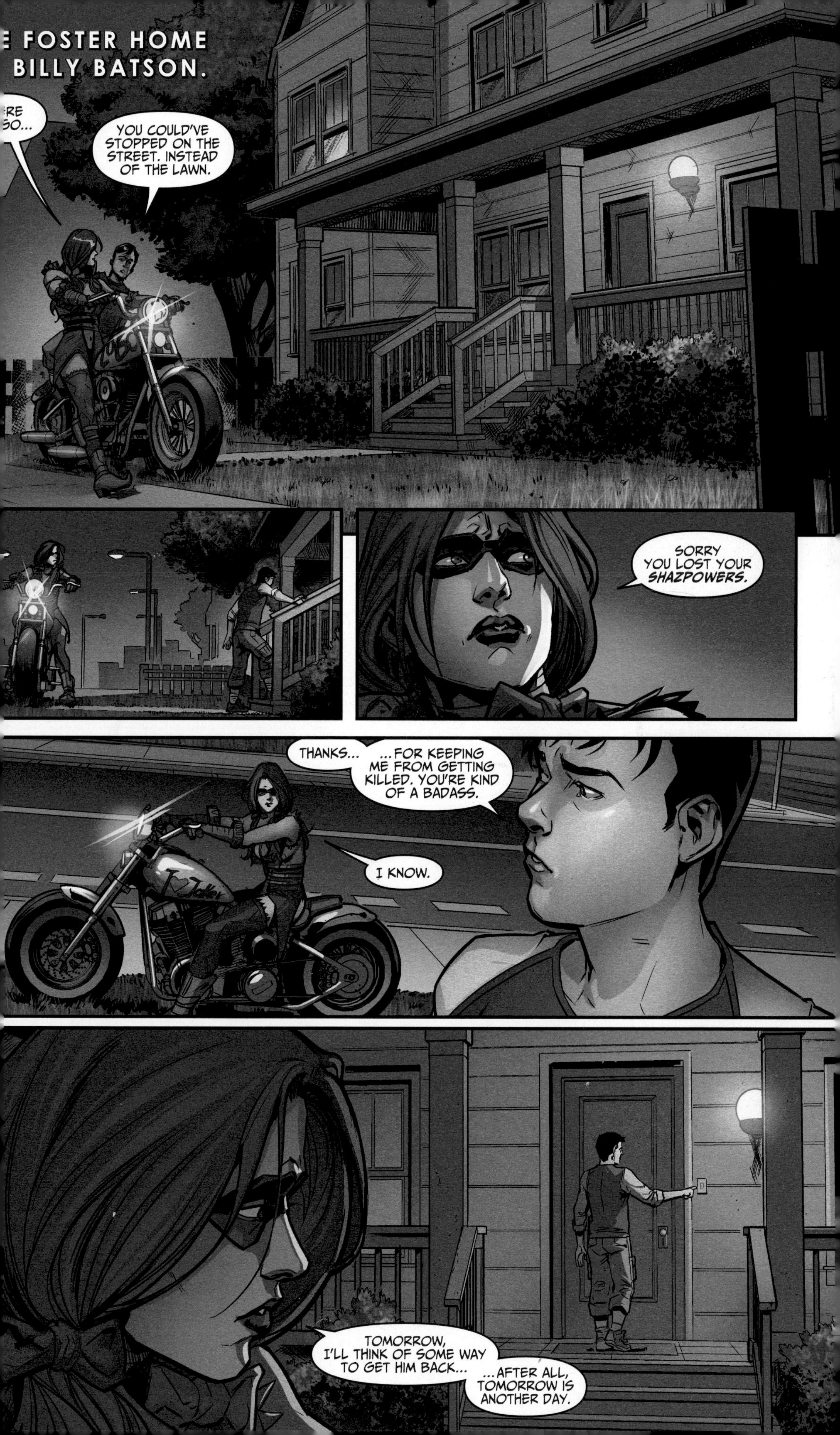
FOSTER HOME
BILLY BATSON.
YOU COULD'VE STOPPED ON THE STREET. INSTEAD OF THE LAWN.
SORRY YOU LOST YOUR SHAZPOWERS.
THANKS...
...FOR KEEPING ME FROM GETTING KILLED. YOU'RE KIND OF A BADASS.
I KNOW.
TOMORROW, I'LL THINK OF SOME WAY TO GET HIM BACK...
...AFTER ALL, TOMORROW IS ANOTHER DAY.

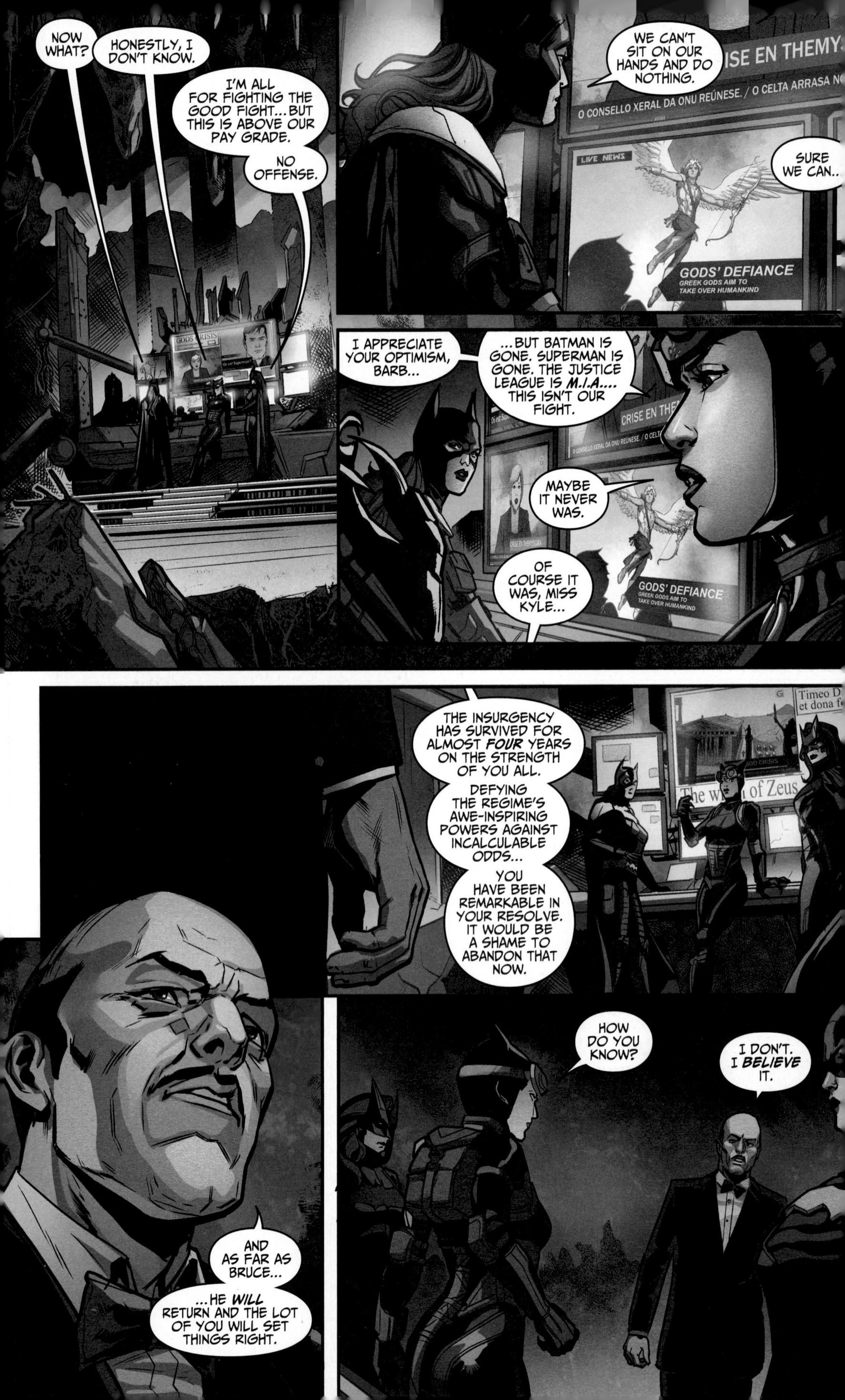
NOW WHAT?
HONESTLY, I DON'T KNOW.
I'M ALL FOR FIGHTING THE GOOD FIGHT... BUT THIS IS ABOVE OUR PAY GRADE.
NO OFFENSE.
WE CAN'T SIT ON OUR HANDS AND DO NOTHING.
O CONSELLO XERAL DA ONU REÚNESE.
LIVE NEWS
GODS' DEFIANCE
GREEK GODS AIM TO TAKE OVER HUMANKIND
SURE WE CAN..
I APPRECIATE YOUR OPTIMISM, BARB...
...BUT BATMAN IS GONE. SUPERMAN IS GONE. THE JUSTICE LEAGUE IS M.I.A.... THIS ISN'T OUR FIGHT.
MAYBE IT NEVER WAS.
GODS' DEFIANCE
GREEK GODS AIM TO TAKE OVER HUMANKIND
OF COURSE IT WAS, MISS KYLE...
THE INSURGENCY HAS SURVIVED FOR ALMOST FOUR YEARS ON THE STRENGTH OF YOU ALL.
DEFYING THE REGIME'S AWE-INSPIRING POWERS AGAINST INCALCULABLE ODDS...
YOU HAVE BEEN REMARKABLE IN YOUR RESOLVE. IT WOULD BE A SHAME TO ABANDON THAT NOW.
AND AS FAR AS BRUCE...
...HE WILL RETURN AND THE LOT OF YOU WILL SET THINGS RIGHT.
HOW DO YOU KNOW?
I DON'T. I BELIEVE IT.

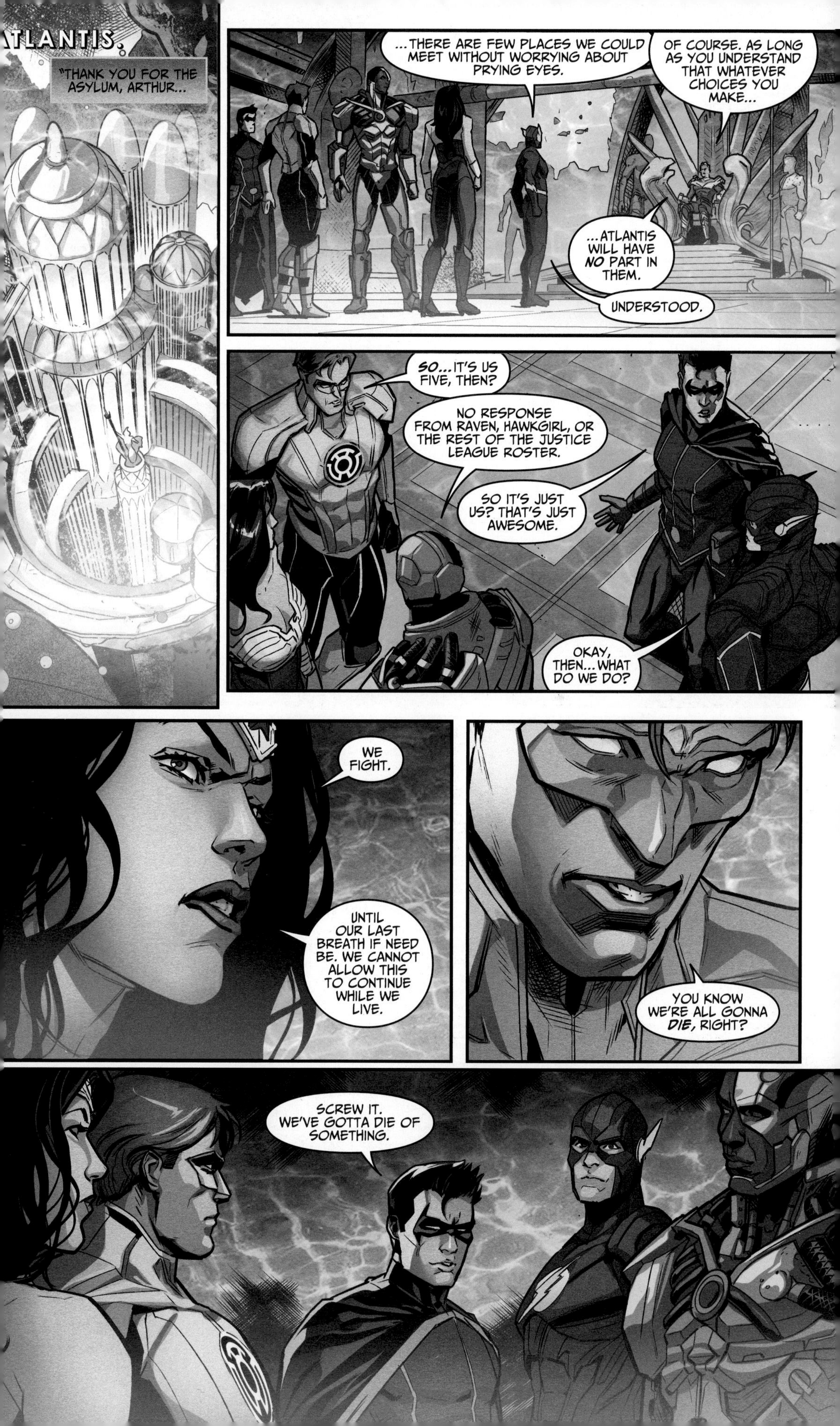

ATLANTIS.
"THANK YOU FOR THE ASYLUM, ARTHUR...
...THERE ARE FEW PLACES WE COULD MEET WITHOUT WORRYING ABOUT PRYING EYES.
OF COURSE. AS LONG AS YOU UNDERSTAND THAT WHATEVER CHOICES YOU MAKE...
...ATLANTIS WILL HAVE NO PART IN THEM.
UNDERSTOOD.
SO...IT'S US FIVE, THEN?
NO RESPONSE FROM RAVEN, HAWKGIRL, OR THE REST OF THE JUSTICE LEAGUE ROSTER.
SO IT'S JUST US? THAT'S JUST AWESOME.
OKAY, THEN...WHAT DO WE DO?
WE FIGHT.
UNTIL OUR LAST BREATH IF NEED BE. WE CANNOT ALLOW THIS TO CONTINUE WHILE WE LIVE.
YOU KNOW WE'RE ALL GONNA DIE, RIGHT?
SCREW IT. WE'VE GOTTA DIE OF SOMETHING.

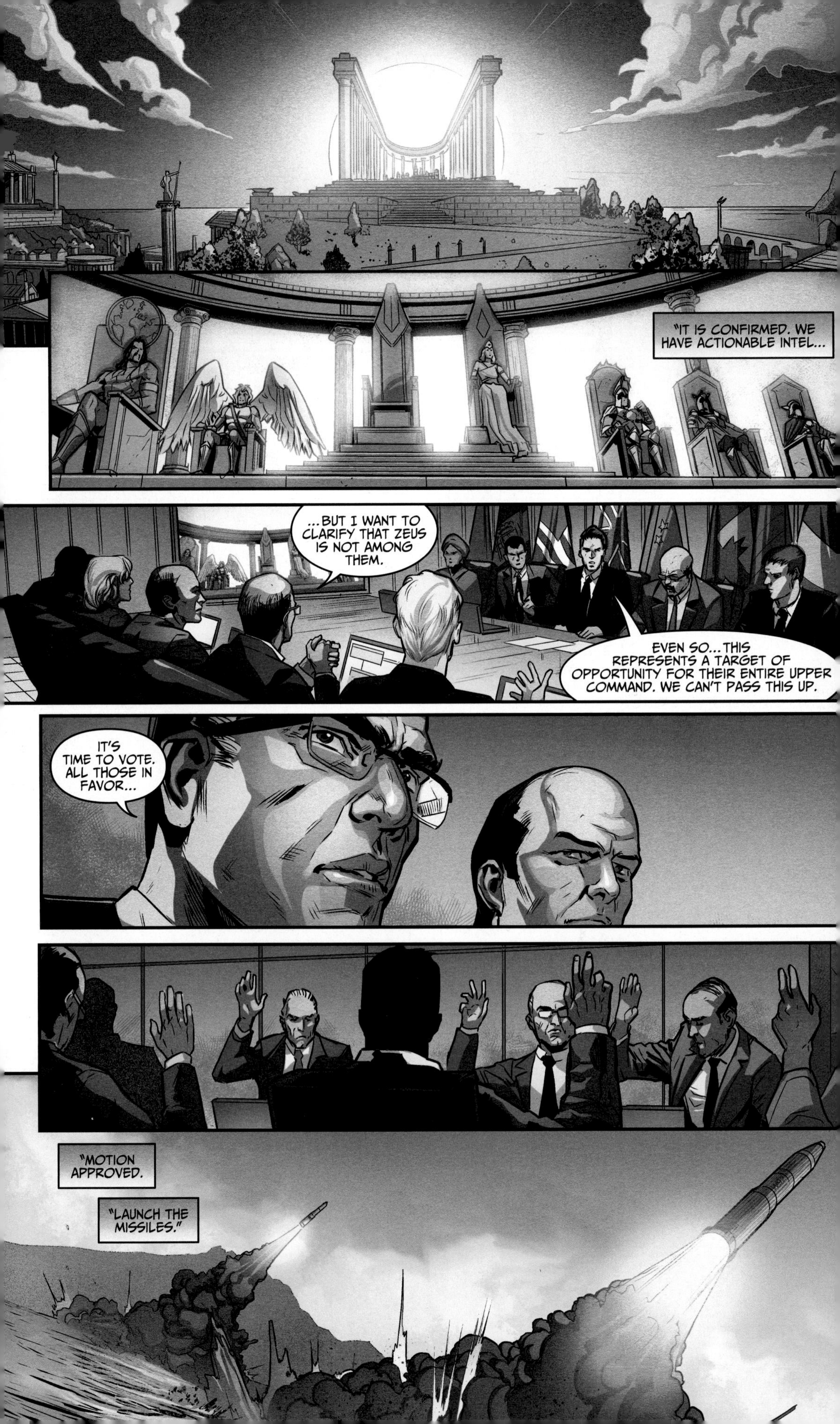
"IT IS CONFIRMED. WE HAVE ACTIONABLE INTEL...
...BUT I WANT TO CLARIFY THAT ZEUS IS NOT AMONG THEM.
EVEN SO...THIS REPRESENTS A TARGET OF OPPORTUNITY FOR THEIR ENTIRE UPPER COMMAND. WE CAN'T PASS THIS UP.
IT'S TIME TO VOTE. ALL THOSE IN FAVOR...
"MOTION APPROVED.
"LAUNCH THE MISSILES."

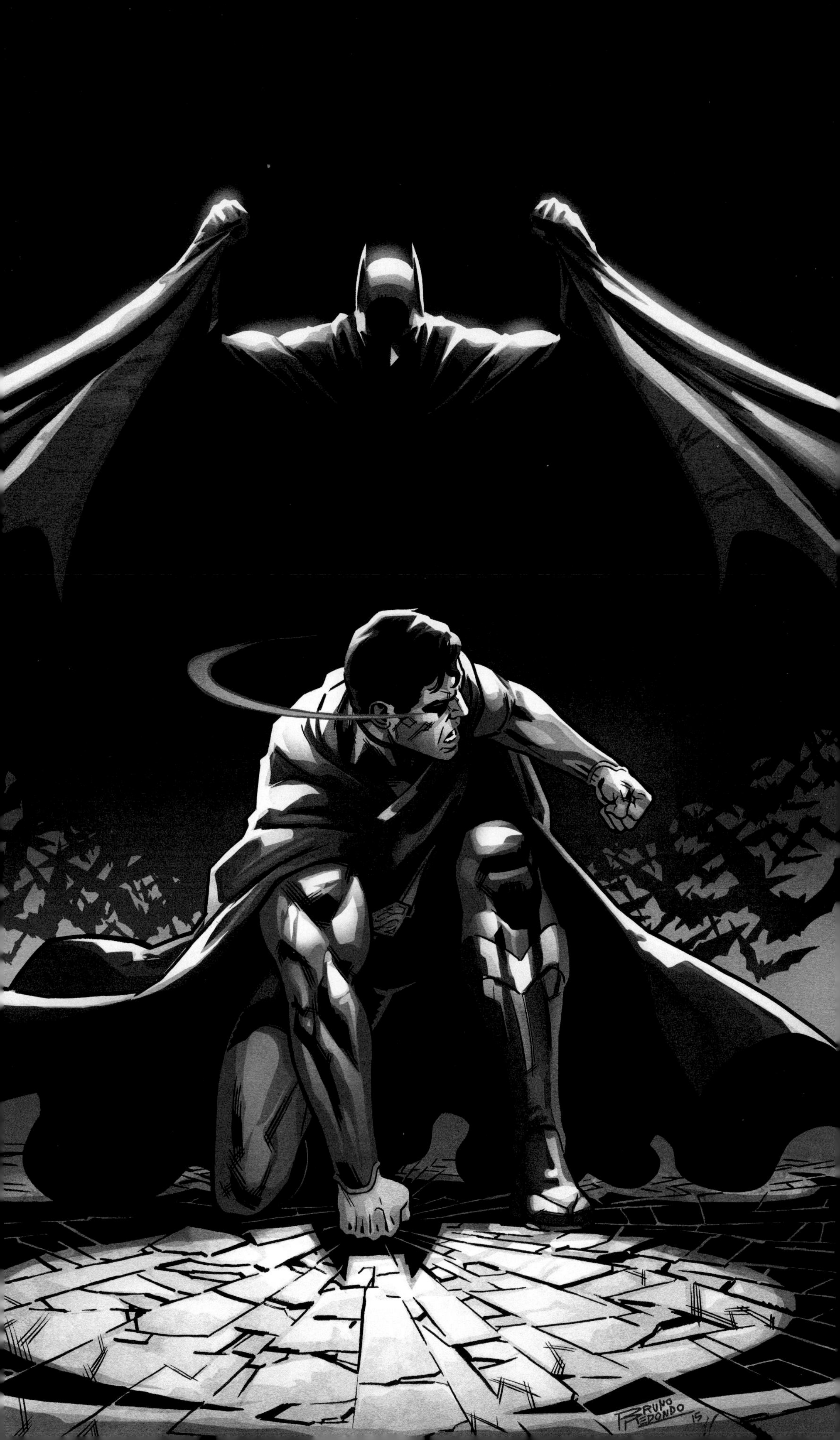
BRUNO REDONDO
15

"Between the Gods" Brian Buccellato Writer Mike S. Miller Bruno Redondo Juan Albarran Artists
J. Nanjan Rex Lokus Colorists Cover Art by Bruno Redondo & Ulises Arreola

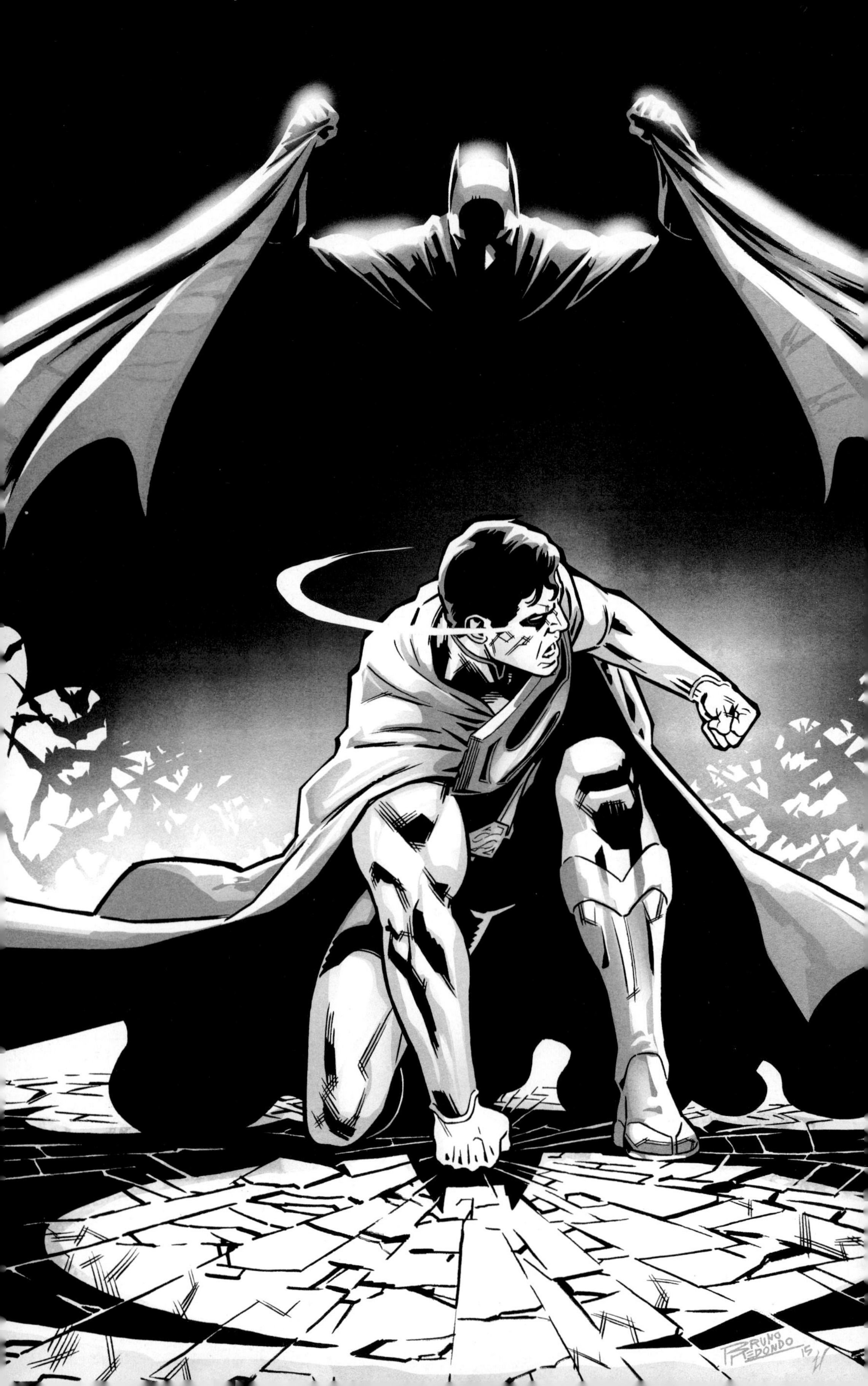
BRUNO REDONDO '15

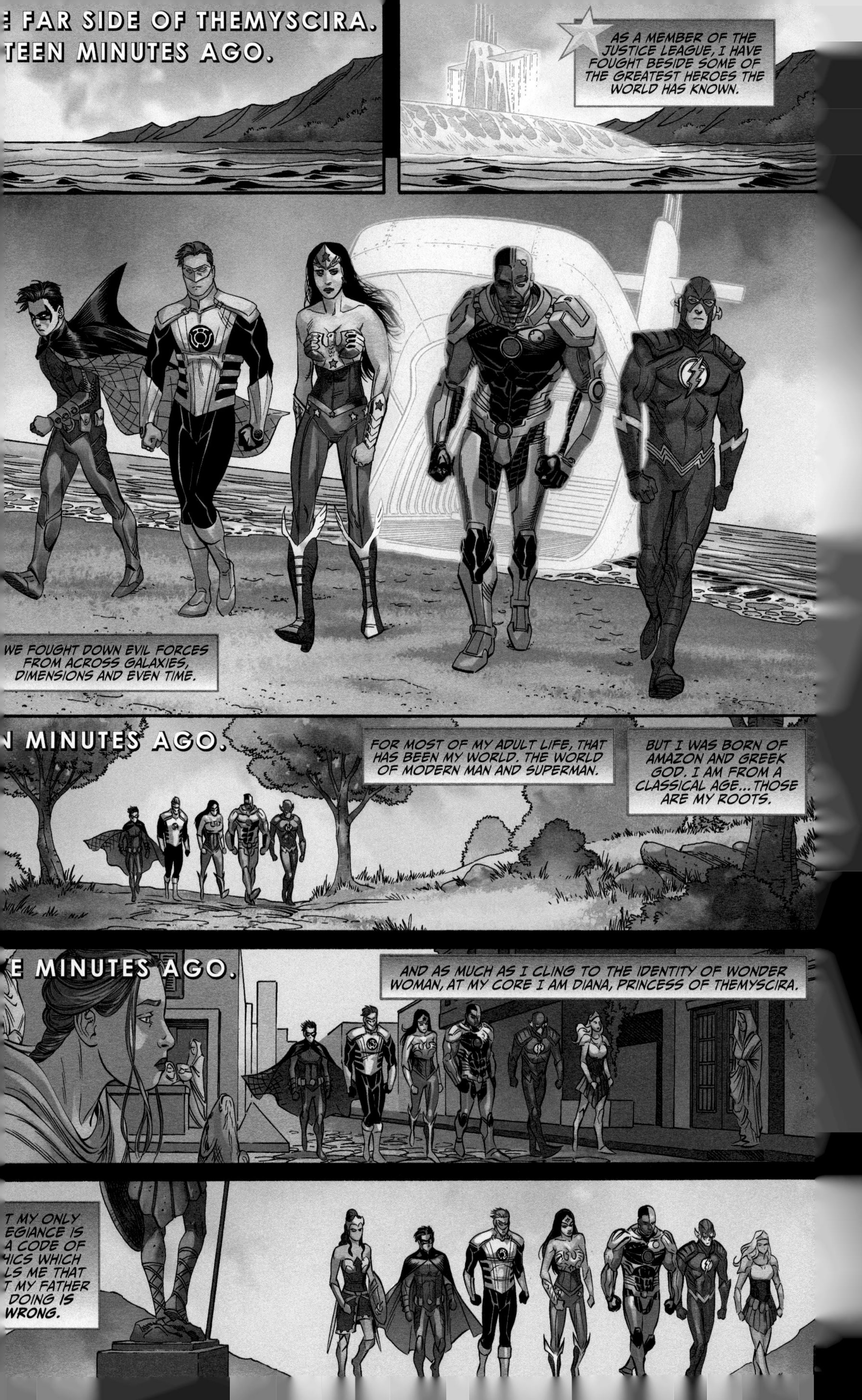
E FAR SIDE OF THEMYSCIRA.
TEEN MINUTES AGO.
AS A MEMBER OF THE JUSTICE LEAGUE, I HAVE FOUGHT BESIDE SOME OF THE GREATEST HEROES THE WORLD HAS KNOWN.
WE FOUGHT DOWN EVIL FORCES FROM ACROSS GALAXIES, DIMENSIONS AND EVEN TIME.
N MINUTES AGO.
FOR MOST OF MY ADULT LIFE, THAT HAS BEEN MY WORLD. THE WORLD OF MODERN MAN AND SUPERMAN.
BUT I WAS BORN OF AMAZON AND GREEK GOD. I AM FROM A CLASSICAL AGE... THOSE ARE MY ROOTS.
E MINUTES AGO.
AND AS MUCH AS I CLING TO THE IDENTITY OF WONDER WOMAN, AT MY CORE I AM DIANA, PRINCESS OF THEMYSCIRA.
T MY ONLY EGIANCE IS A CODE OF HICS WHICH LS ME THAT T MY FATHER DOING IS WRONG.

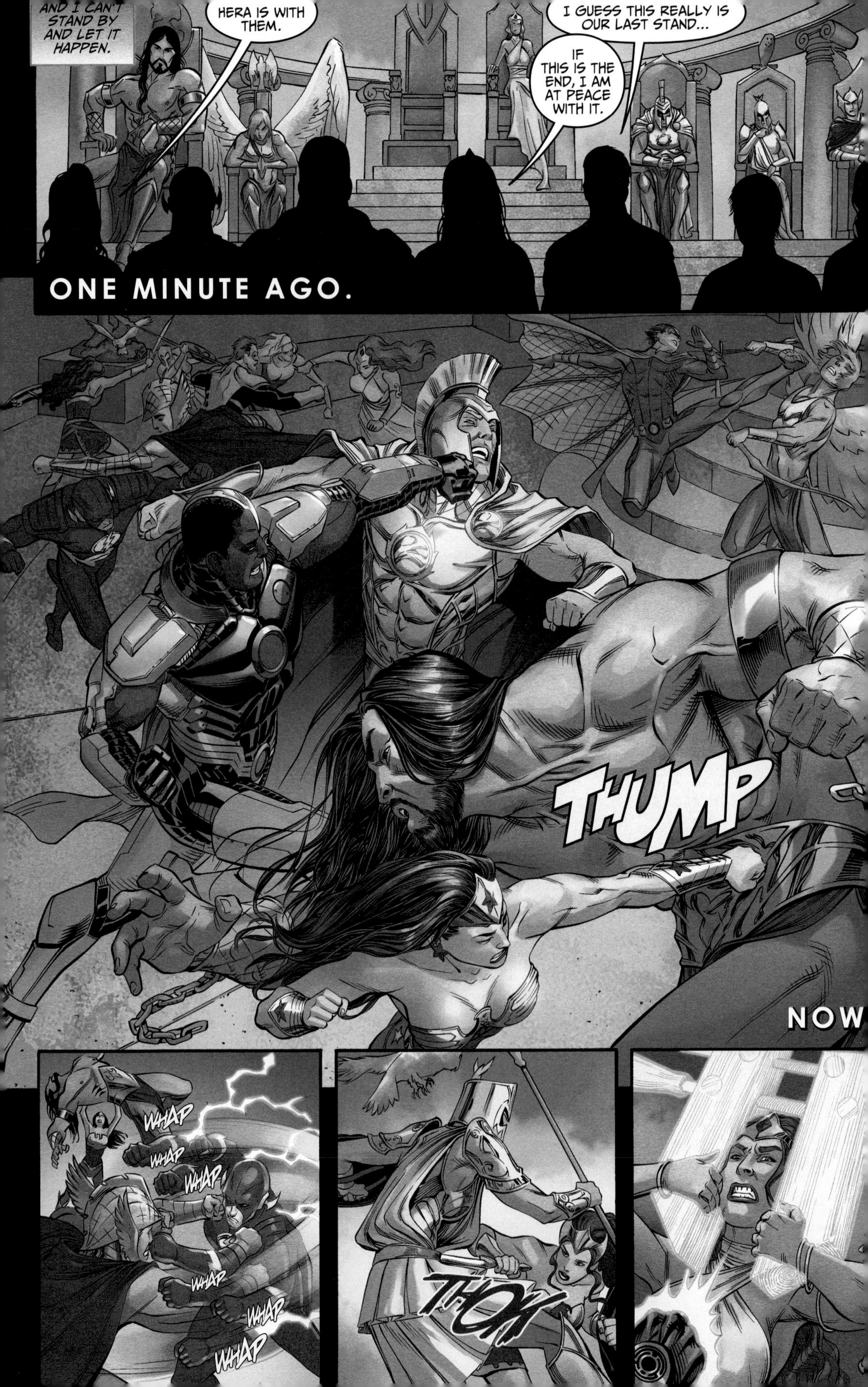

AND I CAN'T STAND BY AND LET IT HAPPEN.
HERA IS WITH THEM.
I GUESS THIS REALLY IS OUR LAST STAND...
IF THIS IS THE END, I AM AT PEACE WITH IT.
ONE MINUTE AGO.
THUMP
NOW
WHAP
WHAP
WHAP
WHAP
WHAP
WHAP
THOK

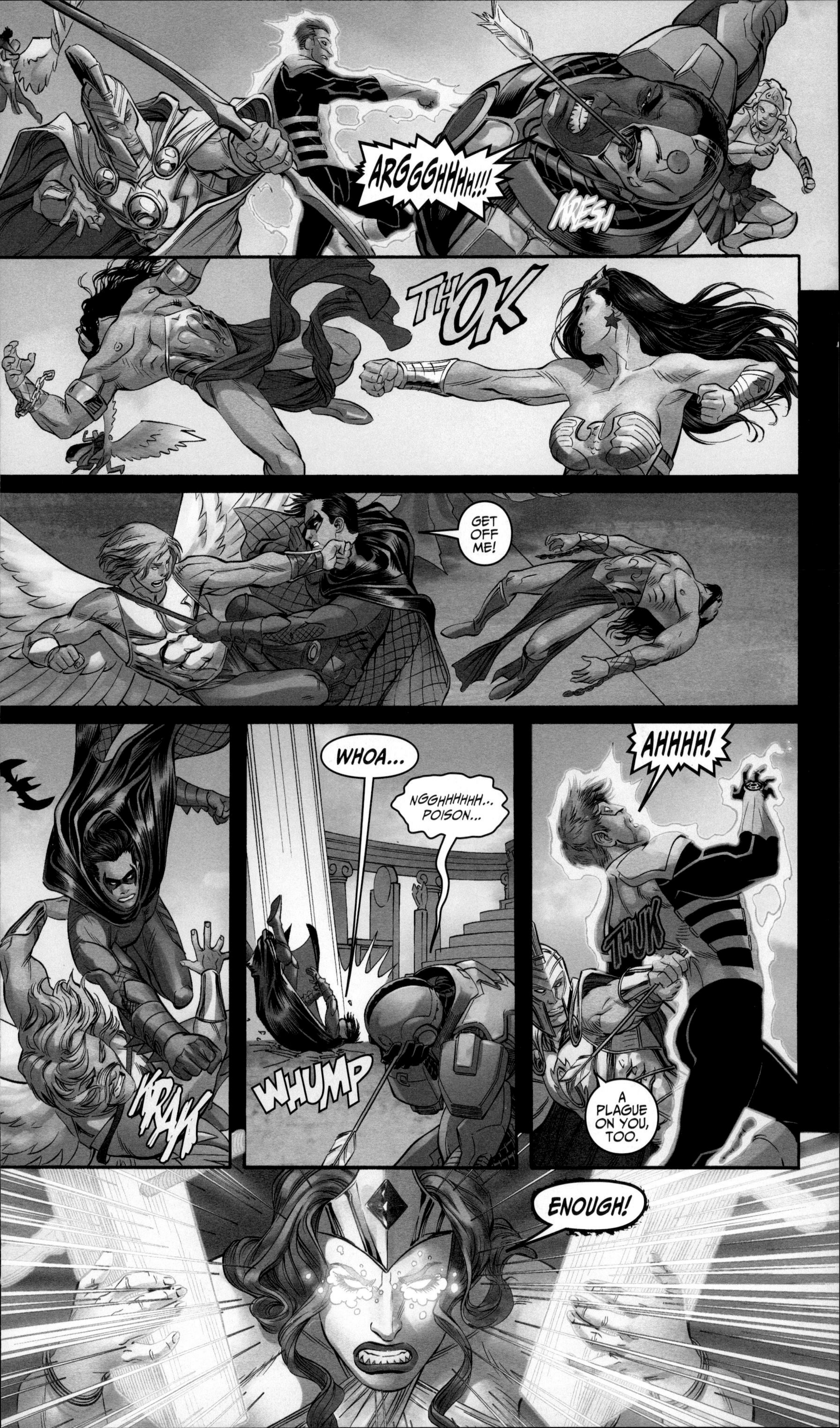
ARGGGHHHH!!!
KRESH
THOK
GET OFF ME!
KRAK
WHOA...
NGGHHHHHH... POISON...
WHUMP
AHHHH!
THUK
A PLAGUE ON YOU, TOO.
ENOUGH!

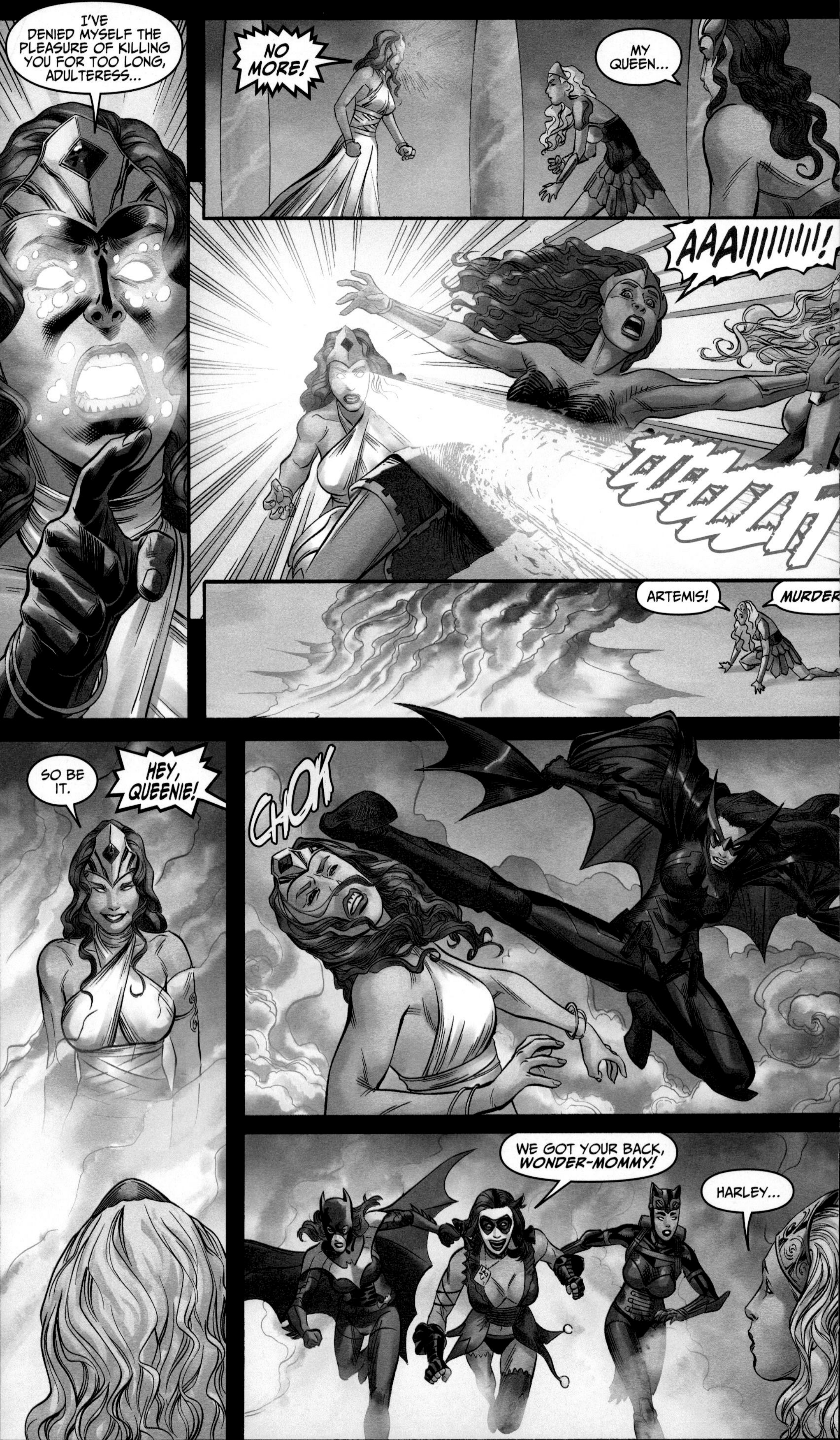
I'VE DENIED MYSELF THE PLEASURE OF KILLING YOU FOR TOO LONG, ADULTERESS...
NO MORE!
MY QUEEN...
AAAIIIIIIIII!
ARTEMIS!
MURDER
SO BE IT.
HEY, QUEENIE!
CHOK
WE GOT YOUR BACK, WONDER-MOMMY!
HARLEY...

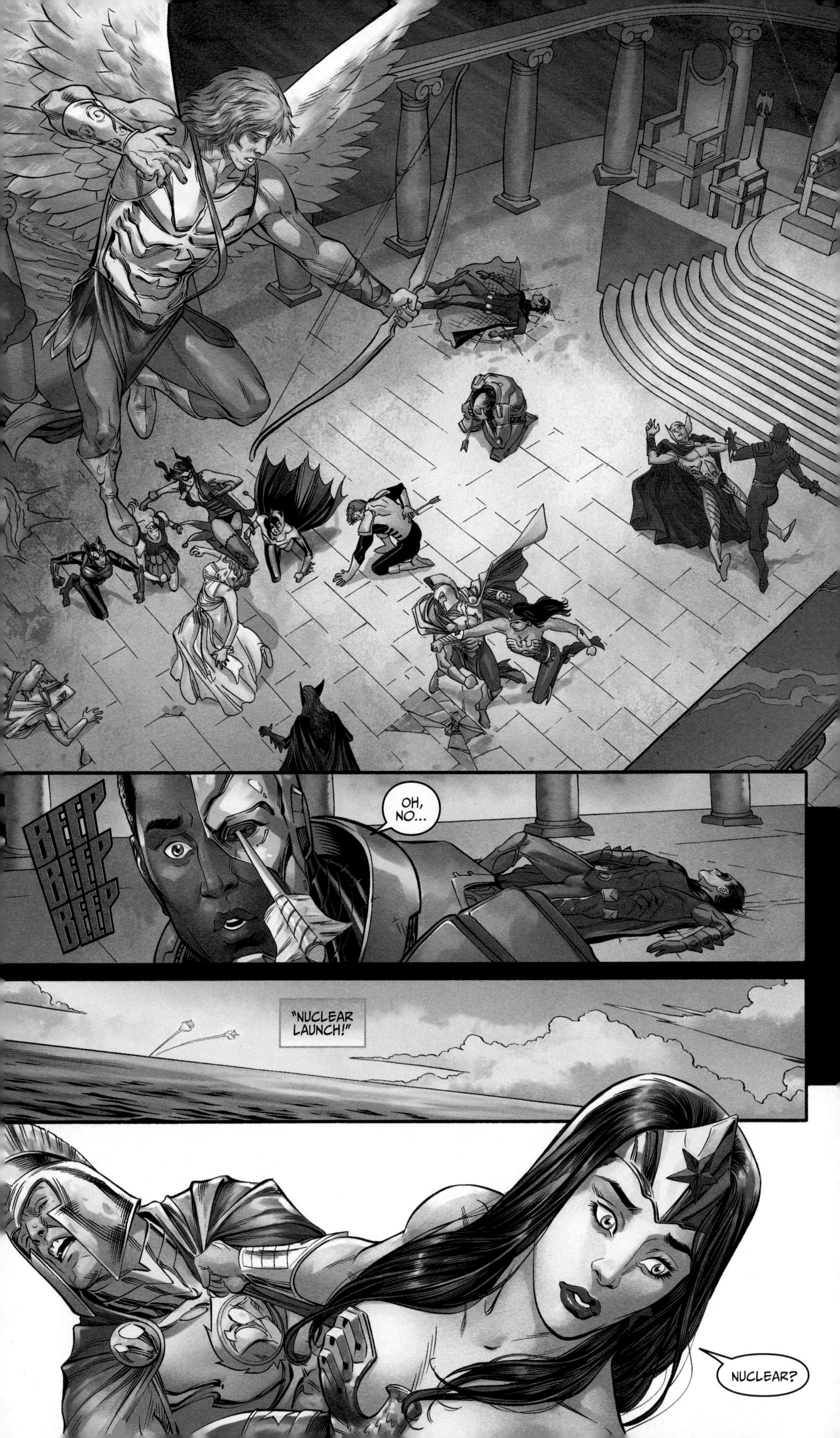
BEEP BEEP BEEP
OH, NO...
"NUCLEAR LAUNCH!"
NUCLEAR?

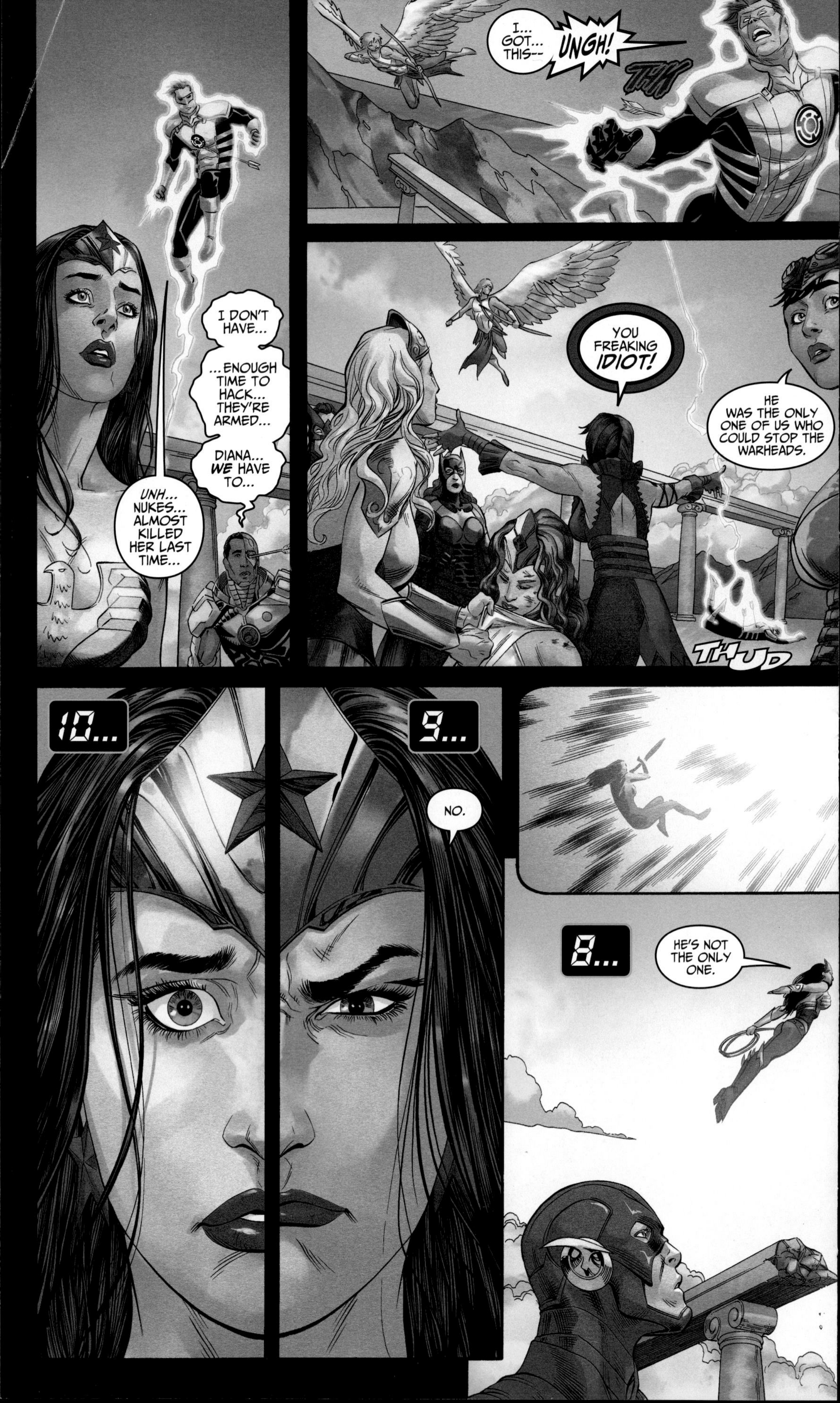
I... GOT... THIS--
UNGH!
THK
I DON'T HAVE...
...ENOUGH TIME TO HACK... THEY'RE ARMED...
DIANA... WE HAVE TO...
UNH... NUKES... ALMOST KILLED HER LAST TIME...
YOU FREAKING IDIOT!
HE WAS THE ONLY ONE OF US WHO COULD STOP THE WARHEADS.
THUD
10...
9...
NO.
8...
HE'S NOT THE ONLY ONE.

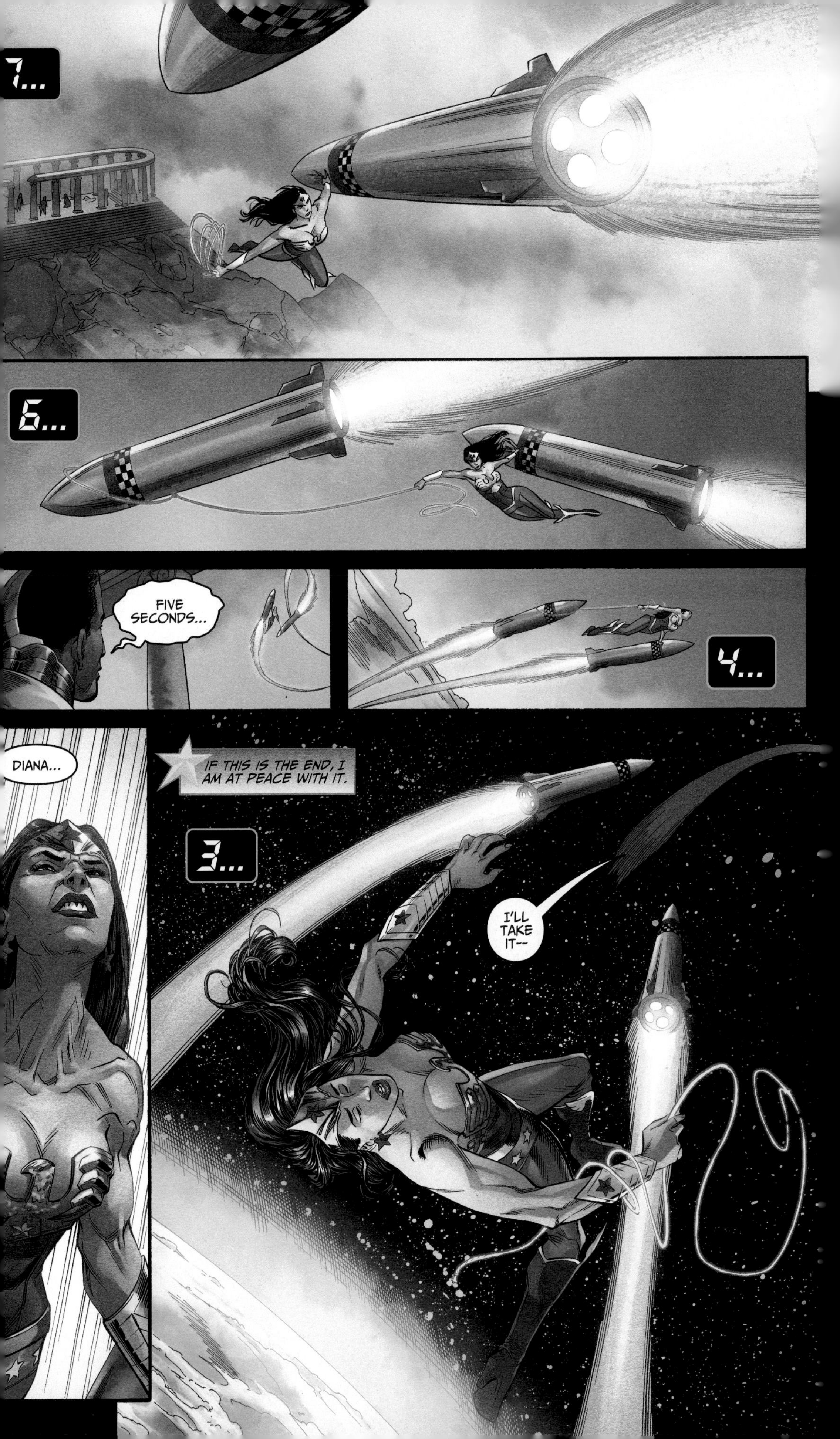
7...
6...
FIVE SECONDS...
4...
DIANA...
IF THIS IS THE END, I AM AT PEACE WITH IT.
3...
I'LL TAKE IT--

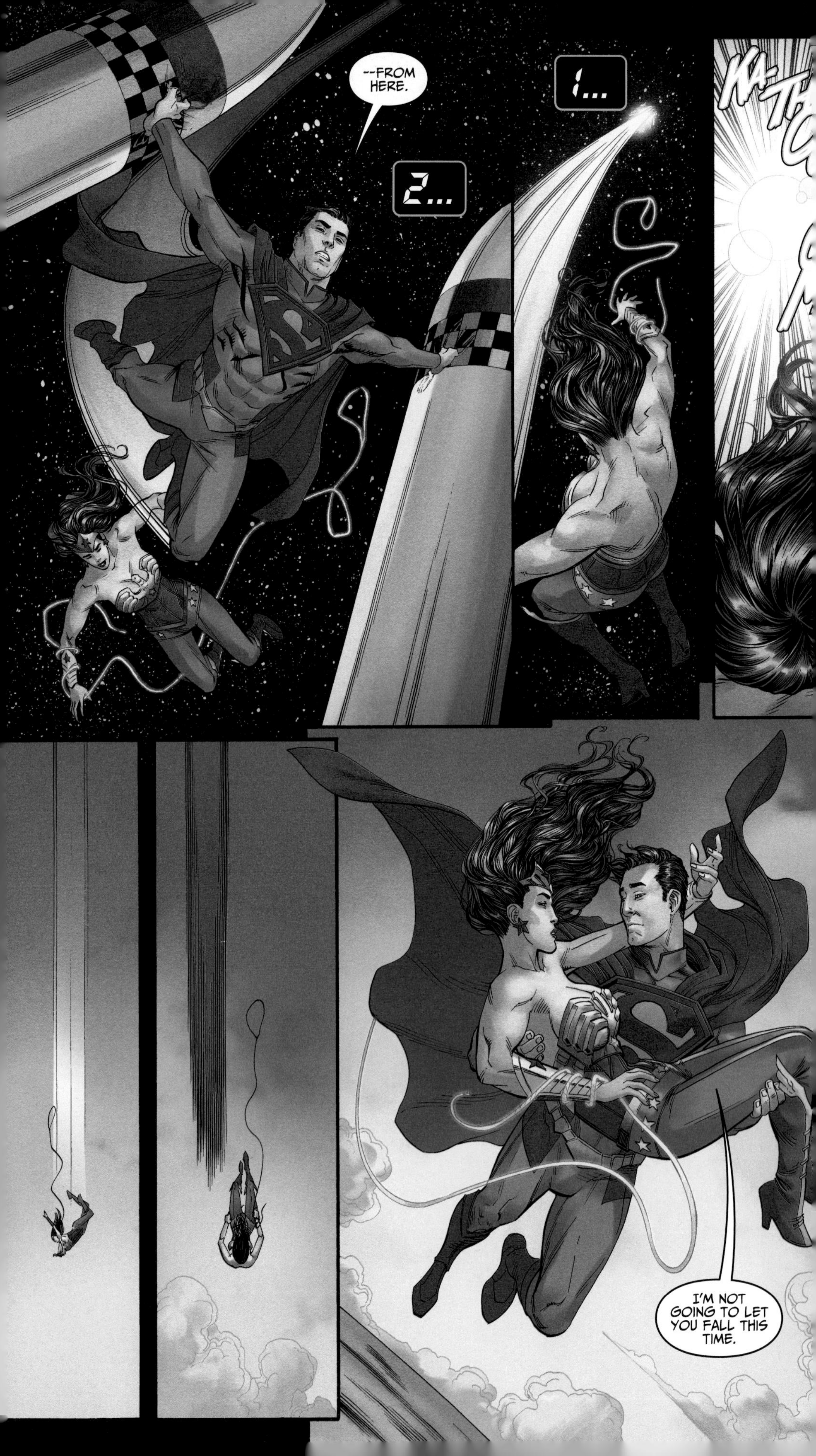

--FROM HERE.
2...
1...
KA-
I'M NOT GOING TO LET YOU FALL THIS TIME.

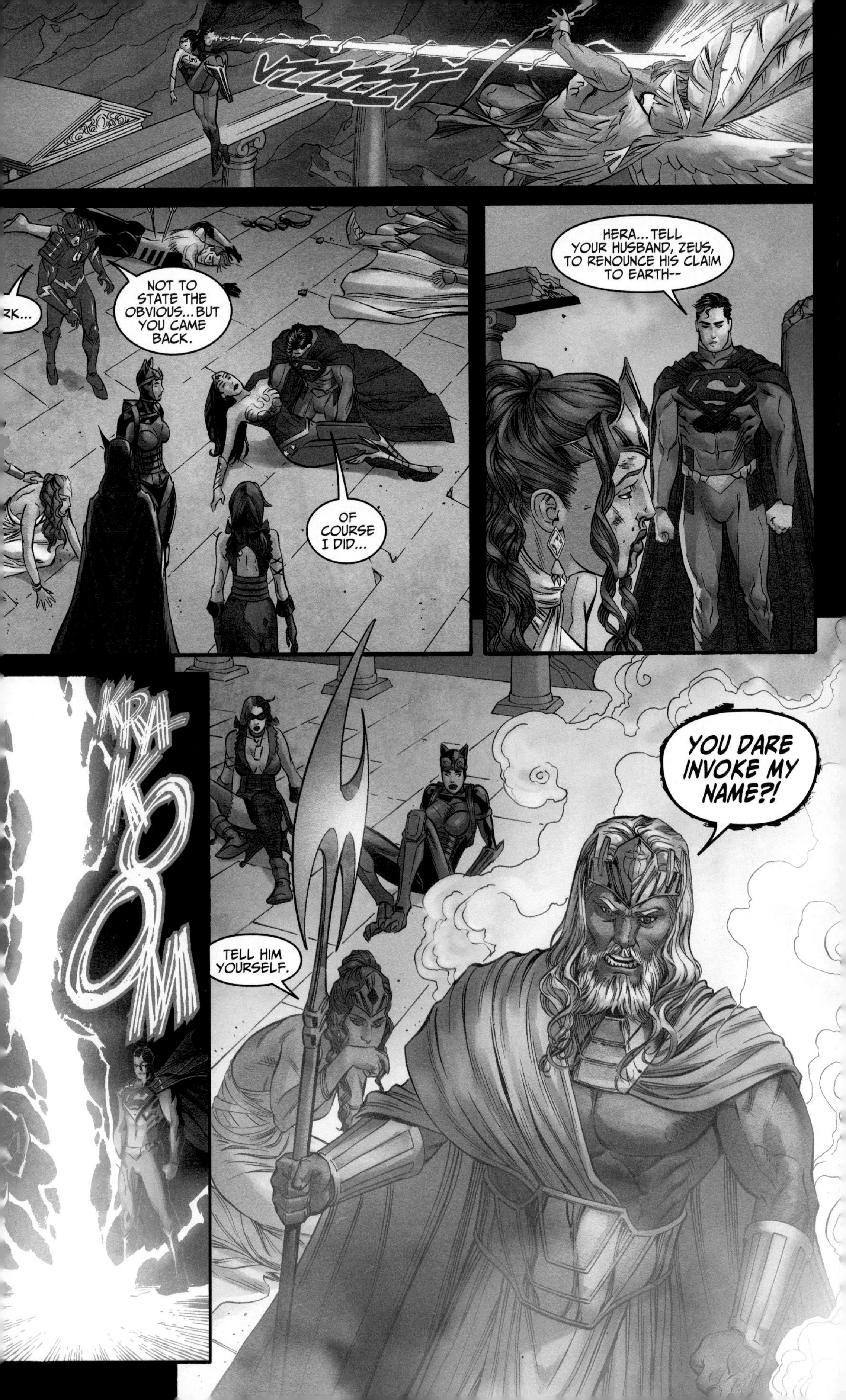
VZZZZT
ZK...
NOT TO STATE THE OBVIOUS...BUT YOU CAME BACK.
OF COURSE I DID...
HERA...TELL YOUR HUSBAND, ZEUS, TO RENOUNCE HIS CLAIM TO EARTH--
KRAKOOM
TELL HIM YOURSELF.
YOU DARE INVOKE MY NAME?!

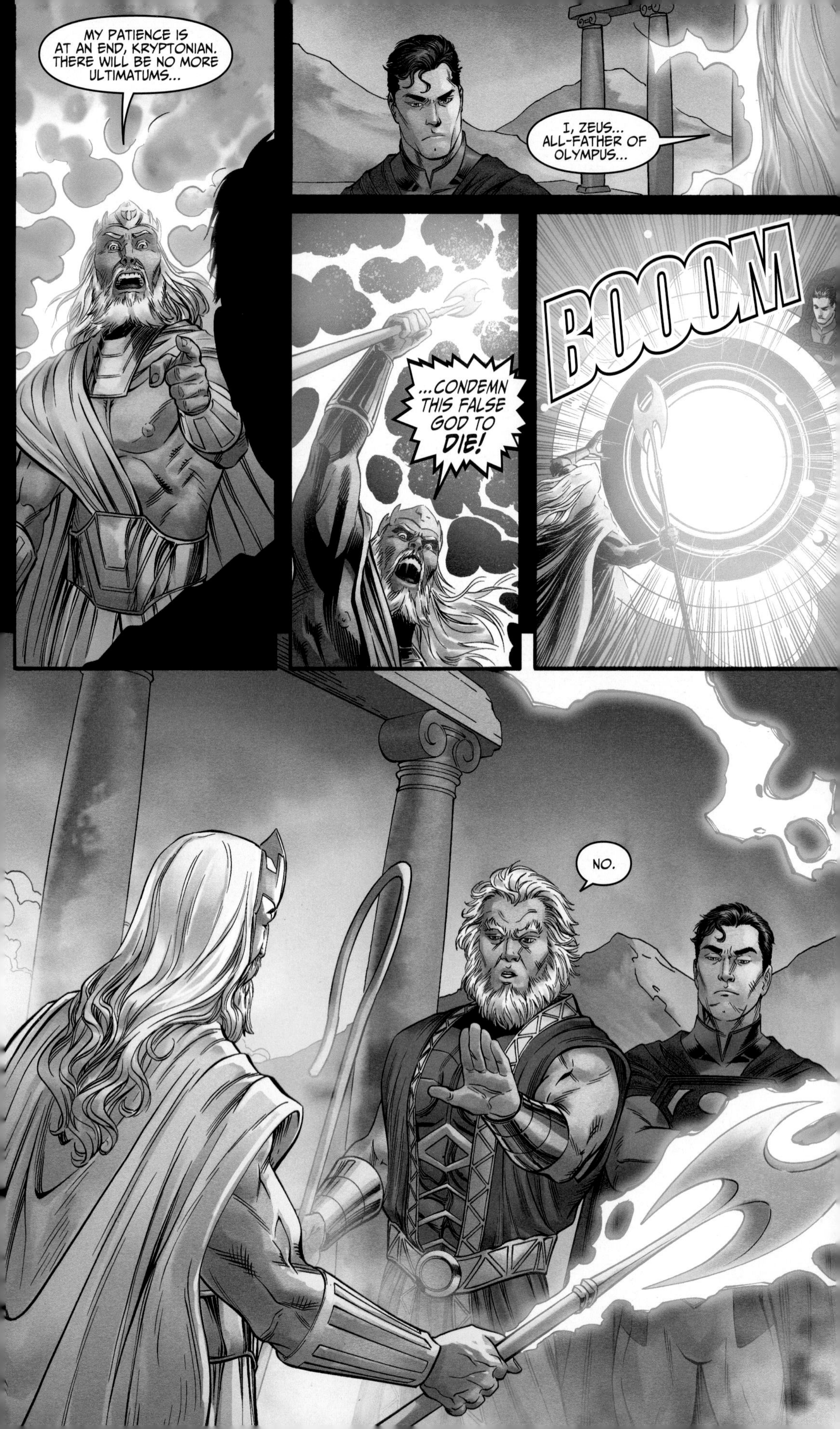
MY PATIENCE IS AT AN END, KRYPTONIAN. THERE WILL BE NO MORE ULTIMATUMS...
I, ZEUS... ALL-FATHER OF OLYMPUS...
...CONDEMN THIS FALSE GOD TO DIE!
BOOOM
NO.

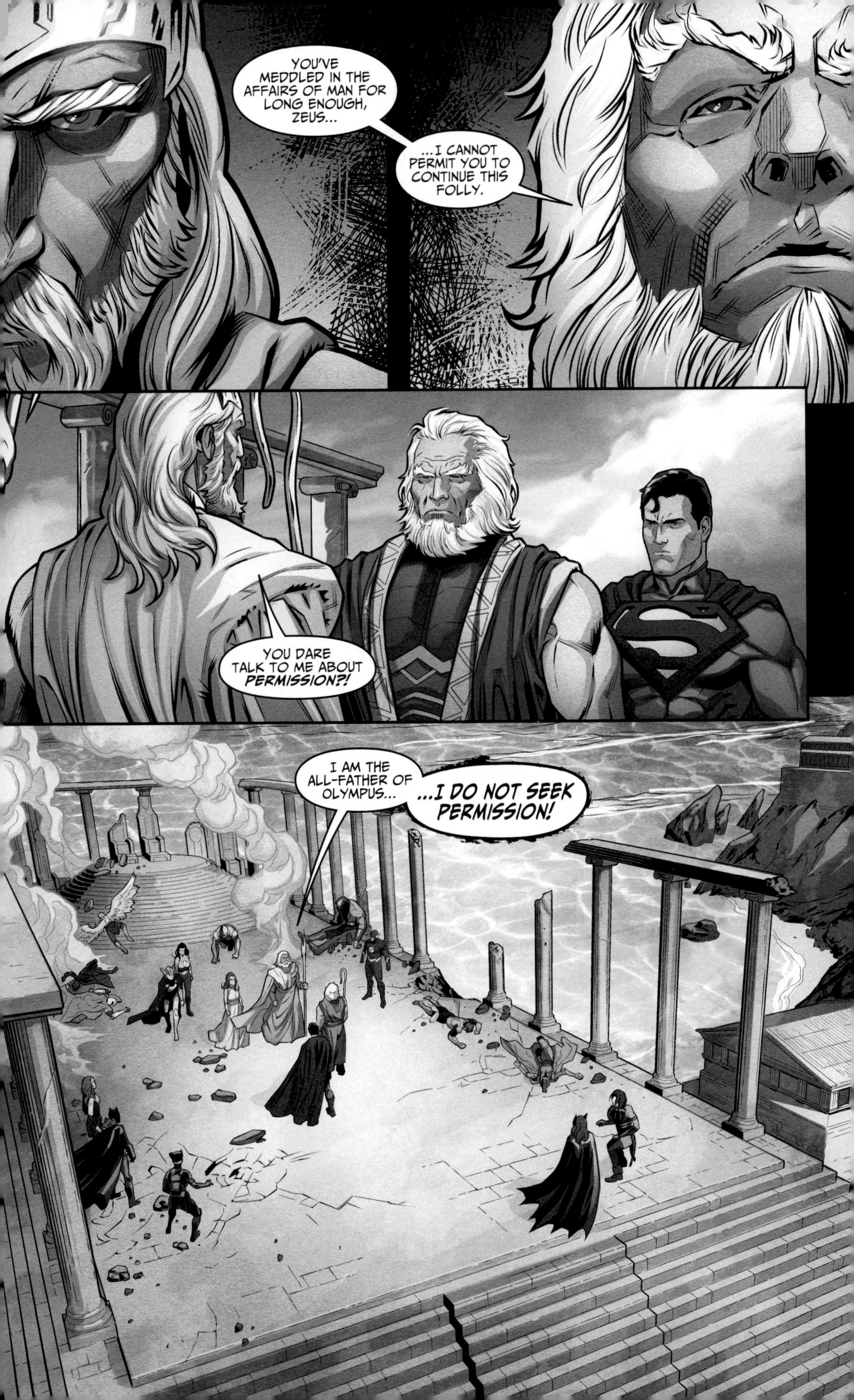
YOU'VE MEDDLED IN THE AFFAIRS OF MAN FOR LONG ENOUGH, ZEUS...
...I CANNOT PERMIT YOU TO CONTINUE THIS FOLLY.
YOU DARE TALK TO ME ABOUT *PERMISSION?!*
I AM THE ALL-FATHER OF OLYMPUS...
...I DO NOT SEEK PERMISSION!

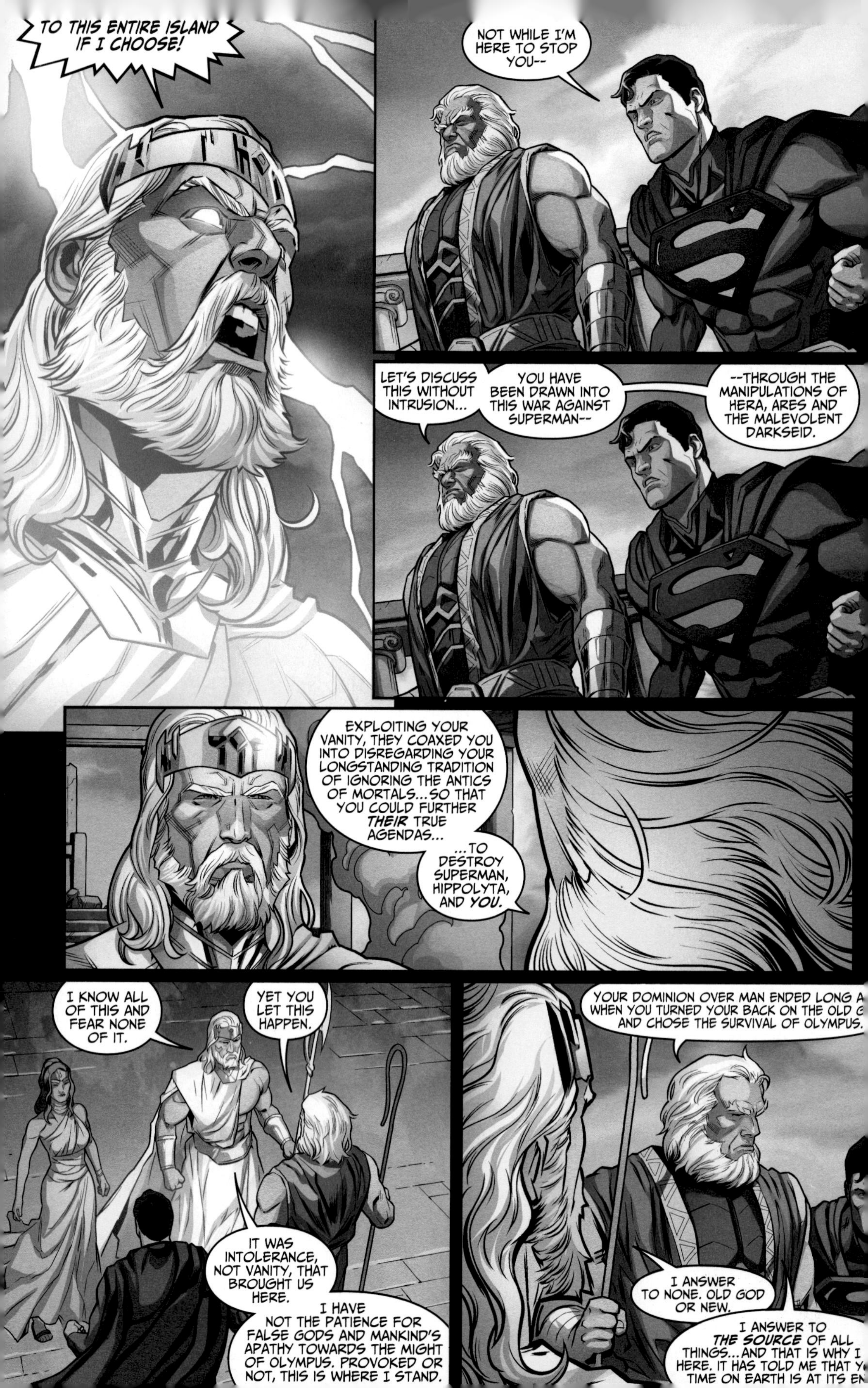
TO THIS ENTIRE ISLAND IF I CHOOSE!
NOT WHILE I'M HERE TO STOP YOU--
LET'S DISCUSS THIS WITHOUT INTRUSION...
YOU HAVE BEEN DRAWN INTO THIS WAR AGAINST SUPERMAN--
--THROUGH THE MANIPULATIONS OF HERA, ARES AND THE MALEVOLENT DARKSEID.
EXPLOITING YOUR VANITY, THEY COAXED YOU INTO DISREGARDING YOUR LONGSTANDING TRADITION OF IGNORING THE ANTICS OF MORTALS...SO THAT YOU COULD FURTHER *THEIR* TRUE AGENDAS...
...TO DESTROY SUPERMAN, HIPPOLYTA, AND *YOU.*
I KNOW ALL OF THIS AND FEAR NONE OF IT.
YET YOU LET THIS HAPPEN.
IT WAS INTOLERANCE, NOT VANITY, THAT BROUGHT US HERE.
I HAVE NOT THE PATIENCE FOR FALSE GODS AND MANKIND'S APATHY TOWARDS THE MIGHT OF OLYMPUS. PROVOKED OR NOT, THIS IS WHERE I STAND.
YOUR DOMINION OVER MAN ENDED LONG A WHEN YOU TURNED YOUR BACK ON THE OLD G AND CHOSE THE SURVIVAL OF OLYMPUS.
I ANSWER TO NONE. OLD GOD OR NEW.
I ANSWER TO *THE SOURCE* OF ALL THINGS...AND THAT IS WHY I HERE. IT HAS TOLD ME THAT Y TIME ON EARTH IS AT ITS EN

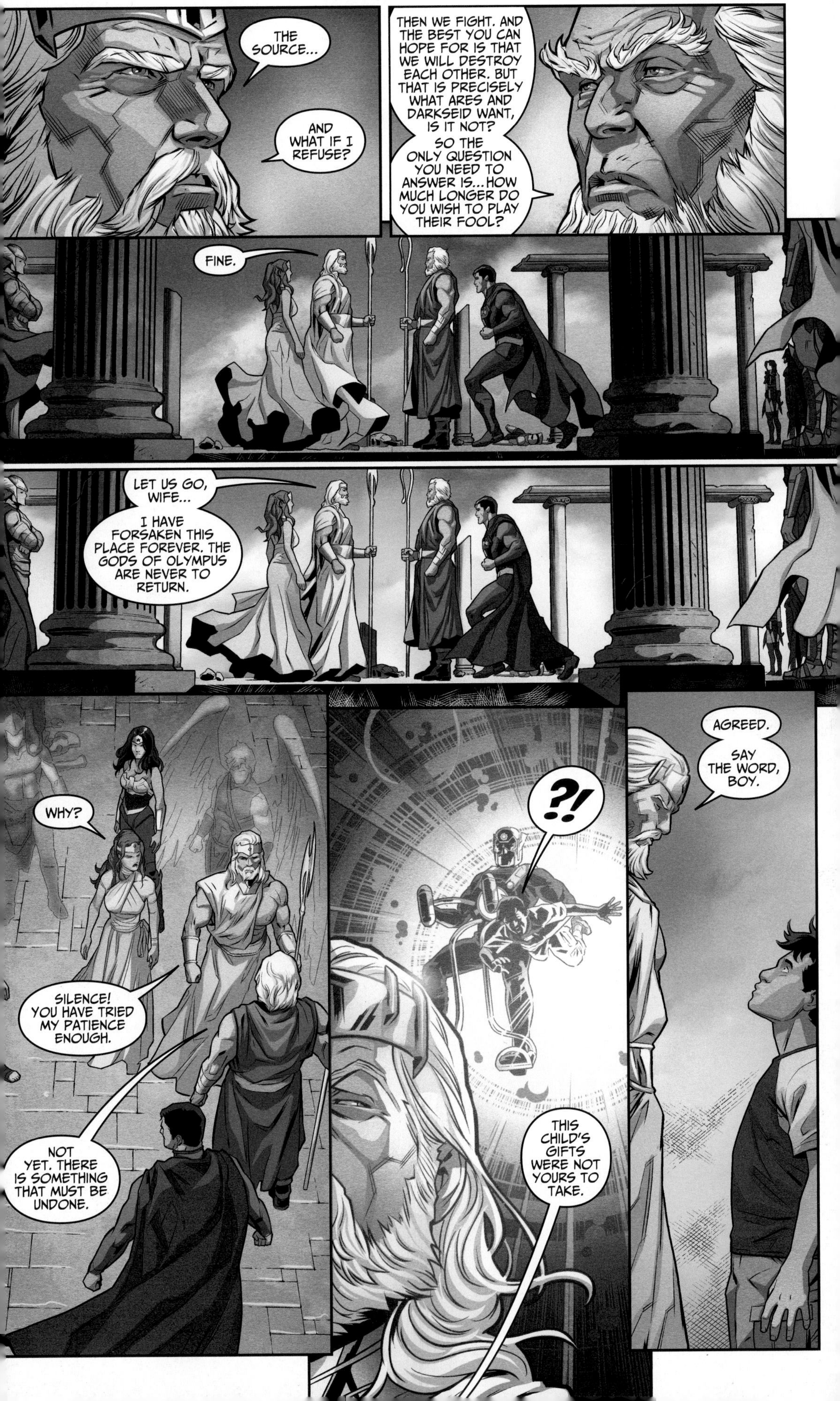
THE SOURCE...
AND WHAT IF I REFUSE?
THEN WE FIGHT. AND THE BEST YOU CAN HOPE FOR IS THAT WE WILL DESTROY EACH OTHER. BUT THAT IS PRECISELY WHAT ARES AND DARKSEID WANT, IS IT NOT?
SO THE ONLY QUESTION YOU NEED TO ANSWER IS...HOW MUCH LONGER DO YOU WISH TO PLAY THEIR FOOL?
FINE.
LET US GO, WIFE...
I HAVE FORSAKEN THIS PLACE FOREVER. THE GODS OF OLYMPUS ARE NEVER TO RETURN.
WHY?
SILENCE! YOU HAVE TRIED MY PATIENCE ENOUGH.
NOT YET. THERE IS SOMETHING THAT MUST BE UNDONE.
?!
THIS CHILD'S GIFTS WERE NOT YOURS TO TAKE.
AGREED.
SAY THE WORD, BOY.

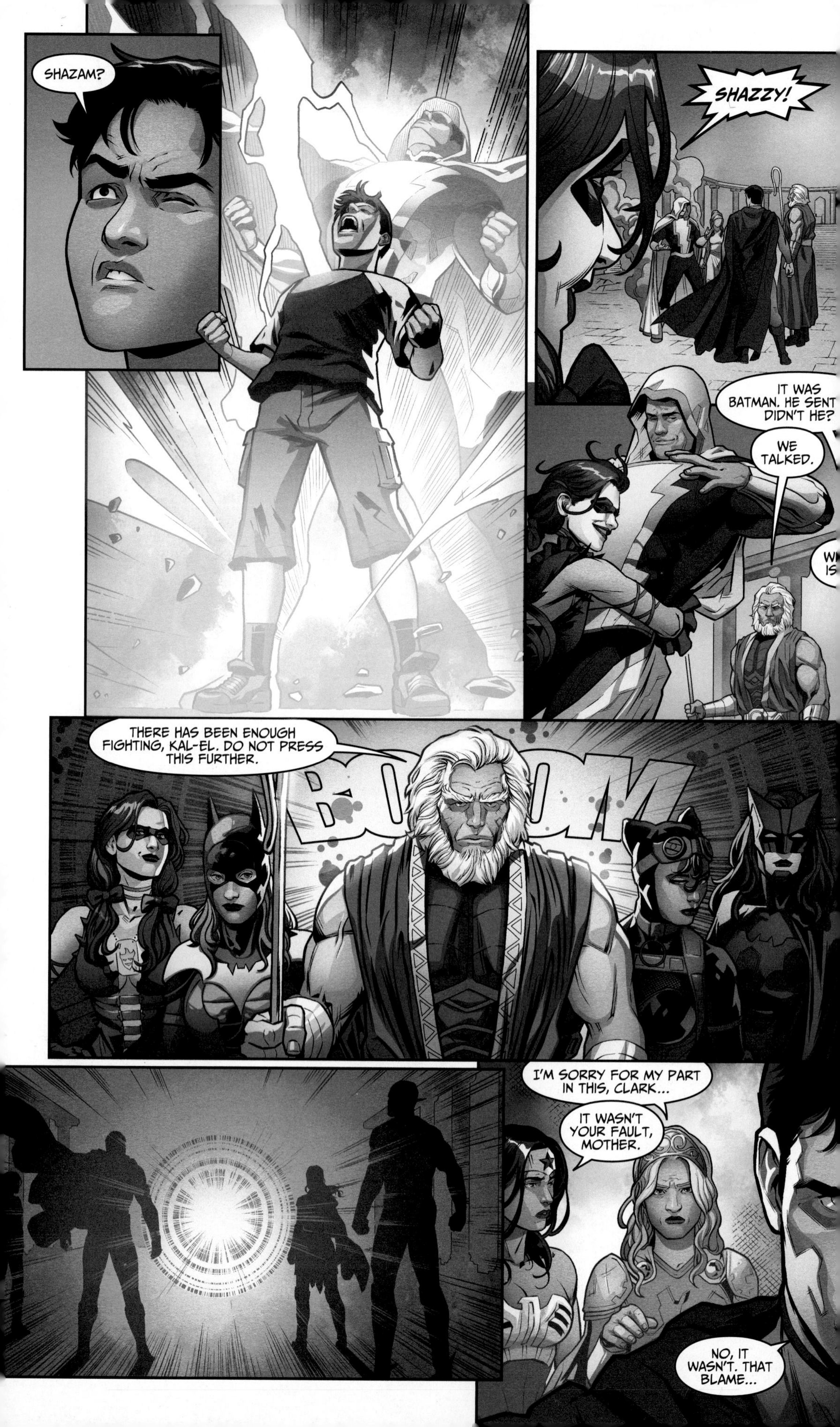
SHAZAM?
SHAZZY!
IT WAS BATMAN. HE SENT DIDN'T HE?
WE TALKED.
THERE HAS BEEN ENOUGH FIGHTING, KAL-EL. DO NOT PRESS THIS FURTHER.
BOOM
I'M SORRY FOR MY PART IN THIS, CLARK...
IT WASN'T YOUR FAULT, MOTHER.
NO, IT WASN'T. THAT BLAME...

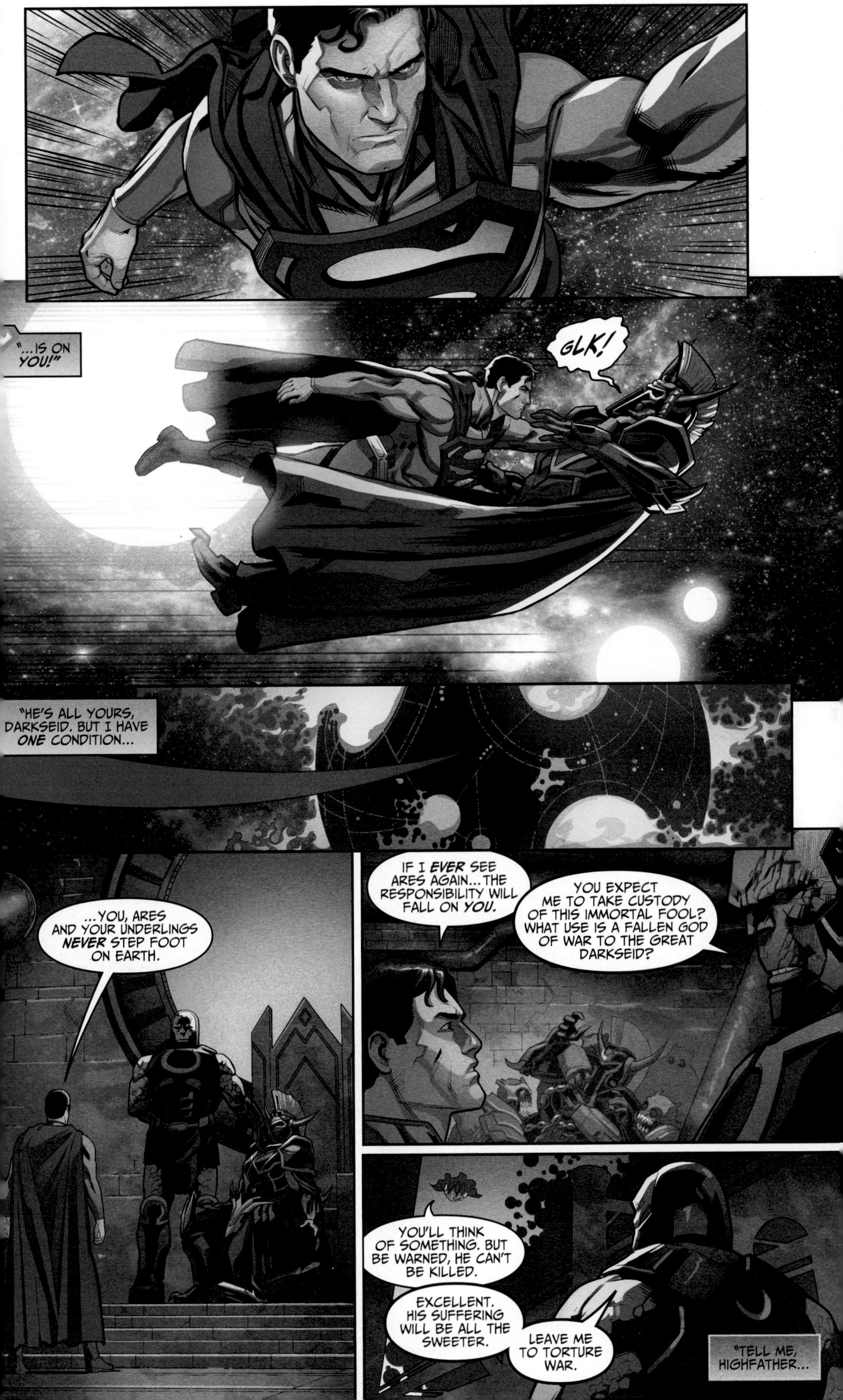
"...IS ON YOU!"
GLK!
"HE'S ALL YOURS, DARKSEID. BUT I HAVE ONE CONDITION...
...YOU, ARES AND YOUR UNDERLINGS NEVER STEP FOOT ON EARTH.
IF I EVER SEE ARES AGAIN... THE RESPONSIBILITY WILL FALL ON YOU.
YOU EXPECT ME TO TAKE CUSTODY OF THIS IMMORTAL FOOL? WHAT USE IS A FALLEN GOD OF WAR TO THE GREAT DARKSEID?
YOU'LL THINK OF SOMETHING. BUT BE WARNED, HE CAN'T BE KILLED.
EXCELLENT. HIS SUFFERING WILL BE ALL THE SWEETER.
LEAVE ME TO TORTURE WAR.
"TELL ME, HIGHFATHER...

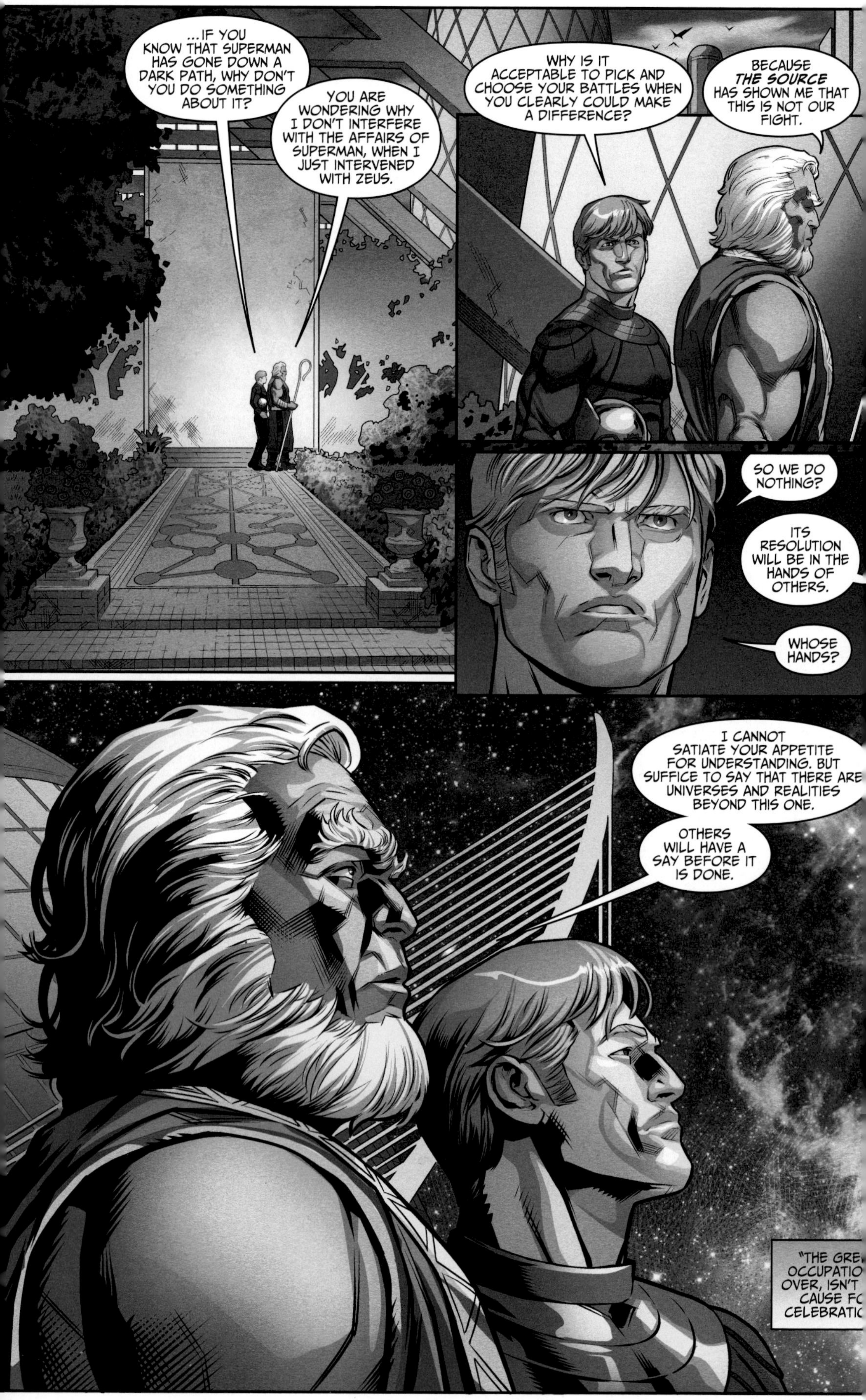
...IF YOU KNOW THAT SUPERMAN HAS GONE DOWN A DARK PATH, WHY DON'T YOU DO SOMETHING ABOUT IT?
YOU ARE WONDERING WHY I DON'T INTERFERE WITH THE AFFAIRS OF SUPERMAN, WHEN I JUST INTERVENED WITH ZEUS.
WHY IS IT ACCEPTABLE TO PICK AND CHOOSE YOUR BATTLES WHEN YOU CLEARLY COULD MAKE A DIFFERENCE?
BECAUSE *THE SOURCE* HAS SHOWN ME THAT THIS IS NOT OUR FIGHT.
SO WE DO NOTHING?
ITS RESOLUTION WILL BE IN THE HANDS OF OTHERS.
WHOSE HANDS?
I CANNOT SATIATE YOUR APPETITE FOR UNDERSTANDING. BUT SUFFICE TO SAY THAT THERE ARE UNIVERSES AND REALITIES BEYOND THIS ONE.
OTHERS WILL HAVE A SAY BEFORE IT IS DONE.

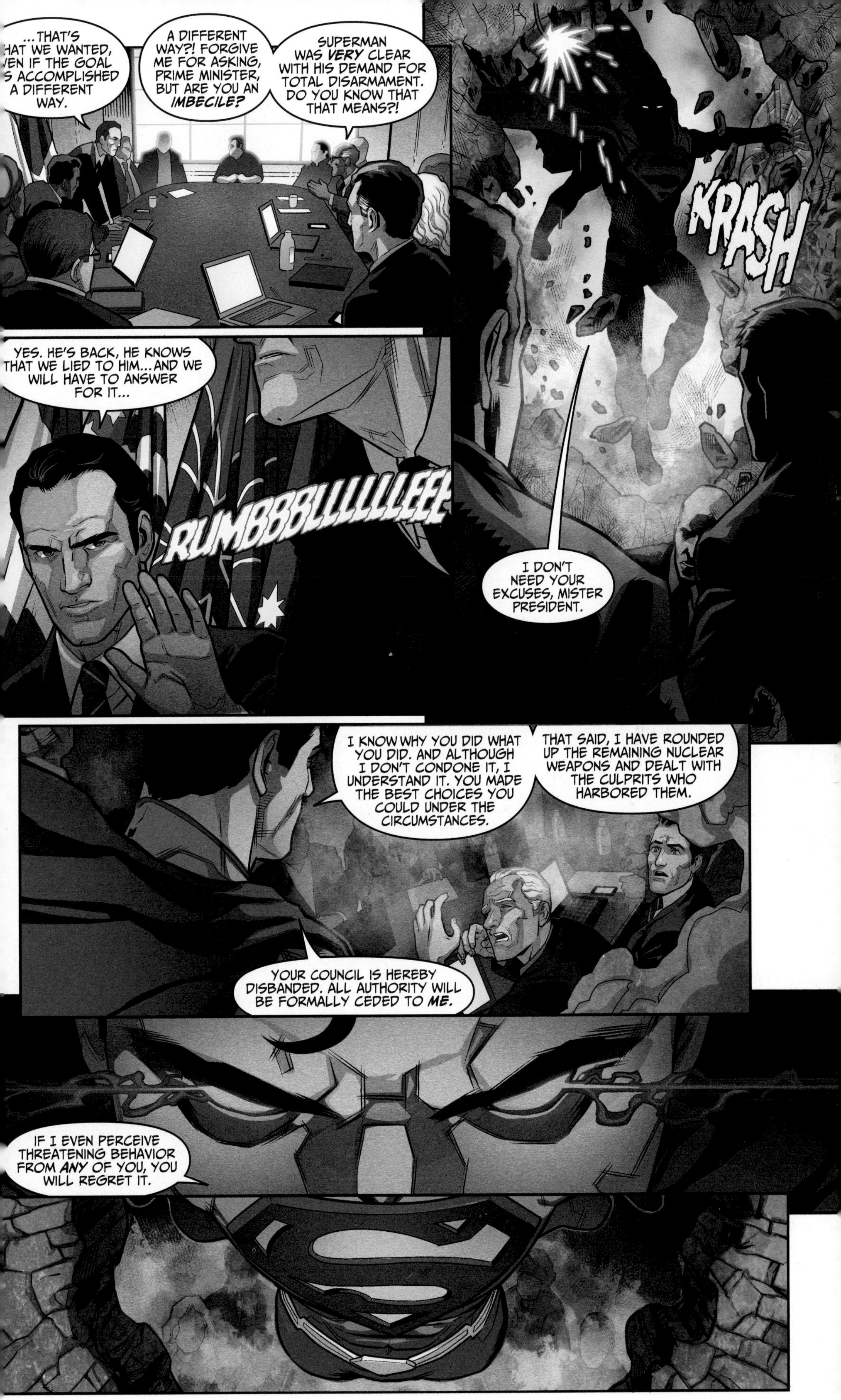
...THAT'S
HAT WE WANTED,
VEN IF THE GOAL
S ACCOMPLISHED
A DIFFERENT
WAY.
A DIFFERENT WAY?! FORGIVE ME FOR ASKING, PRIME MINISTER, BUT ARE YOU AN *IMBECILE?*
SUPERMAN WAS *VERY* CLEAR WITH HIS DEMAND FOR TOTAL DISARMAMENT. DO YOU KNOW THAT THAT MEANS?!
KRASH
YES. HE'S BACK, HE KNOWS THAT WE LIED TO HIM...AND WE WILL HAVE TO ANSWER FOR IT...
RUMBBBLLLLLLLEEE
I DON'T NEED YOUR EXCUSES, MISTER PRESIDENT.
I KNOW WHY YOU DID WHAT YOU DID. AND ALTHOUGH I DON'T CONDONE IT, I UNDERSTAND IT. YOU MADE THE BEST CHOICES YOU COULD UNDER THE CIRCUMSTANCES.
THAT SAID, I HAVE ROUNDED UP THE REMAINING NUCLEAR WEAPONS AND DEALT WITH THE CULPRITS WHO HARBORED THEM.
YOUR COUNCIL IS HEREBY DISBANDED. ALL AUTHORITY WILL BE FORMALLY CEDED TO *ME.*
IF I EVEN PERCEIVE THREATENING BEHAVIOR FROM *ANY* OF YOU, YOU WILL REGRET IT.

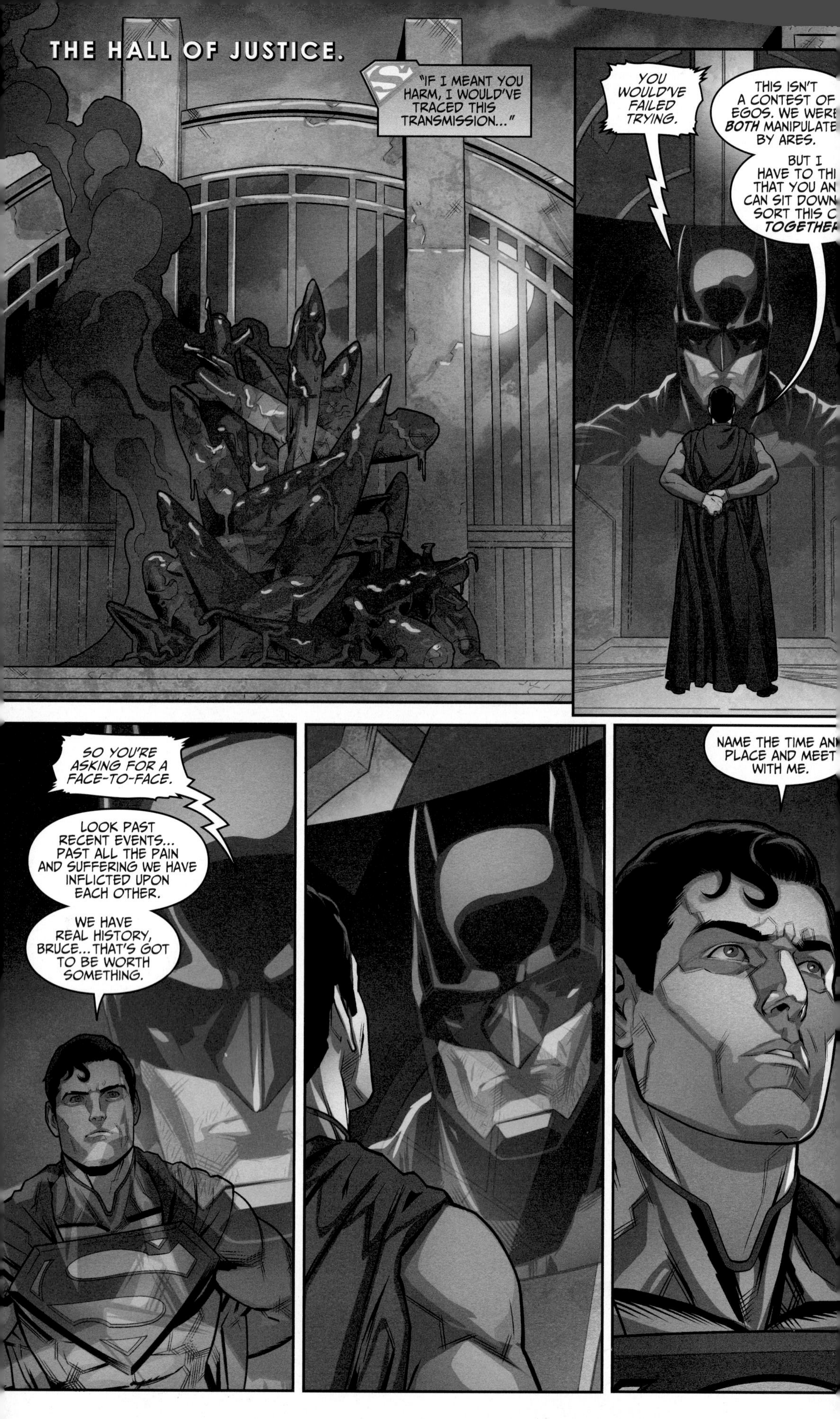
THE HALL OF JUSTICE.
"IF I MEANT YOU HARM, I WOULD'VE TRACED THIS TRANSMISSION..."
YOU WOULD'VE FAILED TRYING.
THIS ISN'T A CONTEST OF EGOS. WE WERE BOTH MANIPULATE BY ARES.
BUT I HAVE TO THI THAT YOU AN CAN SIT DOWN SORT THIS C TOGETHER
SO YOU'RE ASKING FOR A FACE-TO-FACE.
LOOK PAST RECENT EVENTS... PAST ALL THE PAIN AND SUFFERING WE HAVE INFLICTED UPON EACH OTHER.
WE HAVE REAL HISTORY, BRUCE... THAT'S GOT TO BE WORTH SOMETHING.
NAME THE TIME AN PLACE AND MEET WITH ME.

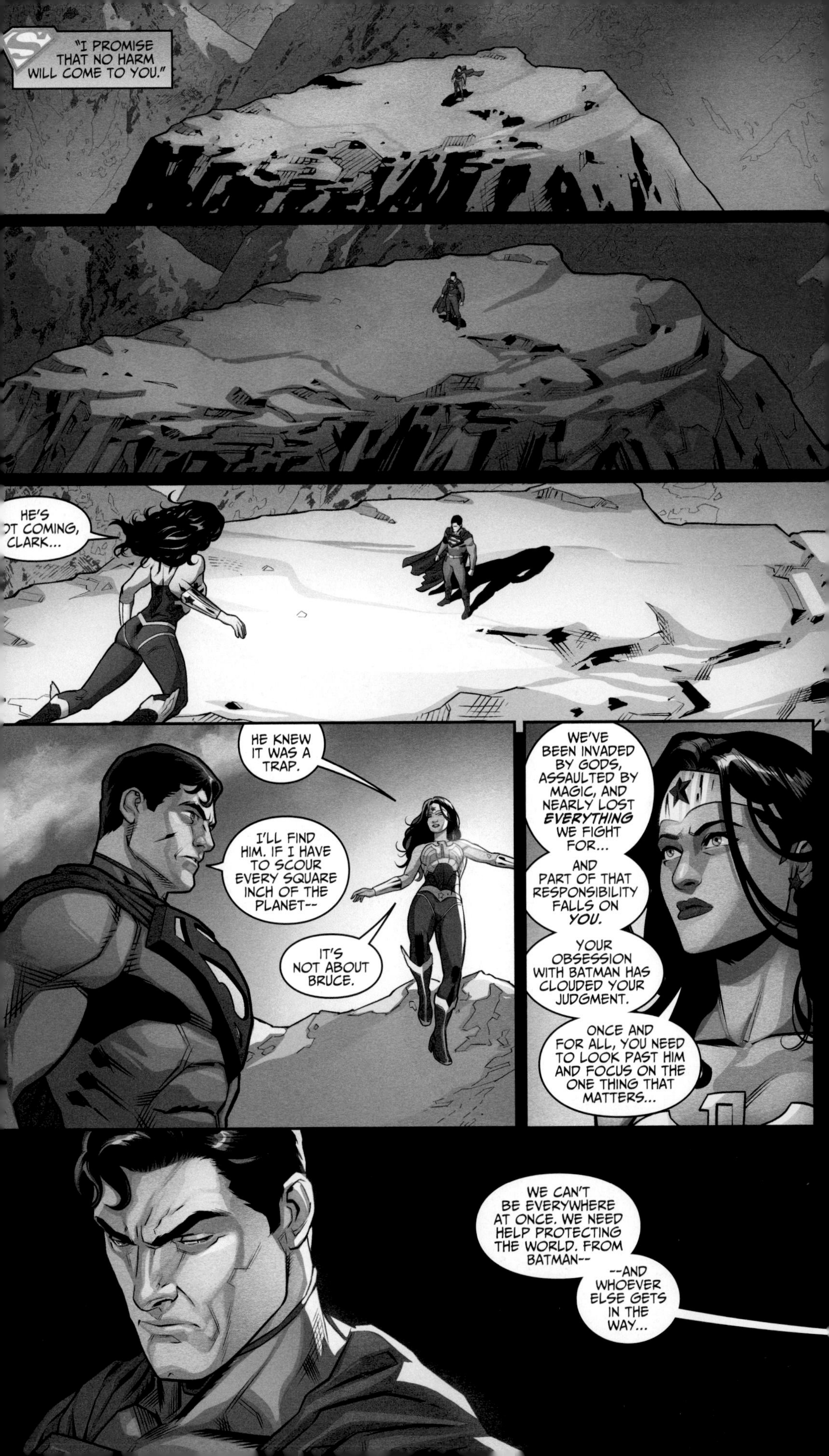

"I PROMISE THAT NO HARM WILL COME TO YOU."
HE'S OT COMING, CLARK...
HE KNEW IT WAS A TRAP.
I'LL FIND HIM. IF I HAVE TO SCOUR EVERY SQUARE INCH OF THE PLANET--
IT'S NOT ABOUT BRUCE.
WE'VE BEEN INVADED BY GODS, ASSAULTED BY MAGIC, AND NEARLY LOST *EVERYTHING* WE FIGHT FOR...
AND PART OF THAT RESPONSIBILITY FALLS ON *YOU.*
YOUR OBSESSION WITH BATMAN HAS CLOUDED YOUR JUDGMENT.
ONCE AND FOR ALL, YOU NEED TO LOOK PAST HIM AND FOCUS ON THE ONE THING THAT MATTERS...
WE CAN'T BE EVERYWHERE AT ONCE. WE NEED HELP PROTECTING THE WORLD. FROM BATMAN--
--AND WHOEVER ELSE GETS IN THE WAY...

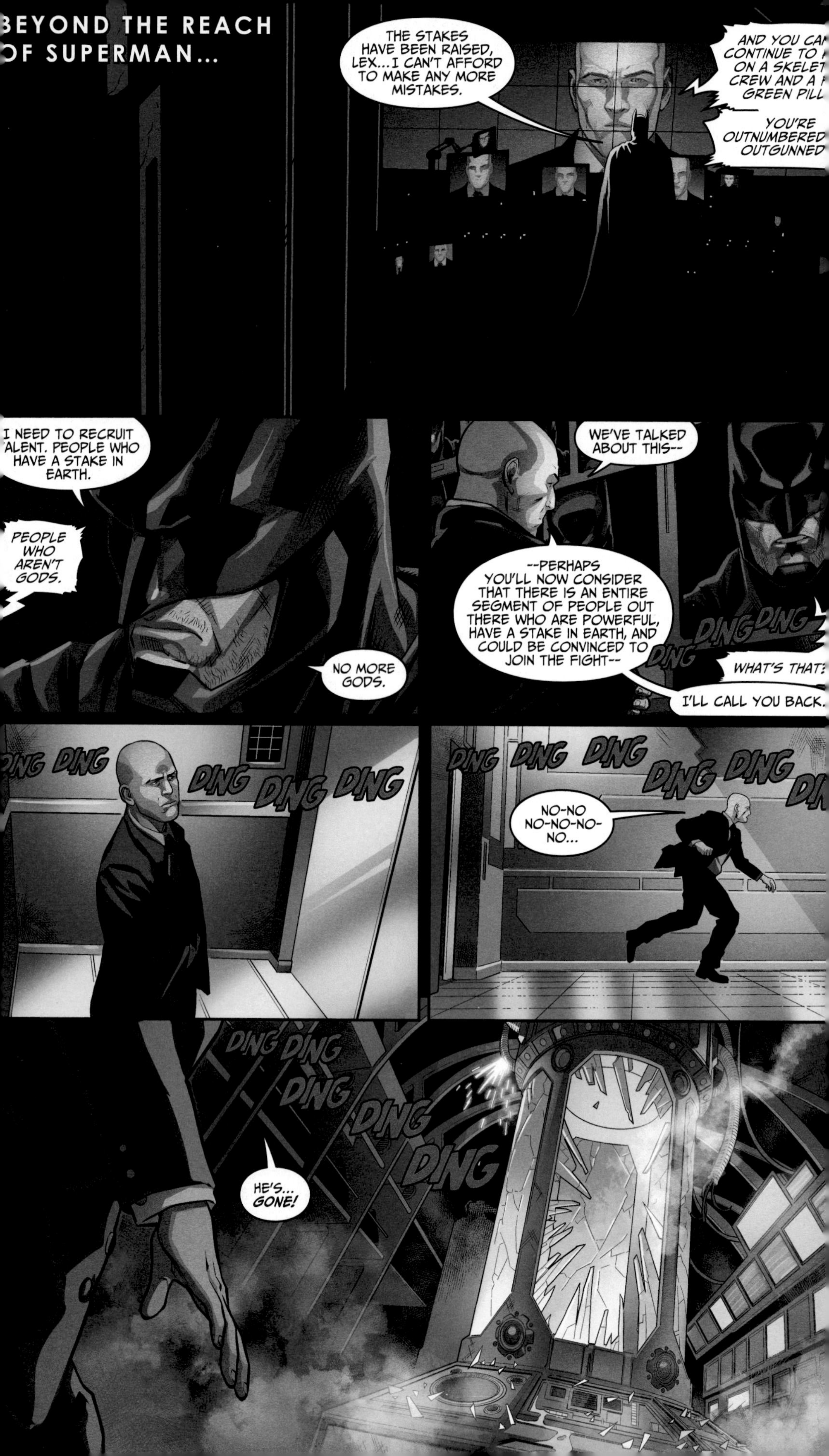
BEYOND THE REACH
OF SUPERMAN...
THE STAKES HAVE BEEN RAISED, LEX...I CAN'T AFFORD TO MAKE ANY MORE MISTAKES.
YOU'RE OUTNUMBERED. OUTGUNNED.
I NEED TO RECRUIT TALENT. PEOPLE WHO HAVE A STAKE IN EARTH.
PEOPLE WHO AREN'T GODS.
NO MORE GODS.
WE'VE TALKED ABOUT THIS--
--PERHAPS YOU'LL NOW CONSIDER THAT THERE IS AN ENTIRE SEGMENT OF PEOPLE OUT THERE WHO ARE POWERFUL, HAVE A STAKE IN EARTH, AND COULD BE CONVINCED TO JOIN THE FIGHT--
DING DING DING
WHAT'S THAT?
I'LL CALL YOU BACK.
DING DING DING DING DING
DING DING DING DING DING DING
NO-NO NO-NO-NO-NO...
DING DING DING DING DING
HE'S... GONE!

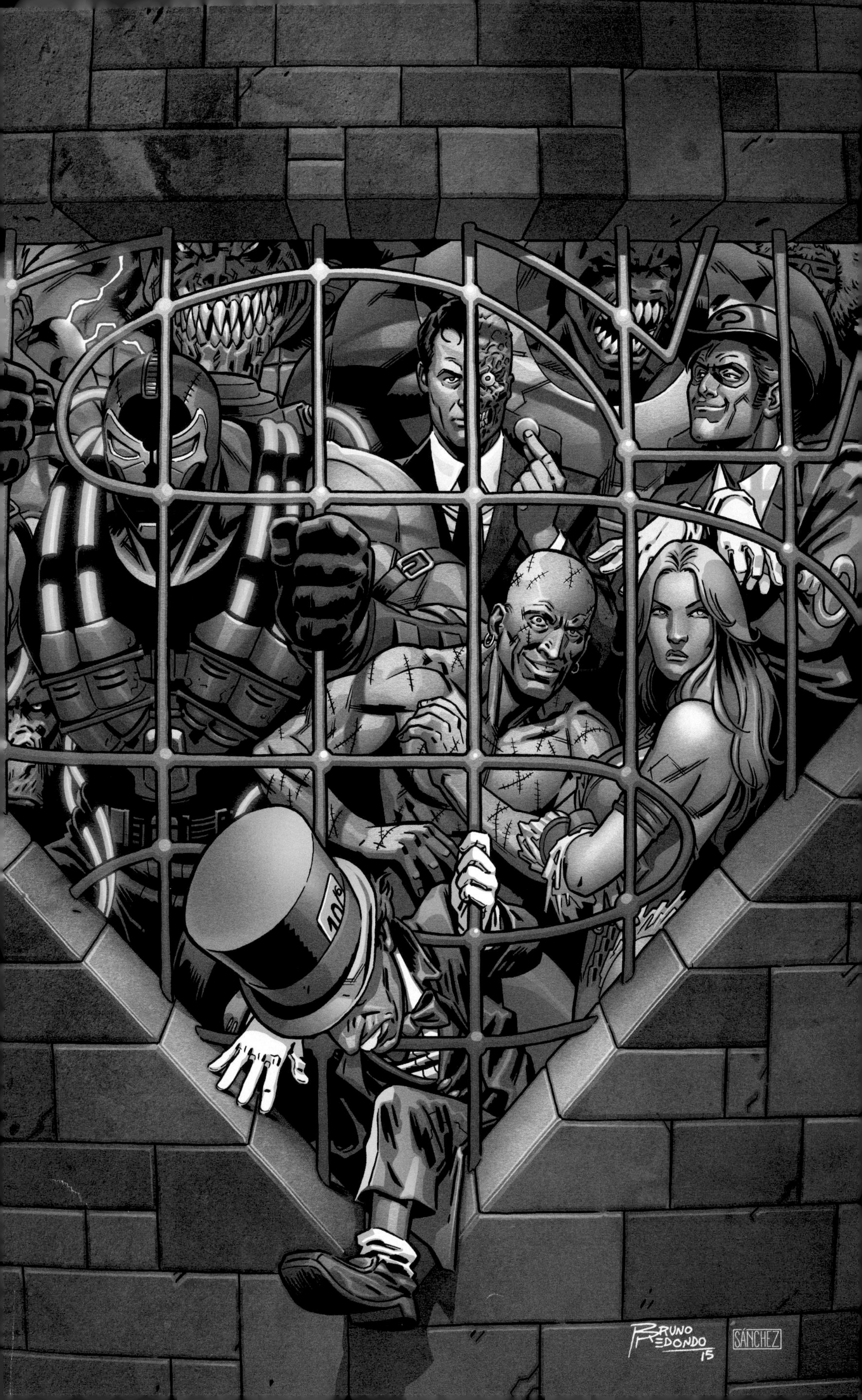
BRUNO REDONDO 15
SÁNCHEZ

"The Trench" **Tom Taylor** Writer **Bruno Redondo** **Sergio Sandoval** **Jordi Tarragona** Artists
Rex Lokus Colorist Cover Art by **Bruno Redondo & Alejandro Sanchez Rodriguez**

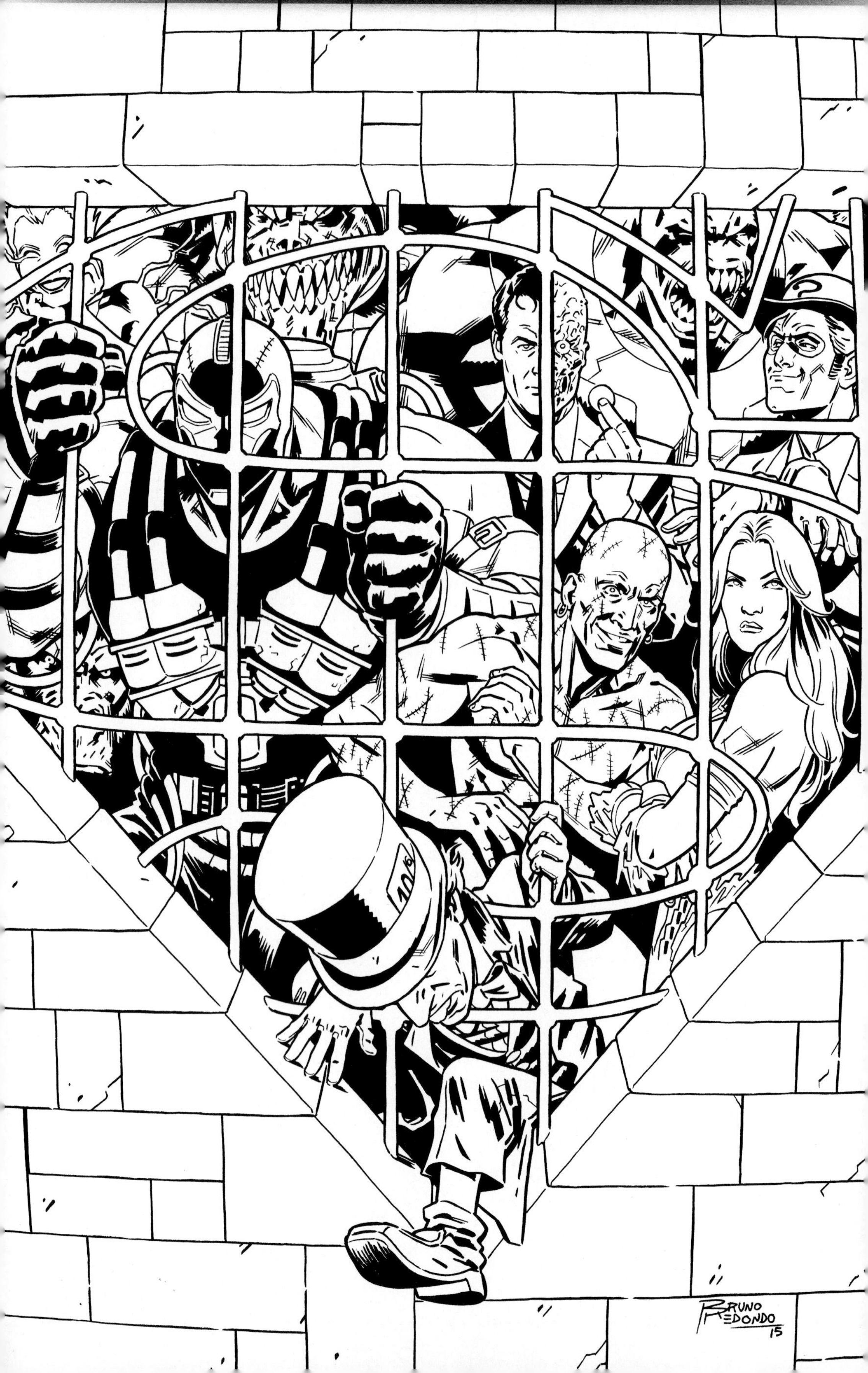
BRUNO REDONDO 15

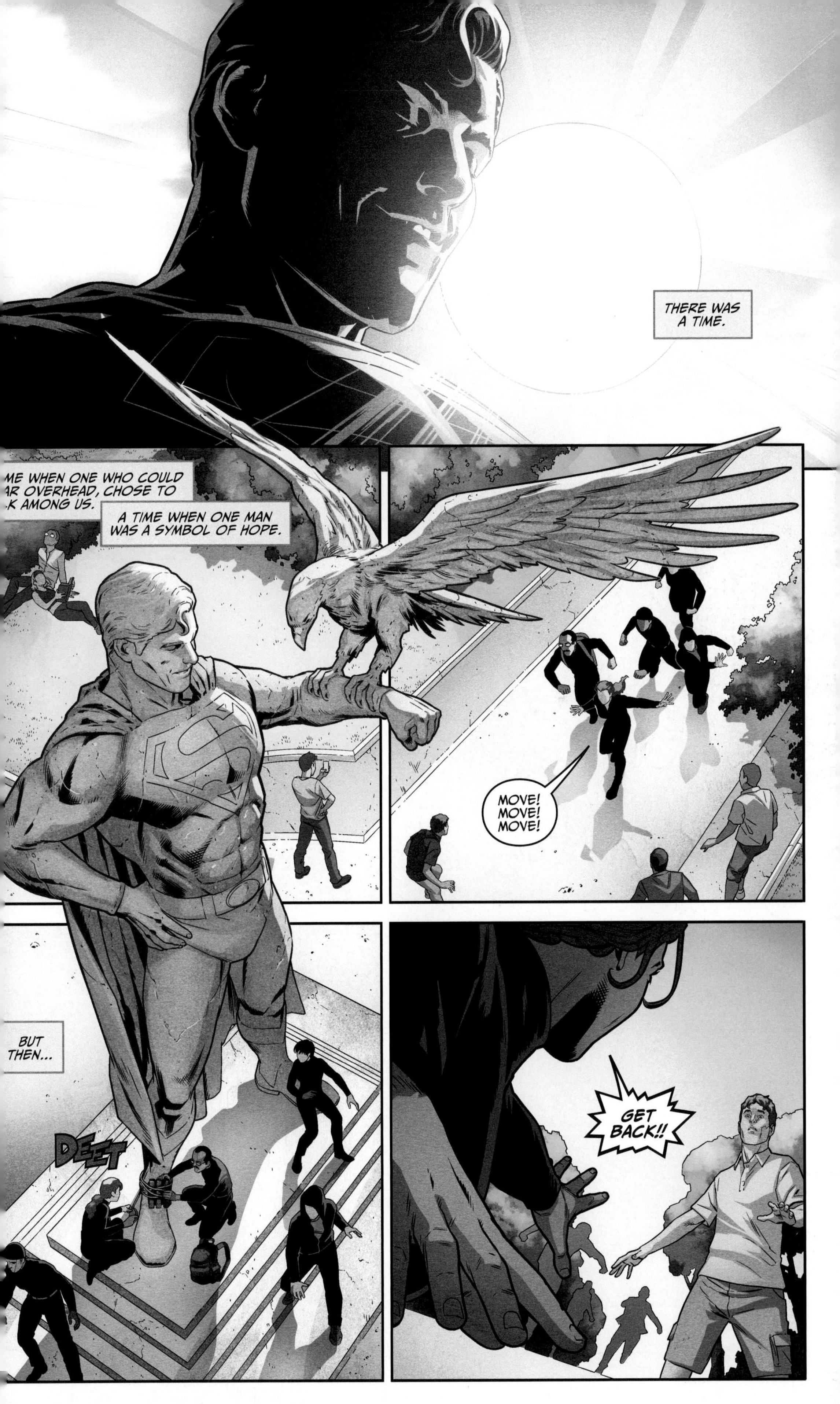
THERE WAS A TIME.
ME WHEN ONE WHO COULD
AR OVERHEAD, CHOSE TO
K AMONG US.
A TIME WHEN ONE MAN WAS A SYMBOL OF HOPE.
MOVE! MOVE! MOVE!
BUT THEN...
DEET
GET BACK!!

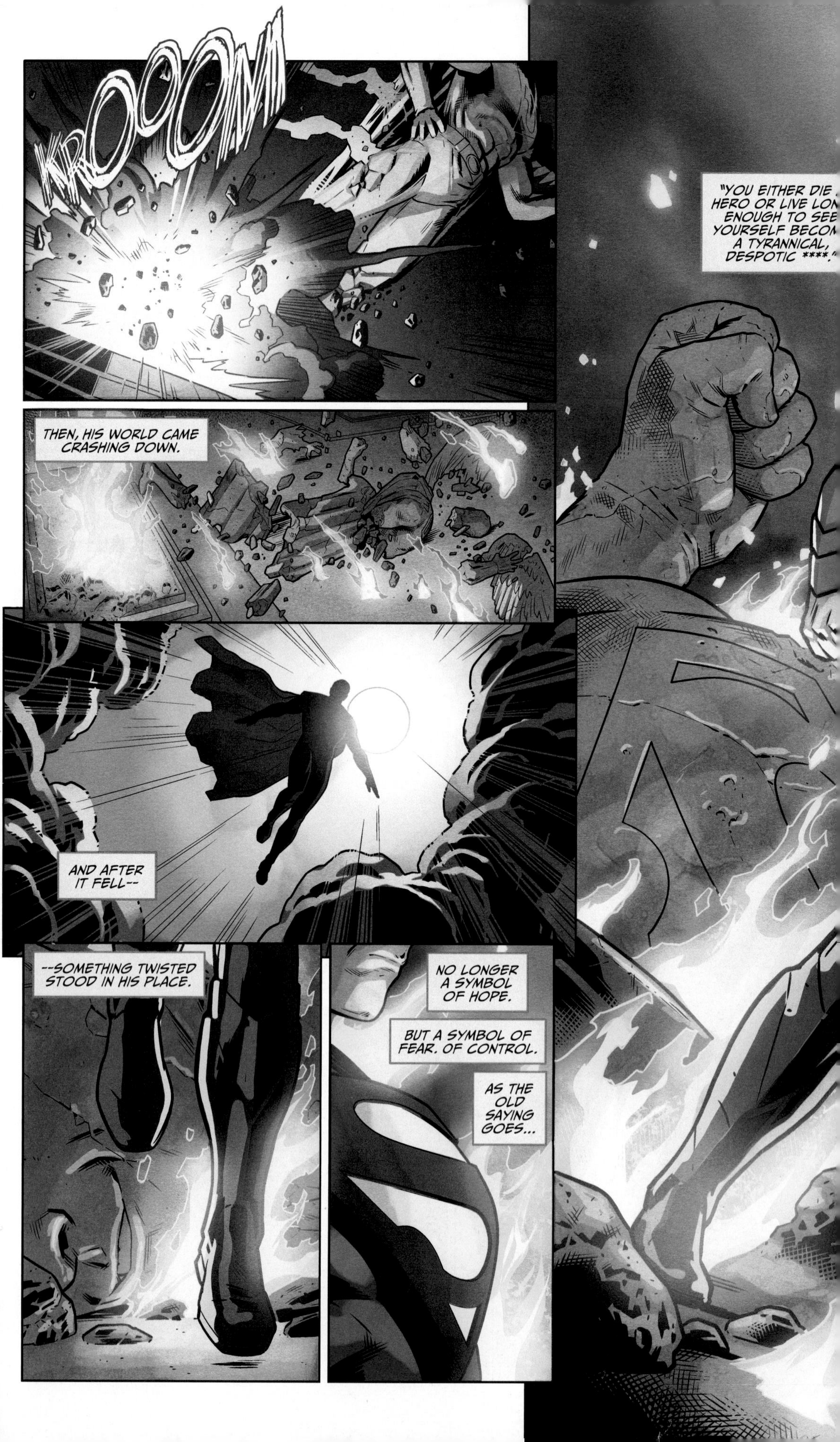
KROOOM!
THEN, HIS WORLD CAME CRASHING DOWN.
AND AFTER IT FELL--
--SOMETHING TWISTED STOOD IN HIS PLACE.
NO LONGER A SYMBOL OF HOPE.
BUT A SYMBOL OF FEAR. OF CONTROL.
AS THE OLD SAYING GOES...
"YOU EITHER DIE A HERO OR LIVE LON ENOUGH TO SEE YOURSELF BECOM A TYRANNICAL, DESPOTIC ****."

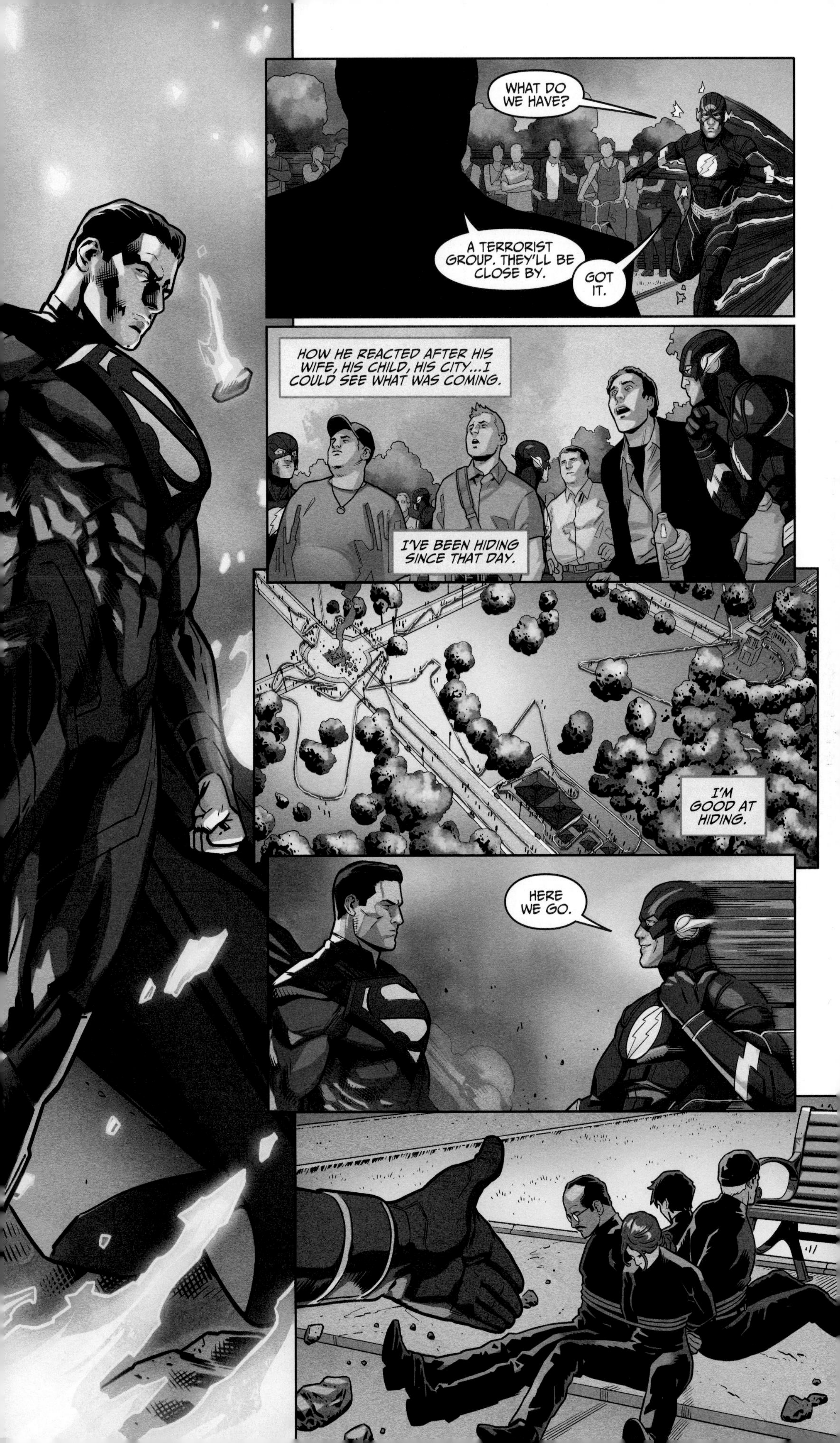
WHAT DO WE HAVE?
A TERRORIST GROUP. THEY'LL BE CLOSE BY.
GOT IT.
HOW HE REACTED AFTER HIS WIFE, HIS CHILD, HIS CITY...I COULD SEE WHAT WAS COMING.
I'VE BEEN HIDING SINCE THAT DAY.
I'M GOOD AT HIDING.
HERE WE GO.

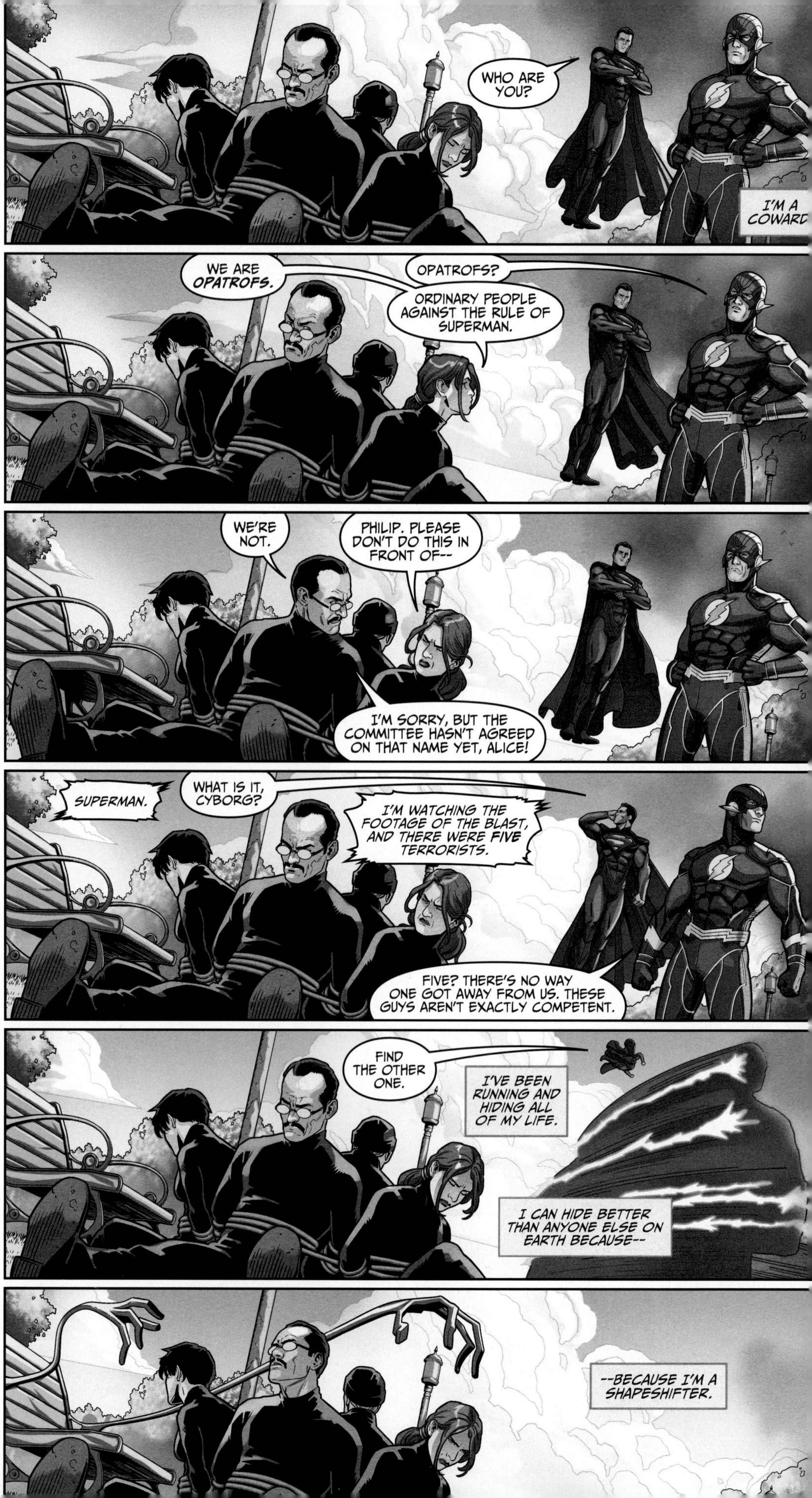
WHO ARE YOU?
I'M A COWARD
WE ARE OPATROFS.
OPATROFS?
ORDINARY PEOPLE AGAINST THE RULE OF SUPERMAN.
WE'RE NOT.
PHILIP. PLEASE DON'T DO THIS IN FRONT OF--
I'M SORRY, BUT THE COMMITTEE HASN'T AGREED ON THAT NAME YET, ALICE!
SUPERMAN.
WHAT IS IT, CYBORG?
I'M WATCHING THE FOOTAGE OF THE BLAST, AND THERE WERE FIVE TERRORISTS.
FIVE? THERE'S NO WAY ONE GOT AWAY FROM US. THESE GUYS AREN'T EXACTLY COMPETENT.
FIND THE OTHER ONE.
I'VE BEEN RUNNING AND HIDING ALL OF MY LIFE.
I CAN HIDE BETTER THAN ANYONE ELSE ON EARTH BECAUSE--
--BECAUSE I'M A SHAPESHIFTER.

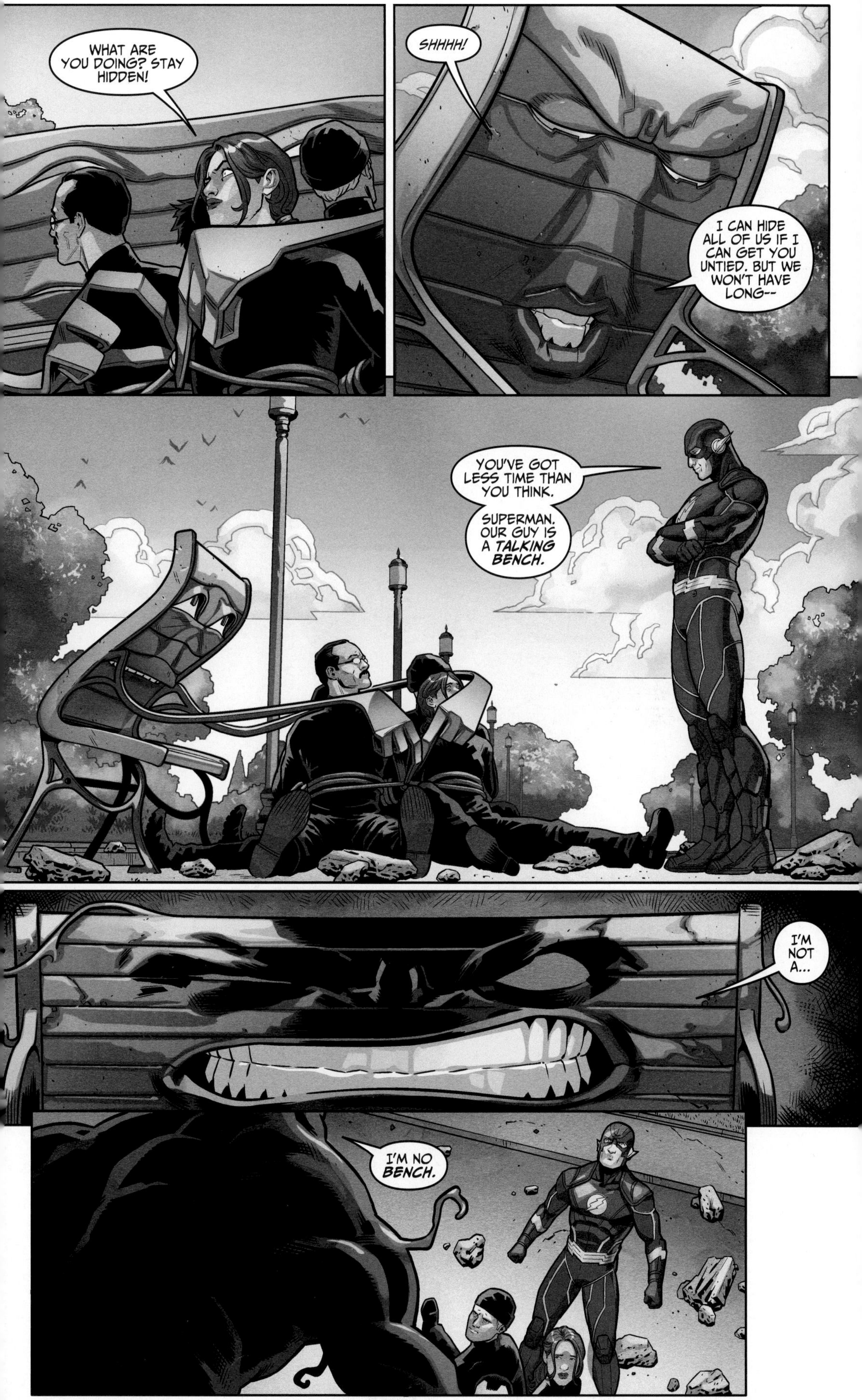
WHAT ARE YOU DOING? STAY HIDDEN!
SHHHH!
I CAN HIDE ALL OF US IF I CAN GET YOU UNTIED. BUT WE WON'T HAVE LONG--
YOU'VE GOT LESS TIME THAN YOU THINK.
SUPERMAN. OUR GUY IS A *TALKING BENCH.*
I'M NOT A...
I'M NO *BENCH.*

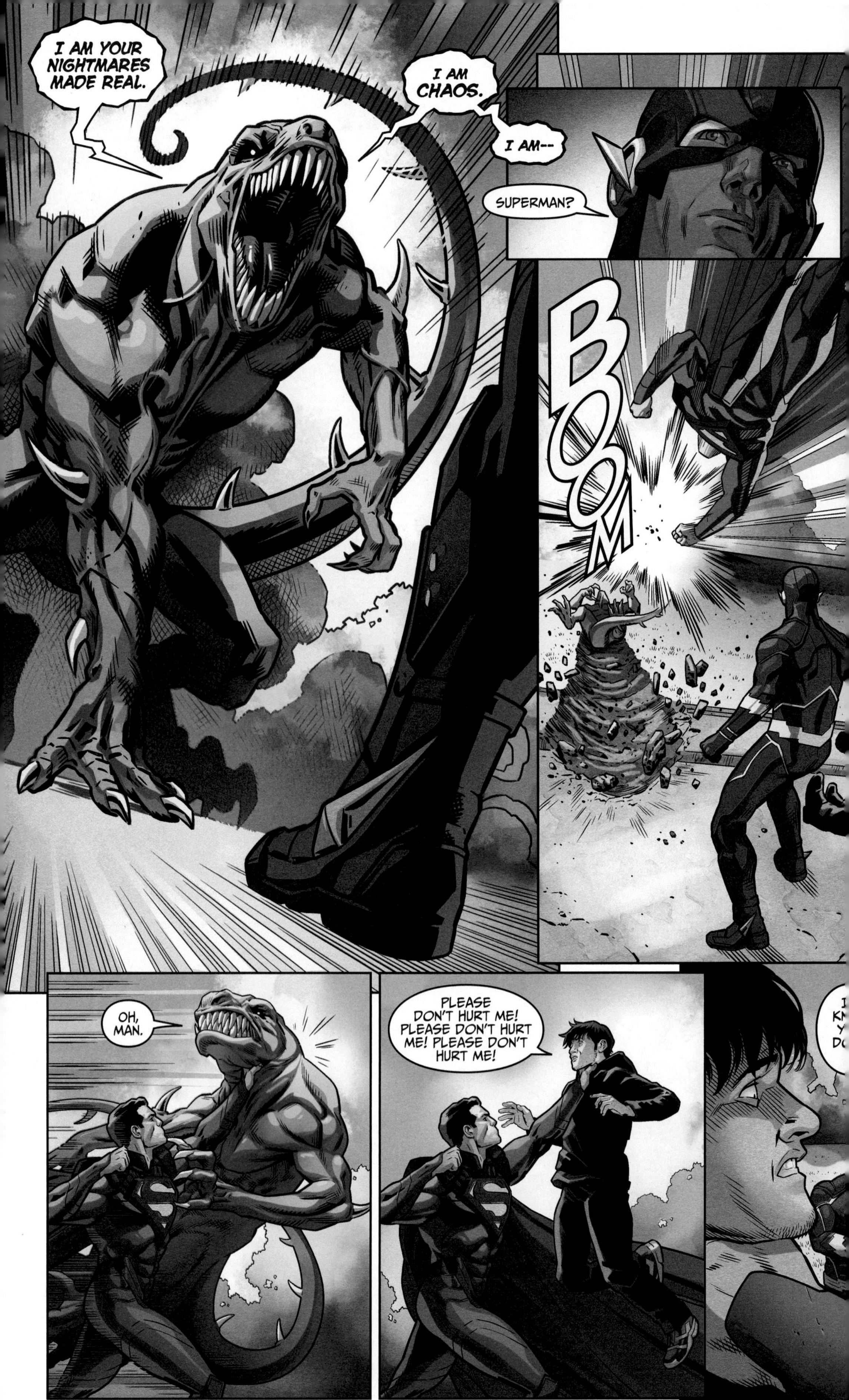

I AM YOUR NIGHTMARES MADE REAL.
I AM CHAOS.
I AM--
SUPERMAN?
BOOM
OH, MAN.
PLEASE DON'T HURT ME! PLEASE DON'T HURT ME! PLEASE DON'T HURT ME!

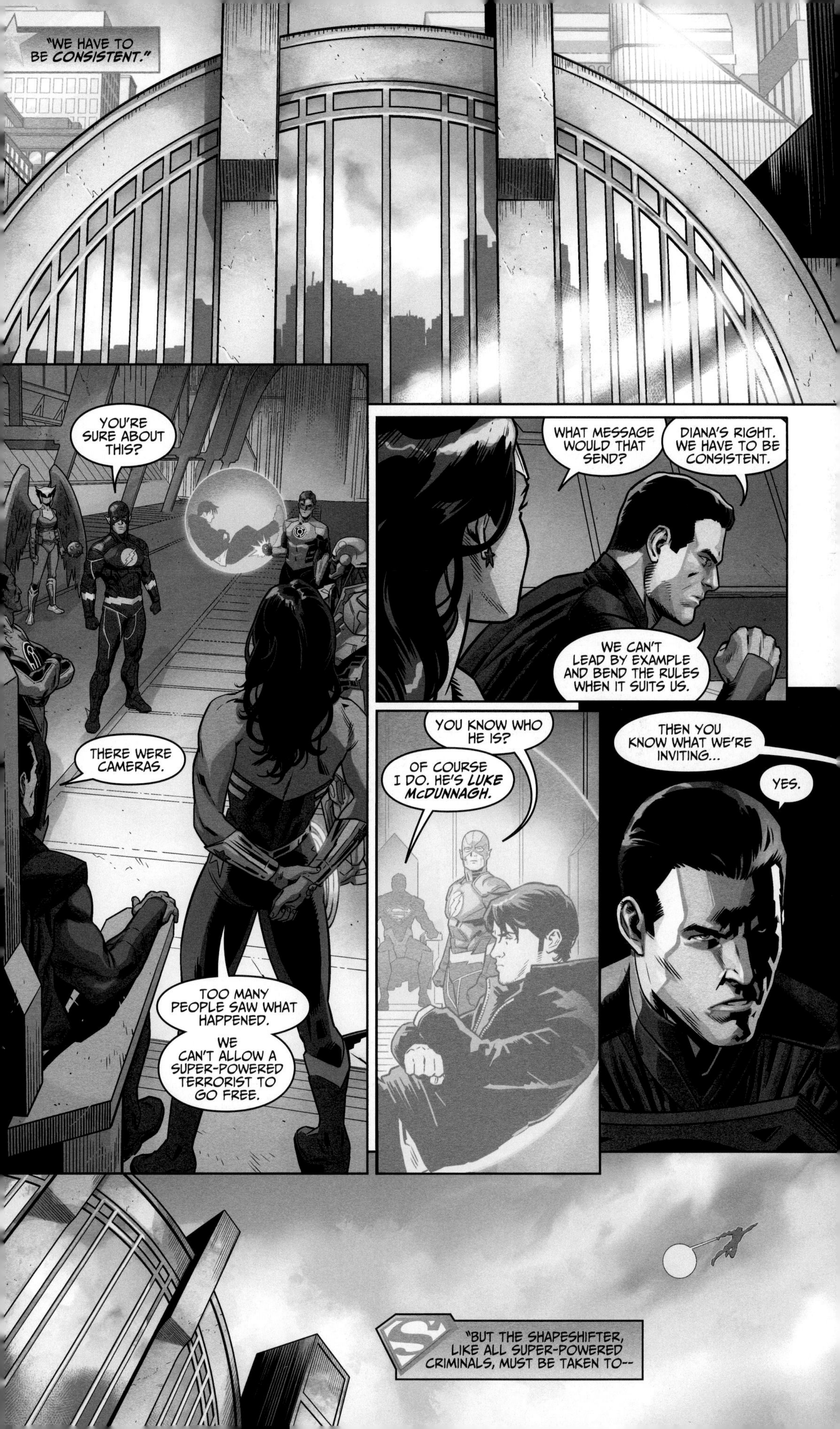
"WE HAVE TO BE CONSISTENT."
YOU'RE SURE ABOUT THIS?
THERE WERE CAMERAS.
TOO MANY PEOPLE SAW WHAT HAPPENED.
WE CAN'T ALLOW A SUPER-POWERED TERRORIST TO GO FREE.
WHAT MESSAGE WOULD THAT SEND?
DIANA'S RIGHT. WE HAVE TO BE CONSISTENT.
WE CAN'T LEAD BY EXAMPLE AND BEND THE RULES WHEN IT SUITS US.
YOU KNOW WHO HE IS?
OF COURSE I DO. HE'S LUKE McDUNNAGH.
THEN YOU KNOW WHAT WE'RE INVITING...
YES.
"BUT THE SHAPESHIFTER, LIKE ALL SUPER-POWERED CRIMINALS, MUST BE TAKEN TO--

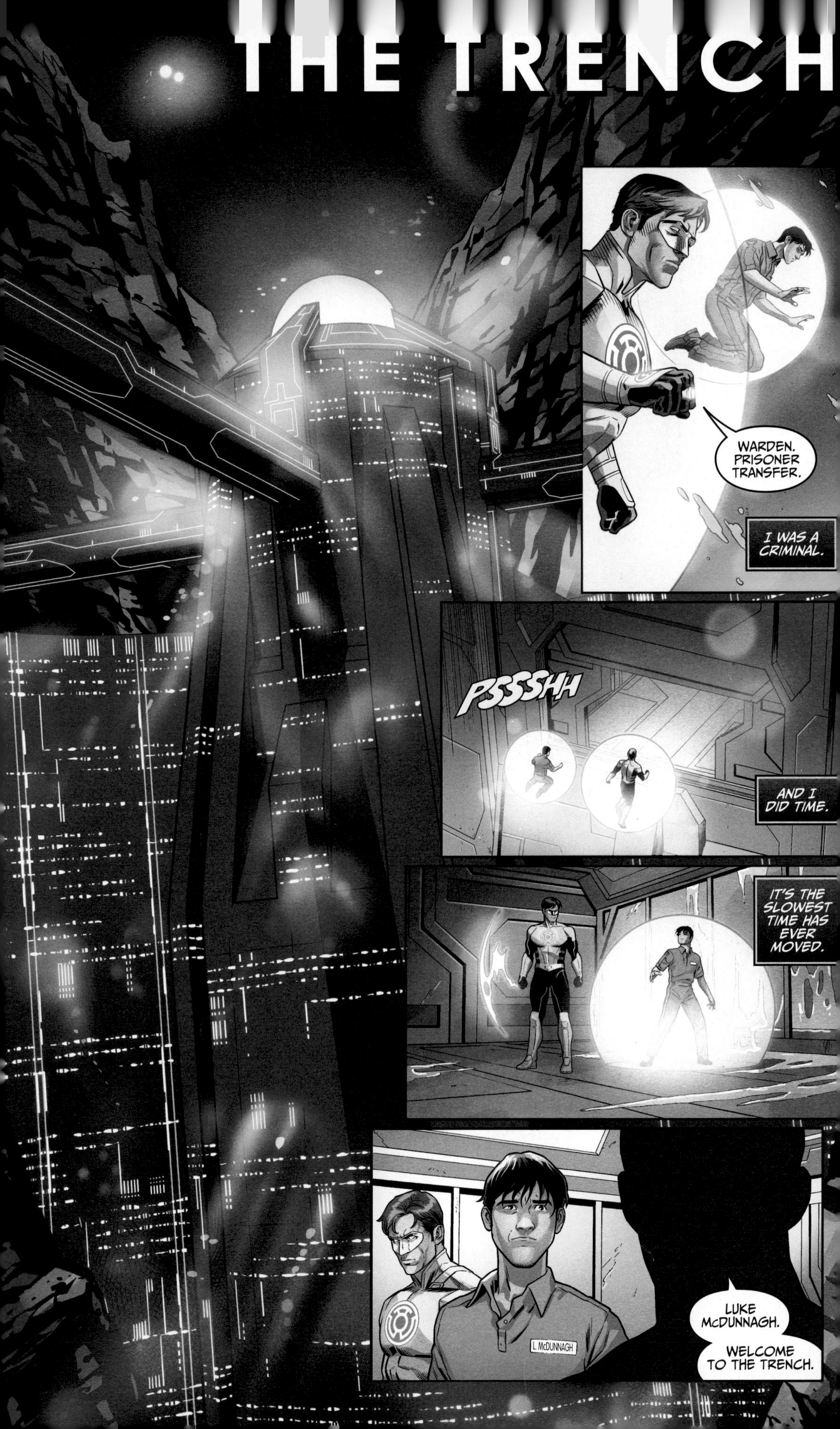
THE TRENCH
WARDEN. PRISONER TRANSFER.
I WAS A CRIMINAL.
PSSSHH
AND I DID TIME.
IT'S THE SLOWEST TIME HAS EVER MOVED.
L. McDUNNAGH
LUKE McDUNNAGH.
WELCOME TO THE TRENCH.

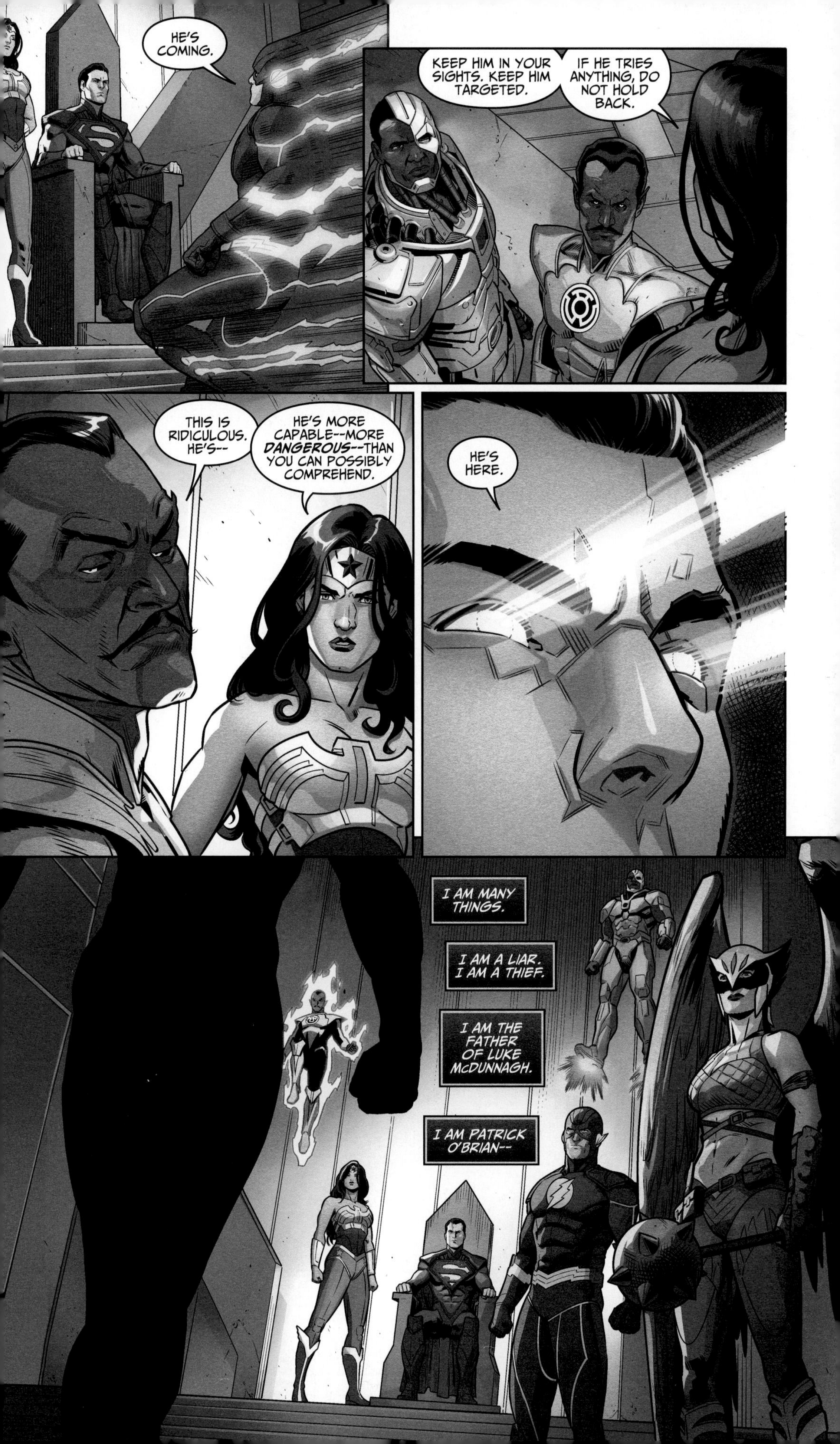
HE'S COMING.
KEEP HIM IN YOUR SIGHTS. KEEP HIM TARGETED.
IF HE TRIES ANYTHING, DO NOT HOLD BACK.
THIS IS RIDICULOUS. HE'S--
HE'S MORE CAPABLE--MORE DANGEROUS--THAN YOU CAN POSSIBLY COMPREHEND.
HE'S HERE.
I AM MANY THINGS.
I AM A LIAR. I AM A THIEF.
I AM THE FATHER OF LUKE McDUNNAGH.
I AM PATRICK O'BRIAN--

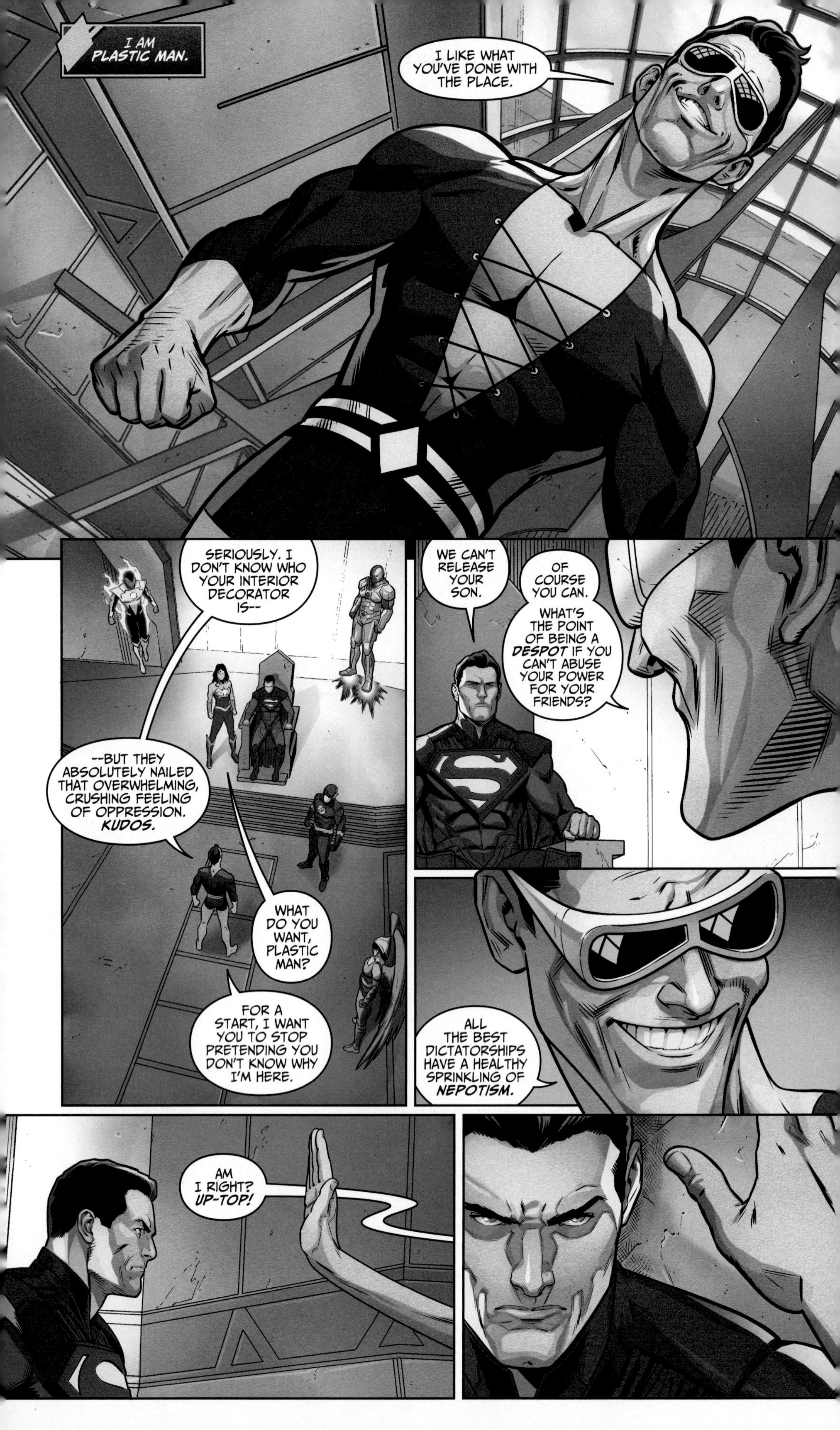
I AM PLASTIC MAN.
I LIKE WHAT YOU'VE DONE WITH THE PLACE.
SERIOUSLY. I DON'T KNOW WHO YOUR INTERIOR DECORATOR IS--
--BUT THEY ABSOLUTELY NAILED THAT OVERWHELMING, CRUSHING FEELING OF OPPRESSION. KUDOS.
WHAT DO YOU WANT, PLASTIC MAN?
FOR A START, I WANT YOU TO STOP PRETENDING YOU DON'T KNOW WHY I'M HERE.
WE CAN'T RELEASE YOUR SON.
OF COURSE YOU CAN.
WHAT'S THE POINT OF BEING A DESPOT IF YOU CAN'T ABUSE YOUR POWER FOR YOUR FRIENDS?
ALL THE BEST DICTATORSHIPS HAVE A HEALTHY SPRINKLING OF NEPOTISM.
AM I RIGHT? UP-TOP!

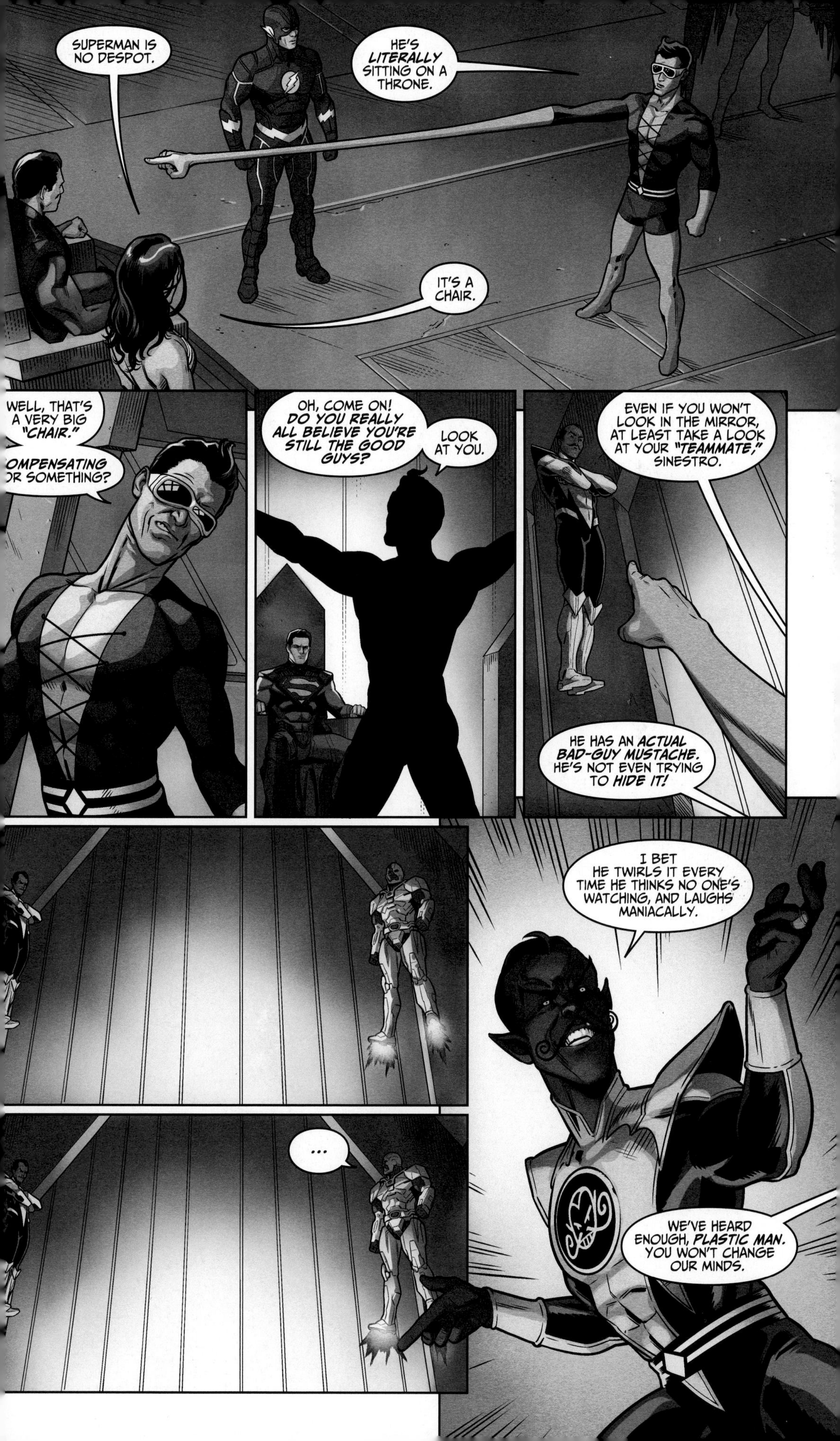

SUPERMAN IS NO DESPOT.
HE'S *LITERALLY* SITTING ON A THRONE.
IT'S A CHAIR.
WELL, THAT'S A VERY BIG *"CHAIR."*
COMPENSATING OR SOMETHING?
OH, COME ON! *DO YOU REALLY ALL BELIEVE YOU'RE STILL THE GOOD GUYS?*
LOOK AT YOU.
EVEN IF YOU WON'T LOOK IN THE MIRROR, AT LEAST TAKE A LOOK AT YOUR *"TEAMMATE,"* SINESTRO.
HE HAS AN *ACTUAL BAD-GUY MUSTACHE.* HE'S NOT EVEN TRYING TO *HIDE IT!*
I BET HE TWIRLS IT EVERY TIME HE THINKS NO ONE'S WATCHING, AND LAUGHS MANIACALLY.
...
WE'VE HEARD ENOUGH, *PLASTIC MAN.* YOU WON'T CHANGE OUR MINDS.

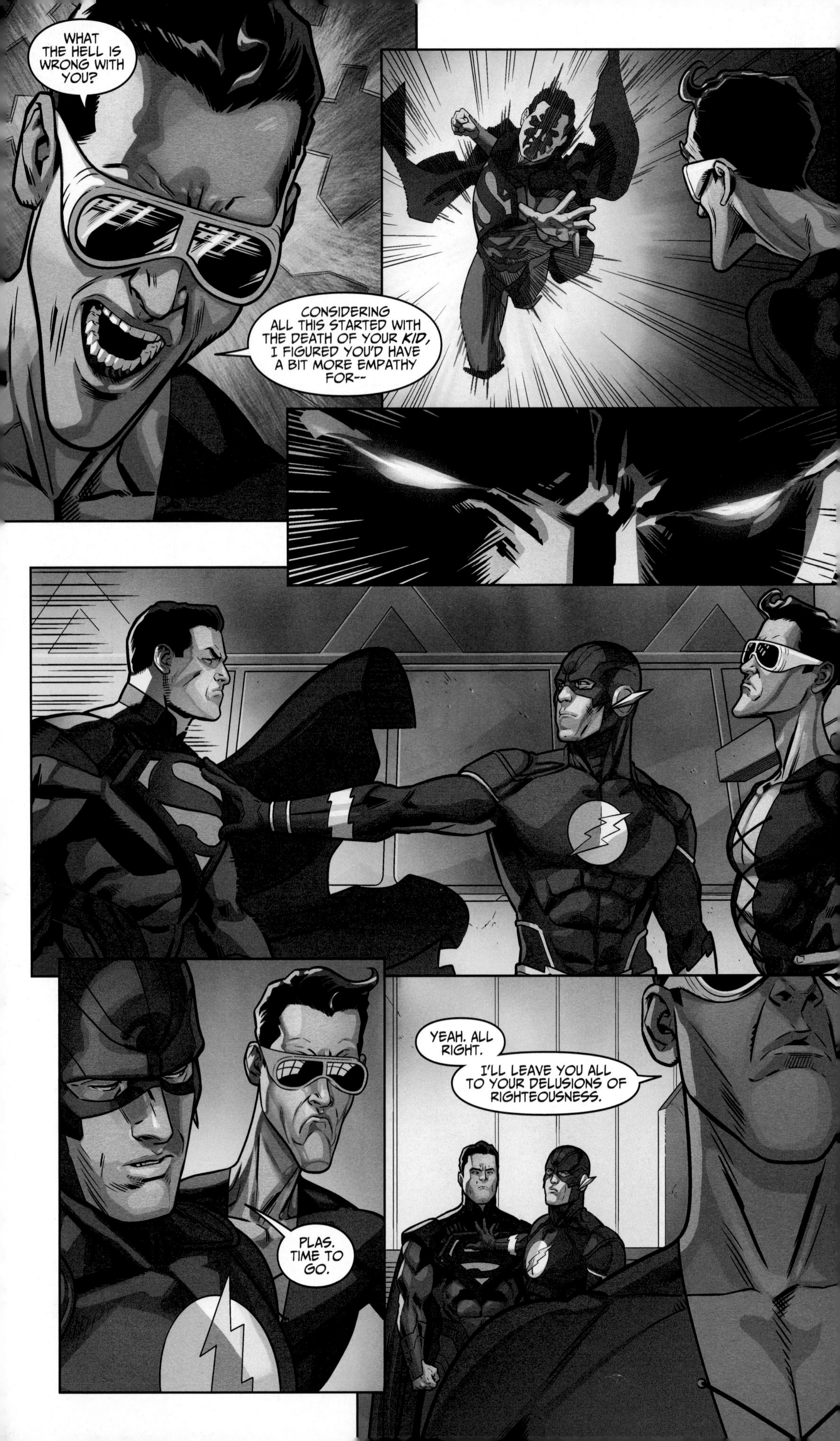
WHAT THE HELL IS WRONG WITH YOU?
CONSIDERING ALL THIS STARTED WITH THE DEATH OF YOUR KID, I FIGURED YOU'D HAVE A BIT MORE EMPATHY FOR--
PLAS. TIME TO GO.
YEAH. ALL RIGHT.
I'LL LEAVE YOU ALL TO YOUR DELUSIONS OF RIGHTEOUSNESS.

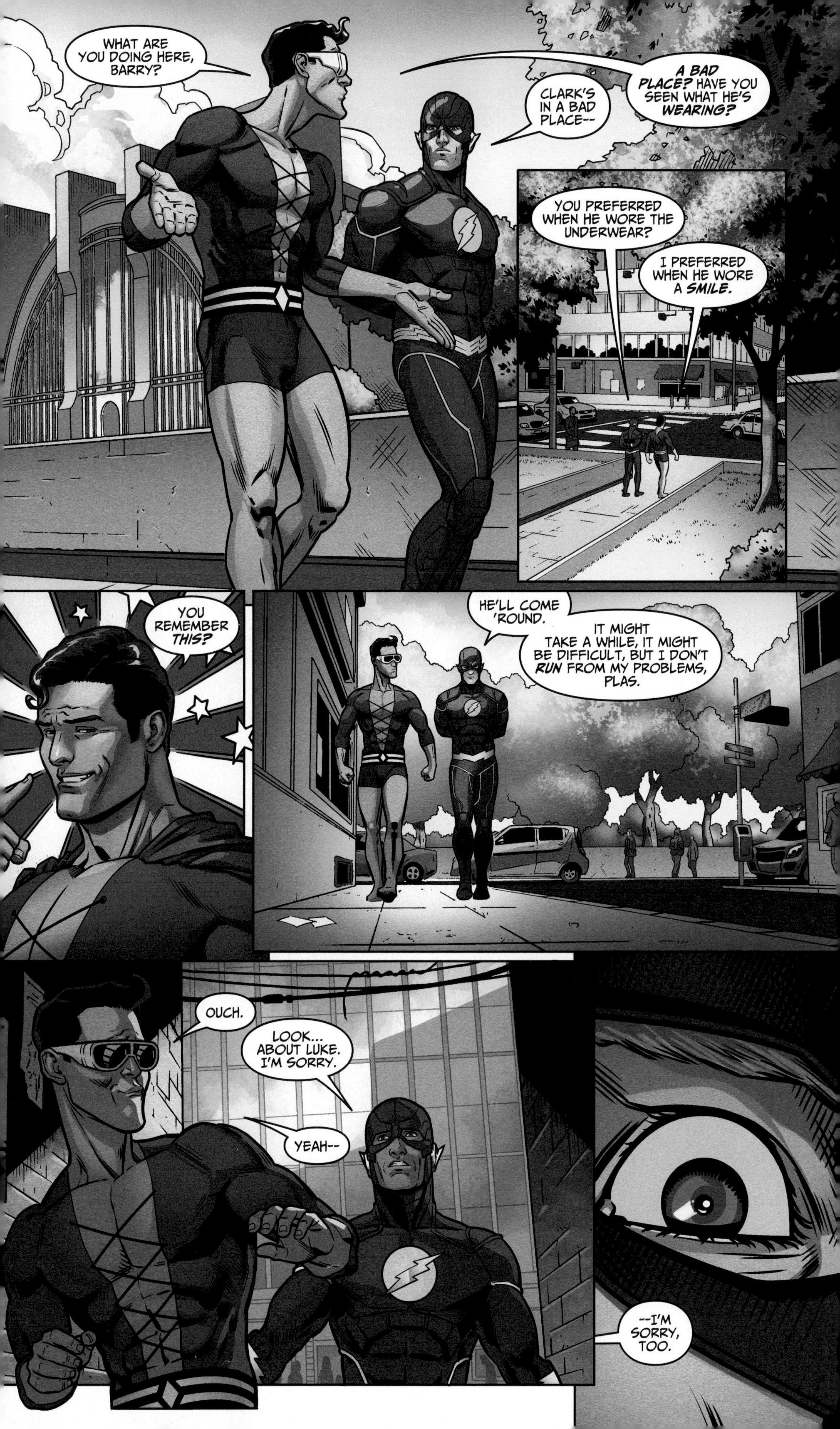
WHAT ARE YOU DOING HERE, BARRY?
CLARK'S IN A BAD PLACE--
A BAD PLACE? HAVE YOU SEEN WHAT HE'S WEARING?
YOU PREFERRED WHEN HE WORE THE UNDERWEAR?
I PREFERRED WHEN HE WORE A SMILE.
YOU REMEMBER THIS?
HE'LL COME 'ROUND.
IT MIGHT TAKE A WHILE, IT MIGHT BE DIFFICULT, BUT I DON'T RUN FROM MY PROBLEMS, PLAS.
OUCH.
LOOK... ABOUT LUKE. I'M SORRY.
YEAH--
--I'M SORRY, TOO.

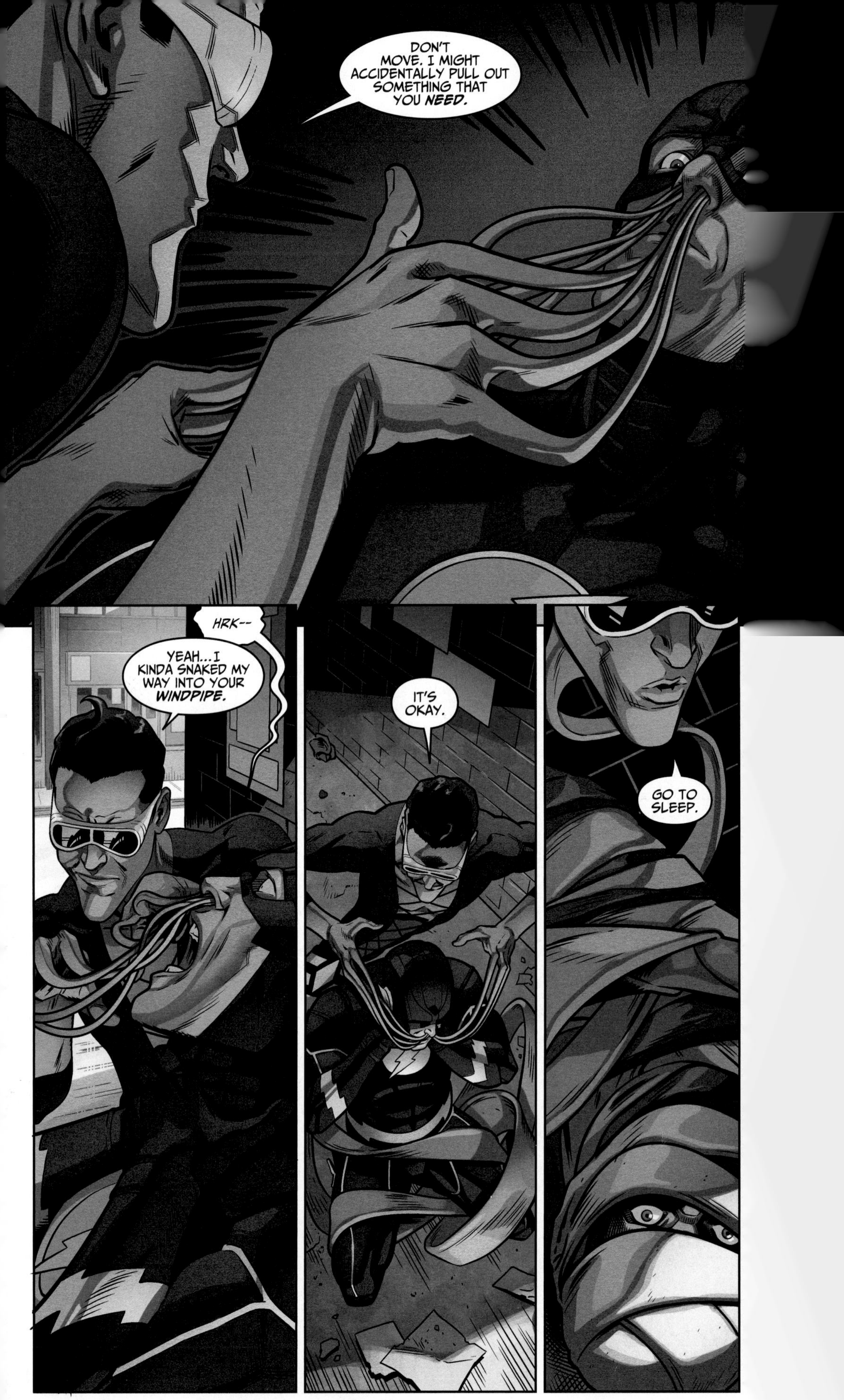
DON'T MOVE. I MIGHT ACCIDENTALLY PULL OUT SOMETHING THAT YOU *NEED.*
HRK--
YEAH...I KINDA SNAKED MY WAY INTO YOUR *WINDPIPE.*
IT'S OKAY.
GO TO SLEEP.

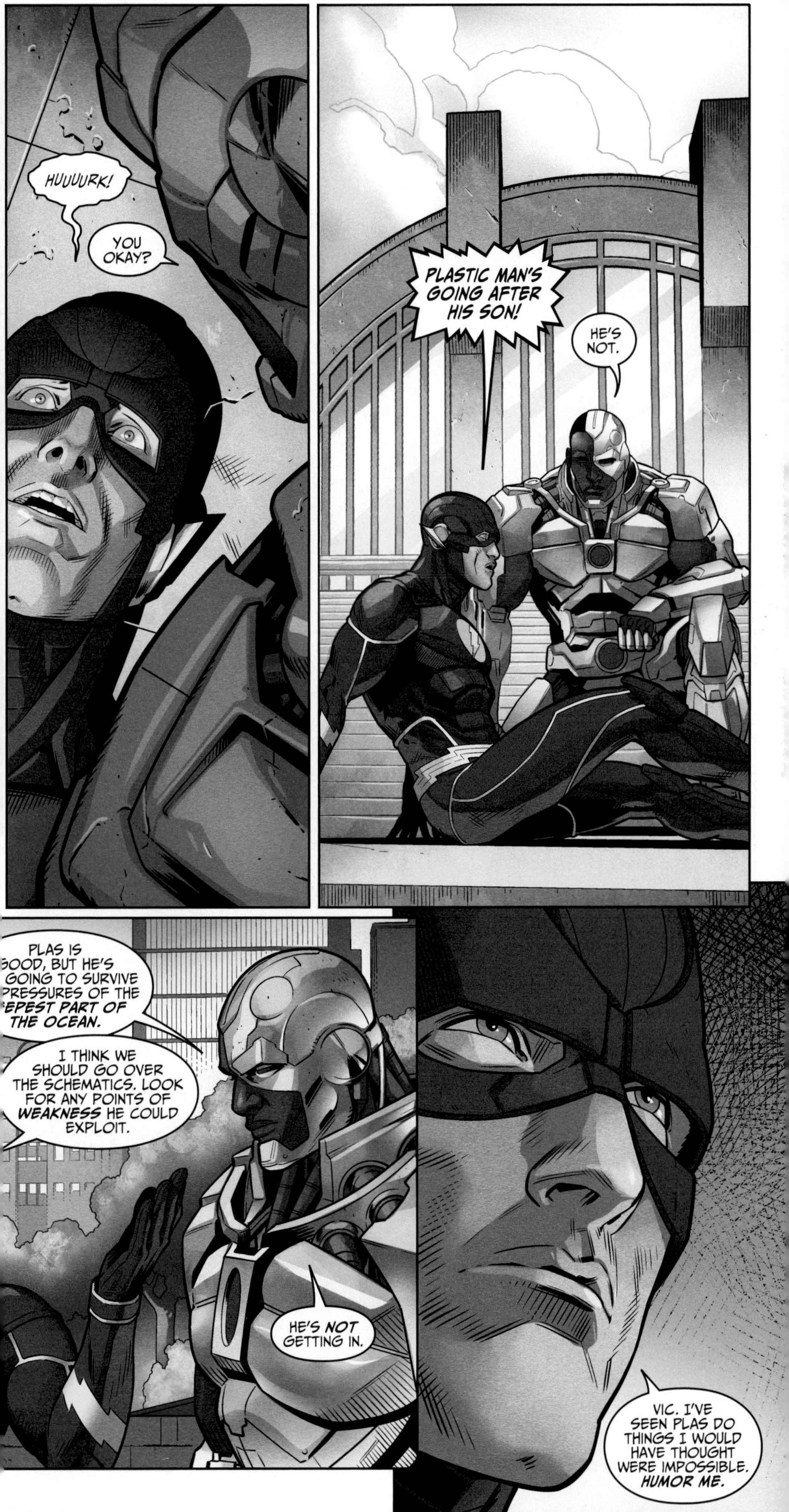
HUUUURK!
YOU OKAY?
PLASTIC MAN'S GOING AFTER HIS SON!
HE'S NOT.
PLAS IS OOD, BUT HE'S GOING TO SURVIVE PRESSURES OF THE EPEST PART OF THE OCEAN.
I THINK WE SHOULD GO OVER THE SCHEMATICS. LOOK FOR ANY POINTS OF WEAKNESS HE COULD EXPLOIT.
HE'S NOT GETTING IN.
VIC. I'VE SEEN PLAS DO THINGS I WOULD HAVE THOUGHT WERE IMPOSSIBLE. HUMOR ME.

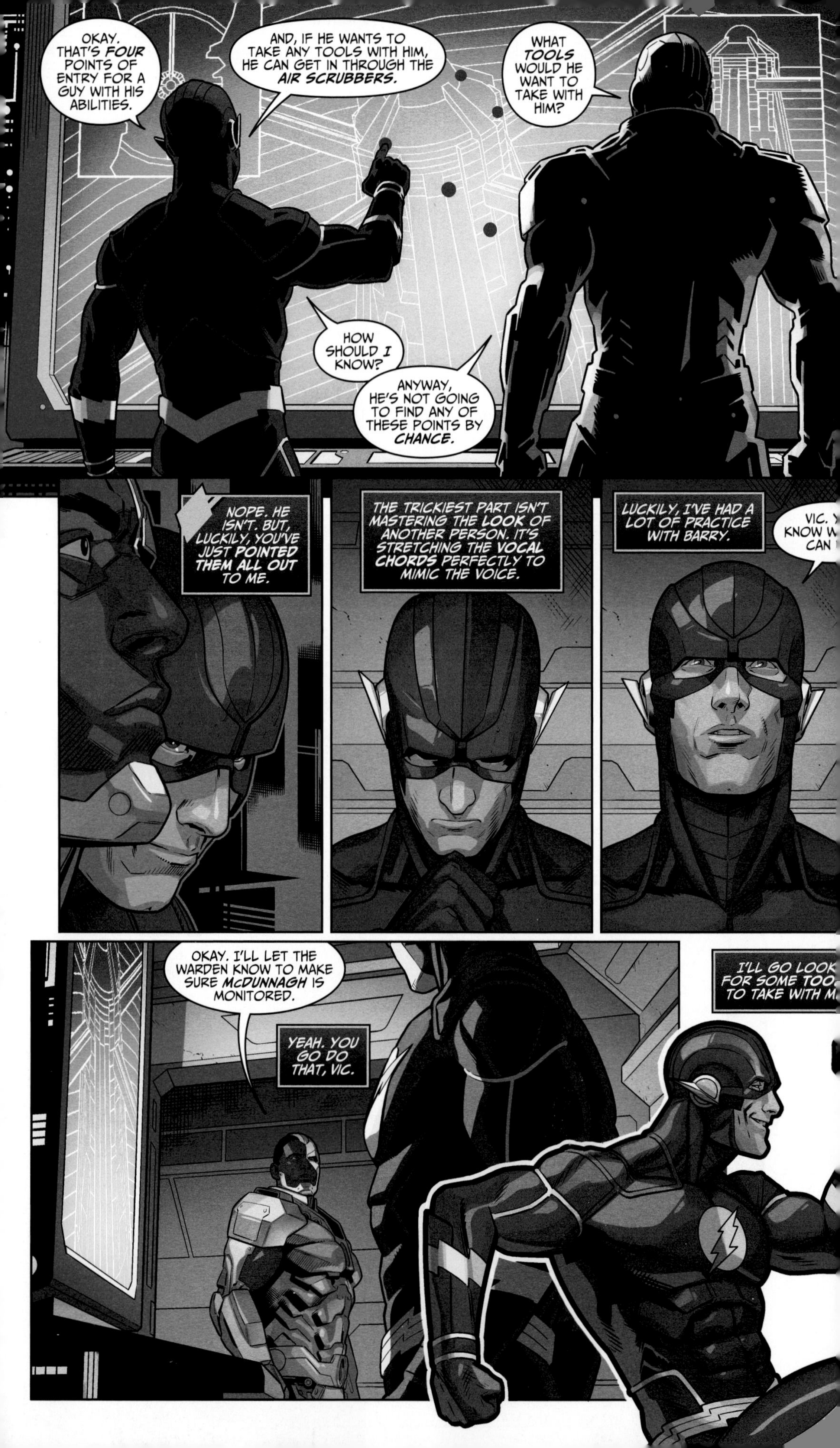
OKAY. THAT'S FOUR POINTS OF ENTRY FOR A GUY WITH HIS ABILITIES.
AND, IF HE WANTS TO TAKE ANY TOOLS WITH HIM, HE CAN GET IN THROUGH THE AIR SCRUBBERS.
WHAT TOOLS WOULD HE WANT TO TAKE WITH HIM?
HOW SHOULD I KNOW?
ANYWAY, HE'S NOT GOING TO FIND ANY OF THESE POINTS BY CHANCE.
NOPE. HE ISN'T. BUT, LUCKILY, YOU'VE JUST POINTED THEM ALL OUT TO ME.
THE TRICKIEST PART ISN'T MASTERING THE LOOK OF ANOTHER PERSON. IT'S STRETCHING THE VOCAL CHORDS PERFECTLY TO MIMIC THE VOICE.
LUCKILY, I'VE HAD A LOT OF PRACTICE WITH BARRY.
OKAY. I'LL LET THE WARDEN KNOW TO MAKE SURE McDUNNAGH IS MONITORED.
YEAH. YOU GO DO THAT, VIC.

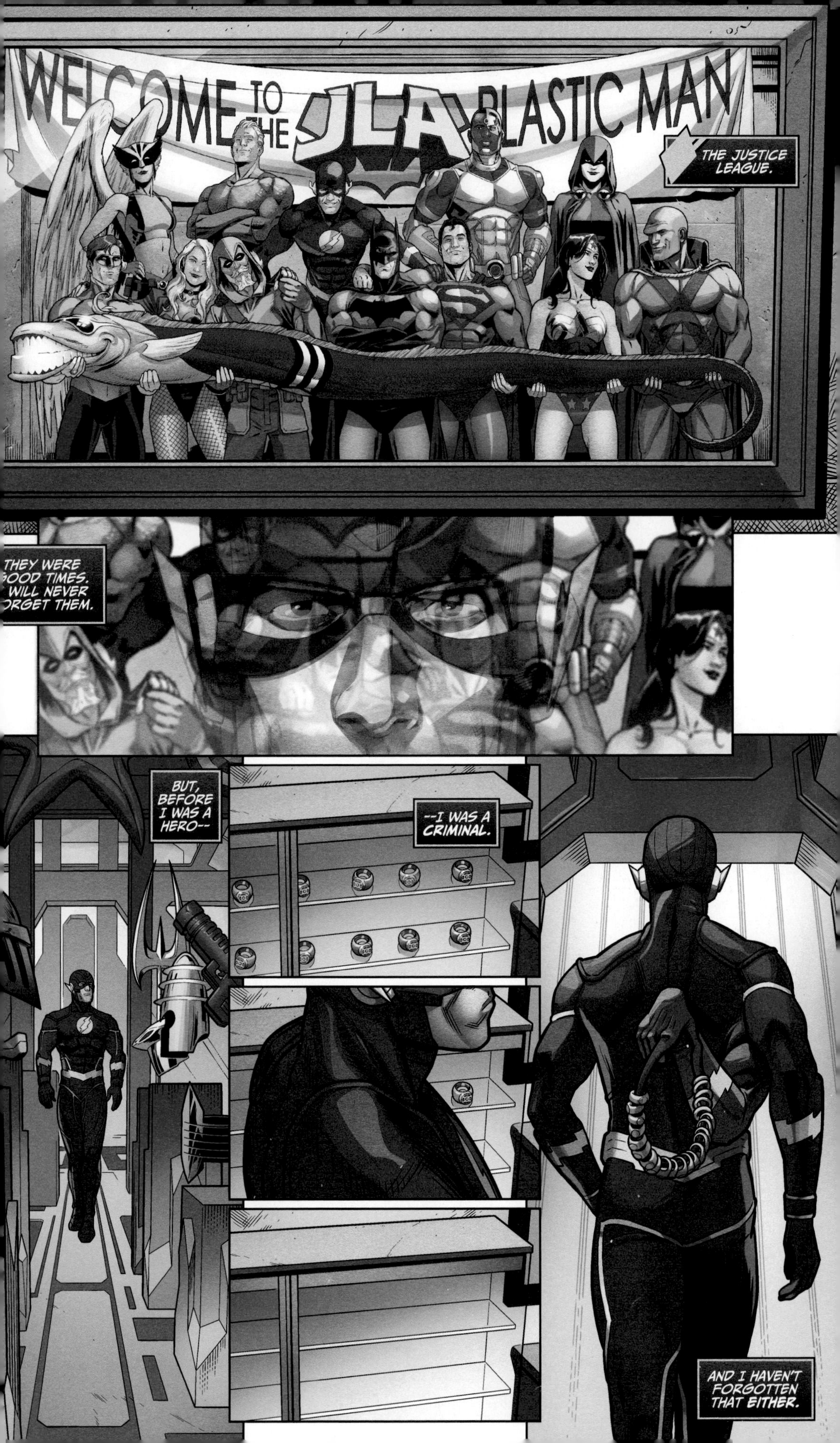
WELCOME TO THE JLA PLASTIC MAN
THE JUSTICE LEAGUE.
THEY WERE GOOD TIMES. I WILL NEVER FORGET THEM.
BUT, BEFORE I WAS A HERO--
--I WAS A CRIMINAL.
AND I HAVEN'T FORGOTTEN THAT EITHER.

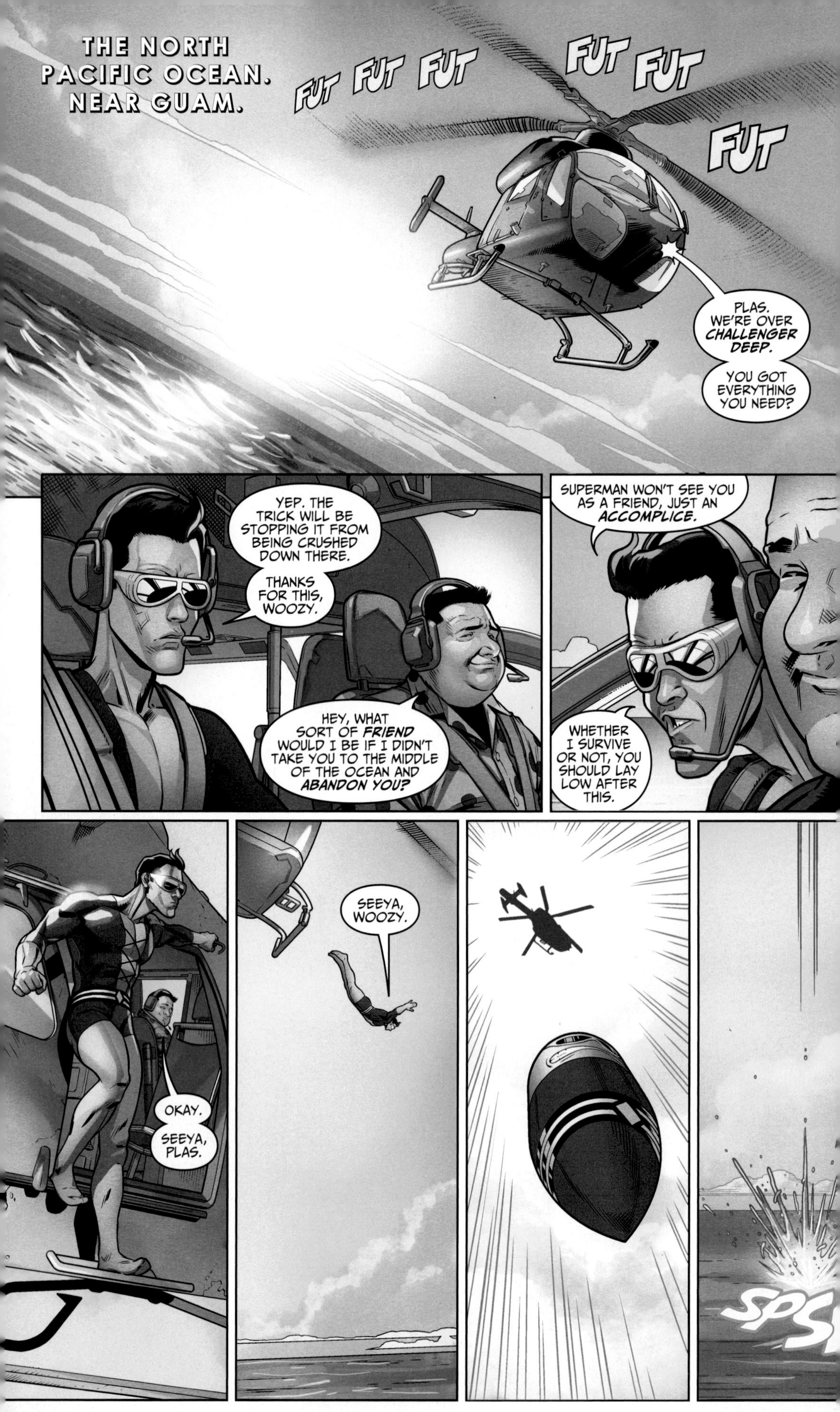
THE NORTH PACIFIC OCEAN. NEAR GUAM.
FUT FUT FUT
FUT FUT
FUT
PLAS. WE'RE OVER CHALLENGER DEEP.
YOU GOT EVERYTHING YOU NEED?
YEP. THE TRICK WILL BE STOPPING IT FROM BEING CRUSHED DOWN THERE.
THANKS FOR THIS, WOOZY.
HEY, WHAT SORT OF FRIEND WOULD I BE IF I DIDN'T TAKE YOU TO THE MIDDLE OF THE OCEAN AND ABANDON YOU?
SUPERMAN WON'T SEE YOU AS A FRIEND, JUST AN ACCOMPLICE.
WHETHER I SURVIVE OR NOT, YOU SHOULD LAY LOW AFTER THIS.
OKAY.
SEEYA, PLAS.
SEEYA, WOOZY.

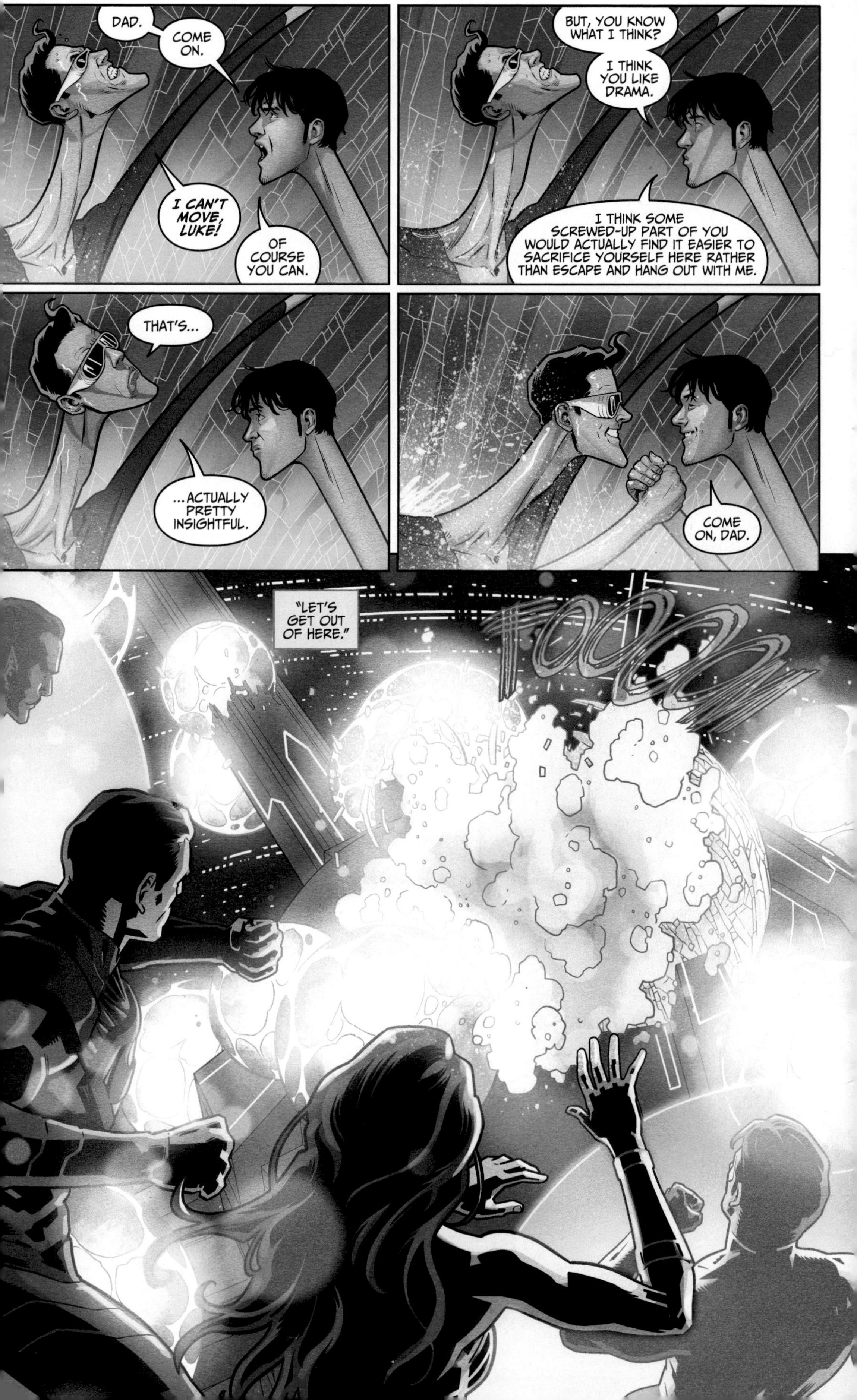
DAD.
COME ON.
I CAN'T MOVE, LUKE!
OF COURSE YOU CAN.
BUT, YOU KNOW WHAT I THINK?
I THINK YOU LIKE DRAMA.
I THINK SOME SCREWED-UP PART OF YOU WOULD ACTUALLY FIND IT EASIER TO SACRIFICE YOURSELF HERE RATHER THAN ESCAPE AND HANG OUT WITH ME.
THAT'S...
...ACTUALLY PRETTY INSIGHTFUL.
COME ON, DAD.
"LET'S GET OUT OF HERE."
TOOOOOM

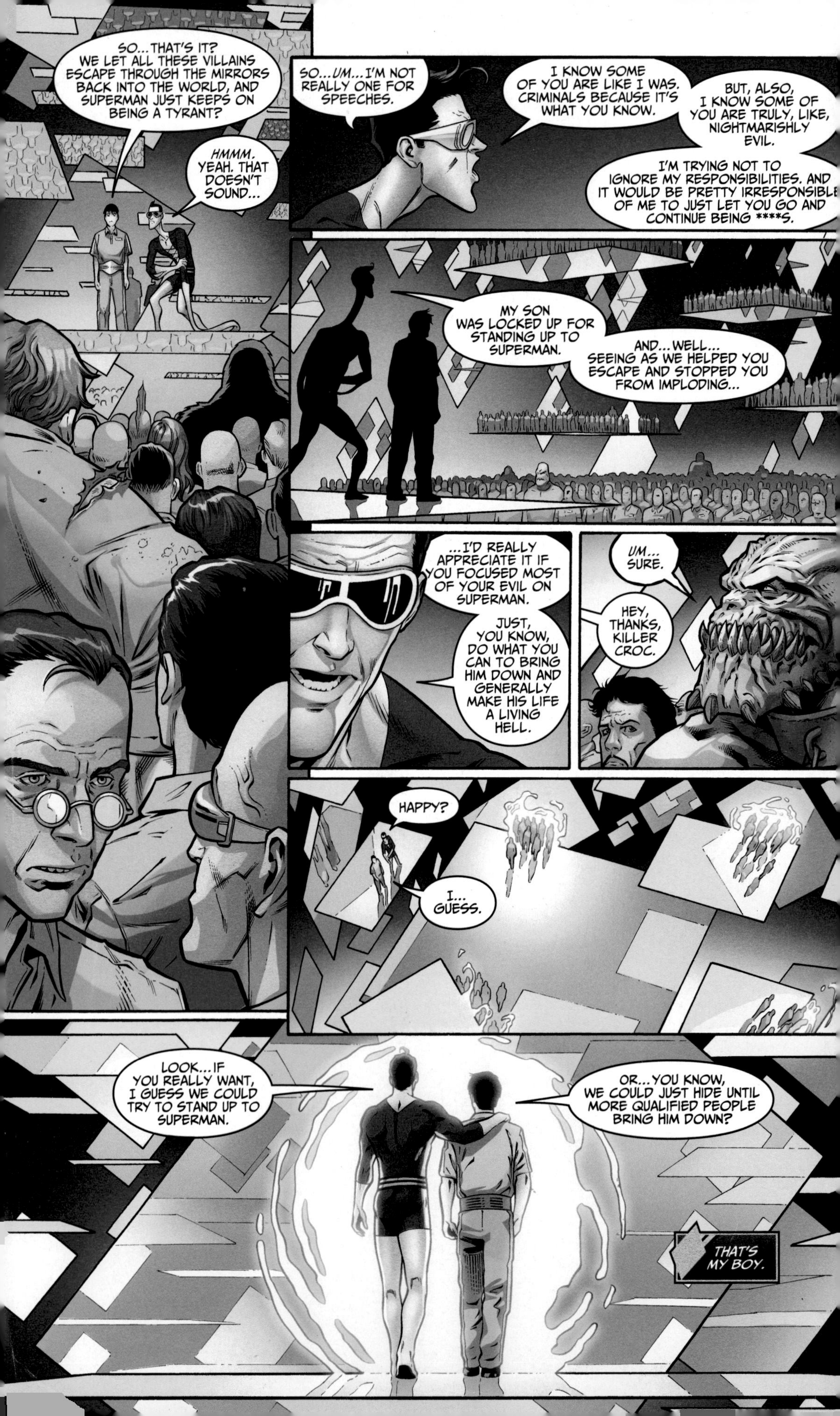
SO...THAT'S IT? WE LET ALL THESE VILLAINS ESCAPE THROUGH THE MIRRORS BACK INTO THE WORLD, AND SUPERMAN JUST KEEPS ON BEING A TYRANT?
HMMM. YEAH. THAT DOESN'T SOUND...
SO...UM...I'M NOT REALLY ONE FOR SPEECHES.
I KNOW SOME OF YOU ARE LIKE I WAS. CRIMINALS BECAUSE IT'S WHAT YOU KNOW.
BUT, ALSO, I KNOW SOME OF YOU ARE TRULY, LIKE, NIGHTMARISHLY EVIL.
I'M TRYING NOT TO IGNORE MY RESPONSIBILITIES. AND IT WOULD BE PRETTY IRRESPONSIBLE OF ME TO JUST LET YOU GO AND CONTINUE BEING ****S.
MY SON WAS LOCKED UP FOR STANDING UP TO SUPERMAN.
AND...WELL... SEEING AS WE HELPED YOU ESCAPE AND STOPPED YOU FROM IMPLODING...
...I'D REALLY APPRECIATE IT IF YOU FOCUSED MOST OF YOUR EVIL ON SUPERMAN.
JUST, YOU KNOW, DO WHAT YOU CAN TO BRING HIM DOWN AND GENERALLY MAKE HIS LIFE A LIVING HELL.
UM... SURE.
HEY, THANKS, KILLER CROC.
HAPPY?
I... GUESS.
LOOK...IF YOU REALLY WANT, I GUESS WE COULD TRY TO STAND UP TO SUPERMAN.
OR...YOU KNOW, WE COULD JUST HIDE UNTIL MORE QUALIFIED PEOPLE BRING HIM DOWN?
THAT'S MY BOY.

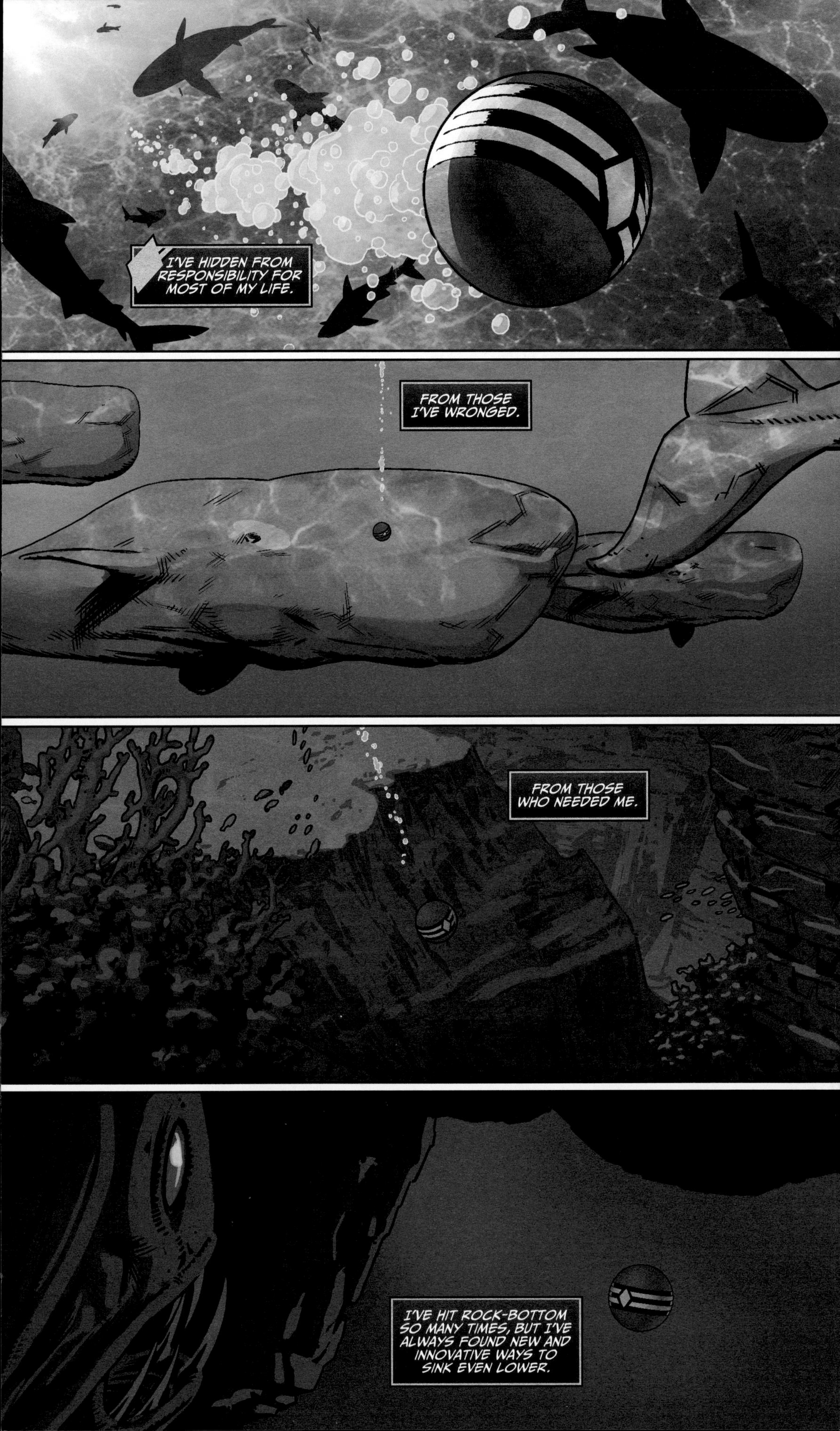
I'VE HIDDEN FROM RESPONSIBILITY FOR MOST OF MY LIFE.
FROM THOSE I'VE WRONGED.
FROM THOSE WHO NEEDED ME.
I'VE HIT ROCK-BOTTOM SO MANY TIMES, BUT I'VE ALWAYS FOUND NEW AND INNOVATIVE WAYS TO SINK EVEN LOWER.

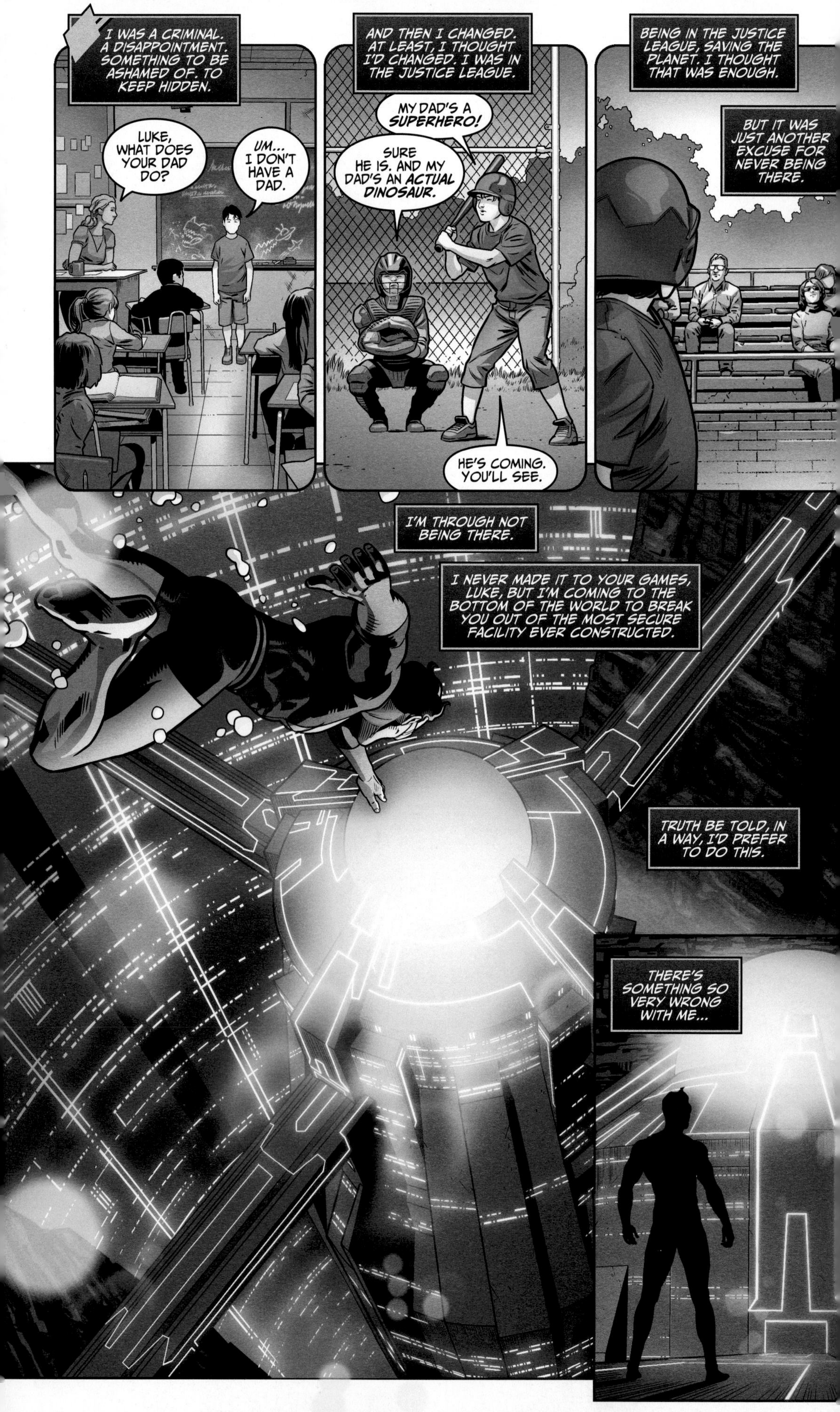
I WAS A CRIMINAL. A DISAPPOINTMENT. SOMETHING TO BE ASHAMED OF. TO KEEP HIDDEN.
LUKE, WHAT DOES YOUR DAD DO?
UM... I DON'T HAVE A DAD.
AND THEN I CHANGED. AT LEAST, I THOUGHT I'D CHANGED. I WAS IN THE JUSTICE LEAGUE.
MY DAD'S A SUPERHERO!
SURE HE IS. AND MY DAD'S AN ACTUAL DINOSAUR.
HE'S COMING. YOU'LL SEE.
BEING IN THE JUSTICE LEAGUE, SAVING THE PLANET. I THOUGHT THAT WAS ENOUGH.
BUT IT WAS JUST ANOTHER EXCUSE FOR NEVER BEING THERE.
I'M THROUGH NOT BEING THERE.
I NEVER MADE IT TO YOUR GAMES, LUKE, BUT I'M COMING TO THE BOTTOM OF THE WORLD TO BREAK YOU OUT OF THE MOST SECURE FACILITY EVER CONSTRUCTED.
TRUTH BE TOLD, IN A WAY, I'D PREFER TO DO THIS.
THERE'S SOMETHING SO VERY WRONG WITH ME...

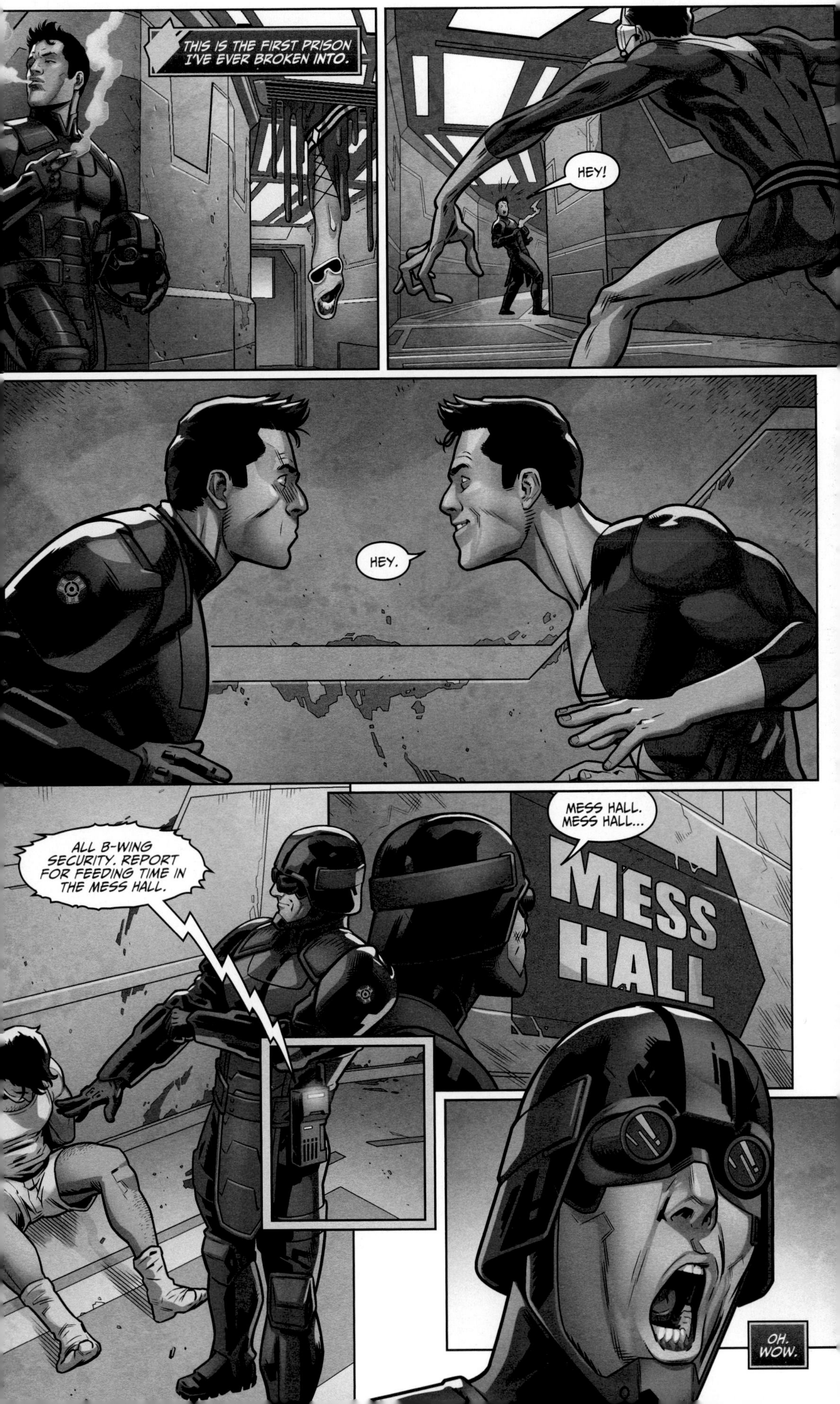
THIS IS THE FIRST PRISON I'VE EVER BROKEN INTO.
HEY!
HEY.
ALL B-WING SECURITY. REPORT FOR FEEDING TIME IN THE MESS HALL.
MESS HALL. MESS HALL...
MESS HALL
OH. WOW.

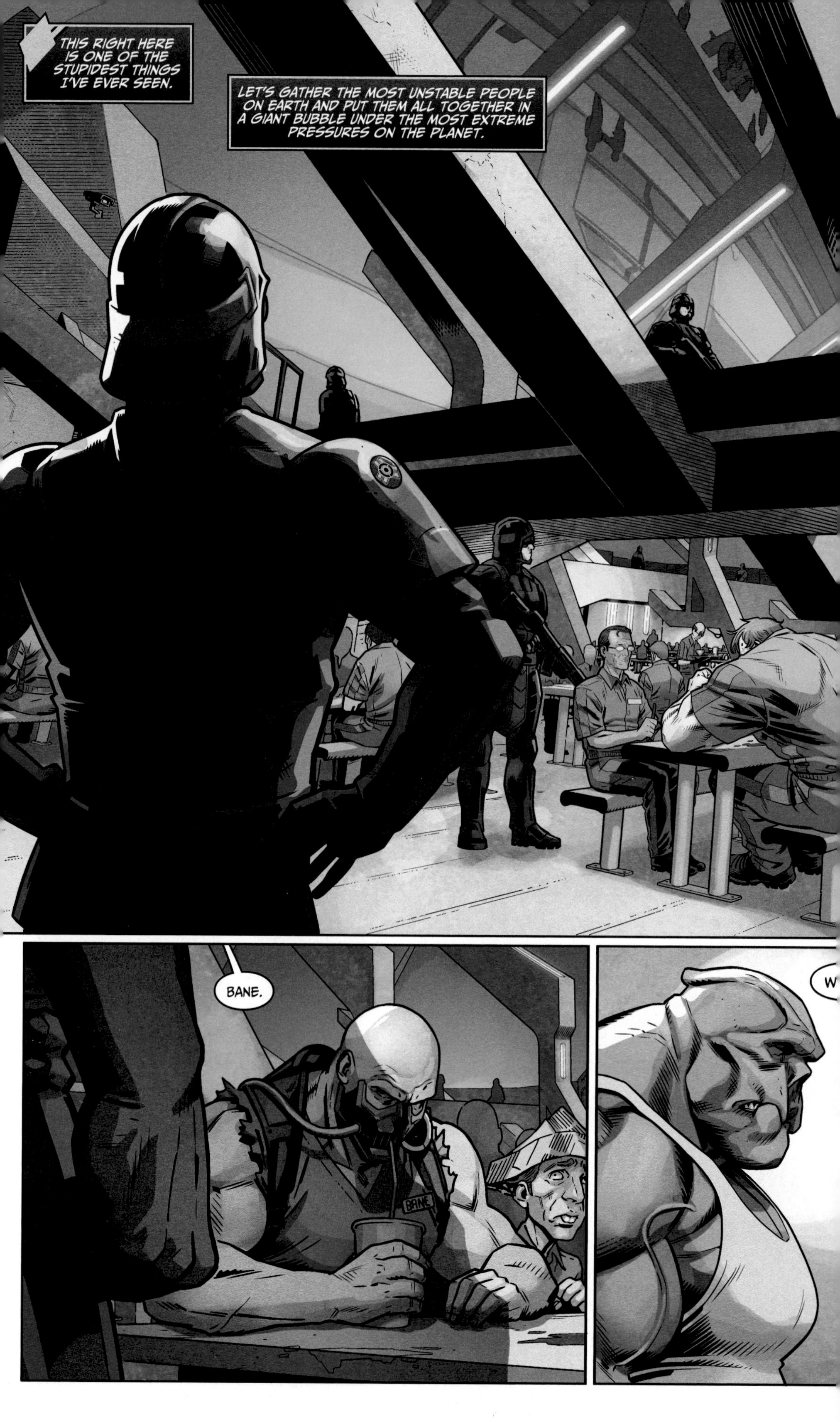
THIS RIGHT HERE IS ONE OF THE STUPIDEST THINGS I'VE EVER SEEN.
LET'S GATHER THE MOST UNSTABLE PEOPLE ON EARTH AND PUT THEM ALL TOGETHER IN A GIANT BUBBLE UNDER THE MOST EXTREME PRESSURES ON THE PLANET.
BANE.
BANE

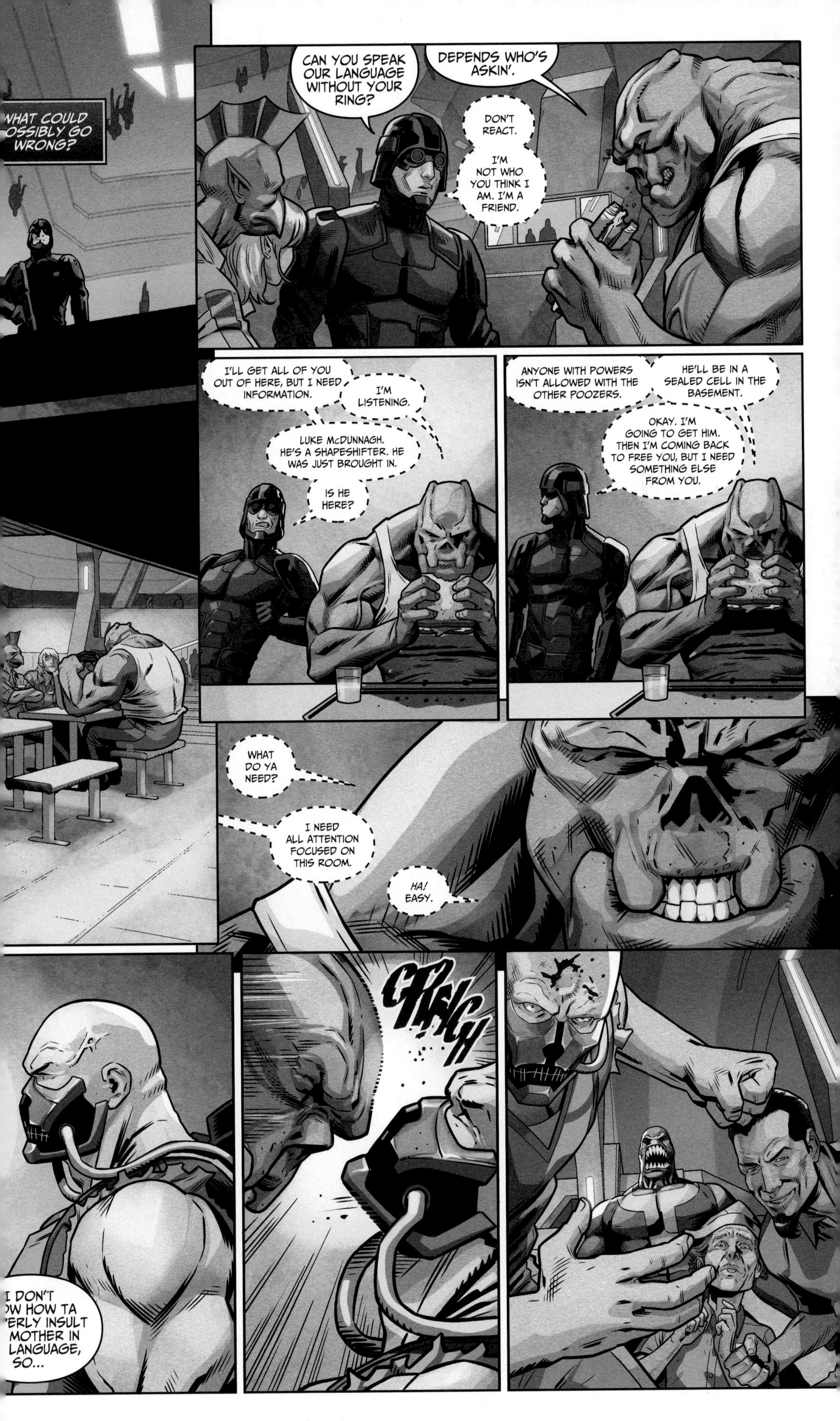
WHAT COULD
OSSIBLY GO
WRONG?
CAN YOU SPEAK OUR LANGUAGE WITHOUT YOUR RING?
DEPENDS WHO'S ASKIN'.
DON'T REACT.
I'M NOT WHO YOU THINK I AM. I'M A FRIEND.
I'LL GET ALL OF YOU OUT OF HERE, BUT I NEED INFORMATION.
I'M LISTENING.
LUKE McDUNNAGH. HE'S A SHAPESHIFTER. HE WAS JUST BROUGHT IN.
IS HE HERE?
ANYONE WITH POWERS ISN'T ALLOWED WITH THE OTHER POOZERS.
HE'LL BE IN A SEALED CELL IN THE BASEMENT.
OKAY. I'M GOING TO GET HIM. THEN I'M COMING BACK TO FREE YOU, BUT I NEED SOMETHING ELSE FROM YOU.
WHAT DO YA NEED?
I NEED ALL ATTENTION FOCUSED ON THIS ROOM.
HA! EASY.
I DON'T
W HOW TA
ERLY INSULT
MOTHER IN
LANGUAGE,
SO...
CRSSH

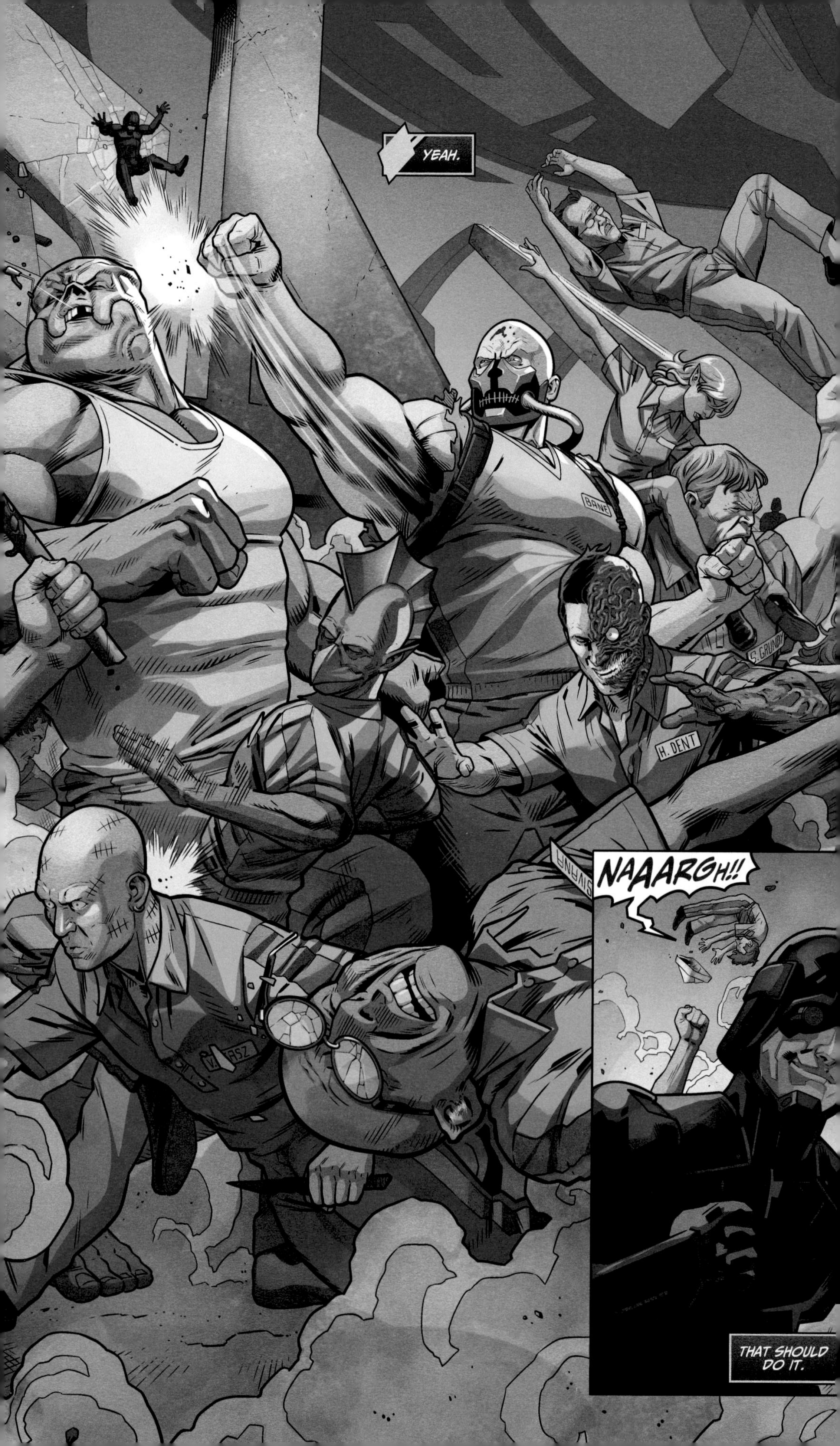
YEAH.
BANE
S. GRUNDY
H. DENT
NAAARGH!!
THAT SHOULD DO IT.

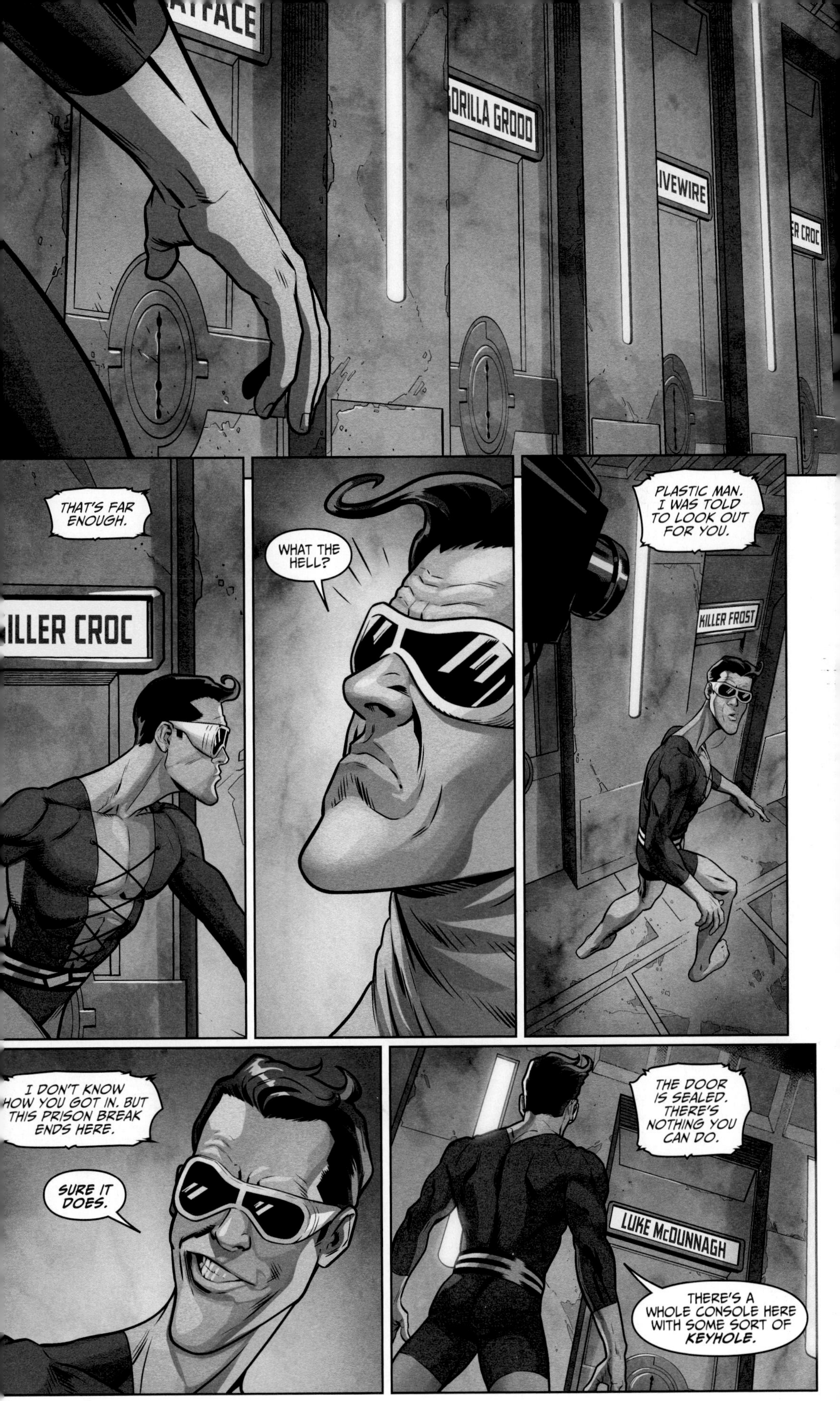

ATFACE
ORILLA GRODD
IVEWIRE
ER CROC
THAT'S FAR ENOUGH.
ILLER CROC
WHAT THE HELL?
PLASTIC MAN. I WAS TOLD TO LOOK OUT FOR YOU.
KILLER FROST
I DON'T KNOW HOW YOU GOT IN. BUT THIS PRISON BREAK ENDS HERE.
SURE IT DOES.
THE DOOR IS SEALED. THERE'S NOTHING YOU CAN DO.
LUKE McDUNNAGH
THERE'S A WHOLE CONSOLE HERE WITH SOME SORT OF KEYHOLE.

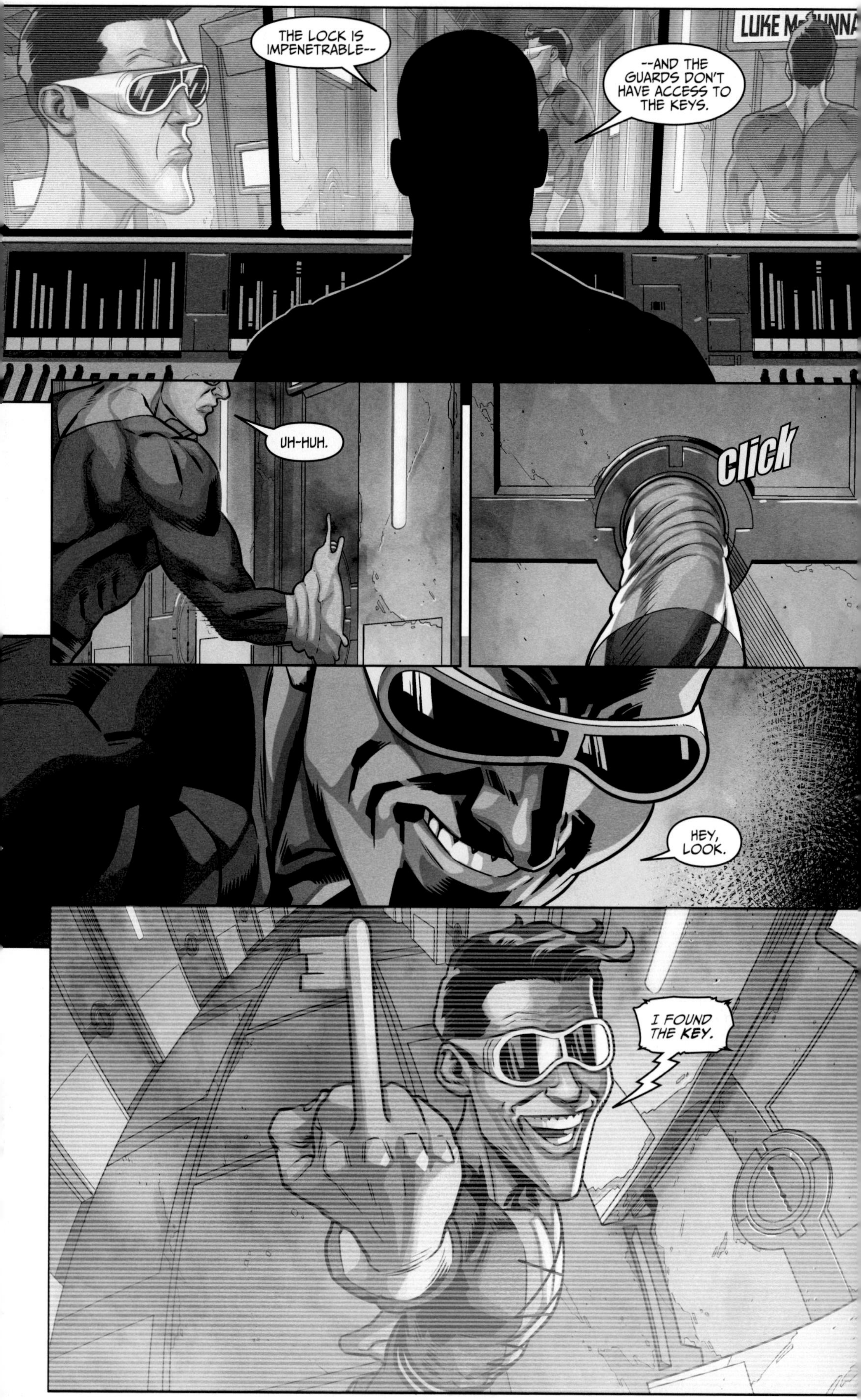
LUKE Mc
THE LOCK IS IMPENETRABLE--
--AND THE GUARDS DON'T HAVE ACCESS TO THE KEYS.
UH-HUH.
CLICK
HEY, LOOK.
I FOUND THE KEY.

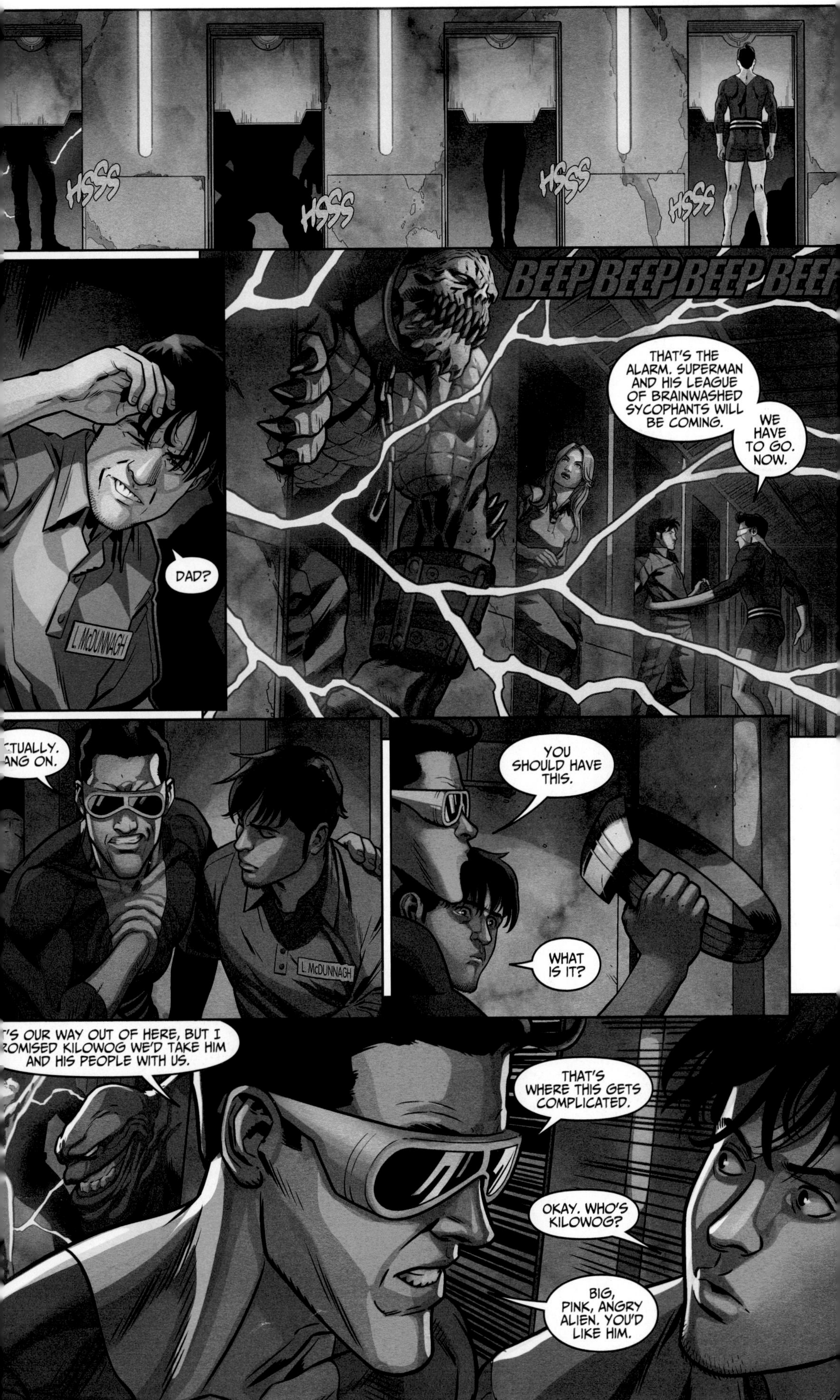
HSSS
HSSS
HSSS
HSSS
BEEP BEEP BEEP BEEP
DAD?
L. McDUNNAGH
THAT'S THE ALARM. SUPERMAN AND HIS LEAGUE OF BRAINWASHED SYCOPHANTS WILL BE COMING.
WE HAVE TO GO. NOW.
TUALLY. ANG ON.
L. McDUNNAGH
YOU SHOULD HAVE THIS.
WHAT IS IT?
'S OUR WAY OUT OF HERE, BUT I ROMISED KILOWOG WE'D TAKE HIM AND HIS PEOPLE WITH US.
THAT'S WHERE THIS GETS COMPLICATED.
OKAY. WHO'S KILOWOG?
BIG, PINK, ANGRY ALIEN. YOU'D LIKE HIM.

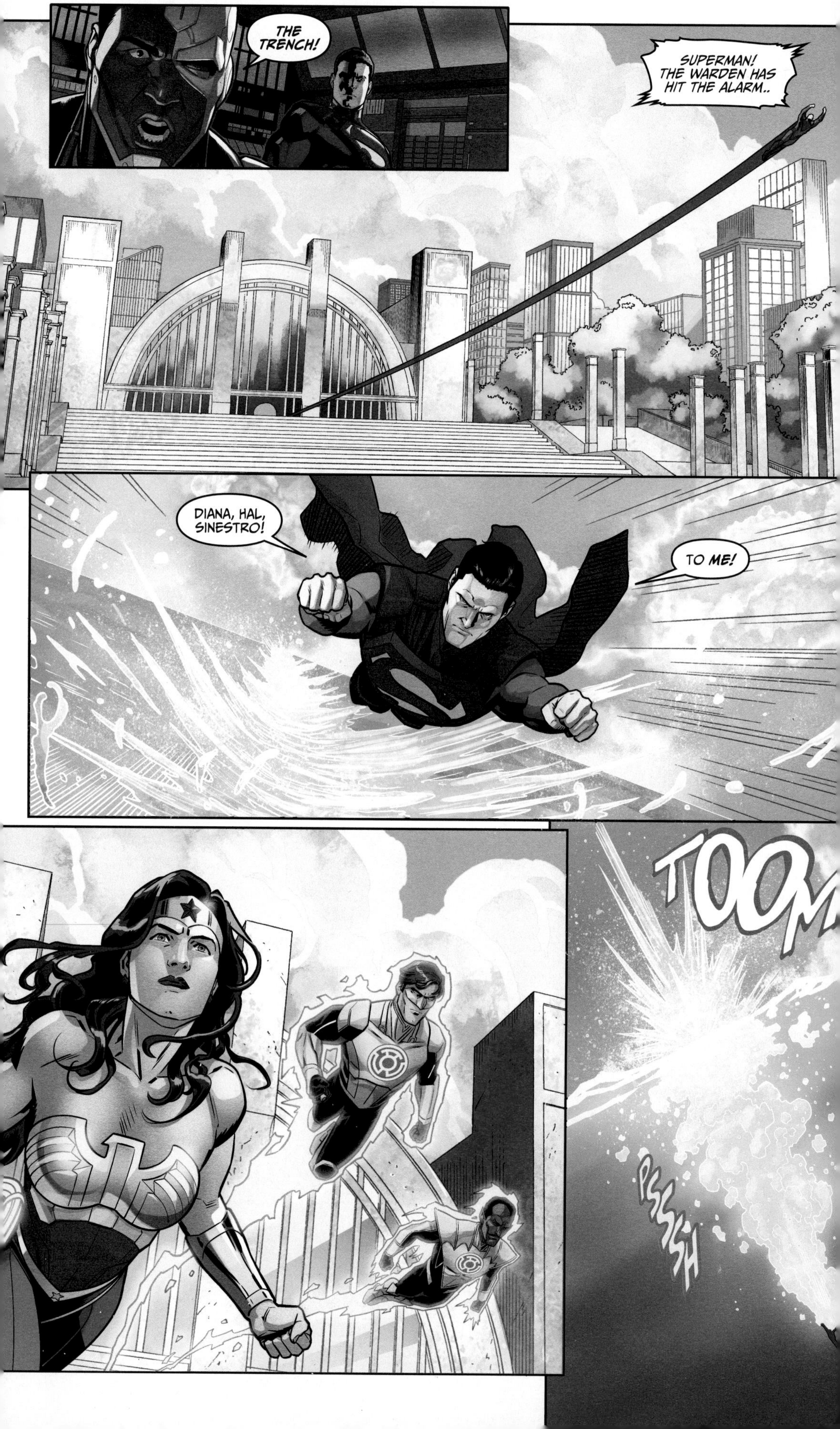
THE TRENCH!
SUPERMAN! THE WARDEN HAS HIT THE ALARM..
DIANA, HAL, SINESTRO!
TO ME!
TOOM
PSSSH

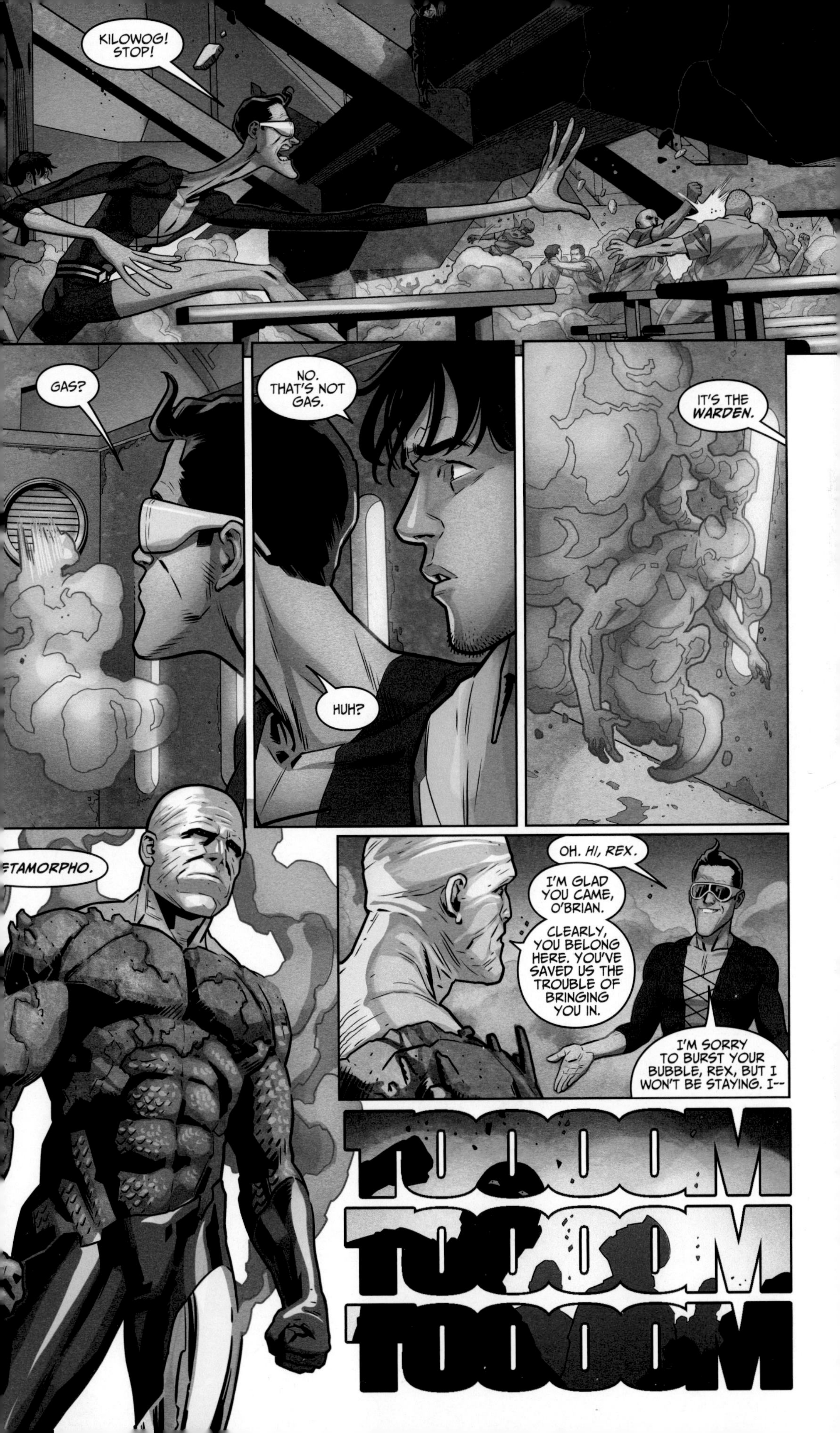
KILOWOG! STOP!
GAS?
NO. THAT'S NOT GAS.
HUH?
IT'S THE *WARDEN.*
ETAMORPHO.
OH. *HI, REX.*
I'M GLAD YOU CAME, O'BRIAN.
CLEARLY, YOU BELONG HERE. YOU'VE SAVED US THE TROUBLE OF BRINGING YOU IN.
I'M SORRY TO BURST YOUR BUBBLE, REX, BUT I WON'T BE STAYING. I--
TOOOOM
TOOOOM
TOOOOM

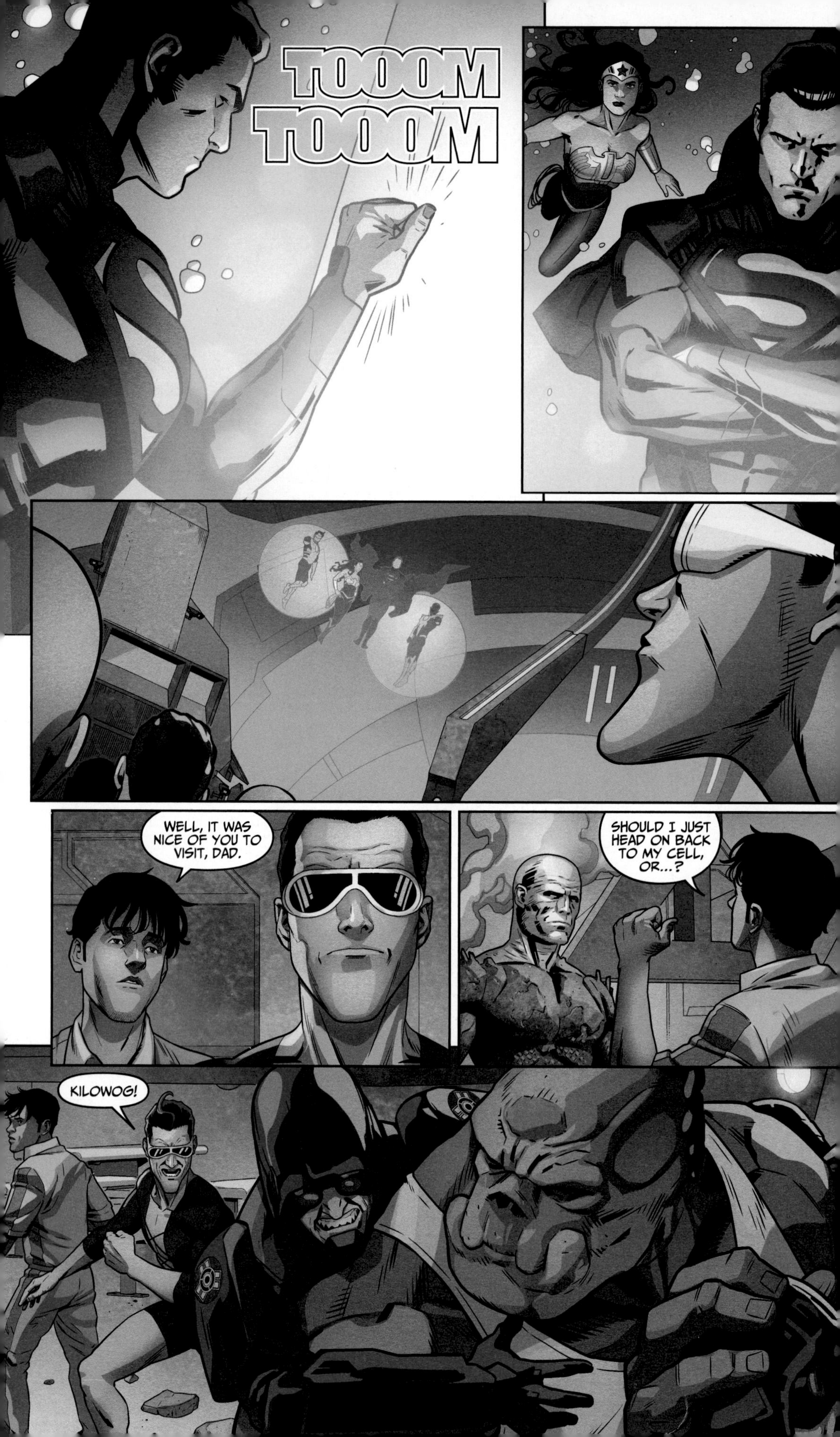
TOOOM
TOOOM
WELL, IT WAS NICE OF YOU TO VISIT, DAD.
SHOULD I JUST HEAD ON BACK TO MY CELL, OR...?
KILOWOG!

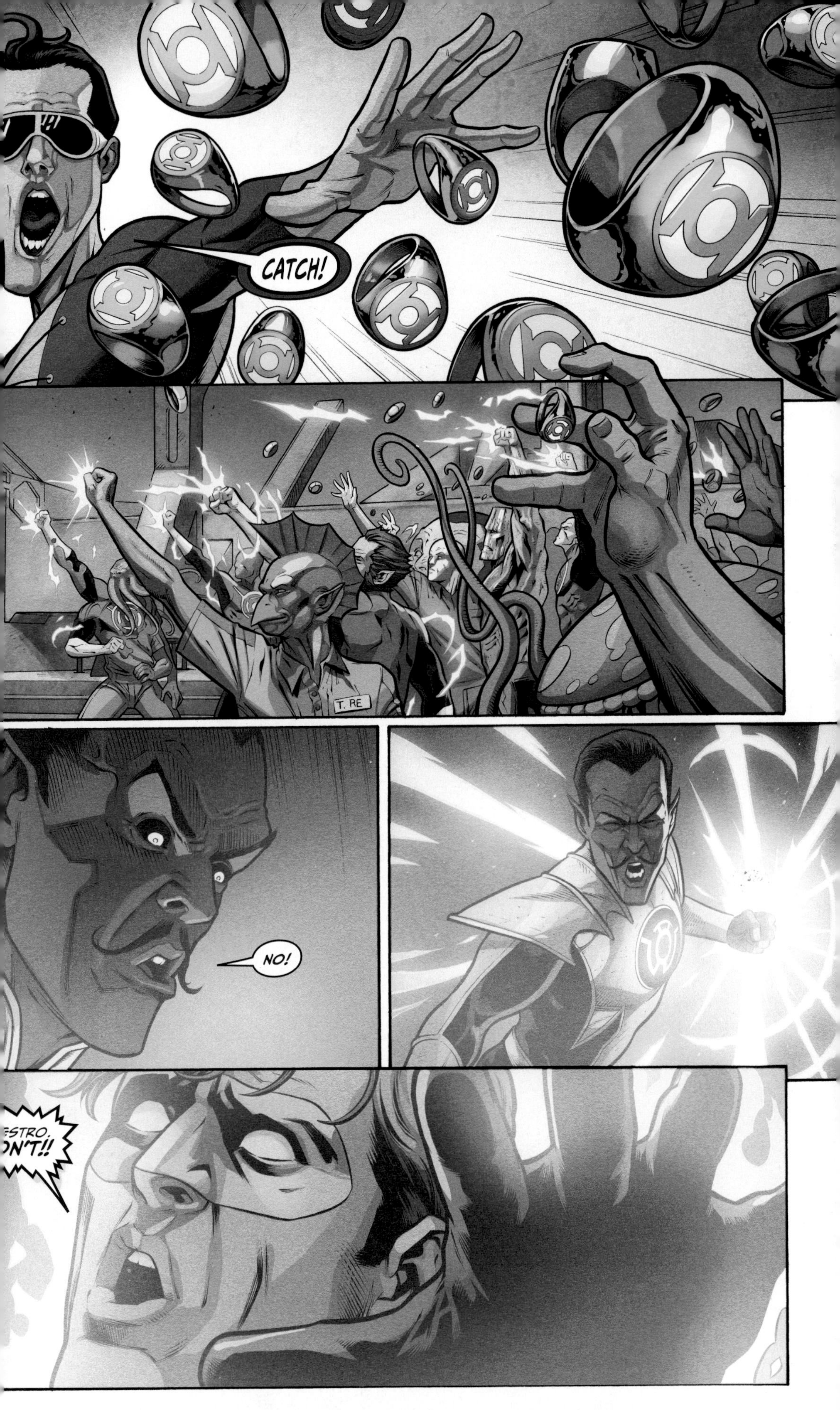
CATCH!
T. RE
NO!
ESTRO,
ON'T!!

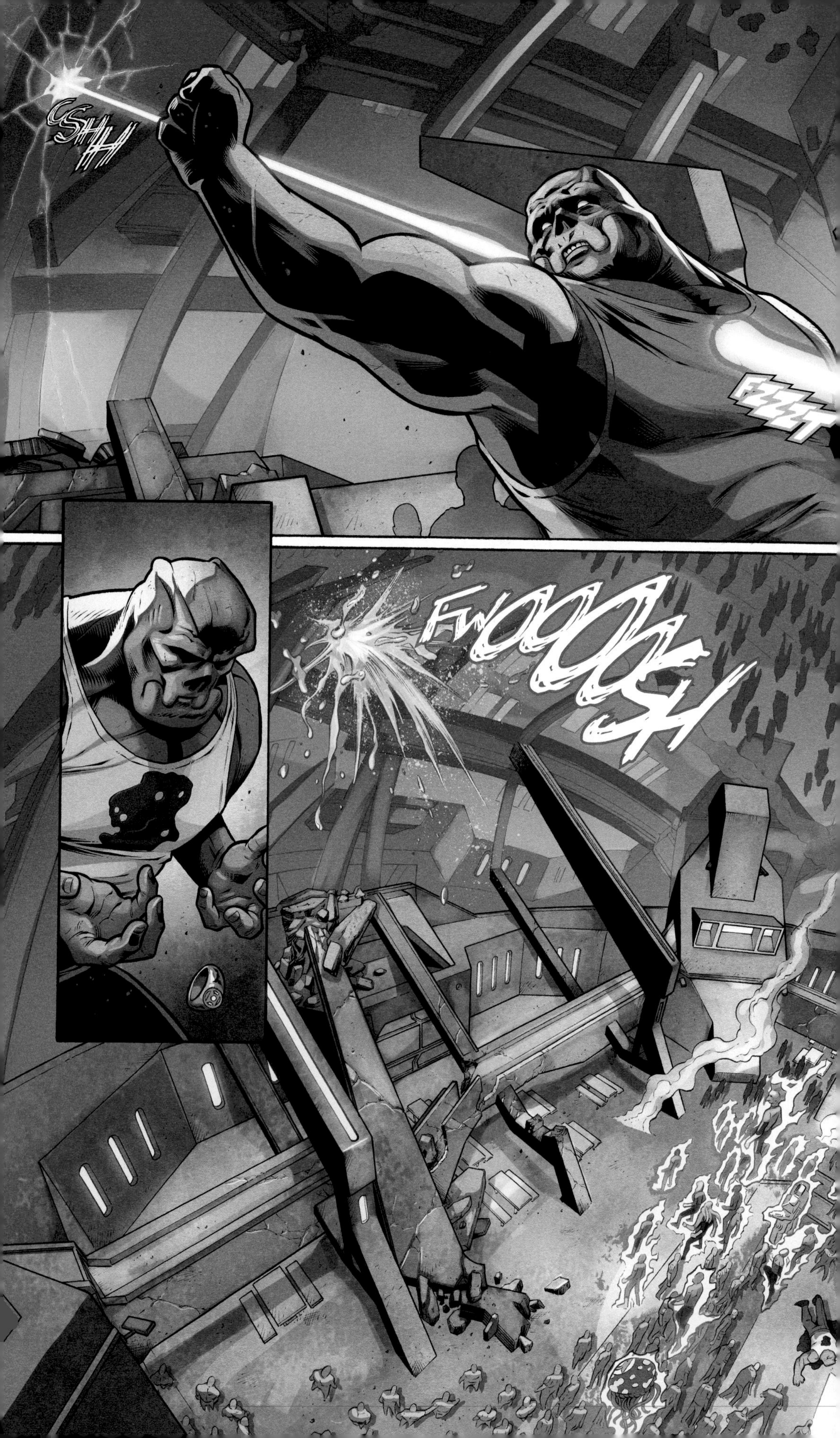
CSHH
FZZZT
FWOOOOSH

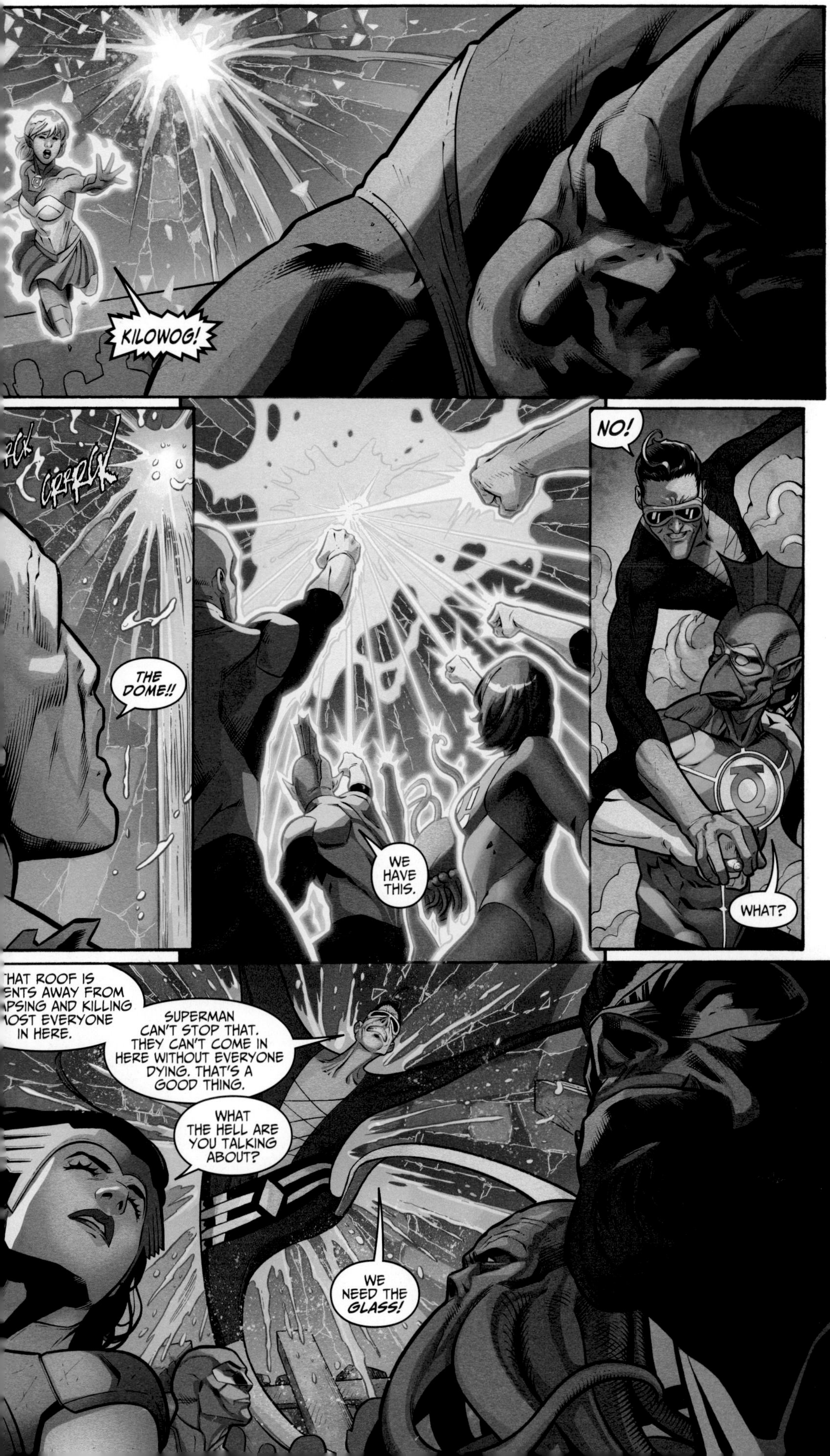
KILOWOG!
CRRRCK
THE DOME!!
WE HAVE THIS.
NO!
WHAT?
THAT ROOF IS
ENTS AWAY FROM
APSING AND KILLING
OST EVERYONE
IN HERE.
SUPERMAN CAN'T STOP THAT. THEY CAN'T COME IN HERE WITHOUT EVERYONE DYING. THAT'S A GOOD THING.
WHAT THE HELL ARE YOU TALKING ABOUT?
WE NEED THE *GLASS!*

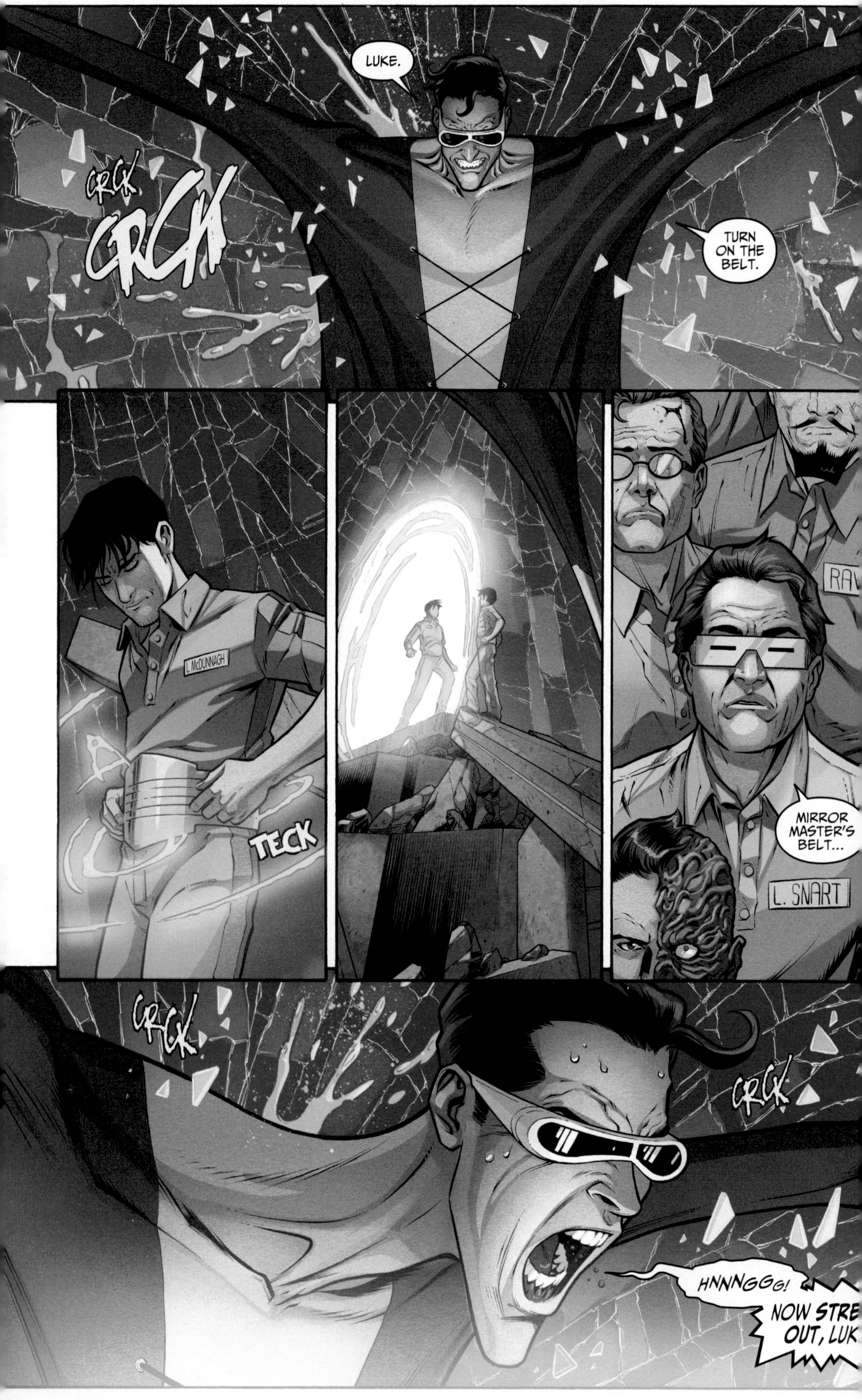
LUKE.
CRCK
CRCK
TURN ON THE BELT.
L. McDUNNAGH
TECK
MIRROR MASTER'S BELT...
L. SNART
CRCK
CRCK
HNNNGGg!
NOW STRE
OUT, LUK

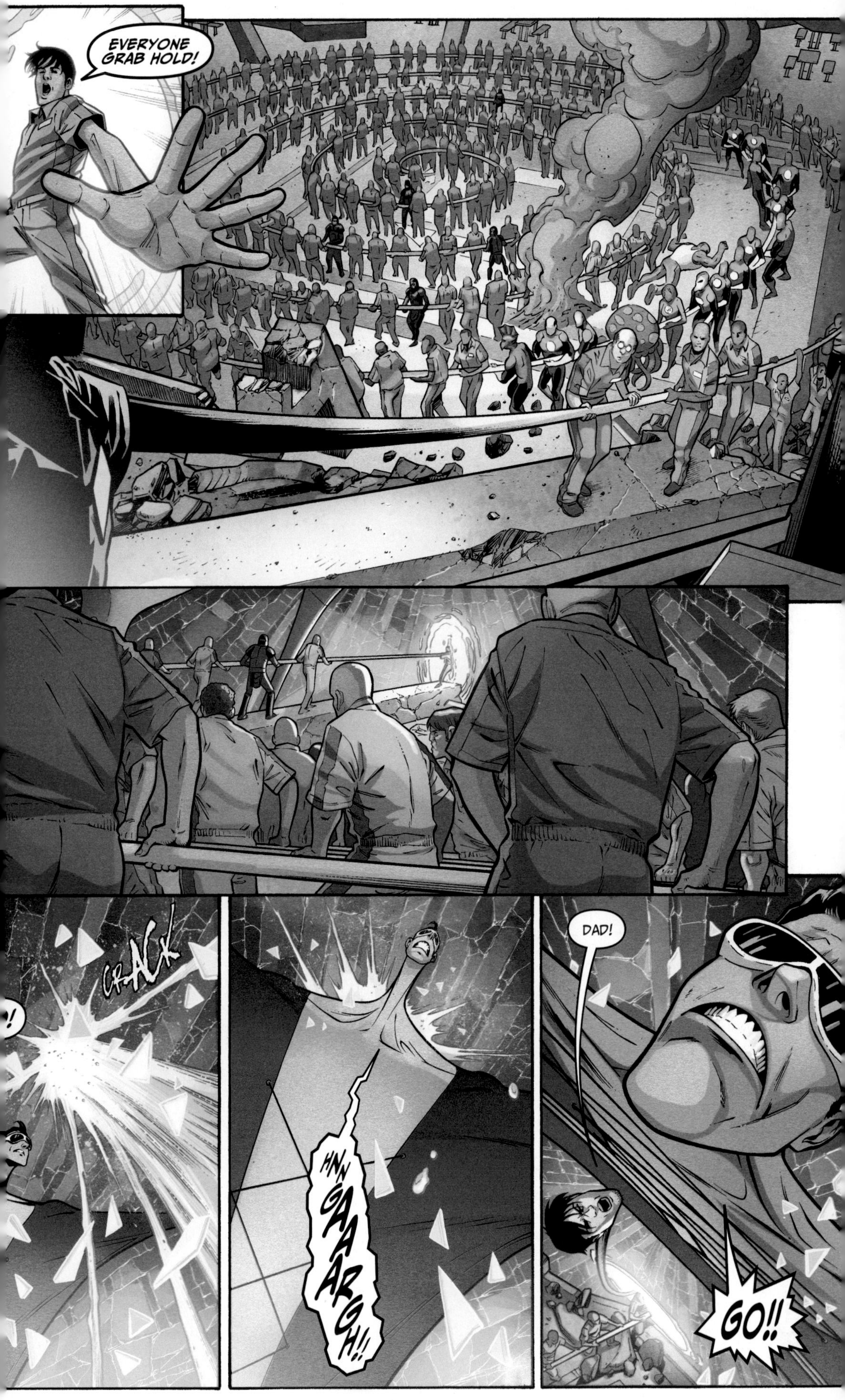
EVERYONE GRAB HOLD!
CRACK
HNN GAAAARGH!!
DAD!
GO!!

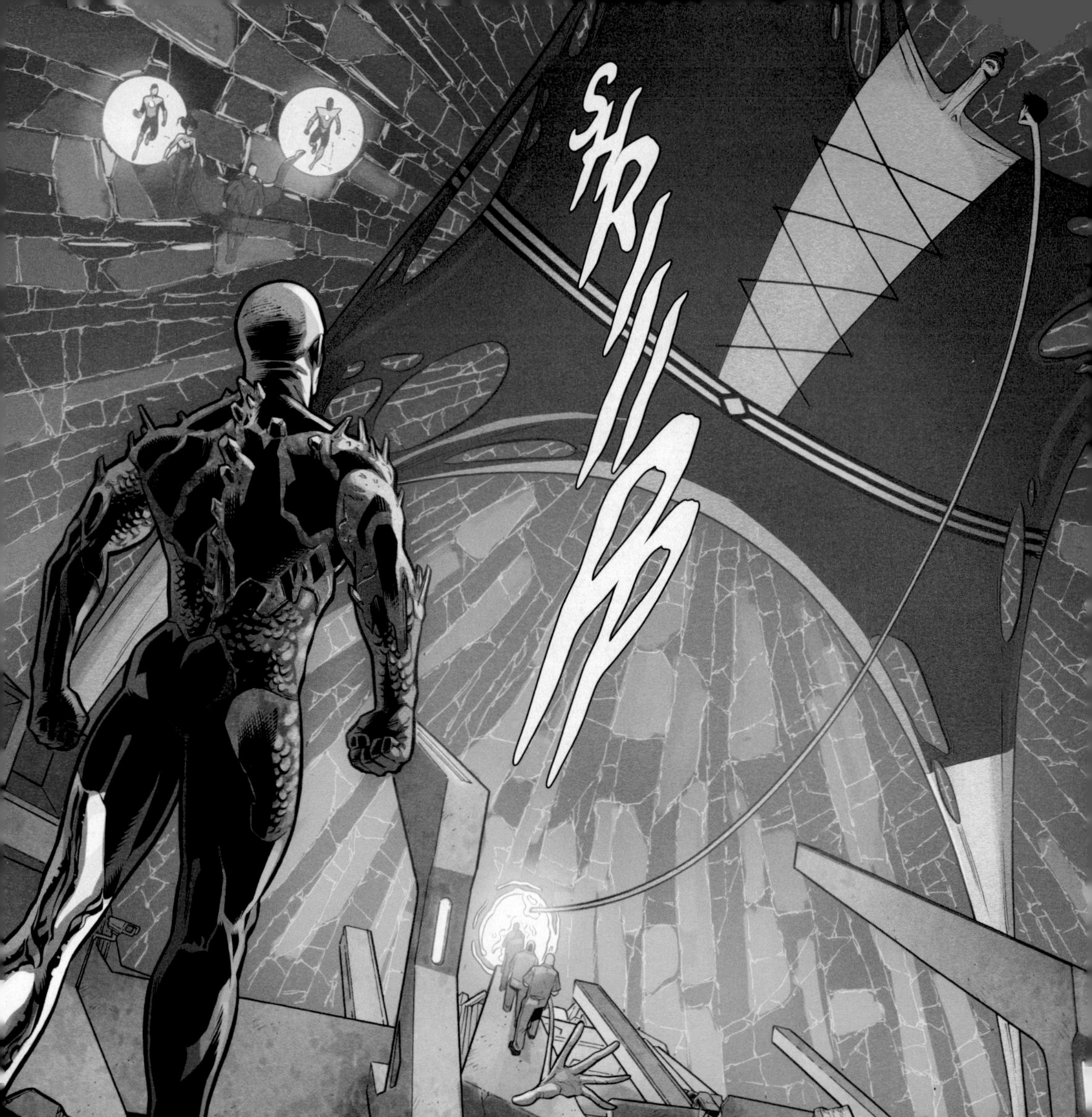

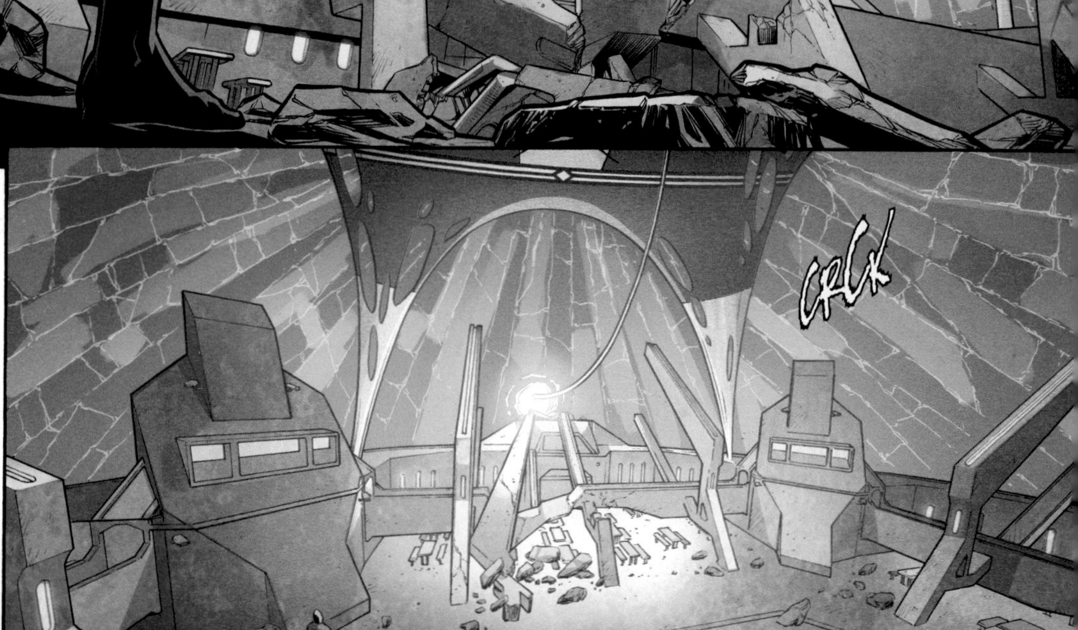
CRCK

INJUSTICE YEAR FOUR #1 variant cover by **MATTHEW CLARK**

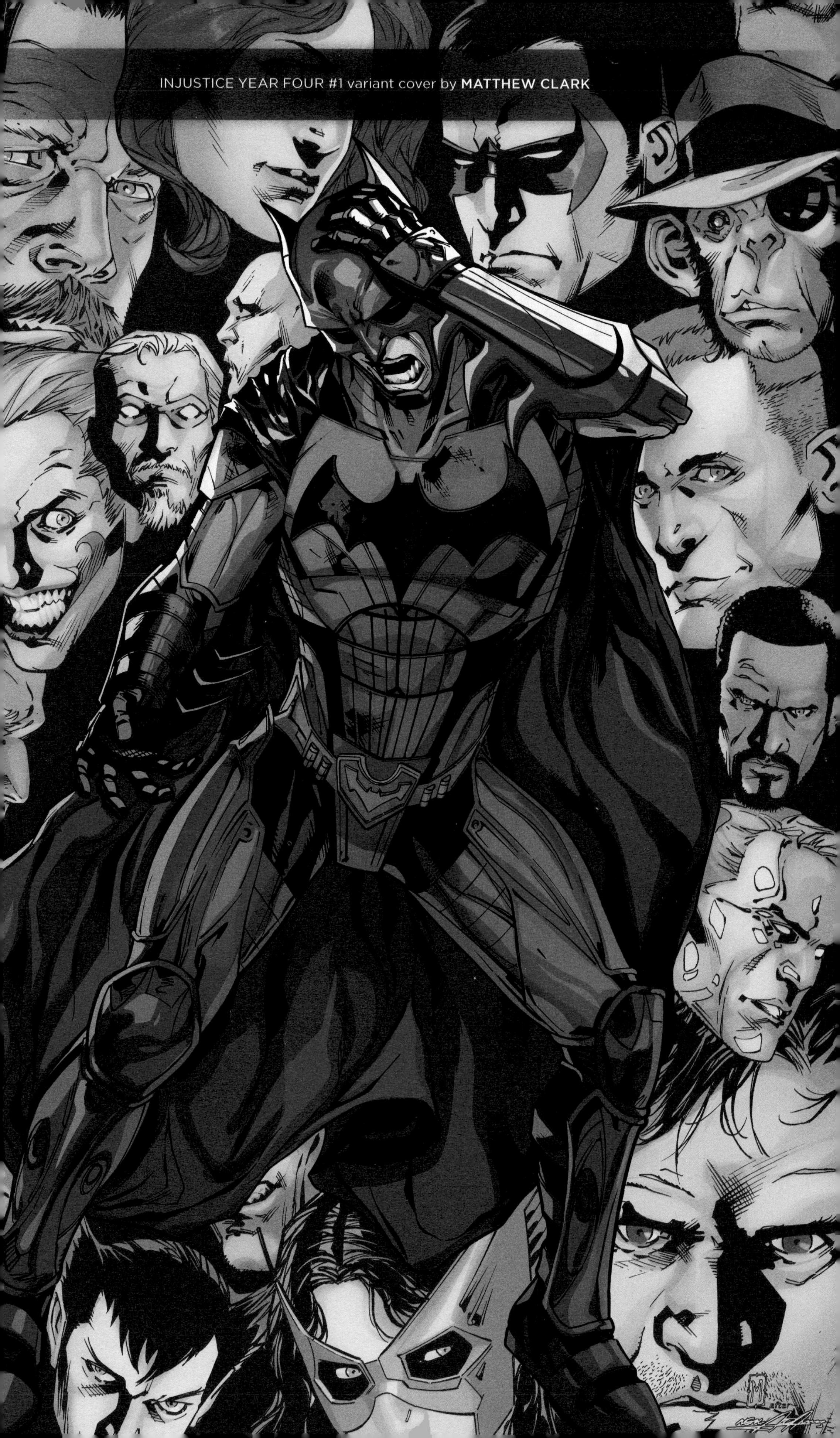

Greek Gods Designs by **Bruno Redondo & Mike S. Miller**

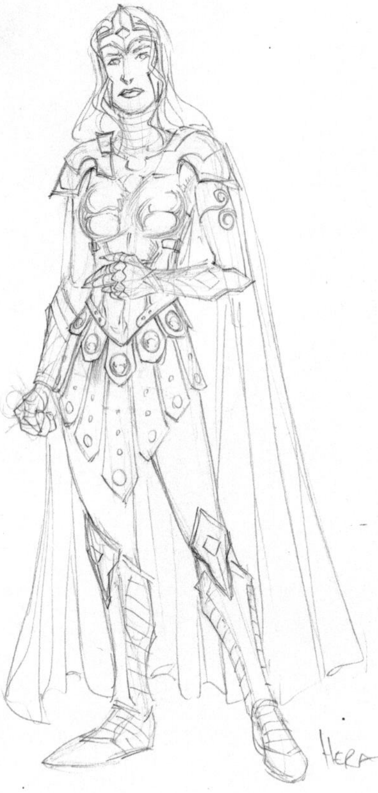
HERA

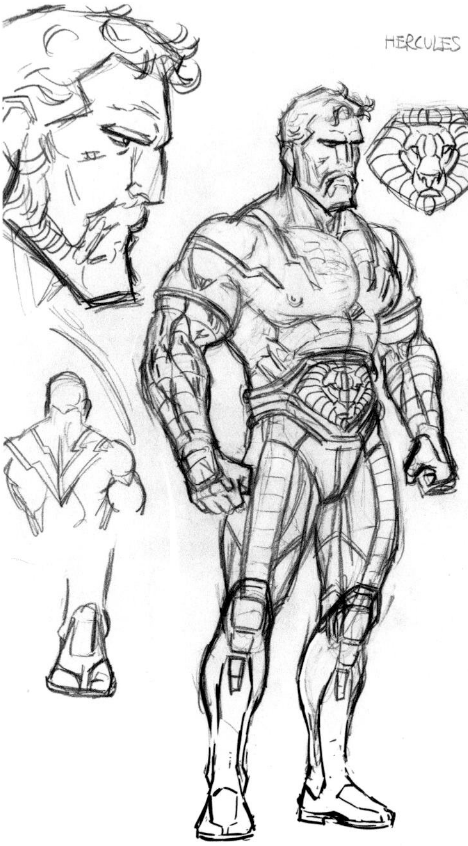
HERCULES

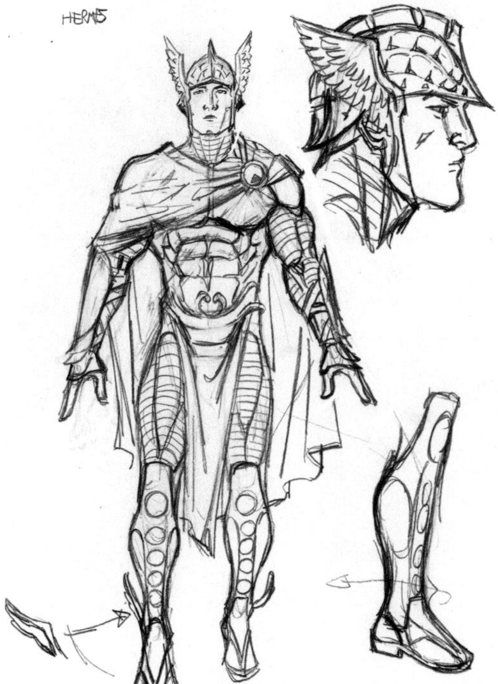
HERMES

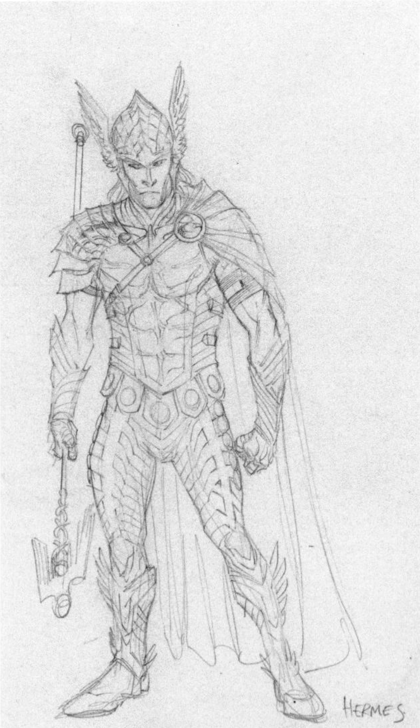
HERMES

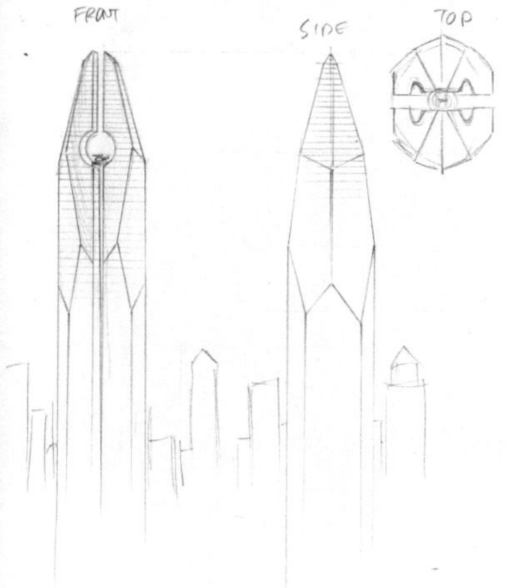
FRONT
SIDE
TOP

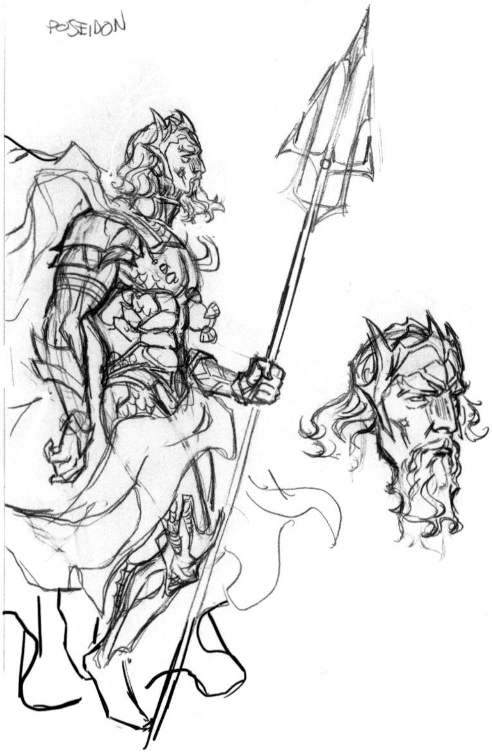
POSEIDON

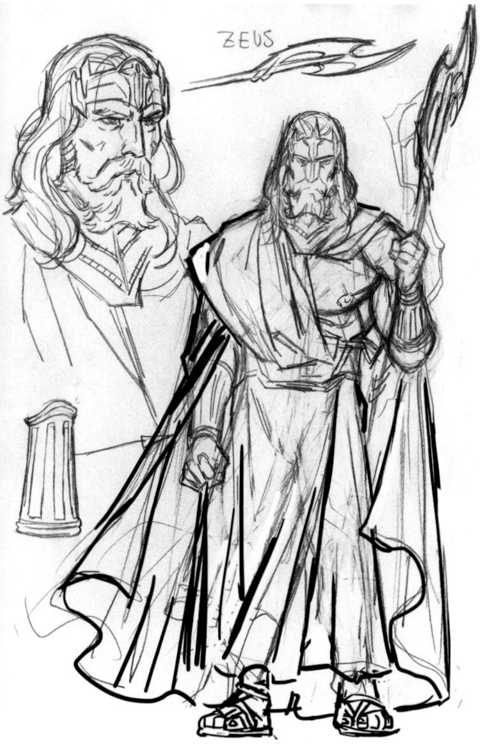
ZEUS

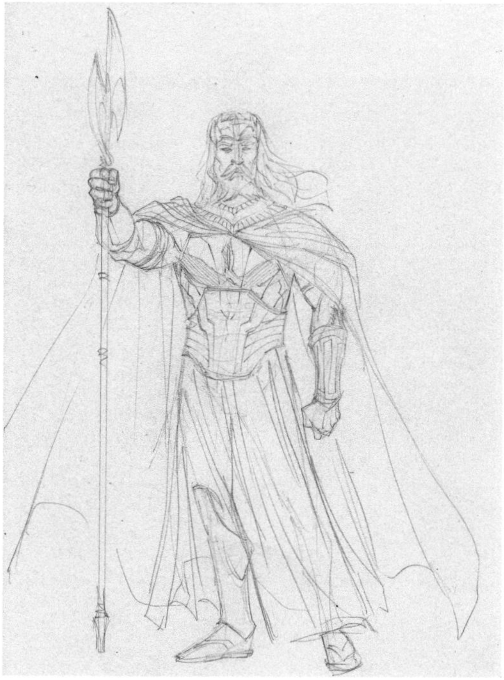

METAMORPHO

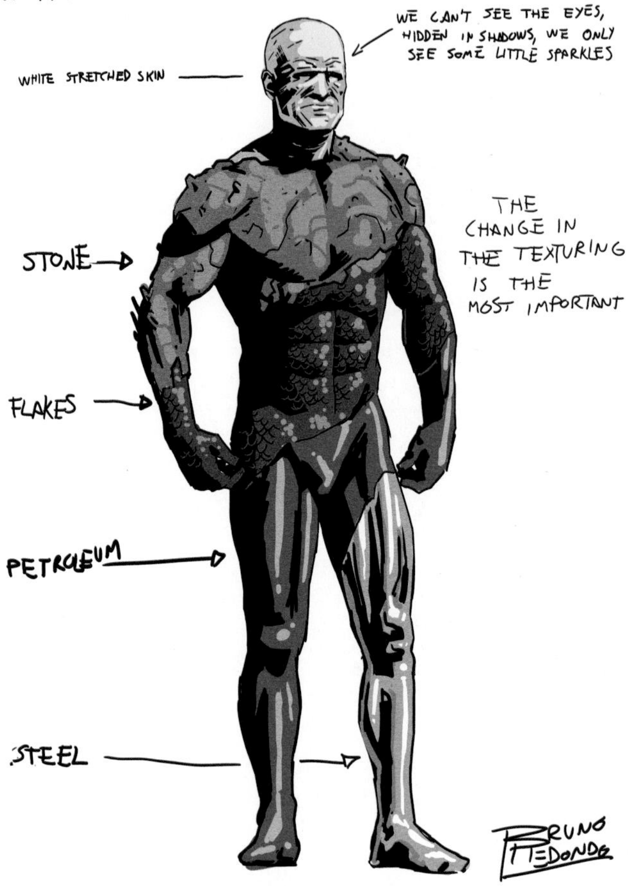
WE CAN'T SEE THE EYES, HIDDEN IN SHADOWS, WE ONLY SEE SOME LITTLE SPARKLES
WHITE STRETCHED SKIN
STONE
THE CHANGE IN THE TEXTURING IS THE MOST IMPORTANT
FLAKES
PETROLEUM
STEEL
BRUNO REDONDO

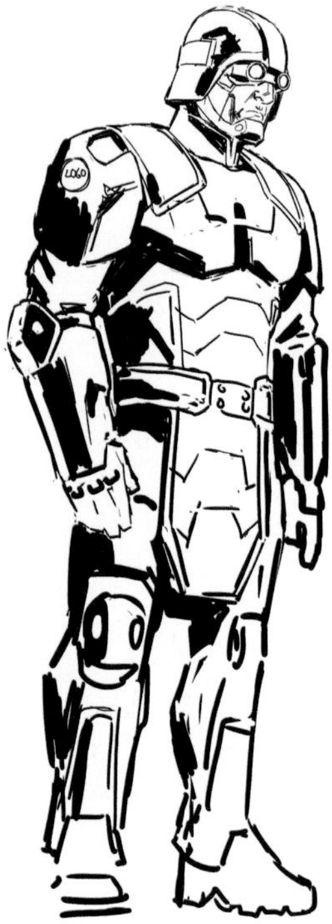
LOGO

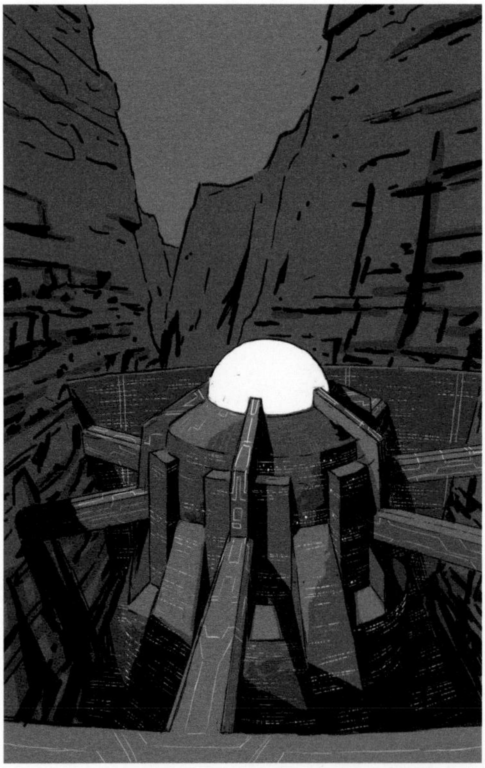

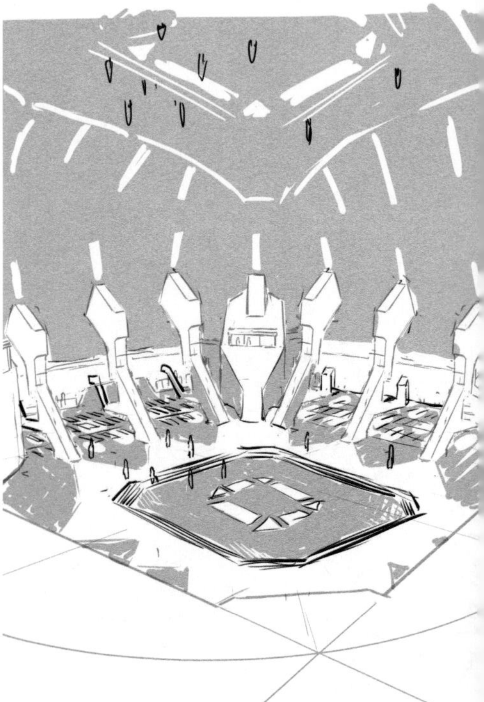

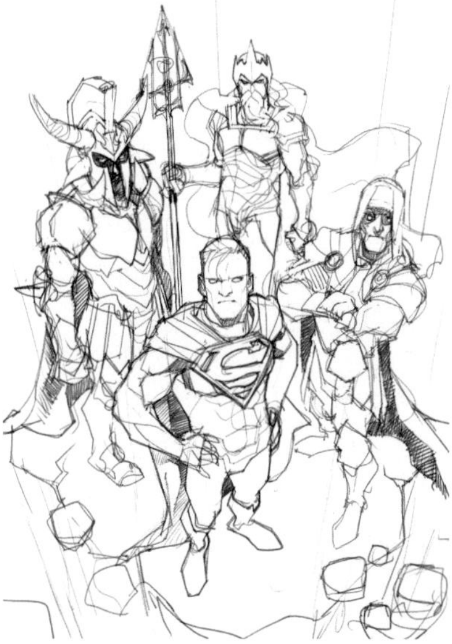

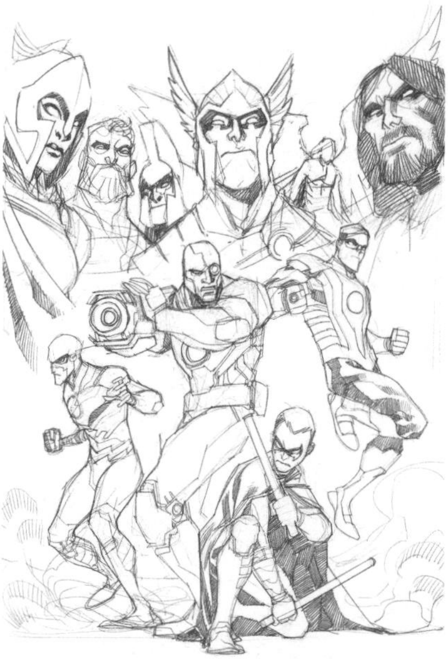

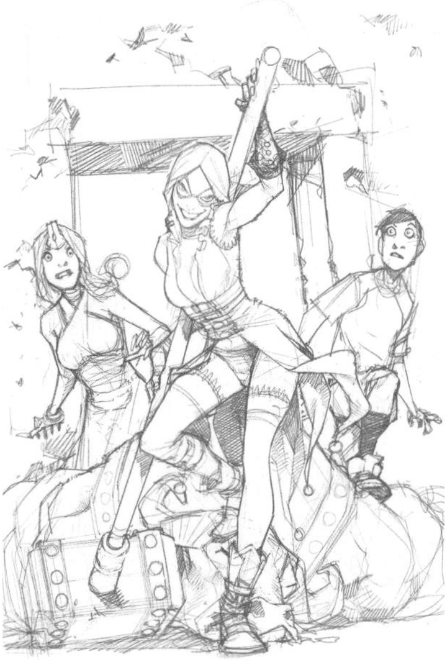

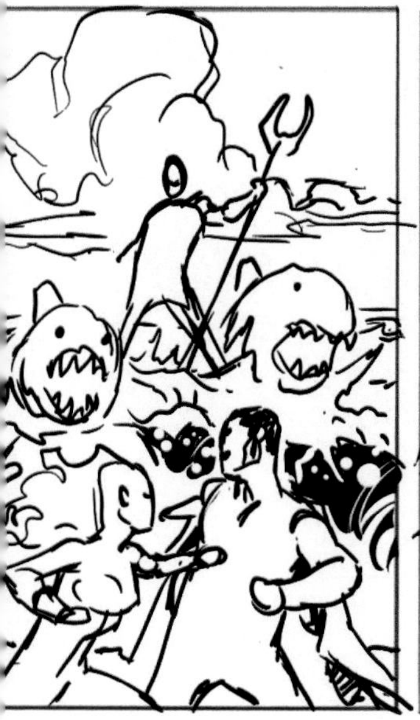

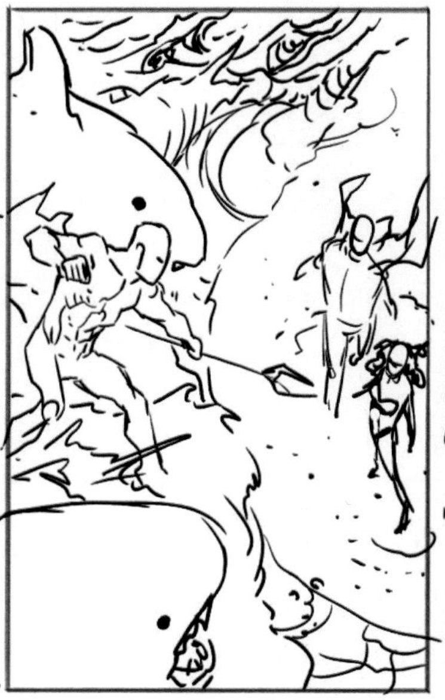

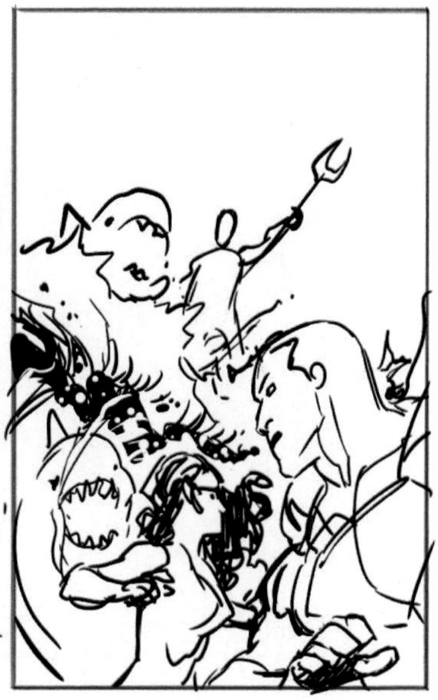

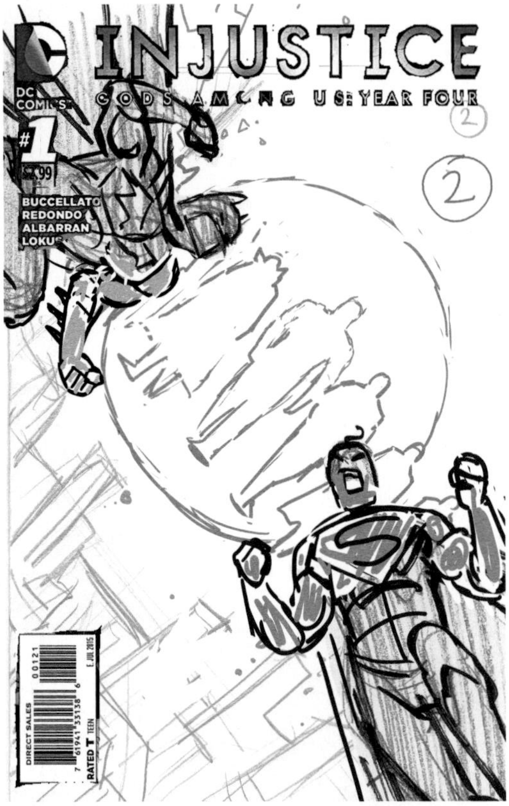
INJUSTICE
DC COMICS
GODS AMONG US: YEAR FOUR
#1
BUCCELLATO
REDONDO
ALBARRAN
LOKUS
DIRECT SALES
RATED T TEEN

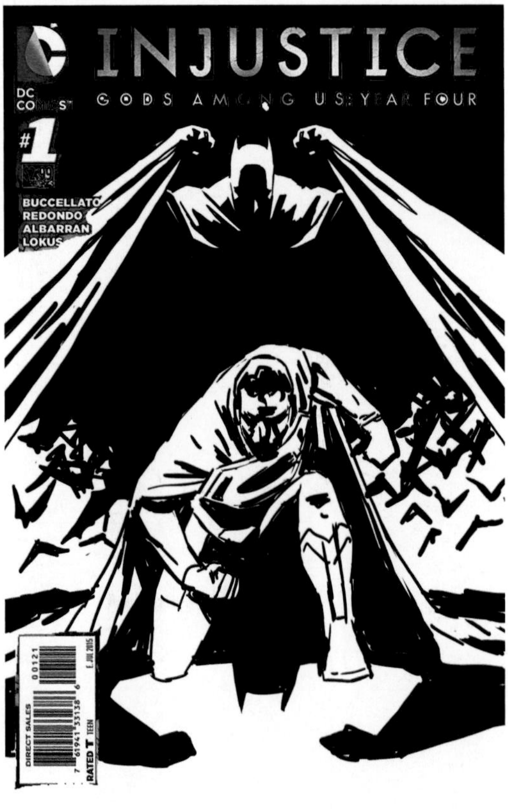
INJUSTICE
DC COMICS
GODS AMONG US: YEAR FOUR
#1
BUCCELLATO
REDONDO
ALBARRAN
LOKUS
DIRECT SALES
RATED T TEEN

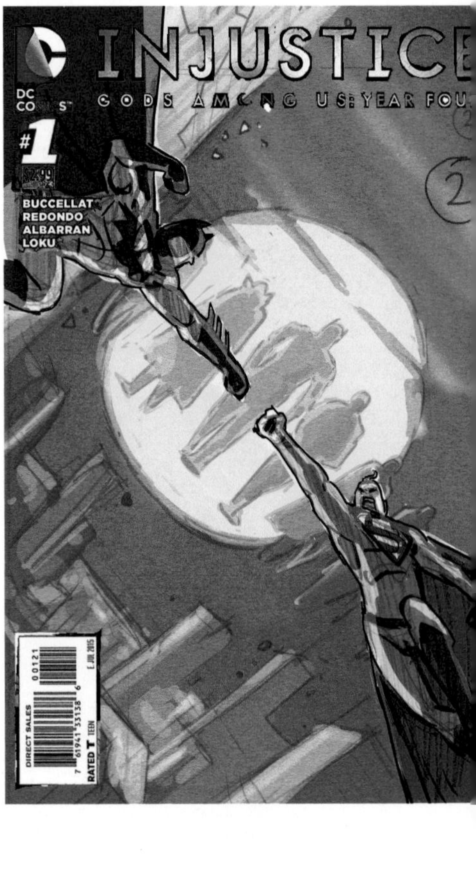
INJUSTICE
DC COMICS
GODS AMONG US: YEAR FOUR
#1
BUCCELLATO
REDONDO
ALBARRAN
LOKUS
DIRECT SALES
RATED T TEEN